CREATIVITY
Is Forever

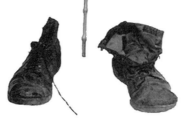

FOURTH EDITION

Gary A. Davis
University of Wisconsin-Madison

KENDALL/HUNT PUBLISHING COMPANY
4050 Westmark Drive   Dubuque, Iowa 52002

Cover photograph courtesy of Wisconsin Center for Film and Theater Research.

Copyright © 1983, 1986, 1992, 1998, 1999 by Kendall/Hunt Publishing Company

Revised Printing

ISBN 0-7872-6429-6

All rights reserved. No part of this publication may be reproduced,
stored in a retrieval system, or transmitted, in any form or by any
means, electronic, mechanical, photocopying, recording, or otherwise,
without the prior written permission of the copyright owner.

Printed in the United States of America

10 9 8 7 6 5 4 3 2

To my mother,
E. Pearl Westwood Davis

contents

4   The Creative Person: Flexible, Funny, and Full of Energy   73

5   The Creative Process: Steps and Stages, Perceptual Changes, and Imagery   113

6   Creative Inspiration through Analogical Thinking   141

preface

Creativity leader E. Paul Torrance (1988) once described creativity as:

Wanting to know	Digging deeper
Looking twice	Crossing out mistakes
Listening for smells	Listening to a cat
Getting in	Getting out
Cutting corners	Cutting holes to see through
Building sand castles	Plugging into the sun
Singing in our own key	Shaking hands with tomorrow
Having a ball	

These metaphors translate approximately as looking for what is not there, viewing the commonplace in unconventional ways, imagining the possibilities, experimenting, solving problems, making mistakes, and above all growing personally, professionally, and uniquely to become what you are capable of becoming. Creativity is essential to one's personal growth and success. It also is vital to society.

This book was prepared for any adult interested in better understanding the topic of creativity, becoming a more creative person, or teaching others to think more creatively. It is absolutely true that much about human creativity remains—and will remain—an intriguing mystery. It is difficult indeed to untangle the drives, thought patterns, and images of a Thomas Edison or Martha Graham. However, it also is absolutely true that we do understand much about creativity and creative people—their energetic and curious personalities, their idea-finding processes and strategies, and the circumstances that support or squelch their lively imaginations and innovative thinking.

It also is absolutely true that despite genetic differences in our cognitive and affective gifts, everyone can become a more flexible, imaginative, and productive thinker. For example, the degree to which motivation—Torrance's (1987a) *blazing drive*—can overcome some limitations in experience and capability is at least astonishing. A central and indispensable ingredient is simply an elevated level of *creativity consciousness*, which is aided directly by a better understanding and appreciation of the topic of creativity.

More specifically, this book will help you better grasp the relationship of creativity to our self-actualization. It will help clarify blocks and barriers to creative thinking, mental processes of creativity, deliberate techniques for solving problems and finding creative ideas, evaluating creativity, the core role of creativity in gifted education, activities for creative dramatics, strategies for strengthening creative attitudes and abilities, and generally "what to teach when you teach creativity." Teachers have a great direct impact on the day-to-day lives of children. This text hopefully will enrich the professional development of teachers and other educators so they may better nurture the creative gifts of students.

The book also addresses some needs of the business person interested in developing his or her own creative thinking potential or in helping others become more creatively productive. Particularly valuable will be the illustrations of creativity and problem solving techniques that, in fact, originated in the business world.

In addition to a sometimes mild updating and polishing of all chapters, improvements to this fourth edition especially include the following. Chapter 3 on definitions and theories is made more complete by adding three-fourths-dozen more contemporary theories and models of creativity. Chapter 4 on characteristics of creative people now includes a section on the nature and making of eminence. (*Creative* is always the missing modifier of *eminence*.) Creative processes in Chapter 5 were made more complete with a still-too-short elaboration of the role of mental imagery in creativity. Chapter 8, formerly restricted to testing, was almost entirely rewritten. One modest purpose was to include a relatively new divergent thinking test born in Hannover, Germany. A more important mission was to review the use of biographical inventories and open-ended questions designed to evaluate creative capability quite independently of formal creativity test scores. If we find that a person has a history of creative activities, can creativity assessment get much better? A section of review exercises now appears at the end of every chapter to help the reader recall some academic highlights of the chapter, and to better internalize suggestions for becoming a more creative thinker.

An understanding of creativity can change your life just as it has changed the lives of many others. The reader will discover that creativity is more than art, theater, new consumer products, and zany TV commercials. These are important. But more important to you personally is the full development of your own capabilities and talents, and an increase in your flexibility, curiosity, open-mindedness, and sense of adventure that also are part of becoming a more creative person. Creative people invest more in life and they reap bigger, more satisfying returns. They live all aspects of life in a more creative, innovative, and enjoyable fashion. They are better prepared to "have a ball."

GAD

how to use the study guides in this book

There are three purposes for the study guides at the end of each chapter:

- To help you master a body of information about creativity
- To provide ideas and strategies for teaching others to develop and use their creativity
- To help you improve your own creative potential

The first goal is based on the principle that you will learn better if you actively respond to printed material, for example, by (1) practicing recalling the information, (2) applying, analyzing, synthesizing, or evaluating the information and skills, (3) thinking about "what's important," and (4) constructing your own interpretations of the knowledge and skills. Therefore, the exercises will ask you to define or explain important concepts and names in each chapter and to "think about" the principles and ideas in various ways—by paraphrasing a particular issue, taking a test that measures an important trait, explaining how the issue might apply to you, or even solving a crossword puzzle that requires using the names and concepts.

The second goal of providing ideas for teaching creativity appears directly, or more often, indirectly, in selected chapters throughout the text, especially Chapter 11. In the Study Guides you occasionally will be asked to relate or apply the ideas and principles to teaching children or adults to think more creatively.

The third purpose, helping YOU develop and use your creative potential, is approached by providing practice in thinking of creative ideas and applying the concepts in the text to yourself and your own creative development. Therefore, you might be asked (1) to think of creative problem solutions, (2) to think of absolutely preposterous ideas, (3) to apply the ideas (e.g., creative personality traits or barriers to creativity) to your own self-concept and creative dispositions, and especially (4) to think about your own creativeness and how it might be improved.

creativity, self-actualization, and you

[*Scene*: *Enchanted forest home of two lovable gnomes, Rodney Dangergnome and Gnome Rickles. The dear friends are trying to help each other with difficult personal problems.*]

Gnome Rickles: Look, dummy, you can't sit around all yer life sweatin' an' straightenin' yer tie an' mumblin' "I don't get no respect! I don't get no respect!" Of course you don't get no respect. Yer a failure! Ya' gotta' get self-actualized an' realize yer potential—like me!

Rodney Dangergnome (*Straightenin' his tie*): You dunno' how tough it's been, Rickles. When I wuz a kid even my mother said she just liked me as a friend! An' I couldn't play hide an' seek 'cause nobody wanted to find me!

Rickles: Maybe it's yer creativity, fish face! Have you ever though of usin' yer imagination? Tryin' to solve a problem once in a while? An' yer personality! Yer neurotic! Self-actualized people ain't neurotic!

Dangergnome: Okay, okay, I'll be self-actualized! But it ain't easy bein' well-adjusted when you're me. My dad took me to the chimp cage at the zoo, an' the zookeeper said "Thanks for bringin' 'im back!" Last week my psychiatrist said I was crazy. I tol' him I wanted a second opinion, so he said I was ugly, too!

Rickles: Just one more time, nincompoop! I'll talk slow. Try to read my lips. Ya' gotta' be more creative, more confident, better adjusted, an' ya' gotta' develop yer skills as much as ya' can. I don't expect much, yer too stupid. But ya' gotta' give it a try!

Dangergnome: Watch it, Rickles! You ain't exactly Prince Charmin', ya' know what I mean? Next to you a sore rattlesnake is a beautiful person! I got problems! When I was a teenager my girlfriend said "Sure, come on over. Nobody's home." So I went over, an' nobody was home!

Rickles: Tell you what. Let's both sit down, you keep yer yap shut, an' let's read Chapter 1 together! Real careful like!

To live creatively is to imagine the possibilities, stay zestful, and grow.
William Wonka

SELF-ACTUALIZATION AND CREATIVITY

Self-Actualization Is Profoundly Important: Abraham Maslow, Carl Rogers

One of the most profoundly important concepts in the field of creativity is the relationship between creativity and self-actualization. Humanistic psychologists Abraham Maslow and Carl Rogers define *self-actualization* as using all of one's talents to become what one is capable of becoming—actualizing one's potential. Further, the self-actualizing person is mentally healthy, self-accepting, forward growing, fully functioning, democratic minded, and more. In Maslow's (1954) words, self-actualization "refers to our desire for self-fulfillment, namely, to the tendency for a person to become actualized in what he or she is potentially . . . the desire to become more and more what one is, to become everything that one is capable of becoming . . . what one can be, one must be.[1] After 14 years of thought, Maslow (1968, p. 138) added, "We are dealing with a fundamental characteristic, inherent in human nature, a potentiality given to all or most human beings at birth, which most often is lost or buried or inhibited as the person gets encultured." Maslow further observed that self-actualization includes an ever-increasing move toward unity, integration, and synergy within the person.

Look carefully at Maslow's description of self-actualized people in Inset 1.1. The thoughtful reader may agree that few things in life are more important that one's self-actualization.

Creativity Is Part of Self-Actualization

Rogers (1962) tied self-actualization to creativity with these words: "The mainspring of creativity appears to be the same tendency which we discover so deeply as the curative force in psychotherapy—one's tendency to actualize oneself, to become one's potentialities . . . the urge to expand, extend, develop, mature—the tendency to express and activate all of the capabilities of the organism" (pp. 65–66).[2] In a scientifically cautious statement, Maslow (1971, p. 57) similarly noted "the concept of creativeness and the concept of the healthy, self-actualizing, fully human person seem to be coming closer and closer together, and may turn out to be the same thing."

Moustakis Agrees

To add further credibility to this paramount relationship, Clark Moustakis (1967), another prominent humanistic psychologist of the time, wrote that "It is this experience of expressing and actualizing one's individual identity in an integrated form in communication and with one's self, with nature, and with other persons that I call creative."

Creativeness is not identical to mentally-healthy *self-actualization*. However, it is an important component. Further, the more you come to define *creativity* as a lifestyle, a way of living and perceiving, the greater is the overlap. Creativity clearly is more than producing zany ideas in art, science, and on divergent thinking tests.

Creativity Is a Lifestyle

Popular Use of "Self-Actualization and Creativity"

In recent decades the bond between self-actualization and creative development has caught on to the point where the relationship is both a semantic trend and virtually a given. For example, Moyer and Wallace (1995) argued that the role of education is not to foster compliance, but to develop the self-actualization that springs from individuality and creative growth. Weiner (1992) stressed a mentor's role in heightening students' anticipation, expectations, feelings of specialness and

Relationship of Creativity to Self-Actualization Is Now Common Assumption

---

[1]"Him" and "he" in the original quote were replaced with the gender neutral "one" and "he or she." Maslow would approve.

[2]"Man's," "himself," and "his" were replaced with "one's" and "oneself." Rogers also would approve.

Inset 1.1
Maslow's 15 Characteristics of Self-Actualized People

In view of the notion that a creative person usually is self-actualized, let's look more closely at Maslow's (1970) description. According to Maslow, self-actualized people:

- Perceive reality more accurately and objectively. They are not threatened by the unknown, and tolerate and even like ambiguity.
- Are spontaneous, natural, and genuine.
- Are problem-centered, not self-centered or egotistical. They have a philosophy of life and probably a mission in life.
- Can concentrate intensely. They need more privacy and solitude than do others.
- Are independent, self-sufficient, and autonomous. They have less need for popularity or praise.
- Have the capacity to appreciate again and again simple and common-place experiences. They have a zest in living and an ability to handle stress.
- Have (and are aware of) their rich, alive, and intensely enjoyable "peak experiences"—moments of intense enjoyment.
- Have a high sense of humor, which tends to be thoughtful, philosophical, and constructive (not destructive).
- Form strong friendship ties with relatively few people, yet are capable of greater love.
- Accept themselves, others, and human nature.
- Are strongly ethical and moral in individual (not necessarily conventional) ways. They are benevolent and altruistic.
- Are democratic and unprejudiced in the deepest possible sense. They have deep feelings of brotherhood with all mankind.
- Enjoy the work in achieving a goal as much as the goal itself. They are patient, for the most part.
- Are capable of detachment from their culture, and can objectively compare cultures. They can take or leave conventions.
- Are creative, original, and inventive, with a fresh, naive, simple, and direct way of looking at life. They tend to do most things creatively, but do not necessarily possess great talent.

Is it important to develop your self-actualized creativity?

---

value—and creativity and self-actualization. Weaver (1990) described techniques to increase the "growth"—job-satisfaction, life-satisfaction, creativity, and self-actualization—of university faculty. We need it. Under the umbrella of *aging individuals*, radio-journalist Goldman (1991) described her "late bloomers'" program that fosters lifelong learning—and self-esteem, self-actualization, and creativity. Kastenbaum (1991) noted that for many senior citizens, creativity and self-actualization continue into later years—they remain open to new experiences, have healthy creative attitudes, and engage in creative activities.

"Growth" Theory of Creativity

The self-actualization approach has been named a *growth* theory of creativity (e.g., Treffinger, Isaksen & Firestien, 1982), since one grows—or should grow—in self-actualization and creativity.

Flow, Entrepreneurship, and Self-Actualization

Flow: Involvement and Enjoyment

Csikszentmihalyi's (pronounced "Smith's"; 1990b) best-selling book *Flow* tries to describe solutions for no less than our search for happiness. "Flow" is involving oneself with an activity to such an extent that nothing else seems to matter—*the experience itself is intensely enjoyable.* Activities that consistently produce flow, noted Smith, are sports, games, art, and hobbies. Further, experts such as artists, athletes, musicians, chess masters, or surgeons experience flow because they are doing exactly what they want to do. It sounds disarmingly simple. Smith also emphasized personal dedication, experiencing exhilaration from taking control of our lives, and the "direct control of experience—the ability to derive moment-by-moment enjoyment from everything we do." According to Gardner's (1993, p. 25–26) interpretation, "those 'in flow' . . . feel that they have been fully alive, totally realized, and involved in a 'peak experience.'" Does flow to relate directly to Maslow's self-actualization? Look again at Inset 1.1.

Entrepreneurship: Freedom, Involvement, and Enjoyment

There also is a literature on *entrepreneurship* with main points that seem identical to Smith's *flow.* For example, Solomon and Winslow (1988) define an entrepreneur as "one who starts and is successful in a venture and/or project that leads to profit (monetary or personal) or benefits society." Fair enough. Rather than great wealth, entrepreneurs described the best thing about being an entrepreneur as, for example, "Freedom to test my ideas and the pleasure of seeing the fruits of my labor" and "Being in complete control of my professional and personal life." They defined *success* as "Doing what I like to do," "Control over my own destiny," "Being happy with myself, doing things I enjoy," and "Seeing my baby live and grow." Does *entrepreneurship* resemble Csikszentmihalyi's *flow* experience? Do both smack of self-actualization and creativity?

Research Relating Self-Actualization and Creativity

The relationship between creativity, on one hand, and mentally healthy, democratic-minded, and forward-growing self-actualization, on the other, has lent itself nicely to empirical research. The perhaps obvious research question is: Does the relationship exist or not?

Measures of Self-Actualization: POI, POD, SI, ROSE, ROSY

As background, the main measure of Maslow's self-actualization has been Shostrom's (1963) *Personal Orientation Inventory* (POI) and slightly newer *Personal Orientation Dimensions* (POD; Shostrom, 1975).[3] Crandall, McCoun, and Robb (1988) described a shortened version—just 15 items—of the POI entitled the *Short Inventory of Self-Actualization.* Buckmaster created the 80-item college-level *Reflections on Self and Environment* (ROSE) inventory (Buckmaster & Davis, 1985). For younger students, Schatz and Buckmaster (1984) built the 62-item *Reflections on Self by Youth* (ROSY). Both the ROSE and the ROSY inventories were based directly on Maslow's 15 characteristics described in Inset 1.1, and both used a rating-scale format.

Maslow's Need Hierarchy and the Maslowian Scale

Now Maslow's (1970) best-known concept is his motivational or "need" hierarchy. Beginning at the bottom, seven levels include *physiological* needs, *safety* needs, *love and belonging* needs, needs for *esteem*, needs to *know and understand*, *aesthetic* needs, and at the top needs for *self-actualization.* Maslow's point was that lower level needs must be met before one addresses even the next higher level. Our point is that the *Maslowian Scale* (Lewis, 1993) is a brief, 12-question test based on this hierarchy that produces a total score reflecting movement toward self-actualization.

---

[3]The POI was considered by Maslow himself to be a sensible test of self-actualization. It has nothing to do with Hawaiian dining.

**High Creativity =
High Self-
Actualization**

Turning to the research, college students' scores on the ROSE measure of self-actualization (Buckmaster & Davis, 1985) were compared with their scores on a shortened version of the creativity inventory *How Do You Think?* (HDYT; Davis, 1975, 1991a; see Chapter 8), which measures personality and biographical characteristics of creative people. The statistical correlation between scores on the two inventories was a whopping .73 (on a scale of 0 to 1.0). Almost every individual who scored high in self-actualization also scored high in creativity, and vice versa, despite the fact that the inventories were constructed based on two supposedly different sets of concepts and literature. Trust me, I was there. Also with college students, Runco, Ebersole, and Mraz (1991) found that intercorrelations between subscales of the HDYT (Davis & Subkoviak, 1978) and the *Short Inventory of Self-Actualization* (SI) again showed good relationships between creativity and self-actualization. The *energetic originality* and *arousal and risk-taking* subscales were the best predictors of SI scores (*rs* = .42 and .46, respectively).

**Creativity and Self-
Actualization Items
Cluster Together**

Research with 302 grade 4, 5, and 6 students who took the ROSY focused on test item interrelationships and clusters (Schatz & Buckmaster, 1984). Two main clusters appeared, one of which was *self-evaluations* whose items related (inversely) to self-acceptance (e.g., "I wish I were more popular," "I worry about what others think of me," and "I wish I were perfect"). The other item cluster was entitled *perceptions*, with the strongest items relating to perceptions of oneself as creative (e.g., "I have a good imagination," "I like to try new and different things," and "I am creative, I can think of many new or unusual ideas"). Importantly, other test items in this cluster reflected other components of self-actualization (e.g., "I am fair to everyone when I work and play," "I speak my opinions without worrying about being right or wrong," and "I can laugh at myself"). Concluded the authors, their research with the ROSE and ROSY "further confirm the relationship between self-actualization and creativity."

**Higher Self-
Actualization = Better
Adjustment**

Lewis, Karnes, and Knight (1995) administered the ROSY, the *Maslowian Scale*, and the *Piers-Harris Children's Self-Concept Scale*, basically a measure of healthy personality adjustment, to 368 high IQ students in grades 4 through 12. Everything was related to everything. Scores on the ROSY and the hierarchy-based *Maslowian Scale* correlated .51. ROSY and the Piers-Harris correlated .43, meaning that the higher their ROSY self-actualization scores, the better were their Piers-Harris self-concept scores.

**Creativity Plus
Intelligence: Highest
Self-Actualization**

Earlier, Yonge (1975) had reviewed research showing positive correlations between scores on the POI and various measures of creativity, for example, scores on a creativity scale for the *Adjective Check List* (Chapter 8). Damm (1970; yes, that's his name) concluded that it helps to be smart, too. While measures of creativity and intelligence each were related to self-actualization scores, the highest levels of self-actualization were reached by his high school students who were both creative and intelligent.

This sample of research confirms that creativeness and self-actualization are indeed related. The next section complicates the issue.

SELF-ACTUALIZED CREATIVITY
AND SPECIAL TALENT CREATIVITY

**Can You Name Some
Neurotic, Highly
Creative People?**

It may or may not have occurred to the thoughtful reader that many world-class creative people have been highly neurotic—not at all self-actualized in the mentally healthy sense. History is full of neurotic creative geniuses. The names of Vincent van Gogh and Edgar Allen Poe come to mind, and perhaps Beethoven, Mozart, Howard Hughes, Judy Garland, John Belushi, Janis Joplin, and introvert Yves St. Laurent. (Can you think of others?)

The solution to this apparent dilemma lies in Maslow's (1954) perceptive distinction between *self-actualized* versus *special talent* creative people. By now you should understand the notion of a general, self-actualized creativeness. In contrast, special talent creative people—by definition—possess an extraordinary creative talent or gift in art, literature, music, theater, science, business, or other area. These people could be well-adjusted and live reasonably happy, self-actualized existences. Or they might be neurotically disturbed and habitually uncomfortable, if not miserable, in their personal, professional, and social lives. As we will see in Chapter 4, a long-standing and continuing literature connects creativity with psychopathology (e.g., Andreason, 1987; Barron, 1969; Flach, 1990; Richards *et al.*, 1988; Walker, Koestner, & Hum, 1995), for example, among entrepreneurs (Solomon & Winslow, 1988) and even regular college students (Schuldberg, 1990; Schuldberg, French, Stone, & Heberle, 1988).

There are at least three important implications of distinguishing between self-actualized versus special talent creativity: (1) being creative without having a specific great talent, (2) the core role of personality and affective traits in creativity, and (3) whether creativity must be taught within a subject area. We will look briefly at each.

One Can Be Creative without a Great Creative Talent

The first implication of the distinction between self-actualized and special talent creativity is tucked into Maslow's last item in Inset 1.1. Under no circumstances should the reader stop and look at the last item in Inset 1.1. Self-actualized creative people are mentally healthy and live full and productive lives; it is a general form of creativeness. Such people tend to approach all aspects of their lives in a flexible, creative fashion. They do not necessarily have an outstanding creative talent in a specific area, for example, one that makes them famous and probably rich. *You need not possess exceptional artistic, literary, scientific, or entrepreneurial talent to consider yourself a creative person and live a creative life.* It is unfortunate that the word *creativity* is associated too strongly with the possession of extraordinary and distinguished talent.

Emphasis on Personality and Affective Traits

The second implication of distinguishing between self-actualized versus special talent creativity is the built-in emphasis on the importance of affective traits of creative people—personality characteristics, attitudes, motivations, and conscious dispositions to think creatively. *Affective traits, not basic intelligence, mark the difference between people who do or do not use their capabilities in a creative way.* We have argued that creativity is a lifestyle, a way of living, a way of perceiving the world, and a way of growing. Living creatively is developing your talents, learning to use your abilities, and striving to become what you are capable of becoming. Being creative is exploring new ideas, new places, and new activities. Being creative is developing a sensitivity to problems of others and problems of humankind. Consider Maslow's list in Inset 1.1. Is this what life is—or should be—about?

The humanistic, self-actualization approach to creativity does not focus only on developing one's creative abilities and creative processes. From this theoretical viewpoint, one's creative abilities and processes are by-products of a larger, more important growth in self-actualization.

In Chapter 4 were will examine the creative personality more closely. Most of the creative personality characteristics described in that chapter—for example, independence, adventurousness, curiosity, humor, perceptiveness, open-mindedness—mesh nicely with Maslow's description of self-actualization and with *flow* and entrepreneurship.

Special Talent Creativity

May or May Not Be Self-Actualized in Mentally Healthy Sense

Creativity and Psychopathology?

Three Implications

Self-Actualized Creative People May Not Have a Great Creative Talent

Highlights Importance of Affective Traits

Creative Thinking Is a Way of Living

Creativity Need Not Be Taught within a Subject Matter

A third implication of the self-actualized versus special talent distinction relates to whether creativity must be taught within a subject area. The matter is a long-standing inaccuracy. For example, Keating (1980) and Schiever and Maker (1997) claim that creativity cannot be taught in the abstract and must be tied to subject matter. The seemingly logical arguments are that students "need something to think about" and that creativity taught in the abstract will not transfer to content areas (Schiever and Maker, 1997, p. 113–114). Wrong. Both are realistic and effective—creativity may be taught in a completely abstract, content-free setting, or the training may be embedded within a specific content or subject area, for example, photography or 18th century theater costuming.

Again, self-actualized creativity is a *general* creativeness that is content free. Many successful creative courses, programs, workshops, and educational workbooks try to:

- Raise creativity consciousness
- Strengthen creative attitudes, such as valuing novel ideas
- Teach idea finding and creative problem solving techniques
- Strengthen underlying creative abilities through exercise

All creativity courses and workshops stress the nature of creativity and creative persons, and all encourage learners to approach personal, academic, and professional problems in a more creative fashion. This approach to teaching creativity is sensible, common, and effective (e.g., Davis & Bull, 1978; Edwards, 1968; Parnes, 1978, 1981; Smith, 1985; Stanish, 1979, 1981, 1988; Torrance, 1987b, 1995; von Oech, 1983, 1986). The general approach is characteristic of teaching *brainstorming* and the *Creative Problem Solving* (CPS) model of the Creative Education Foundation (Chapters 5 and 7). Consistent with self-actualized creativity, creativity training need not be tied to a particular subject or content.

On the other hand, a goal might well be to strengthen creative thinking and problem solving skills as they relate directly to a specific subject such as creative writing, photography, theater, botany, architecture, astronomy, or dinosaurs. With the typical independent projects approach, students are given (or find) a project or problem and proceed to clarify it, consider various approaches, settle on a main solution or resolution, and then create or prepare the project or problem for presentation. Throughout, students identify and resolve numerous subproblems, evaluate their methods and results, acquire knowledge and develop technical skills in the content area, and their creative abilities and skills are strengthened. This strategy clearly fits Maslow's special talent type of creativeness. It also is an appropriate and effective teaching method.

We will see in Chapter 9 that independent projects are a common strategy for teaching academic content, technical skills, and creativity to gifted children. Content-free creativity training also is widely employed, for example, in brainstorming sessions that teach creativity consciousness, receptiveness to wild ideas, deferring criticism and evaluation, and principles of looking for many ideas and building upon others' ideas.

SELF-ACTUALIZED AND SPECIAL TALENT CREATIVITY: TWO CONTINUA

While Maslow identified the two types—self-actualized and special-talent creativity—it seems more logical that each of the two traits lies on an independent

---

Sidebar notes (left margin):

Self-Actualized Creativity Is Content Free

And May Be Taught and Learned

Creativity Consciousness, Attitudes, Techniques, Abilities

Brainstorming and CPS Model Are Content Free

Special Talent Creativity Is Taught within a Subject Area

Independent Projects

Teaches Knowledge, Technical Skills, Creativity

Creativity Training May Be in a Content Area or Content Free

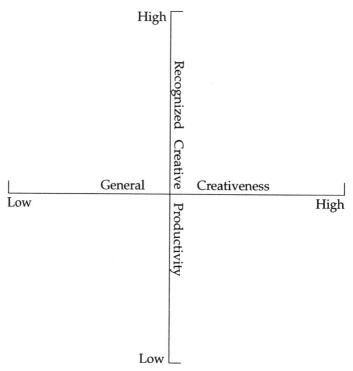

Figure 1.1. Two-dimensional illustration of personal creativeness. A person may low to high in general creativeness, which is a life style and a thinking style (Maslow's self-actualized creativity), and low to high in recognized creative achievement (Maslow's special-talent creativity).

Independent Continua

continuum. As illustrated on the horizontal axis of Figure 1.1, any given person will be low to high in Maslow's general, *self-actualized creativity*. As we have seen, a person high in this trait takes a creative approach to most aspects of life; it is a way of living, growing, and perceiving one's world, as well as a way of thinking and solving problems. Such a person is mentally healthy, self-accepting, and grows toward self-realization. As represented on the vertical axis of Figure 1.1, a person also may be low to high in recognized creative productivity, Maslow's *special talent creativity*. By definition, a person high in this dimension has achieved recognition for socially-judged creative achievement, for example, in art, science, or business. He or she may or may not be mentally healthy in the self-actualization sense.

Everyone Can Be More Creative

This broad conception of creativity acknowledges the obvious—that many people think and act creatively, some in just a few areas, some in all areas of their lives, and a handful achieve recognition and eminence. This view also acknowledges the truism that everyone has an opportunity to live a more creative life and become a more fulfilled and creatively productive person. The word *creative* must not be restricted only to persons who have achieved creative eminence, as is claimed by some (Chapter 3). By exclusion, 99+ percent of everyone necessarily—and unrealistically—would be *not creative*.

Bad Odds

CIVILIZATION: A HISTORY OF CREATIVE IDEAS

Civilization: History of Creative Ideas

Because the main purpose of this chapter is to increase awareness of the importance of creativity, we might remind the reader that the history of civilization

The history of civilization is a history of creative innovations. Traffic accidents were reduced to zero when this dangerous intersection became the site of the world's first stop-and-go signal. Unfortunately, the policeman operating the signal was immobilized by a tuna sandwich from the corner restaurant. (Wisconsin Center for Film and Theater Research.)

Cottontail Drumstick Anyone?

is more than a sequence of famous wars. Civilization is a history of creative ideas that have been modified, combined, transformed, and transferred—building upon each other—into ever new creations. It has happened, and continues to happen, in any area we might look at—art, science, mathematics, technology, law, medicine, politics, music, philosophy, agriculture, economics, consumer products, and even more imaginative ways to conduct those wars.[4] Without creative ideas and creative thinkers, we still would be living in caves and trees, picking berries and clubbing bunny rabbits for breakfast.

Civilization will continue to have problems and aesthetic needs, and creative people will continue to provide solutions and aesthetic experiences.

---

[4]Creativity may be used constructively or, regrettably, destructively.

COMPLEXITY OF CREATIVITY

Mystery of Creativity

It may be trivial to point out that creativity is intricate and complicated. Artistic and scientific creativity reflect enticingly mysterious processes, capabilities, and experiences that have baffled scholars, philosophers, and creative people themselves for centuries. The ambiguity continues to encourage unusual and superstitious beliefs about creativity.

Lots of Poppycock

For example, ancient Greek poets, composers, and others credited their ideas to inspiration from the Muses, nine sister goddesses, daughters of Zeus and Mnemosyne, who presided over the arts (which curiously included astronomy). Plato suggested that a state of "divine madness" helps the inspiration. Chalking up creativity to inspiration from gods seems an unscientific idea with remarkable endurance. A few ancient and contemporary people, with more imagination than objectivity, attribute creativity to somehow tapping a *universal mind* or *universal consciousness*—a mysterious information source said to float throughout the universe.

Freud's Neurotic Conflict

In our theory chapter (Chapter 4) we will see that Sigmund Freud assumed creativity to be motivated by an unconscious conflict between the sex drive (*libido*) of the *id* and one's learned social conscience (*superego*). The neurotic conflict supposedly is resolved by rechanneling the sex urge into creative outlets—so the id is happy, the superego is happy, the ego (self) is well-adjusted, and everybody goes to Mexico for a vacation.[5] No one any longer believes this. Another classic theorist, Carl Jung, proposed that true creativity involves accessing your "primordial archetypes," mental images genetically passed down through the ages which provide ideas for your creative efforts. Jungians continue to believe this.

Jung's Primordial Archetypes

Gardner Murphy, APA, ESP, and Creativity

Former American Psychological Association President Gardner Murphy cited examples of paranormal experiences by Mark Twain, Robert Schumann, Goethe, and other creative persons, and argued that psychical ability and creativeness are related because similar processes are involved, such as access to one's unconscious mind (Krippner & Murphy, 1976; Murphy, 1963).

Complexity Limits Creativity Test Validity

Let's look at additional reasons why we perceive *creativity* to be complicated, complex, and perhaps mysterious. To anticipate later chapters, these are reasons why measuring creative potential and predicting future creative productivity is difficult and prone to error. That is, these are reasons why the validity of any creativity test or other predictive method necessarily is limited.

Affective Traits Central to Creativity

- There are many attitudes, personality traits, motivations (commitment, enthusiasm, adventurousness, drive for accomplishment and recognition), cognitive abilities and information processes, and family and school experiences that combine to orient students toward creativity thinking—or combine to squelch creative thinking. Their role is essential.

Infinite Forms of Creativity

- Individuals can be creative in any one part or combination of parts of their personal, educational, or adult professional lives. Said Torrance (1979), we can be creative in an infinite number of ways.

Can Be Forced or Intuitive and Unexpected

- Creativity can be "forced," as when we set a time and place for classroom brainstorming; it also happens suddenly and unpredictably, as when problem solutions unexpectedly pop into consciousness, composers hear symphonies in their heads, or as Hemingway once said, "The stuff comes alive and turns crazy on ya'" (Bass, 1968).

---

[5]Freud also said that only men can be creative because women's creative urges are fulfilled in reproduction. So much for Freud's credibility.

Small Creativity, Big Creativity

- We have small-scale creative insights and projects, as when a child creates a poem or solves a problem in a novel way; we also have larger-scale creative productivity, as when a student writes and directs a high school play.

Self-Actualized, Special Talent Creativity

- As we have seen, Maslow (1954, 1970) distinguished between *self-actualized creativity* versus *special-talent creativity*. Some students will be high in general self-actualized creativity, others will show high creativity in a special talent area, and still others will have both.

Psychopathology?

- We also noted that creativeness seems related to psychopathology (e.g., Barron, 1969; Flach, 1990; Walker, Koestner, & Hum, 1995).

Hard Work? Inspiration?

- Creative innovation may stem from visible planning and hard work, which can hide "inspiration" and "insight" components. For example, analogical connections may appear in an instant, as when Cartoonist Gary Larson substitutes house flies for adoring mothers: "Oh my, what a cute little maggot!"

Suprarational

- Creativity authority Paul Torrance (1979) emphasized that creative processes are *suprarational*. *Suprarational* means that creativity involves not only the intellect and voluntary factors, but such nonrational tendencies as to be playful, fanciful, illogical, farfetched, and even emotional, particularly in one's commitment or "blazing drive."

Age?

- Children can be innovative and creative, yet so were Grandma Moses and Picasso at 90.

Same Process in Art and Science?

- Some experts assume that the creative process is the same in art as in science; others claim with equal confidence that there are as many creative processes as their are creative people. Both likely are true, since we find commonalities across virtually all types of creativity, yet unique features in regard to the person and the medium. This resolution should not be a great surprise.

Psychologically Safe Environment

Society Judges Creativeness

- Creative talent will remain repressed and hidden without, to use Carl Rogers' (1962) apt phrase, a *psychologically safe* social and cultural environment that supplies opportunities and reinforcement. In fact, claims Csikszentmihalyi (1988; still pronounced "Smith"), society itself will select which products and ideas are valued and hence judged "creative." There clearly is a huge role of social circumstance, which can support or repress creativity.

Problem Finding Important

- Several authors emphasize that *problem finding* is a hallmark of creative accomplishment in artistic and scientific creativity (e.g., Getzels & Csikszentmihalyi, 1976; Okuda, Runco, & Berger, 1991; Subotnik, 1988). Truly creative people can identify problems worth working on. They also tolerate the ambiguity of assuming that their work always can be improved. Said Albert Einstein, "The identification of the problem is more important than the solution, which may merely be a matter of mathematical or experimental skills.

Creative Adaptors and Creative Innovators: KAI

- Research with extreme scorers on the *Kirton Adaption-Innovation Inventory* (KAI; Kirton, 1987) tells us that Adaptors solve problems and create within a conforming structure; they "try to do things better." More imaginative and fluent Innovators redefine the problem, break restraints, and "try to do things differently." Adaptors think Innovators are "unsound, impractical, risky, abrasive, often shocking ... and create dissonance" (Mudd, 1995, p. 242).

Motivation Is Important

- Farley (1986) argued, with supporting research data (e.g., Davis, Peterson, & Farley, 1973), that *motivation* in the form of high sensation seeking, arousal seeking, and adventurousness by itself is an adequate and parsimonious explanation of why some people are creatively productive and others are not. Certainly, high energy and drive are core traits of creativity, traits that are shared by all creatively productive persons.

Years of Training and Experience Important

- There is a big role of training and experience in a content area. If we are talking big-time, special-talent creative contributions, such as making major medical discoveries, writing Broadway plays, or creating a successful business or corporation, it can take years of training, experience, and skill development before high-level creative achievements are possible.

Chance Remains Important

- Finally, while planning and hard work play an obvious role, chance and randomness also are important in creative discovery and problem solving. Simonton (1988a), for example, stressed the role of chance in both the production (or selection) of the novel idea combination and in its social acceptance. Many inventions and discoveries are accidental, as when Eli Whitney saw a cat reach through a fence to grab a chicken, but came back only with a pawful of feathers, thus inspiring the cotton gin. Pasteur's pasteurization also was rooted in chance, as was Roentgen's discovery of x-rays, Nobel's research with dynamite, Fleming's penicillin, Foucault's discovery that a pendulum would illustrate the rotation of the earth, Galvani's discovery that electricity could be chemically produced, and several discoveries by Edison. Columbus accidentally found a Caribbean island while looking for China (was he ever lost!). If you wish to be a successful ballerina or Sumo wrestler you must possess the right genes for the right physique. Great accomplishments in most areas require the existence of appropriate cultural knowledge and technology and high-level instruction; one cannot—by chance—be born too soon.

Comment

Creativity: Partly Genetic, Partly Environment

Despite its intrinsically puzzling nature, there is much we do understand about creativity. This book will help clarify creativity by examining definitions and theories, characteristics and traits, internal creative processes, idea-finding techniques used by creative people, creativity tests and their assumptions, and realistic strategies for teaching for creative growth.

But Can Be Increased

A core message of this book is that everyone can increase their creative potential and live more creative lives. It is important.

SUMMARY

Self-actualization is developing your talents to become what you are capable of becoming. It includes being mentally healthy, forward growing, democratic-minded, and more. Creativity and self-actualization are intimately related, perhaps identical, say humanists Carl Rogers, Abraham Maslow, and Clark Moustakis.

Popular usage assumes a relationship between creativity and self-actualization. Csikszentmihalyi's *flow* and the topic of entrepreneurship both relate to self-actualization and creativity.

Measures of self-actualization include the POI, the POD, the shorter SI (based on the POI), the ROSE, the ROSY, and the Maslowian Scale. Research with these instruments supports a fairly strong relationship between self-actualization and measures of creativity. A measure of personal adjustment was related to scores on both. Self-actualization scores were highest for students who were creative and bright.

The self-actualized creative person approaches all aspects of life in a creative fashion. The special talent creative person has a great creative talent, but may or may not be self-actualized in the mentally healthy sense. The relationship between creativity and psychopathology is a longstanding one.

The first implication of this distinction is that one need not possess a great creative talent to consider oneself creative and live a creative life. A second implication stresses the importance of affective, personality characteristics in creativeness. A third implication is that general, self-actualized creativeness can and is successfully taught in a content-free fashion. Special talent creativity must be taught within a content area, most often by engaging students in independent projects.

It may be logical to view self-actualized and special talent creativity as independent continua; a person may be low or high on either dimension.

The history of civilization is a history of creative ideas in every area.

For centuries creativity has confused scholars, philosophers, and even creative people, leading, for example, to the invocation of Muses, a "universal mind," Freud's unconscious neurotic conflict, and other seemingly superstitious explanations.

Some aspects of the complexity of creativity include the following:

Affective, dispositional personality traits are important for creativity.

There are infinite forms of personal, education, and occupational creativity.

Creativity can be "forced" with techniques, or can appear unexpectedly.

We have small-scale and large-scale "creative" accomplishments.

We have Maslow's distinction between a general, self-actualized creativeness versus special-talent creativity.

Creativity relates to psychopathology.

Visible planning and hard work may obscure "insight" and "inspiration" components.

Torrance emphasized suprarational components—such as being fanciful, playful, illogical, farfetched, and having a "blazing drive."

Children and senior citizens can be creative.

Some parts of the creative process are the same in art as in science; other components are unique to the person and the medium.

A psychological safe environment is essential. According to Csikszentmihalyi, society itself decides what is creative and what is not.

Problem finding probably is a long-overlooked, essential part of creativeness.

Kirton and others distinguish between creative Adaptors versus creative Innovators.

Farley reduces creativity to high motivation (arousal seeking, adventurousness).

The role of training and experience should not be ignored.

Chance and randomness also play a role in discovery and innovation.

Nonetheless, there is much we do know about creativity.

Everyone can increase their creative capability.

Creativity, Self-Actualization, and You

Self-Test: Key Concepts, Terms, and Names

Briefly define or explain each of these:

Self-actualization _____

_____

Self-actualized creativity _____

_____

Special-talent creativity _____

_____

Why does your author think these names are important?

Abraham Maslow _____

Carl Rogers _____

Clark Moustakis _____

Mihaly Csikszentmihalyi[6] _____

Let's Think about It

1. a. Did you recently do something creative? _____

    b. What was it? _____

    c. What led you to be creative? _____

    _____

_____

[6]Pronounced CHICK-sent-mi-HIGH. Now try spelling it.

2. According to the book, why is creativity important?

    _____

    _____

    _____

3. According to YOU, why is creativity important?

    _____

    _____

    _____

4. Do you agree that the relationship between self-actualization and creativity is important? Why?

    _____

    _____

    _____

5. According to the text, in what ways is creativity complex?

    _____

    _____

    _____

    _____

    Can you add to this list? (That is, what mystifies YOU about "creativity"?)

    _____

    _____

    _____

    _____

6. How is being self-actualized like being an eagle?

    _____

    _____

    _____

7. What would be two implications FOR YOU of being high in *self-actualized* creativity?

Implication 1 _____

_____

Implication 2 _____

_____

What would be two implications FOR YOU of being high in *special-talent* creativity?

Implication 1 _____

_____

Implication 2 _____

8. *Self-test.* Define or explain each of the following to yourself:

Flow   Maslow's Need Hierarchy

Entrepreneurship   Maslowian Scale

POI, POD   Vincent van Gogh

ROSE, ROSY

9. *Thought and study question:* Which points in the chapter are likely to appear on a test?

Self-Actualization Test

Indicate the degree to which each statement applies to you, or the degree to which you agree with the statement. Use the following scale:

1 = No
2 = To a small degree
3 = Average
4 = More than average
5 = Definitely

_____ 1. I enjoy some ambiguity and "unknowns" in my life.

_____ 2. Most people are basically good.

_____ 3. I am a spontaneous and natural person.

_____ 4. I have a philosophy about life.

_____ 5. I accept myself; I like who I am.

_____ 6. I feel I have a mission in life—a vision about what I am and what I will achieve.

	7.	I am independent and self-sufficient.
_____	8.	I can concentrate very intensely on my work.
_____	9.	I am a democratic-minded person; that is, strongly unprejudiced.
_____	10.	I have a great zest for life.
_____	11.	I am creative.
_____	12.	I can appreciate again and again simple and commonplace experiences.
_____	13.	I handle stress well.
_____	14.	I have marvelous moments of intense enjoyment.
_____	15.	I have strong feelings of brotherhood with all people.
_____	16.	I am a kind, considerate, and charitable person.
_____	17.	I enjoy working toward a goal as much as the goal itself.
_____	18.	I define right and wrong according to my own standards more so than society's conventions.
_____	19.	I am working to become what I am capable of becoming.
_____	20.	I feel I am high in self-actualization.

Scoring: Add up your ratings. The following is a guideline for interpretation:

20–40	Low Self-Actualization
41–53	Below Average
54–69	Average
70–83	Above Average
84–100	High Self-Actualization

Whatever your score, review Maslow's traits in Inset 1.1. Do you think you can improve on many of them?

barriers, blocks, and squelchers
why we are not more creative

[*Scene: Small girl scout camp deep in forest of Southern California. Scout Leader Rita Rambo is discussing plans to rescue pet duck, held hostage without sardines by disgruntled political group. Small girl scouts Darcy, Jennifer, and others listen intently. Darcy opens the creative problem solving.*]

Darcy: We need a plan. Something creative to surprise those people—maybe distract them while we sneak in and grab Daffy!

Rita Rambo: No thanks, kiddo! Somebody would have suggested it before if it were any good! You've got to be kidding. What bubblehead thought that up! I say let's hit 'em with everything we got. Jennifer, did you bring your little bazooka?

Jennifer: No, Ms. Rambo, but I have my brother's baseball bat.

Darcy: But Ms. Rambo, we shouldn't be violent. Besides, we might hurt Daffy!

Rambo: You don't understand the situation, small fry! And don't forget the chain of command. I learned how to deal with duck-nappers on Wake Island! Soften 'em up with artillery, then we go in! That's the way it's always been done!

Darcy: What about disguising ourselves as Groucho Marx, Ben Turpin, Charlie Chaplin, and W. C. Fields. We could walk in, argue about who is the funniest, and when Jennifer says "That's the most ridiculous thing I ever hoid!" I'll sneak off with Daffy!

Rambo: Not this girl scout, cookie! It just won't work, we've never done that before, too blue sky, we need more lead time. I don't see the connection, the comedians' union will scream, it'll mean more work, don't step on any toes, don't rock the boat, and you can't teach this old dog new tricks!

Jennifer: Do you imagine that . . .

Rambo: No, I never imagine.

Jennifer: Well, do you suppose sometimes?

Rambo: Sometimes I suppose, if it's not difficult.

Jennifer: Suppose we hire a mariachi band. While everyone is drinking margueritas and dancing the New Mexican Hat Dance, Darcy could pop Daffy into her big siesta.

Darcy: You mean my sombrero.

Rambo: We did all right without a mariachi band, our people won't accept it, let's be practical, and what will the other Girl Scouts think? Besides, we tried that before!

Darcy: Maybe we could negotiate a trade—a dozen Big Macs, some french fries, and a winning season for the Los Angeles Rams!

Jennifer: Let's just buy a new duck! Daffy's in the soup by now anyway!

> *To give a fair chance to creativity is a matter of life and death for any society.*
> Arnold Toynbee

A good case could be made for the notion that all of us would be more creative if it were not for external and internal barriers, blocks, and squelchers. That is, because of well-learned habits, an unsupportive or even repressive environment, or our fears and insecurities, most people do not use their creative imaginations and abilities. Some have taken the argument so far as to assume that everyone is born creative, but in our earliest years the social pressures of home, school, and community flatten our lively imaginations to produce legions of dutiful conformers.

In this chapter we will look more closely at some common barriers to creative thinking and productivity: habit and learning, rules and traditions, perceptual blocks, cultural blocks, emotional blocks, and resource blocks, at least the first four of which are interrelated and stem from lifelong learning. We also will review von Oech's (1983) 10 types of mental blocks, which may take a whack on the side of the head to jar loose. Finally, we will itemize probably-too-familiar "idea squelchers," a list that has been growing for nearly half a century.

The challenge to anyone wishing to increase his or her personal creativeness is to understand, expect, and be ready to cope with barriers to creativity from the environment or from inside oneself.

We Do Not Use the Creative Abilities We Have

Lots of Blocks and Barriers

Understand and Be Ready

HABIT AND LEARNING

The first and most obvious barrier to creative thinking and innovation is just *habit*, our well-learned and customary ways of thinking and responding. It begins when we are munchkins. We learn the "correct" responses, routines, and patterns of behavior. We learn language habits and the conceptual categories that things and ideas belong in. We learn "the way things have always been done" and "the way things are supposed to be done." Over the years it becomes more and more difficult to break away from these habits, to see and create new possibilities.

When did you last try something truly new? An exotic restaurant? A new sport? A college course in some intriguing topic? When *did* you last do something truly novel? Are your old habits and expectations interfering with new ideas and activities?

Of course, the ability to form habits and expectations is an adaptive and necessary capability for humankind and lower animals. It would be troublesome indeed to open your eyes each morning and wonder what you are supposed to do next. Being a "creature of habit" is a boon and a curse.

Routines, Language Habits, Correct Categories

Have You Been Creative Lately?

Habits Are Necessary

RULES AND TRADITIONS

It should be obvious that social groups—from the family to educational, corporate, national, and international groups—could not function without the rules,

Rules and Traditions: Necessary but Restrictive

Inflexible School Systems?

Organizational Paralysis?

Industrial Era and Brain-Damaged?

regulations, policies, and traditions that guide personal, social, and institutional behavior. However, *guide* often means *restrict* or *inhibit*.

Ambrose (1996), for example, recently took a few shots at inflexible school systems. He claimed they suffer from a lack of creative flexibility because of top-heavy, bureaucratic structures that cubbyhole people into highly distinct roles. Such specialized people focus on the detail of everyday concerns within their own departments and lose any capability for big-picture, visionary thought. Said Ambrose, they seldom have good reason to take risks beyond the confines of established procedures, particularly since "mistakes are routinely punished in our right-answer-fixated bureaucracies" (p. 28).

Criticizing the rigidity of traditional organizations, while suggesting positive and creative changes, has become an accepted catharsis (e.g., Drucker, 1989; Kanter, 1989; Peters, 1992; Tapscott & Caston, 1993). Ambrose (1995), injured only mildly while hopping on the bandwagon, listed these traits of "dullard ... brain-damaged bureaucracies ... inherited from the old industrial era":

- Myopic and coercive leadership that treats employees as automatons
- Premature judgment
- Repressed creativity
- Anger, frustration, and resentment
- Inflexible conformity
- Reflexive ritual
- Plus habit bound; narrow focus; slow; and with poorly integrated subsystems

Habit, tradition, rules, regulations—all will interfere with versatile creative problem solving. "Sure, chief, we're all trained up an' ready to give out them parking tickets! Before we can move, the boys gotta' know if they should use a number 2 or a number 3 pencil!" (Wisconsin Center for Film and Theater Research.)

Versus Genius and Creatively Intelligent

The opposite characterized well-functioning "genius . . . creatively intelligent post-industrial organizations":

- Visionary leadership
- Critical analysis and judgment
- Creative thinkers and creative teamwork
- Excitement, pride, and purpose
- Plus flexibility; sensitivity; responsiveness; and dynamism

Van Gundy (1987) described additional organizational barriers to creative innovation that also are rooted in rules and traditions. While aimed at corporate organizations, these barriers seem to apply to educational and other organizations as well.

Status Hierarchy

One barrier lies in the *status hierarchy*. Lower-status persons are reluctant to suggest ideas to those in higher positions due to insecurity and fear of evaluation. When there is little lower-level participation in decision-making, it is unlikely that new ideas will "trickle up."

Further, if a new idea threatens to reduce status differences ("Hey, we can increase sales if we make everybody a vice president!"), the idea is sure to be resisted by higher status persons.

Enforcement of Rule Following

Understatement?

The *formalization* barrier refers to the degree to which following rules and procedures is enforced. Observed Van Gundy in a mild-mannered understatement: "It is thought that formalization is detrimental to initiation of innovations. . . . If organizational members are expected to behave in prescribed ways, and innovation is not prescribed, fewer idea proposals will be generated" (p. 361). However, he also observed that after an innovation is accepted, an efficient formal structure expedites its implementation.

Procedural Barriers

Van Gundy's *procedural* barriers include policies, procedures, and regulations (including unwritten ones) that inhibit creative innovation. Some examples are:

Promoting administrators based on analytic skills, not on their ability to encourage a creative atmosphere.

Emphasizing short-term (translation: short-sighted) planning.

Avoiding expenditures that do not produce an immediate payback.

Overemphasizing external rewards rather than internal, personal commitment.

Insisting on an orderly advancement with an innovation, with excessive detailed control early in its development.

Rules and traditions keep the system working. However, like habits, such predetermined guides can work against creative thinking.

PERCEPTUAL BLOCKS

Perceptual Set, Mental Set, Functional Fixedness

Perceptual blocks also are based in learning and habit. We become accustomed to perceiving things in familiar ways and it is difficult to see new meanings, new relationships, or new applications and uses. Psychologists refer to our predisposition to perceive things in certain ways as *perceptual set*, *mental set*, or *functional fixedness*. Perceptual sets are different for different people, rooted in our unique interested, needs, biases, values, and past learning.

Jumping to Conclusions

Perceptual sets also are tied to our tendency to make quick decisions and jump to conclusions, rather than flexibly see alternatives. One old problem solving experiment demonstrated that when a piece of string was needed to solve a problem, the string would be perceived and used if it were dangling from a nail on the wall—but not if it were engaged hanging a *No Smoking* sign, mirror, or calendar (Sheerer, 1963).

Perceptual barriers lead us to "kick ourselves" for not seeing a solution sooner. Try the following puzzles. The solutions appear at the end of the chapter summary.

1. Punctuate the following set of words to make a meaningful statement:

   TIME FLIES YOU CANNOT THEY FLY TOO FAST

Puzzles

2. Consider this puzzle:

   The police entered the gym containing five wrestlers just as the dying man looked at the cciling and mumbled the words, "He did it." They immediately arrested one of the wrestlers. How did they know which one?

3. Remove six letters from ASIPXPLETLTERES. What word is left?

Can Miss the "Real" Problem

Perceptual blocks can prevent one from identifying "the real problem." For example, based on symptoms that seem familiar, a physician or auto mechanic may persist in misclassifying a problem and will treat it incorrectly.

Failure to See Other Possibilities

Perceptual blocks also prevent us from getting a more complete and accurate picture of the world around us. For example, school teachers who fixate on IQ scores will fail to perceive students who are highly creative, artistic, or gifted in just one area. A teacher who has successfully used a particular teaching technique for many years will not recognize another technique as being even more effective. If a salesperson is invited by a client to demonstrate a computer desk, and is "mentally set" to do just that, he or she may fail to perceive that the client needs other products and supplies. A new product developer, who tries to make his or her product exactly right for one purpose, may fail to see other uses or markets for modified versions of the product.

Making the Familiar Strange: Seeing New Possibilities

Creativity leader William J. J. Gordon (1961) described how *making the familiar strange*—perceiving common objects and ideas in new ways—is a central creative process. Indeed it is. Much creativity involves a mental transformation, the perception of new meanings, combinations, and relationships that depend upon overcoming perceptual blocks.

CULTURAL BLOCKS

Expectations, Conformity

Cultural blocks amount to social influence, expectations, and conformity pressures, all based on social or institutional norms. Cultural blocks thus include more than a dab of learning and habit and rules and traditions. There are several dabs of "fear of being different" and a few dashes of "the way we think others expect us to behave." The result is a loss of individuality and creativity.

Fear of Being Different

Torrance (1968, 1977, 1979, 1984a, 1984b) concluded that creativity (fantasy, imagination) drops when children enter kindergarten, an early time when conformity and regimentation suddenly become the rule. Said Torrance (1977, p. 21), "this drop . . . is a societal or cultural phenomenon rather than a biological or natural one."

Kindergarten Slump

Fourth-Grade Slump

There has been an even larger drop in creativity at the fourth grade—Torrance's famous *fourth-grade slump*. Repeated Torrance (1977, p. 22), "the drop which occurs in the fourth grade is a societal rather than a biological phenomenon." The cultural

Fifth-Grade Slump in Korea

Fourth-Grade Slump Disappearing

Seventh-Grade Slump, Too

Dynamics: Uncomfortable to Be Different

Expectations, Stereotypes

Be Practical and Economical, but Not Nosy

Reason and Logic, but Not Fantasy

Cooperation or Competition Can Stifle Creativity

Additional Subtle Creativity Squelchers

source of the fourth-grade slump was confirmed in a study of 1,100 Korean elementary children by Kang (1989). Kang also found a substantial drop in creativity test scores, but in the fifth grade rather than fourth. The fourth-grade slump cannot be biological in origin if it occurs at age 9–10 in one country and age 10–11 in another.

There is a silver lining around the dark fourth-grade cloud, particularly in western cultures. A growing emphasis on teaching for creative development has helped offset the conformity-based fourth-grade slump.

Perhaps the most visible monkey-see monkey-do conformity pressures exert themselves at adolescence, when new-found abstract thinking abilities (Piaget's formal operational thinking) increase students' self-awareness and self-consciousness. Is it surprising that Torrance (1977) described another drop in creative thinking at the seventh-grade level? This drop is not as large as the notorious fourth-grade slump.

On the surface, the dynamics of conformity pressures are not particularly mysterious: It simply is uncomfortable to be different, to challenge accepted ways of thinking and behaving.[1] We learn that it is good to be correct and bad to make mistakes. Rewards normally follow correctness, but being wrong can elicit disapproval, criticism, or even sarcasm and ridicule. "Being different" or "being wrong" raises fears of being judged foolish, incompetent, or just plain stupid.[2]

Expectations and conformity pressures also work in more subtle ways. The traditionally perceived role of females—overloaded with expectations and stereotypes—is a perennial and slow-changing difficulty that is yet to be overcome (see, e.g., Davis & Rimm, 1998). There are pressures on us all to be practical and economical, which can be inconsistent with innovative, creative thinking. We also learn not to be "nosy," not to ask too many questions. However, as Simberg (1978, p. 126) noted, "By stifling questioning, we are cutting out the very heart of creativity—curiosity." There also is a backstairs belief that *fantasy* is a waste of time. (Where would creativity be without fantasy?) Moreover, society tells us to have faith in reason and logic, tendencies that can delicately repress imagination and innovation.

Simberg (1978) also noted that, especially in corporate settings, an overemphasis either on cooperation *or* competition can be barriers to creativeness. If high cooperation is stressed, a person must temper his or her creative ideas in order to "fit in," to conform and please others. On the other hand, an overemphasis on competition can orient us toward "beating somebody else to it," rather than toward finding good creative solutions.

Van Gundy (1987) described subtle *social/political* barriers to creative innovation, which include any organizational norms that reinforce conformity, inhibit innovation, discourage "idea people," or otherwise ban rocking the boat. For example:

Attitudes of secrecy

A reluctance to share ideas

The attitude that creative types do not fit in

A fear that innovation may change the uniqueness of an organization

A desire to protect the status quo

A fear that innovation will reduce jobs

---

[1]Note: "Unconventional" young people—beatniks of the '60s, hippies of the '70s, punkers of the '80s and '90s—may be viewed as conforming to different norms.

[2]As we will see in Chapter 4, however, the creative person must take risks and sometimes fail; that's part of being an innovator.

**Culture Itself:
Traditions, Roles,
Customs, Beliefs**

Finally, the greatest cultural barrier to creativity probably is—*the culture itself*. Western psychology traditionally ignores monumental cultural differences that exist elsewhere, for example, in their influence on one's creative personality, creative productivity, and general self-actualization. Think for a moment of the role of tradition, conformity, and especially the role (or place) of women in Spanish- and Arabic-speaking countries and many spots in India, Africa, and Asia.

Your author attended an all-Arabic (except for two Americans) creativity conference held in Doha, Qatar, located on the north edge of Saudi Arabia (Davis Kogan, & Soliman, submitted). About half of the women in the audience, many of whom were participants, wore Western clothes, but some of these felt compelled to keep their hair covered. Among the half wearing traditional black Arabic costumes, some exposed their faces and some only their eyes. On Doha streets many women were totally covered, peering out through a black veil.[3] Women were never on the streets in the evening, and almost none drove cars, although legally allowed to do so. The relatively new University of Qatar includes two duplicated and equivalent campuses—one for men and one for women—which are separated by the tongue-in-cheek "Berlin Wall."

Separate Campuses

At the conference, at least three women speakers blasted the flagrant Arabic discrimination against women because of its repressive effect on their creative development and contributions, which all participants had agreed was necessary for contemporary Arabic growth. Male participants seemed in agreement. Regrettably, by the time I left nothing had changed.

**Koran Favors
Individual
Development**

A recurrent topic—or dilemma—of the conference was the development of creativity in a traditional and religious Arabic society. One resolution was that, in the Koran, Mohammed's writings clearly favored the development of individuality and, by inference, creativity.

While unrelated to the conference, two recent papers also addressed the development of creativity in a traditional, conformist, and authoritarian (their words) Arab culture, Sudanese in this case. Khaleefa, Erdos, and Ashria (1996b) confirmed that in "tight sociocultural systems" females receive less education, experience less freedom and independence, and generally there is more conformity and authoritarianism. As a result, girls usually (but not always) score lower than boys on creativity tests. In this study, males (ages 15 to 20) scored higher on a test of creative personality, which measures independence, adventurousness, individuality, activity, curiosity, responsibility, motivation, and freedom. Big surprise. Females scored higher on a test that assesses actual past creative activities (linguistic, artistic, social, and scientific), a test whose scores, according to the authors, are influenced by the higher verbal creativity of females.

**Discrimination
Confirmed**

**Creativity Traits
Reinforced in Males**

**Culture Represses
Creativity Traits**

In another study, Khaleefa, Erdos, and Ashria (1996a) noted that the creative personality includes traits quite oppositional to traditional cultures, for example, being self-assertive, self-sufficient, unconventional, radical, expressive, non-authoritarian, having an individual and unique value system, and being willing to break with custom. (Whoa!) Clearly, this portrait works against nonconformity. The authors contrasted Western individualism, autonomy, self-reliance, and independence with Afro-Arabic Sudanese obedience, duty, conformity, sacrifice for the group, and low tolerance for deviating from the norms. In two memorable statements: *"Conformity to sociocultural institutions and to the expectations of others involves a substantial limitation of one's individuality"* and *"There is small scope for individuals to be creative"* (Khaleefa, Erdos, & Ashria, 1996a, pp. 270, 274). On the positive side, the authors noted that to be creative, as many wish to be, they must learn how to "attach to the sociocultural system, and at the same time how to

**Obedience, Duty
Conformity**

---

[3]The difference, I was told, was not in having different religions, but in varying degrees of belief and commitment to the same religion.

There Is a Time to Conform, a Time to Be Creative

detach from it." A creative individual must learn when to conform and how to be creative within the system. Another point is that original ideas are more likely to be accepted if they are placed within the values of the sociocultural system.

As a general guideline, and one consistent with even severe cultural blocks: *There is a time to conform and a time to think independently and creatively.*

EMOTIONAL BLOCKS

Strong Emotions Interfere

Emotional blocks, which may or may not be rooted in early learning or cultural traditions, interfere with clear thinking, sometimes by preoccupying and distracting our creative minds, other times by making us "freeze" in our thinking. Simberg (1978) imagined a balance scale with emotions on one side and clear thinking on the other; as one side goes up, the other goes down. Some familiar emotional blocks are anger, fear, anxiety, hate, and even love. Some are temporary states, caused perhaps by problems with peers, parents, partners, or children, or by pressures at school or work, financial stresses, or poor health. More permanent emotional blocks include such chronic sources of insecurity and anxiety as fear of failure, fear of being different, fear of criticism or ridicule, fear of rejection, fear of supervisors, timidity, or poor self-concepts.

Particularly Chronic Anxieties

Fears, Values, Needs

Van Gundy (1987) noted that some attitudinal barriers, such as fear of taking risks, fear of uncertainty and ambiguity, differences in values, or differences in personal needs, will block either the creation of innovations or their adoption and implementation.

Emotional states will interfere with creativity. This woman got upset over a simple game of hide-and-seek. (The Museum of Modern Art/Film Stills Archive.)

Can Take a Problem Solving Approach to Emotional Blocks

While this book does not deal in psychotherapy, we should note that moderate amounts of tension and anxiety are normal. In fact, some feelings of urgency or motivation are required for creative thinking and problem solving. However, if emotional blocks are interfering with thinking, it may help to take a creative problem-solving approach to dealing with them. That is, ask "What is the problem?" and "What can I/we do about it?" Chapter 5 will present the *Creative Problem Solving* (CPS) model that also may be used effectively with personal problems.

RESOURCE BARRIERS

Resource Barriers Not in Short Supply

Van Gundy (1987) described one last type of organizational block, to creative innovation, *resource barriers*, which is just that—a shortage of people, money, time, supplies, or information. Innovation requires such resources, beyond what is needed for routine organizational procedures. Internal conflicts, a type of social/political (or cultural) barrier, are likely if resources are pirated from one department to develop an innovation in another department.

A WHACK ON THE SIDE OF THE HEAD

Von Oech: Being Creative = Removing Mental Blocks

One fine book on stimulating creativity, written for corporate readers, was entitled *A Whack on the Side of the Head* (von Oech, 1983). The entire book focused on 10 mental blocks of the variety discussed above. It is noteworthy that to von Oech—a successful consultant and author in the area of corporate creativity—stimulating creativity is almost entirely as a matter of removing mental blocks. As his book title suggests, it can take a whack on the side of the head to jolt us out of our anti-creative mental blocks.

A Second Right Answer?

The first of von Oech's mental blocks, *The Right Answer*, is the usual assumption that there is just one right answer. Not so. We should look for a second right answer, a third right answer, and more. A later "right answer" is likely to be more creative than the first right answer. In Chapter 6 we will see that brainstorming, a creativity technique, is based squarely on deferring judgment until many possible solutions are produced.

This One Makes Sense

Von Oech's second block, *That's Not Logical*, is based on our culturally-rooted assumption that logical thinking is better than illogical thinking. However, illogical thinking can provide the imaginative play and new perspectives necessary for a creative breakthrough. In contrast to strictly logical thinking, von Oech listed other possibilities: speculative thinking, fantasy thinking, analogical thinking, divergent thinking, lyrical thinking, mythical thinking, poetic thinking, visual thinking, symbolic thinking, foolish thinking, ambiguous thinking, surreal thinking, and others. Instead of "getting down to brass tacks" we should consider steel tacks, copper tacks, plastic tacks, sailing tacks, income tax, syntax, or contacts.

We Should Inspect the Rules We Follow

A third block to creative thinking is *Follow the Rules*. Following rules includes thinking of things only as they are. Instead of following the rules, says von Oech, we should play the revolutionary and challenge rules. He recommended holding "rule-inspecting and rule-discarding" sessions within one's organization. (We might add "tradition-inspecting" and "tradition-discarding" sessions as well.)

Ask "What If" Questions

Be Practical is his fourth block. Instead of being inhibited by pressures toward practicality, we should ask creativity stimulating "what if" questions, and encourage "what-iffing" in others. Sometimes preposterous "what-iffing" leads to practical ideas. In von Oech's example, an engineer at a large chemical company asked this question: "What if we put gunpowder in our house paint? . . . [When it got old] we could just blow it right off the house!" This led to adding an inert

An Explosive Idea!

These political reformers are stymied in their creative thinking because of their strong beliefs that "We Must Follow The Rules," "We Must Be Practical," "We Must Not Be Foolish," and "To Err is Wrong." "Oh, what the heck," said Abe, honestly, "let's just serve broccoli and see what happens!" (The Museum of Modern Art/Film Stills Archive.)

Never Ambiguity Is Always Helpful

Fear of Making Mistakes

Thomas Edison, Thomas Watson: Mistakes Lead to Success

Errors = Whacks

Play with Ideas

chemical additive to the paint which, when another additive later was applied, a reaction would take place and the paint would easily strip off.

Avoid Ambiguity is the fifth block. In fact, ambiguity serves as a subtle form of motivation that inspires imaginative ideas. One can pose problems in deliberately ambiguous ways to induce imaginative answers. We will see in Chapter 7 that Gordon's "book titles" or "compressed conflicts" are ambiguous two-word statements that are deliberately created to provoke new viewpoints. Does the book title *motionless exertion* suggest ideas for physical exercises? Further, whenever one is engaged in creative problem solving a period of ambiguity always exists. A tolerance for or even liking of ambiguity is an essential creative trait.

Von Oech's sixth block is *To Err is Wrong*, which we noted earlier is a well-reinforced habit. A fear of making mistakes inhibits trying new things—but creative innovation necessarily requires making errors and even failing. One story claims that while working on the light bulb, Edison tried nearly 2,000 ideas. Edison optimistically reported that he now knew 2,000 ways *not* to build a light bulb! One probably surprising strategy for increasing creative productivity is to deliberately *increase* your failure rate. Creative person Thomas Watson, founder and president of IBM, claimed that "The way to succeed is to double your failure rate" (von Oech, 1983, p. 93). Observed von Oech, "Errors [serve] as stepping stones. . . . We learn by our failure. A person's errors are the whacks that lead him or her to think something different" (pp. 90–92).

Another block, von Oech's seventh, is the notion that *Play is Frivolous*. Countless creative innovations and scientific discoveries have been born by playing with ideas. As we will see in Chapter 4, childlike thinking, humor, and playing with ideas are exceedingly common characteristics of creative people. Necessity may be the mother of invention, said von Oech, but play is the father!

I Know Nothing about This Topic, It's Not My Area

Block number eight is *That's not My Area*. This block is rich with implications for creative thinking and problem solving. Especially, it is an excuse for not even trying to solve a problem because of presumed ignorance. Moreover, such a thinker certainly will not look for ideas and inspiration in other fields. In fact, many innovations are born by adapting ideas from outside of one's own field—

Analogical Thinking

as we will see in Chapter 7 on analogical thinking. Von Oech suggested finding idea in old science magazines, history, want ads, and "studying a subject on a shallow level" (p. 109). Many innovations come from people outside of an area, or who know little about the given problem situation.

C'Mon von Oech, Get Serious!

Don't be Foolish, block nine, is another cultural barrier rooted in conformity. Says von Oech, you occasionally should play the fool, and you certainly should be aware of when you or others are putting down a creative "fool." Prince's (1968) "get fired" technique, in which you propose an idea so totally foolish that your boss will immediately fire you, helps create the playfulness and craziness that can lead to creative ideas.

Self-Squelcher Will Be Accurate

Finally, we have the tenth block, the self-squelcher *I'm Not Creative. If you seriously believe this, you will be correct.* It is a self-fulfilling prophecy.

Do you need an occasional whack on the side of the head?

IDEA SQUELCHERS

It is bad enough to be uncreative. It's worse to squelch your own or other people's creative thinking. This list of *idea squelchers* is based on one created by Warren (1974), who modified a list by Clark (1958) in his book *Brainstorming*, plus a few more from two covers of the *Journal of Creative Behavior* (1974, Issue 2, and 1996, Issue 3), and a couple from Biondi (1980).

Popular Ways to Demolish Creativity

You never would make any of these comments, would you?

We've never done it before.	See? It didn't work!
We've already tried that before.	We haven't the teacher-student ratio.
It can't be done.	It's not in the budget.
It won't work.	It has limited possibilities.
Too blue sky.	We're not ready for it yet.
No way.	All right in theory, but can you put it into practice?
Are you nuts?	Too academic.
It's a waste of time.	Not academic enough; we need supporting theory.
I'm telling you, it won't work.	
I just know it won't work.	Won't we be held accountable?
What will the parents think?	Let's form a committee.
Somebody would have suggested it before if it were any good.	Let's put it in writing.
	We need more lead time.
Too modern.	Walk, don't run.
Too old-fashioned.	You'll never sell it to the union.
Not that way.	Don't forget the chain of command.
Let's discuss it at some other time.	Let's not fight city hall.
This is the last try.	Stay on their good side.
You've got to be kidding.	Don't step on any toes.
You ask too many questions.	

You don't understand our situation.

You don't understand the problem.

We're to small for that.

We're too big for that.

We're too new for that.

Let's not bother.

We have too many projects now.

It's been the same for 20 years, so it must be good.

This is how it's done.

Let's use proven methods.

What bubble head thought that up?

That's trouble.

Don't rock the boat.

I'll bet some professor suggested that.

We have to be practical.

It's not in the plan.

It's not in the curriculum.

We did all right without it.

You can't argue with success.

It'll mean more work.

It's too early.

It's too late.

Be practical.

Let's wait and see.

I don't see the connection.

It won't work in our neighborhood.

We can't do it under the regulations.

There's no regulations covering it.

The Board will faint.

That's not our responsibility.

That's not our department.

That's not our job.

That's not our role.

It's low in our priorities.

It will offend.

What's the use?

Why bother?

It doesn't matter.

Our people won't accept it.

You can't teach an old dog new tricks.

Have you checked with . . . ?

And you stand there saying . . . .

No adolescent is going to tell me how to run this operation!

Understand, Be Ready

The main advantage of understanding external barriers to creativity is that it forces you to plan ahead—to anticipate the resistance that may greet your innovative ideas and plans. Understanding internal barriers can help us deal with them in a mentally healthy, creativity-consistent way.

SUMMARY

We all would be more creative if it were not for blocks and barriers to creative thinking.

Habit and learning, which are necessary for humankind, also can be blocks to creative thinking.

Rules and traditions, too, are essential for society, but can inhibit imagination and innovation. Some recent shots at traditional, imagination-stifling educational and other organizations emphasized bureaucratic structures, over-specialized roles, punishment for taking risks and making mistakes, near-sighted and coercive leadership, frustration, conformity, ritual, narrow focus, and poorly integrated subsystems.

"Creatively intelligent" organizations showed visionary leadership, creativity, excitement, flexibility, and dynamism.

Van Gundy's organizational barriers included the status hierarchy, formalization (rule following), and procedural barriers, e.g., promotions based on analytic skills, short-term planning, emphasis on external (not personal) rewards, and tight control in developing innovations.

Perceptual blocks—mental set, perceptual set, functional fixity—are based in learning. They prevent us from seeing new meanings, relations, applications, and new possibilities generally. Perceptual blocks are related to "jumping to conclusions," prevent us from "seeing the real problem," and prevent us from getting an accurate picture of our world.

Cultural blocks are social influence, expectations, and conformity pressures, which combine with our "fear of being different" to squelch creative thinking. Torrance's fourth-grade slump, and his smaller kindergarten and seventh-grade slumps, are due to conformity pressures and expectations.

Regarding dynamics, we simply do not like to be different, make mistakes, be wrong, look stupid, or "ask too many questions." Traditional expectations and stereotypes of females persist.

A traditional belief in reason and logic can repress fantasy and innovation.

Excessive cooperation—fitting in—or competition can stifle creativity.

Van Gundy described such social/political barriers as attitudes of secrecy, dislike for creative types, and protecting the status quo.

The most problematic cultural block is the culture itself, particularly in the repressed roles of females, along with traditions, beliefs, authoritarianism, and conformity that are inconsistent with creative personalities and creative productivity. One suggestion was to be creative, but within the traditional value system.

Emotional blocks may be temporary states or more chronic insecurities and fears, particularly fear of failure, ridicule, being different, or taking risks.

One can take a creative problem solving approach to emotional blocks.

Resource barriers are shortages of people, money, supplies, time, or information.

Von Oech's Whack on the Side of the Head approach to increasing creativity amounted to unlocking 10 mental blocks: The Right Answer; That's Not Logical; Follow the Rules; Be Practical; Avoid Ambiguity; To Err Is Wrong; Play Is Frivolous; That's Not My Area; Don't Be Foolish; and "I'm Not Creative."

Our list of idea squelchers affords an excellent list of suggestions for nipping creativity in its bud.

As a general principle, as one proceeds down the yellow brick road of life, there is a time to conform and a time to be creative.

Solutions to Puzzles:

1. Time flies? You cannot, they fly too fast.

2. The other four wrestlers were women.

3. Try removing S-I-X L-E-T-T-E-R-S.

Barriers, Blocks, and Squelchers: Why We Are Not More Creative

Self-Test: Key Concepts and Terms

Give an example of how each of these barriers can depress YOUR creativity:

Habit and learning _____

_____

Rules and traditions _____

_____

Perceptual blocks _____

_____

Cultural blocks _____

_____

Emotional blocks _____

_____

Resource barriers _____

_____

Briefly define or explain each of these:

A Whack on the Side of the Head

_____

Idea squelchers _____

Let's Think about It

1. Problem: Rules, traditions, social expectations, and conformity pressures squelch our creativity and our independence.

   Solution(s): _____

   _____

   _____

   _____

2. Regarding creativity, how are the effects of conformity pressures and insecurity like being a *slug* (soft-shelled snail).

   _____

   _____

3. Make up at least five absolutely ridiculous, preposterous blocks to creativity, i.e., things that STOP you from thinking creatively, or reasons you are not more creative (for example, "EEG says I am brain dead").

   a. _____

   b. _____

   c. _____

   d. _____

   e. _____

4. Which four or five of von Oech's 10 barriers do you HEAR the most?

   a. _____

   b. _____

   c. _____

   d. _____

   e. _____

   Which do you USE the most?

   a. _____

   b. _____

   c. _____

5. Which idea squelchers do you think are the most common?

a. _____

b. _____

c. _____

d. _____

e. _____

f. _____

Which do you use? (None? Terrific!)

_____

_____

_____

6. Look over the list of idea squelchers in this chapter. Create a half-dozen more.

a. _____

b. _____

c. _____

d. _____

e. _____

f. _____

Self-Rating of Creativity

I AM A CREATIVE PERSON

Strongly Disagree		Unsure		Strongly Agree
1	2	3	4	5

Creativity Test

Indicate the degree to which each statement applies to you. Use the following scale:

1 = No
2 = To a small degree
3 = Average
4 = More than average
5 = Definitely

_____   1.   I am unconventional in many ways.

_____   2.   I am very artistic.

_____   3.   I am quite absent-minded.

_____   4.   I try to use metaphors and analogies in my writing.

_____   5.   I am a very active, energetic person.

_____   6.   I enjoy thinking of new and better ways of doing things.

_____   7.   I am very curious.

_____   8.   I am quite original and inventive.

_____   9.   Some of my past or present hobbies would be considered "unusual."

_____   10. I like the nonsense forms and bright colors of modern art.

_____   11. My ideas are often considered impractical or even "wild."

_____   12. I would rate myself high on "intuition" or "insightfulness."

_____   13. I like some body smells.

_____   14. I am able to work intensely on a project for many hours.

_____   15. I like trying new ideas and new approaches to problems.

_____   16. I often become totally engrossed in a new idea.

_____   17. Most of my friends are unconventional.

_____   18. The word "quick" describes me.

_____   19. I could be considered a spontaneous person.

_____   20. I have engaged in a lot of creative activities.

_____   21. I would rate myself high in self-confidence.

_____   22. I am always open to new ideas and new activities.

_____ 23. Sometimes I get so interested in a new idea that I neglect what I should be doing.

_____ 24. I am often inventive or ingenious.

_____ 25. I enjoy trying new approaches to problems.

_____ 26. I have taken things apart just to find out how they work.

_____ 27. I have participated in theatrical productions.

_____ 28. I have a great sense of humor.

_____ 29. Many stories of mysterious, psychical happenings are true.

_____ 30. When I was young, I was always building or making things.

Scoring: Add up your ratings. The following is a guideline for interpretation:

30–55	Low in creative personality traits
56–79	Below average
80–102	Average
103–126	Above average
127–150	High in creative personality traits

Does your test score agree with your initial rating?

Does your test score generally agree with your Self-Actualization score at the end of Chapter 1?

Regardless of your score (but especially if it is below about 90), try developing your creative personality traits—see Chapter 4.

3

definitions and theories
what is creativity?

[*Scene: Austrian court room. Judge Heinrich Hangum is reading the charges against defendant Sigmund Freud.*]

Judge Hangum: Herr Doktor Freud, you bin charged mit using schmutty ideas in your creativity theory und offendink the sensitivities of delicate folks. How do you plead, you guilty rascal?

Sigmund Freud: Not guilty, Herr Judge. I bin writin' und speakin' only die truth!

Judge: But die truth is, you bin sayin' we're bein' creative because we got a big sexy sex drive! You bin guilty as Cain!

Freud: But Herr Judge, dot isn't schmutty! We're bein' creative 'cause our id got sex needs, our superego got a clean conscience, und so our ego—dot's our "self"—puts the sex needs into creative fantasies!

Judge: Schmutty fantasies?

Freud: Nein, nein! Creative idea fantasies—poetry und painting, nice tings like dot.

Judge: Sounds fischy to me! Herr Doktor Freud, are you sure?

Freud: I am not die world's greatest psychoanalyst for nothink, you know.

Judge: I sink I vill give you six months in das schlammer to clean up your theory.

Freud: I sink you love your mama, hate your papa, und so you bin pickin' on defenseless psychoanalysts!

Judge: Make dot a year.

> *The creative writer does the same as the child at play. The writer creates a world of phantasy which he or she takes very seriously . . . while separating it sharply from reality.*
>
> Sigmund Freud

39

There are many definitions and theories of creativity. To complicate matters, definitions sometimes are considered theories, and theories sometimes are definitions. Elaborate definitions are especially likely to be called a theory. If the statements are presented as a theory, they are certain to include a definition of creativity. Further, every test of creativity absolutely must define what the test purports to measure, and so the testing literature is another source of definitions. The problem is complicated, or delicate, as we soon will see.

The commonality among definitions and theories is that both seek to simplify and explain a complex phenomena. To impose some structure, this chapter will review five categories of definitions of creativity, three classic theoretical approaches to creativity, and then summarize eight more contemporary theories, including the "investment" and "interactionist" models of creativity. For a more extensive review of creativity definitions and theories, the reader might begin with the olde-but-excellent *The Creativity Question* (Rothenberg & Hausman, 1976), which includes, for example, Plato (inspiration from the gods through the Muses); behaviorist Burrhus Frederick Skinner (his friends called him "Fred"; reinforcement of creative responses); Paul Torrance (the creativity man himself; Millar, 1995); Frank Barron (creative personality); and Joseph Bogen and Glenda Bogen (creativity and brain hemispheres). The book also presents a selection by my favorite classic scholar Cesare Lombroso, who in 1895 related creativity to insanity—and therefore to degeneration of the brain—because both the creative and the insane tend to be original.[1] Another anthology, *The Creative Process* (Ghiselin, 1952), presents original writings by historically creative persons, for example, Einstein, Mozart, van Gogh, Wordsworth, and Nietzsche. A recent eloquent volume presents relevant parts of the lives of seven creatively eminent persons (Gardner, 1993), Freud, Einstein, Picasso, Stravinsky, T. S. Eliot, Martha Graham, and Gandhi. Other theoretical works are Arietti (1976), Dacey (1989), Runco and Albert (1990), and Sternberg (1988b; especially the chapter by Taylor).

To set the tone, there are about as many definitions, theories, and ideas about creativity as there are people who have set their opinions on paper. As a few pertinent quotes, Freeman, Butcher, and Christie (1968) concluded that "there is no unified psychological theory of creativity" and that we freely use such terms as *imagination, ingenuity, innovation, intuition, invention, discovery,* and *originality* interchangeably with *creativity.* Nicholls (1972) added that "the term *creativity* is used with something approaching [reckless] abandon by psychologists ... and people in general."

Tardif and Sternberg (1988, p. 429), in an attempt to review commonalities and differences among the theoretical explanations in Sternberg's (1988b) anthology on creativity, concluded that "Different levels of analysis were used to address the concepts; within levels, different components were put forth; and even when similar components were discussed, differences were seen in how these components are defined and how crucial they were claimed to be for the larger concept of creativity." Translation: Gee whiz, even experts have different ideas about what's important for "creativity."

A recent Asian viewpoint explained *Ninja Secrets of Creativity* (Petkus, 1994). A state of emptiness (*Ku*; e.g., having a problem) leads one to draw from four bipolar centers: *chi* (earth; stability [+] versus resistance to change [−]); *sui* (water; flexibility [+] versus over-emotionalization [−]): *ka* (fire; dynamic vitality [+] versus fear [−]); and *fu* (wind; wisdom and love [+] versus over-intellectualization [−]). One's personality, cognitive style, and situational requirements are said to influ-

---

[1]Lombroso would have loved Rosanne Barr, Steve Martin, Jim Carrey, and Howard Hughes.

ence the selection. For example, losing your job (a problem, *ku*) might involve assessing strengths (*chi*, stability), vigorously and flexibly pursuing new jobs (*sui* and *ka*), and taking into account what was learned in the earlier job (*fu*). Western tastes may find excess terms and concepts in this view, but it illustrates the complexity issue.

Creativity Is Complex, Multifaceted

A main problem in pinning down "creativity" is its complexity and multifaceted nature. We can choose to examine, theorize, or conduct research about any minuscule or global part of creativity, and we do. Said Carl Jung (1959), "the creative aspect of life . . . baffles all attempts at rational formulation." Well, not entirely. Two traits of creative people are attraction to complexity and tolerance for ambiguity, which also seem to characterize anyone interested in pursuing this topic.

DEFINITIONS OF CREATIVITY

Four Interrelated P's

It is convenient and conventional to organize creativity around at least three *P*s: The creative *person*, the creative *product*, and the creative *process*. There also is an indispensable fourth *P*, the creative *press*—the environment or climate. For example, sections of Arietti's (1976) classic book are organized around the creative person, product, and environment. Tardif and Sternberg (1988) reviewed their creativity chapters in regard to contributions to each of the four areas; and Taylor (1988) already had organized his chapter around the four words. Person, product, process, and press (environment) are classic ways to classify creativity research, creativity definitions and theories, and other discussions of the topic.

Simonton's *P*: Persuasion

Simonton (1988a, 1990), incidentally, added a fifth *P*, *persuasion*, to emphasize the role of *leadership* in impressing others with one's creativity. "A creator [must] claim appreciators or admirers to be legitimatized as a true creator" (p. 387). We also will see this social-interpersonal part of creativity in the theories of Csikszentmihalyi (1988; pronounced "Smith") and Gardner (1993). For now, we will sample definitions included under the first four *P*s—person, product, process, and press.

4 *P*s Are Related

The four *P*s are interrelated in the obvious way: Creative products are the outcome of creative processes engaged in by creative people, all of which is supported by a creative environment. Torrance (1988) relates the creative process, person, product, and press with these words: "I chose a process definition of creativity for research purposes. I thought that if I chose a process as a focus, I could then ask what kind of person one must be to engage in the process successfully, what kinds of environments will facilitate it, and what kinds of products will result from successful operation of the processes" (p. 47).

To the four *P*s we add a fifth class of definitions: *mysterious mental happenings*, a pesky category that cannot be ignored despite the best struggles of contemporary objective thinking.

CREATIVE PERSON

Creative Persons Possess Particular Traits

In Chapter 4 we will review many recurrent personality and biographical traits of creative people, for example, confidence, energy, risk-taking, humor, and a history of creative activities. Definitions with a person orientation respond to the question "What is creativity?" with an answer such as, "Well, a creative person is someone who . . . [possesses particular traits that influence his or her creativeness]."

Cesare Lombroso

There are several historically notable and unique definitions of creativity with a distinct person emphasis. Consider, for example, Lombroso's degenerate brain definition (or theory). Naming specific famous persons, Lombroso (1895) noted that "signs of degeneration in men of genius" include stuttering, short stature, general emaciation, sickly color, rickets (leading to club-footedness, lameness, or being hunch-backed), baldness, amnesia/forgetfulness, sterility, and that awful symptom of brain degeneration—left-handedness! While rating high in entertainment value, the characteristics are not related to creative potential, except possibly the left-handedness.[2]

Otto Rank

Rank's (1945) description of his *creative type*, also referred to as the *artist* or the *man of will and deed*, resembles strongly Maslow's self-actualized creativity. This creative person has a strong, positive, integrated personality and "is at one with himself . . . what he does, he does fully and completely in harmony with all his powers and ideals." Rank's creative type contrasts with his "average man" and his "conflicted and neurotic man." A former glass blower, Rank himself probably was an artist.

Carl Jung

Jung was a noteworthy colleague of Freud's. He was a regular guest at the weekly meetings of Freud's Wednesday Psychological Society. Quoting Society member Ernest Jones, Gardner (1993) noted that "the particular collection of men . . . were mostly of second rank. . . . it was hard to secure a pupil with a reputation to lose" (pp. 50–51). In 1909 Freud and Jung traveled together to Clark University in Massachusetts to promote psychoanalysis, and in 1910 Freud offered Jung the presidency of his new International Psychoanalytic Association (Gardner, 1993).

Jung (1933, 1959, 1976) described the creative works of novelists and poets, particularly Goethe, and identified two types of artistically creative people, the *psychological type* and the *visionary type*. The psychological type of creator draws from the realm of human consciousness—lessons of life, emotional shocks, and experiences of passion and human crises. For example, said Jung, the poet's work is an interpretation of conscious life that raises the reader to greater clarity and understanding. Novels about love, crime, the family, or society, along with didactic poetry and much drama, is of the psychological type. According to Jung, the material is understandable, based in experience, and fully explains itself.

More interesting and mystical is his visionary type. "It is a strange something that derives its existence from the hinterland of man's mind. . . . It is a primordial experience which surpasses man's understanding" (Jung, 1933). This "primordial experience" is said to be an activation of one's "archetypes" or "primordial images." Jung claimed that "The archetypal image . . . lies buried and dormant in man's unconscious since the dawn of culture . . . they are activated—one might say 'instinctively'—[in the] visions of artists and seers." When exposed to such archetypes, said Jung, we may be astonished, taken aback, confused, and perhaps even disgusted. They remind us of nothing in everyday life, but they may remind us of dreams, nighttime fears, and "dark recesses of the mind" about which we have misgivings.

---

[2]As elaborated slightly in Chapter 4, the suggestion is that left-handers, most of whom are ambidextrous, have superior access to both brain hemispheres, which helps creativity. The jury is still out.

"I got primordial archetypes and you-ou don't. I got primordial archetypes and you-ou don't!" gloated Harpo. "They're probably in that stupid hat!" replied Zeppo. (Wisconsin Center for Film and Theater Research.) Copyright by Universal City Studios, Inc. Courtesy of Universal Studios Publishing Rights. All rights reserved.

The visionary creative person, due to dissatisfaction with current circumstances, is said to reach out to this collective unconscious. "The creative process, in so far as we are able to follow it at all, consists in an unconscious animation of the archetype, and in a development and shaping of this image till the work is completed" (Jung, 1976, p. 125–126).

Thin Evidence!

Is there evidence for this eyebrow-raising explanation of the creative person? Said Jung (1976), the assumption that an artist has tapped his collective unconscious for an unfathomable idea can be derived only from *a posteriori* analysis of the work of art itself. That is, the material seems not to be a reflection of the poet's personality, experience, or psychic disposition. However, noted Jung (1933), "we cannot doubt that the vision is a genuine, primordial experience, regardless of what reason-mongers may say." The critical reader, presumably a reason-monger, might mentally place Jung's archetypes with Plato's Muses and the tooth fairy.

Later in this chapter many theories of creativity, particularly that of Sternberg, also focus heavily on characteristics of the creative person.

CREATIVE PROCESS

E. Paul Torrance

Torrance's Definition

Torrance's (1988, 1995) definition of creativity describes a process that resembles steps in the scientific method: "I have tried to describe creative thinking as taking place in the process of [1] sensing difficulties, problems, gaps in information, or missing elements; [2] making guesses or formulating hypotheses about these deficiencies; [3] testing these guesses and possibly revising and retesting them; and finally [4] communicating the results. I like this definition because it describes such a natural process" (Torrance, 1995, p. 72). Torrance's process definition is unique in including the entire creative episode, from detecting a problem to presenting the results. We noted earlier that Torrance's process definition implicitly or explicitly includes the creative person (someone who can do this), the creative product (the successful result), and the creative press (the environment that facilitates the process).

Graham Wallas

Wallas Stages

In Chapter 5 we will look at several proposed sets of stages in creativity, each of which has been described as "the creative process." For now, we will mention just briefly Wallas' (1926) ancient-but-still-healthy four steps of *preparation, incubation, illumination,* and *verification*. The terms are almost self-defining, but you may peek at Chapter 5 if you wish.

Creative Problem Solving (CPS) Model

Six CPS Stages

Or Five

The currently most useful set of stages, in the sense of helping one to creatively solve real problems, is the Creative Problem Solving (CPS) model (e.g., Parnes, 1981; Treffinger, Isaksen, & Dorval, 1994a). To anticipate Chapter 5, the six thought-and-work guiding stages are entitled (1) *Mess Finding* (locating a problem needing solution), (2) *Fact Finding* (examining what you know about the problem), (3) *Problem Finding* (selecting a specific problem definition), (4) *Idea Finding* (e.g., through brainstorming), (5) *Solution Finding* (evaluating ideas), and (6) *Acceptance Finding* (implementing ideas). The CPS model sometimes is presented without the first step, that is, as a five-stage model (e.g., Parnes, 1981).

Combining Ideas

Many process definitions assume that a creative idea is a combination of previously unrelated ideas, or looking at it another way, a new relationship among existing ideas. The creative process, therefore, is the process of combining the ideas or perceiving the relationships.

To note a few notables:

"It is obvious that invention or discovery, be it in mathematics or anywhere else, takes place by combining ideas" (Hadamard, 1945).

"The ability to relate and to connect, sometimes in odd and yet striking fashion, lies at the very heart of any creative use of the mind, no matter in what field or discipline" (Seidel, 1962).

"The intersection of two ideas for the first time" (Keep, cited in Taylor, 1988).

"The integration of facts, impressions, or feelings into a new form" (Porshe, 1955).

"That quality of the mind which allows an individual to juggle scraps of knowledge until they fall into new and more useful patterns" (Read, 1955).

"The creative process is the emergence in action of a novel relational product, growing out of the uniqueness of the individual" (Rogers, 1962, p. 65).

"Creativity is a marvelous capacity to grasp two mutually distinct realities without going beyond the field of our experience and to draw a spark from their juxtaposition" (Preface to Max Ernst Exhibition, cited in Fabun, 1968).

Perkins' (1988) explanation of creativity focused on how a creative person deals with idea combinations. Perkins began by posing the hypothetical question of

Many creative ideas are the product of combining previously unrelated ideas. In this historic photo Winchester Arms inventor Wally Boome combined the idea of "big oaf" with the idea of "cannon" to produce the first self-propelled, self-aiming artillery piece that runs on a daily fuel supply of five chickens and 25 pounds of potatoes. "A little rhubarb pie, too," adds Olaf Oaf, carefully taking aim. (The Museum of Modern Art/Film Stills Archive.)

How Can Something Come from Nothing?

Generation, Selection, Preservation of Ideas: Perkins

whether invention is possible, the *ex nihilo* question: How can something come out of nothing? His solution, in brief, includes a process analogous to natural selection—the *generation*, *selection*, and *preservation* of ideas. Unlike natural selection, the generation process is not random. The potential "combinatorial explosion" of possibilities is "mindfully directed" by creative people, who are motivated, have creative "patterns of deployment" or "personal maneuvers of thought," and have raw ability in a discipline. Such people mentally represent and "operate on" traditional boundaries, producing practical innovations (e.g., the light bulb) and impractical ones (e.g., poetry—his example).

High Intuitive Appeal

Defining creative ideas as new combinations of existing ideas has strong intuitive appeal. For example, virtually any consumer product, from bread makers and roller blades to Chinese pizza and glowing golf balls, easily can be dissected into the parts that were combined into the innovative wholes. The same usually applies to scientific, medical, technological, and—perhaps with more difficulty—to artistic and literary creations.

Creative Combinations Require a Creative Person

Assembling high quality creative combinations normally requires experience, highly-developed technical and stylistic skills, high energy, a lively imagination, and a polished aesthetic taste to know when the idea combination is good. The final creation may be a simple idea combination, such as chocolate ants, or a complex one, such Beethoven's Ninth or your student union building.

CREATIVE PRODUCT

Product and Process Related

Some definitions of creativity in the *process* category are a hair-width (or less) from definitions in the creative *product* category and easily could appear in this section.

Originality

And Social Worth

He's a Good Egg!

Definitions that focus on the creative product typically emphasize *originality*, a word sometimes used interchangeably with *creativity*. If the person penning the definition thinks a few seconds longer, he or she usually will include some notion of correctness, appropriateness, value, usefulness, or social worth. Such terms exclude the bizarre, off-the-wall—but unquestionably original—scribblings of a chimpanzee or babblings of a child, mentally deranged person, or politician. Said Briskman (1980, p. 95), "The novelty of a creative product clearly is only a necessary condition of its creativity, not a sufficient condition; for the man who, in Russell's apt phrase, believes himself to be a poached egg may very well be uttering a novel thought, but few of us, I imagine, would want to say that he was producing a creative one."

Some definitions emphasizing just originality are:

"Creative ability appears simply to be a special class of psychological activity characterized by novelty" (Newell, Shaw, & Simon, 1962).

Creativity is "the process of bringing something new into birth" (May, 1959).

"Creativity . . . is a noun naming the phenomenon in which a person communicates a new concept (which is the product)" (Rhodes, 1961).

Adding a dash of appropriateness, value, or social worth we get:

"Creativeness, in the best sense of the word, requires two things: an original concept, or 'idea,' and a benefit to someone" (Mason, 1960).

"To be considered creative, a product or response must be novel . . . and appropriate" (Hennessey & Amabile, 1988).

"Creativity is the occurrence of a composition which is both new and valuable" (Murray, cited in Fabun, 1968).

"Creativity is the disposition to make and to recognize valuable innovations" (Lasswell, cited in Fabun, 1968).

"The creative process in any thinking process which solves a problem in an original and useful way" (Fox, cited in Fabun, 1968).

"A creative person, by definition, . . . more or less regularly produces outcomes in one or more fields that appear both original and appropriate" (Perkins, 1988).

Barron: Newness, Purposefulness, Fitness

Emphasizing both originality and worth, Barron (1988, p. 80) wrote that "Creativity is an ability to respond *adaptively* to the needs for new approaches and new products. It is essentially the ability to bring something new into existence purposefully." Expanding on the purposefulness of innovations, Barron emphasized "their aptness, their validity, their adequacy in meeting a need, and a rather subtle additional property that may be called, simply, *fitness*—aesthetic fitness, ecological fitness, optimum form, [and] being 'right' as well as original at the moment. The emphasis is on whatever is fresh, novel, unusual, ingenious, clever, and apt."

This Circular Definition Is an Implicit Definition

If you are willing to concede that you more-or-less know a creative product when you see one, a convenient circular definition is that *a creative person is someone who does creative things*. The focus is on the product, with creativeness generalizing to the person who created it. The definition seems to encompass both Maslow's self-actualized creativity and his special talent creativity. It also accepts the inherently creative nature of many occupations and pastimes, for example, art, architecture, theater, writing, music composition and expression, science research, marketing and advertising, business entrepreneurship, industrial design work, and hosts of others. We will see "implicit theories" of creativity again later.

CREATIVE PRESS

Environment Has Central Role

A fourth category of definitions of creativity emphasizes the creative *press*, the social and psychological environment.[3] We do not find definitions or theories that are based solely on the presence or absence of a creative environment. We do find continual reference to the role of society and culture in virtually all thoughtful writings on creativity, including most theories, as we soon will see.

Press May Repress Creativity

We know that the environment may repress imagination and innovation, for example, as described in our cultural barriers section of Chapter 2. We saw that organizations or nations can squelch creativity by stressing conformity, tradition, duty, obedience, role obligations, inflexible rules, and the *status quo* in general. To anticipate Freud's theory, he combined virtually all social pressures into his word *superego*, which usually translates "social conscience."

Or Support Creativity

We find an emphasis on a favorable creative press in brainstorming, with its defining principle of *deferred judgment* (no criticism, no evaluation; Chapter 6), in Carl Rogers' (1962) emphasis on *psychological safety*, and in any classroom or corporate setting where a *creative climate* encourages creative thinking and innovation. Isaksen (1987, p. 14) noted as "necessary conditions for the healthy functioning of the preconscious mental processes which produce creativity: The absence of serious threat to the self, the willingness to risk, . . . [and] openness to the ideas of others."

Responses to Social Needs: Rhodes

Response to Social Needs. Rhodes (1987) mentioned two aspects of the environment that are important for creativity. First, many innovations are in response to social needs—the world needed a cotton gin, a telephone, a Xerox machine, good Broadway shows, heart transplants and angioplasties, CAT Scans, microcomputers, modems, the internet, and awful-tasting TV dinners. Current highly visible needs—such as a cure for AIDS and fewer guns, gangs, and joints in the elementary school—are motivating near-frantic levels of creative problem solving and innovation. Second, for most creations, especially those based in technology, the environment must offer "a sufficiently advanced state of culture and a proper technical heritage" (Rhodes, 1987, p. 220).

And Sufficient Technology

Environment Provides Judges

Below, in the theories of Csikszentmihalyi, Gardner, and Simonton we will see a perhaps surprising, but to them essential, role of society in the provision of sophisticated judges to decide what products, and therefore what people, truly are *creative*.

MYSTERIOUS MENTAL HAPPENINGS

Descriptions of mysterious mental happenings come from people who should be best qualified to understand the process of creativity—creatively eminent people themselves. A main point is that creativity either is inexplicable or just sort of happens. Peanuts cartoonist Shulz, for example, claimed that many of his ideas came from "things that go bump in the night." Despite his own suggestions, Jung (1933) noted that "Any reaction to a stimulus may be causally explained; but the creative act, which is the absolute antithesis of mere reaction, will forever elude human understanding."

Things That Go Bump: Shulz

Creativity Eludes Understanding: Jung

Intriguing Combinations

John Livingstone Lowes (1927) analyzed Samuel Coleridge's writing of *Kubla Khan* in a way that hints of combining mental ideas, but in a deeper and more intriguing way. Coleridge had reported that he composed over two hundred lines while in a deep opium sleep, and published it almost without modification. Lowes

---

[3]Mnemonic device: Think of *social pressure*.

proposed that Coleridge's prior readings and writings filled his mind with the ideas and images that combined into the poetic *Kubla Khan*. Said Lowes in dry social science journalese, "Facts which sank at intervals out of conscious recollection drew together beneath the surface through almost chemical affinities of common elements . . . there in the darkness moved phantasms of fishes and animiculae and serpentine forms of his vicarious voyages, thrusting out tentacles of association and interweaving beyond disengagement."

In a letter, Mozart (1963) described unconscious processes in creativity:

Mozart Hears Completed Compositions "All at Once"

> When I am, as it were, completely myself, entirely alone, and of good cheer—say traveling in a carriage, or walking after a good meal, or during the night when I cannot sleep—it is on such occasions that my ideas flow best and most abundantly. *Whence* and *how* they come, I know not; nor can I force them. Those ideas that please me I retain in memory, and am accustomed, as I have been told, to hum them to myself. If I continue in this way, it soon occurs to me how I may turn this . . . agreeably to the rules of counterpoint, to the peculiarities of the various instruments, etc. All this fires my soul, and, provided I am not disturbed, my subject enlarges itself, becomes methodized and defined, and the whole, though it be long, stands almost complete and finished in my mind, so that I can survey it, like a fine picture or a beautiful statue, at a glance. Nor do I hear in my imagination the parts *successively*, but I hear them, as it were, all at once. . . . All this inventing, this producing, takes place in a pleasing lively dream . . . the committing to paper is done quickly enough, for everything is . . . already finished; and it rarely differs on paper from what it was in my imagination. (pp. 44–45)

Fabun (1968) provided additional brief examples:

> "It is like diving into a pond—then you start to swim . . . Once the instinct and intuition get into the brush tip, the picture happens, if it is to be a picture at all" (D. H. Lawrence).

> Gertrude Stein reflected, "Think of writing in terms of discovery, which is to say that creation must take place between the pen and the paper, not before in thought or afterwards in a recasting . . . It will come if it is there and if you will let it come."

> "I have no idea whence this tide comes, or where it goes, but when it begins to rise in my heart I know that a story is in the offing" (Dorothy Canfield).

Martindale (1975) also described creative people whose idea sources mystified even them:

> William Blake reported that he wrote one poem "from immediate dictation, 12 or sometimes 20 or 30 lines at a time without premeditation, and even against my will."

> Beethoven, as with Mozart, heard symphonies in his head and had only to scribble out the notes.

> Mathematician Poincare reported that after some stiff coffee, "ideas rose in crowds, I felt them collide until pairs interlocked, making a stable combination. By the next morning I had established the existence of a class of fuchsian functions . . . I had only to write out the results."

Poet A. E. Housman said that, after a few beers, "As I went along, thinking nothing in particular, . . . there would flow into my mind with sudden and unaccountable emotion, sometimes a line or two of verse, sometimes a whole stanza at once."

Poet Jean Nicolas Rimbaud wrote, "I witness the breaking forth of my thoughts. I watch them, I listen to them."

Socrates: Divine Power

Plato (Cooper, 1961) had Socrates explain this account of the poetic process: "A poet is a light and winged thing, and holy, and never able to compose until he has become inspired, and is beside himself and reason is no longer in him . . . for not by art do they utter these, but by power divine."

She Later Discovers the Meaning

Contemporary writer Gloria Naylor stated that she discovers the meaning of her writing after it is completed. "I'm like a filter for these stories . . . The process starts with images that I am haunted by and I will not know why . . . You just feel a dis-ease until somehow you go into the whole, complicated, painful process of writing and find out what the image means." She referred to the images as "waking, psychic revelations" (Perry, 1993).

Much about Creativity Remains a Mystery

The lesson in this series of definitions and analyses is that although we do understand much about creative people and creative processes, much also remains a mystery, even to our most creative people.

CLASSIC THEORIES OF CREATIVITY

Three Traditional Approaches

There are a large number of ideas that are considered "theories of creativity," including many of the definitions and descriptions above. This section will briefly review three traditional approaches, the *psychoanalytic*, *behavioristic*, and *self-actualization* views.

PSYCHOANALYTIC THEORIES

There is not a single, unitary psychoanalytic interpretation of creativity. Rather, there are several.

A Bright Child

Sigmund Freud.   The best-known and least-liked psychoanalytic theory of creativity is that of the great man himself, Sigmund Freud. Freud was extremely intelligent and well read. As a child he topped his school class for many years. His family catered to his talent, giving him his own room and even his own "eating chamber." When his sister's piano practicing annoyed him, the piano was removed from the house (!) (Gardner, 1993, p. 52). As an adult thinker, dream analysis led him to conclude that sexual themes lay behind the unconscious, and that defense mechanisms, such as repression and sublimation (redirection), deal with the disturbing sexual notions.

Freud: Conflict between Libido and Social Conscience

Freud's explanation of creativity focused on the motivation to create. Creative productivity is said to result from an unconscious conflict between the primitive sexual urges (*libido*) of the *id* and the repressive influences of our learned social conscience, the *superego*. Because one cannot freely indulge one's urges, the sexual energy is redirected (sublimated) into acceptable forms—creative fantasies and products. The id is happy, the superego is happy, and the self (ego) has fended off an attack of neurosis stemming from the conflict.

Sublimation into Acceptable Outlet: Creativity

Freud concedes that everyone has the innate sexual urges which must be sublimated; however, not everyone is highly or even moderately creative. The solu-

Psychoanalyst Ernst Kris tells us that aggressive instincts find outlets in creative productivity. "Oh, how I wish our students would have had some crayons!" laments teacher Rose Busch, left. "Maybe they'll do better in first grade," answers the student teacher. (The Museum of Modern Art/Film Stills Archive.)

Uncreative Person Represses Fantasies: Freud

tion to this dilemma is that the creative person accepts the libido-stimulated fantasies and elaborates upon them, while the uncreative person represses them.

Freud (1976) described the special case of creative writers, at least novelists, which more-or-less fits his model of unconscious desires and conflict. He assumed first that common daydreams or fantasies arise from unsatisfied and unacceptable erotic wishes. After all, "the well-brought-up young woman is only allowed a minimum of erotic desire, and the young man [must] suppress the excess of self-regard he brings . . . from childhood" (p. 50). The writer "creates a situation relating to the future which represents a fulfilment of the wish." A fantasy thus is created, often including a heroine who, in novels, always falls in love with an invulnerable hero—thus satisfying female erotic fantasies and male egoistic and ambitious ones.

Fantasies from Erotic and Egoistic Wishes

If you were psychoanalyst Sigmund Freud, and had read a few steamy novels, you also might arrive at this interpretation of the novelist's mental life.

Childlike Regression

Freud noted also that fantasy and creative thinking include a *regression* to more childlike modes of thought—a still-popular idea that relates creativeness to childlike thinking, humor, and a lively imagination. In fact, to Freud creativity is a continuation of and substitute for the free play of childhood. As a vocabulary lesson, we might note that the regression is to *primary process* thinking, which contrasts with *secondary process* thinking, two terms that remain useful. Developmentally, primary process thinking occurs before secondary process thinking. It happens during relaxation and includes the chaotic realm of dreams, reveries, free associations, and fantasies—your basic stuff of creativity. Secondary process thinking is more "grown up"—more logical, analytical, and oriented toward reality.

Primary Process Thinking

Secondary Process Thinking

A Negative View

The basic Freudian view is a rather negative one: Creativity is said to be the outcome of an unconscious neurotic conflict. Most of us prefer a more positive explanation of the motivation behind creativity, such as responding to the challenge of a problem or difficulty, or else meeting our innate needs to construct, create, achieve success, or improve the lot of humanity. The desire to make a pile of money also has stimulated lots of entrepreneurial creativity. Compton (1952) described the motive to create simply as "the decision to do something when you are irritated." Amabile (1983, 1987) emphasized the importance of intrinsic rewards, contrasted with extrinsic (high grades, money) rewards. Farley (1986) argued simply that a strong innate drive, in the form of thrill seeking or sensation seeking, virtually always motivates high creative productivity.

Many Motives to Create

Strong Innate Thrill Seeking Drive: Farley

Ernst Kris. A more recent psychoanalyst, Ernst Kris (1952), presented a view that is just a slight modification of Freud's creativity theory. The main distinctions are that (1) creativity is motivated by two main instincts of the *id*, the libido (sex drive) and aggressive instincts; and (2) instead of *unconscious* neurotic conflicts, Kris emphasizes *preconscious* and *conscious* mental activity. Said Kris, "Fantastic, freely wandering thought processes [creativity] tend to discharge . . . libido and aggression." According to Kris, creative fantasies occur in the preconscious mind. The preconscious mental activity can be understood most easily in terms of idle fantasies and daydreaming, which often occur on the fringes of consciousness. The shift of creative ideas from the preconscious to the conscious is felt as a sudden "Eureka!" or illuminating experience, following the preconscious incubation of the problem. As with Freud, Kris also accepts regression to more childlike thought processes—primary process thinking—as part of the preconscious activity.

Kris: Sex Plus Aggression Drives are "Discharged"

Emphasis on Preconscious and Conscious Activity

An important theoretical distinction between Freud and Kris is that, to Freud, creativity is said to "be in the service of the *id*," since creativity unconsciously releases libidinal (id) energy. To Kris, however, creativity is said to "be in the service of the ego," since the ego exercises some voluntary control over regression and over the shifting of preconscious ideas to the conscious mind. It is unclear to whom this distinction is important.

Freud: Id

Kris: Ego

Lawrence Kubie. A third psychoanalytic theory of creativity is that of Kubie (1958). While Kubie ignores ids, egos, libidos, and superegos, like Kris he does emphasize preconscious mental activity. Imagine a continuum of consciousness. At one end is conscious mental life and conscious symbolic processes (e.g., language). With these conscious symbolic processes we communicate, we think, we examine our thinking, we also rearrange our experiences into logical categories. Such conscious processes have their roots in learning and experience. Since these processes are anchored in reality, there is little flexibility or imaginative free play, said Kubie.

Kubie: Preconscious Activity

Conscious End of Continuum: Anchored in Reality

At the other end of the continuum are unconscious, symbolic processes. According to Kubie, in the unconscious symbolic meanings are hidden, lost, or repressed and can only be made conscious by special techniques, for example, psychoanalysis, hypnosis, or drugs. This unconscious system of symbols, meanings, and relationships is said to be even more fixed and rigid than the conscious system—not flexible nor creative at all. This rigidity of the unconscious, said Kubie, leads artists, composers, and poets to repeatedly use the same recognizable style and content in their works.

Unconscious Is Rigid, Not Creative

Creative activity takes place *between* the conscious and the unconscious, that is, in the *preconscious*. The preconscious is not tied strictly to the everyday pedestrian realities of the conscious mind, nor is it anchored to the even more rigid symbolic relationships of the unconscious. Rather, the preconscious can engage in free play

Creativity Takes Place in the Preconscious, on the Fringe of Consciousness

Conscious Mind _____ [   ] _____ Unconscious Mind

Transliminal
Chamber

Figure 3.1. Illustration of Harold Rugg's Transliminal Chamber, an area of preconscious, fringe conscious, or off-conscious creative thinking that draws from the conscious and unconscious minds.

with ideas, meanings and relationships, thereby producing the new and unexpected connections, metaphorical relationships, overlapping meanings, puns, and allegories that we call *creativity*.

Education: Ties Preconscious to Conscious

On education, Kubie says, "The price we pay for traditional educational methods is that they . . . tie our preconscious symbolic processes prematurely to precise [conscious] realities."

Freud/Kris Theory Misleading: Kubie

On the Freud-Kris explanation of creativity, Kubie says, "the ad hoc postulate that there is a separate and special mechanism known as the sublimation of unconscious processes may not be needed to explain creativity, and may actually be misleading . . . Neurosis corrupts, mars, distorts, and blocks creativity in every field" (Kubie, 1958).

Rugg: Similar to Kubie

Harold Rugg.   Finally, Rugg's (1963) formulation of creativity is extremely similar to that of Kubie. The difference, in fact, seems mostly semantic. Rugg emphasized "off-conscious" mental activity or thinking in the "transliminal chamber," which he located midway between the unconscious mind and conscious mental activity (Figure 3.1). The transliminal chamber was called "the center of creative energy." Here, the mind is free to draw from the vast store of experiences in the unconscious, and to creatively use these in conscious everyday living.

Transliminal Chamber: Midway between Conscious, Unconscious

Privacy, Day Dreaming: Good for Creativity

Both Kubie and Rugg thus emphasize the importance of preconscious, fringe-conscious, or off-conscious thinking in creativity. Perhaps this relates to why creative people have strong needs for privacy, away from the demands of conscious realities, and why daydreaming and incubation—both of which are forms of preconscious activity—can produce creative inspirations.

BEHAVIORISTIC AND LEARNING THEORIES

Learning theorists do not agree either. To review your introductory psychology, traditional learning theory emphasizes the reinforcement (reward) of correct responses plus stimulus-stimulus associations. You may recall Skinner's hungry rats who learned to press a bar to earn lunch, and Pavlov's dog who learned the association between bells and food, causing him (the dog) to spit whenever the bell rang. The approach is called *behaviorism* because the focus is on the visible behavior itself, rather than the unseen mental events that control the behavior.

B. F. Skinner: No Such Thing as Creativity(!)

Burrhus F. Skinner.   The big gun behaviorist, of course, is B. F. Skinner—a highly creative person who creatively argues that there is no such thing as creativity. In *Beyond Freedom and Dignity* (Skinner, 1971), he argued that we have no *freedom*, since all of our behavior is controlled by those who dispense reinforcements and punishments (parents, teachers, peers, police, and others who enforce laws, traditions, customs, mores, social expectations, etc.). Nor should we accept the *dignity* which comes from personal accomplishment, since again those achievements were determined by our history of rewards and punishments.

No Freedom or Dignity Either

Creativity Due to Genetics, Environment, Learning

Let's examine how he deprives us of our creativeness. Basically, the behavior of a creative person such as a poet is "merely the product of his genetic and environmental history" (Skinner, 1972).[4] The act of composing a poem out of "bits and pieces" is not an act of creativity, since in the experience of the poet he or she "had to learn how to put them together." In behavioristic terms, "the behavior [response] was ... triggered by the environment [stimulus] ... [and] the consequences [reward] may strengthen his tendencies to act in the same way again." While creating a poem may indeed require exploration and discovery, these are tied to the history of the poet and to trial-and-error learning activities, according to Skinner.

Since the poet is not aware of all of his or her history, he or she does not know where the poetic ideas (behavior) come from. Therefore, the poet erroneously attributes his or her own creations to a creative mind, an unconscious mind, or perhaps "to a Muse, ... whom he has invoked to come and write his poem for him." Even Shakespeare is given little credit for his own works because "Possibly all their parts could be traced by an omniscient scholar to Shakespeare's verbal and nonverbal histories." Shakespeare himself merely put the bits and pieces together in a fashion that produced rewarding consequences.

Even Shakespeare deserves no dignity.

Irving Maltzman.   Moving to a second and related behavioristic theory of creativity, in a well-known article published in a journal with high social status, experimental psychologist Maltzman (1960) argued that we can increase original behavior simply by rewarding it. He also reviewed his own research which proved beyond doubt that when original word associations were rewarded, the frequency of original word associations increased.

One scientific study, entitled "The Creative Porpoise," showed that if porpoises were given a dead fish only when they performed a new, creative stunt—but not when they repeated an old one—they quickly learned to put a lot of variety and creativity into their act (Pryor, Haag, & O'Reilly, 1969).

It is comforting to have this scientific confirmation that creativity will increase when it is encouraged and rewarded. However, something seems amiss when porpoises are called *creative* but William Shakespeare is not.

Arthur Staats.   A third behavioristic analysis of creative thinking also is straightforward. Staats (1968) described how S-R psychology can explain the production of novel, creative behavior through "complex stimulus control." We begin with the existence of two unrelated stimulus-response (S-R) relationships, each established by previous reinforcement. For example, the stimulus "Berlin Wall" elicits images of the Berlin Wall guarded by East German Soldiers. The stimulus of "people leaving" can elicit the verbal direction "Turn out the lights when you leave." In the fall of 1989, when East Germans were first allowed to leave their country, at least three cartoonists created a cartoon showing exiting East Germans telling a border guard to "Turn out the lights when you leave!"

This approach (theory?) assumes that creative ideas are new combinations of previously unrelated ideas. The approach simply describes in stimulus-response language how two previously unrelated stimuli, when encountered together, can elicit a creative response combination. The description applies, according to Staats (1968), to any creative act from a child uttering a novel sentence to a scientist creating a theory.

Sarnoff Mednick.   Finally a fourth behavioristic view of creativity focuses upon *mental associations*. Mental associations—for example, the word *carrot* might

History Plus Trial-and-Error

Poet is Unaware of Source of Ideas: Skinner

Shakespeare: No Creativity Here Either

Maltzman: Increase Original Behavior with Reinforcement

The Dead Fish Approach

Is Something Amiss?

Staats: Complex Stimulus Control

Two Unrelated Stimuli Elicit Novel Response Combination

---

[4]This section presents many direct quotes from Skinner in order to decrease the suspicion that your author fabricated Skinner's unusual position on creativity. Skinner really said these things.

A Creative Person Has Many Available Mental Associations: Mednick and Mednick

elicit *rabbit*—are assumed to be learned on a stimulus-stimulus contiguity basis. That is, carrots and rabbits have been repeatedly experienced together, and so a mental association between them is formed much as Pavlov's dog Rin-Tin-Tinovich formed the association between the bell and the Alpo. According to psychologist Mednick (1962; also Martha Mednick & Andrews, 1967), a highly creative person is one who possesses a large number of verbal and non-verbal mental associations which are available for recombination into creative ideas. A less creative person is one who is able to respond with just a few, highly dominant mental associations. For example, in listing unusual uses for a brick, the low creativity person, with few-but-strong associations, would quickly snap off, "Well, . . . uh . . . you might build a house or a garage with 'em . . . if you had enough. That's all I can think of."

The Mednicks' RAT

Mednick (1967) published the *Remote Associates Test* (RAT; now out of print), which was supposed to measure differences in the availability of verbal associations; that is, differences in creative ability. The test taker would be given three words (*birthday, surprise, line; shopping, washer, picture*) and was asked to produce a fourth word somehow associated with all three (*party; window*). The two main criticisms of the test are that (1) truly imaginative answers—those not on the scoring guide—will *lower* your score (what's this?), and (2) the test corre-

Originality Lowers Your Score

High Verbal IQ Raises Your Score

lates too highly with verbal intelligence, .40 to .60 in research by the Mednicks (Mednick, 1962, 1967; Mednick & Andrews, 1967) and .69 in a study by Davis and Belcher (1971). Other tests seem to focus more clearly upon creative potential, separate from intelligence.

Oversimplification

The traditional criticism of stimulus-response psychology is that of oversimplification or *reductionism*. Such complex human behavior as hopes, plans, aspirations, neuroses, speech, reading this book, chuckling at the jokes, or solving chemistry problems, writing poetry, or designing a marketing plan theoretically could be "reduced to" principles of Pavlovian (classical) conditioning or Skinnerian (instrumental) conditioning. Much of the beauty and complexity of learning and mental life is lost in such oversimplification.

SELF-ACTUALIZATION APPROACH

Self-Actualization Equals Mental Health

The essence of the *self-actualization* approach to creativity was presented in Chapter 1. The central point was that the creative person also is a self-actualized person—a fully-functioning, mentally healthy, forward-growing human being who is using his or her talents to become what he or she is capable of becoming (Maslow, 1968, 1970; Rogers, 1962). Some, even today, refer to this as a *mental health* or *psychological growth* explanation of creativity. To account for creative neurotics, or neurotic creatives, the reader should recall Maslows' distinction between

Self-Actualized and Special Talent Creativity

self-actualized creativity, the mentally healthy tendency to approach all aspects of one's life in a creative way, and *special talent* creativity, having a strong creative talent in a particular area with or without mental health and self-actualization. The reader also should recall Maslow's 15 characteristics of a self-actualized person summarized in Inset 1.1. (Yes, you may look again at Inset 1.1).

Carl Rogers (1962) added additional important conditions for creativity that relate to growth in self-actualization:

Rogers: Psychological Safety

1. *Psychological safety.* This is the creative atmosphere, a flexible and receptive environment. It is entirely a matter of attitudes.

Internal Locus of Evaluation

2. *Internal locus of evaluation.* This refers to personal characteristics of self-confidence and independence, a tendency to make one's own judgments, and a willingness to accept responsibility for one's successes and failures.

Playfulness

Openness to Experience: External and Internal

3. *A willingness to toy with ideas, to play with new possibilities.*

4. *Openness to experience.* This includes a receptiveness to new ideas and an attraction to new interests and experiences in the external world. It also includes a willingness to acknowledge internal wants, needs, and habits, some of which could be of questionable social acceptability. For example, a creative male is more willing to accept traditionally feminine interests or behaviors, such as petting a cat, making baby formula, or baking a cake (Bem, 1974).

From Rogers' humanistic point of view, one stimulates creativity by creating a psychologically safe environment, modeling openness to experience and an internal locus of control, and encouraging students to play with possibilities.

MORE CONTEMPORARY THEORIES OF CREATIVITY[5]

The following includes brief summaries of eight theoretical explanations of creativity, plus a description of our *implicit* theories. It is not an exhaustive list. The views represent some of the better-known contemporary speculations about the nature of creativity, creative processes, and creative persons.

Arthur Koestler: Bisociation

Koestler: Bisociation of Ideas

Koestler's (1967; see also Mudd, 1995) *bisociation of ideas* theory of creativity is an eloquent statement that extends the notion of combining ideas presented earlier. Said Koestler: "Let me recapitulate the criteria which distinguish bisociative originality from associative routine . . . The first [is] the previous independence of the mental skills or universes of discourse which are transformed and integrated into the novel synthesis of the creative act . . . [Creativity is] the amalgamation of two realms as wholes, and the integration of the laws of both realms into a unified code of greater universality . . . The more unlikely or more 'far-fetched' the [idea combination], the more unexpected and impressive the achievement." Koestler's broad theory emphasizes the commonality of creativity processes in jokes, artistic representations, and intellectual insights generally. He applied it to genetic codes and amino acids, on one molecular hand, and to aesthetics and organizational behavior, on the other much larger other one. If it helps the reader's visualization, a "realm" (domain) is conceived as a two-dimensional plane—a flat matrix containing coded ideas, rules, and action sequences—whose intersection with another plane sparks the creative combination. Said Koestler (1967, p. 36), "The creative act . . . always operates on more than one plane," and "The bisociative act connects previously unconnected matrices of experience" (p. 45).

The More Unlikely the Combination, the More Creative It Is

Highly General

Who Smokes 'Em?

Woody Allen once combined a religion plane with a cigarette plane to produce an innovative commercial for *New Testament* cigarettes: The priest proclaims "I smoke 'em, He smokes 'em."

Robert Sternberg: Three-Facet Model

Based on Creative Personality Traits

Sternberg's (1988a) three-facet model of creativity focuses on characteristics of the creative person. In a summary statement (p. 126), "creativity is . . . a peculiar intersection between three psychological attributes: intelligence, cognitive style,

---

[5]If the reader wishes a list of cues to help remember all eight theories, plus the "implicit" idea (definitely a good way to keep the grades up), he or she might try: A GI IS SICK. (Amabile is "A," Gardner is "G," Interactionist is "I," etc.)

and personality/motivation. Taken together, these three facets of the mind help us understand what lies behind the creative individual."

1. Intelligence

Intelligence, from Sternberg's information processing and triarchic theory perspectives, cannot be summarized briefly. Let's just call it *intelligence*, with an emphasis on verbal ability, fluent thought, knowledge, planning, problem defining, strategy formulation, mental representation, decisional skill, and a general intellectual balance (see Sternberg, 1988a, 1997).

2. Cognitive Style

The *cognitive style* (or *intellectual style* or *mental self-government*) found in a creative person evolves around low conventionality—a preference for creating one's own rules and doing things one's own way; a liking for problems that are not prestructured; an enjoyment of writing, designing, and creating; and a preference for creative occupations, such as creative writer, scientist, artist, investment banker, or architect. Sternberg included in creative intellectual styles an *anarchic* form of mental self-government, characterized by a potpourri of needs and goals, a random approach to problems, motivation from "muddle," frequent lack of clear goals, tendencies to simplify, an inability to set priorities, and more. Said Sternberg

Anarchics May Not Be Popular

(1988a, pp. 140–141), "Anarchics have the ability to remove themselves from existing constraints, ways of seeing things, and ways of doing things . . . Anarchics are not to the tastes of either teachers or parents, because the anarchics go against the existing grain."

3. Personality and Motivation

The *personality/motivation* dimension includes creative traits that duplicate those to be described in Chapter 4, for example, tolerance for ambiguity, flexibility, drive for accomplishment and recognition, perseverance in the face of obstacles, willingness to grow in creative performance, and moderate risk-taking.

Concluded Sternberg, "People are creative by virtue of a combination of intellectual, stylistic, and personality attributes" (p. 145).

Therese Amabile's Three-Part Model

Amabile (1983, 1988; Conti, Coon, & Amabile, 1996; Hennessey, 1997) proposed another three-part model of creative productivity. Her first component is *domain-relevant skills*—skills that produce competent performance within a domain, for example, writing or drawing. This part of the model includes knowledge about the domain, technical skills, and special domain-relevant talent. *Creativity-relevant skills*, the second component, contribute to one's creative performance across domains. Conti, Coon, and Amabile mentioned appropriate cognitive styles, favorable working styles, and divergent thinking abilities. The third component is *task*

You Are Talented

Creative

And Motivated

motivation, a factor we will see often in descriptions of creative and eminent people. Task motivation was said to include one's attitude toward the task, perceptions of one's motivation for beginning the task, one's initial level of intrinsic motivation toward the task, and the ability to mentally minimize external constraints.

The Sternberg and Amabile models are similar in several ways. Both include motivation and thinking styles, although their precise descriptions vary. For example, Sternberg includes creative personality characteristics in the descriptions of both his *cognitive style* and *personality/motivation* dimensions, and seems to assume the existence of Amabile's *domain-relevant skills*. Amabile substitutes a more specific *domain-relevant talent* for Sternberg's *intelligence*.

Mihalhyi Csikszentmihalyi: Where Is Creativity? Person, Domain, and Field

Before he invented *flow*, Csikszentmihalyi (1988, 1990a; pronounced "Smith") assembled a three-part theory of creativity consisting of (1) the creative *person*, (2) the person's *domain* or discipline, and (3) the *field* (institutions, experts, or society).[6] The creative person supplies the necessary ability, talent, and affective traits. He or she receives formal training in the domain, for example, piano or mathematics, which includes exposure to rules, structures, and practices and within which the individual is expected to produce. Society, or the larger field, provides judges who, snobs that they are, pass judgment on the creativeness of the output. *All three elements must interact to produce true creativity*, defined as an innovation that—if it receives society's blessing—permanently alters the domain.

Person, Domain, and Field Must Interact

Where Is Creativity?

The model evolves around the question "Where is creativity?" The obvious answers of "in the person's head" or "in the creative product" are unacceptable, said Smith, because without the larger field or society passing judgment ("We hereby stamp this creative"), the person and the product simply are not recognized nor accepted as "creative." Genuine creativity does not reside in the object itself, said Smith, rather "the reason we believe that Leonardo or Einstein was creative is that we have read that that is the case" (Csikszentmihalyi, 1988, p. 327). It is the more sophisticated artistic and scientific establishments, in whom we place great trust, that make such judgments; it is social agreement that decides what is "an adaptive innovation" (p. 326). According to Smith, in regard to the notoriously fickle realm of the arts, the "critics and viewers who have looked . . . closely at Botticelli's work are just as indispensable to Botticelli's creativity as was the painter himself" (p. 328). In math, physics, and chemistry, the attribution of creativity again is a social process which, as in the arts, can be "relative, fallible, and sometimes reversed by posterity" (p. 328).

Poor van Gogh!

So that's why van Gogh died poor—the field had not yet made up its mind. In October, 1989, one of his paintings was offered for sale at 40 million dollars, which sounds high but the frame and little light were included.

Aha! Creativity versus Creative Eminence!

What's wrong? If you have not found it, the flaw in Csikszentmihalyi's thinking is to use *creativity* synonymously with *creative eminence*. Certainly, only a handful of people are sufficiently creative and produce sufficiently creative products such that, as judged by the larger field or society, they permanently impact the domain (e.g., math, chess, art, literature, theater, business, industry, science). But are the rest of us chopped liver?

Howard Gardner: Person, Domain, and Field

Of MI Fame

You should recognize the name Howard Gardner, who has impacted psychology and gifted education by replacing the single IQ number with his seven-part theory of multiple intelligences, which appears in *Frames Of Mind* (Gardner, 1983) and elsewhere (e.g., Ramos-Ford & Gardner, 1997).

Person, Domain, and Field Again

In *Creating Minds*, Gardner (1993) presents a case study of the lives of seven creatively eminent persons, Sigmund Freud, Albert Einstein, Pablo Picasso, Igor Stravinsky, T. S. Eliot, Martha Graham, and Mahatma Gandhi, "whose impact on our time has been compelling" (p. 4).[7] Gardner adopts totally the three-part Csikszentmihalyi (1988) definition of true creativity, which requires a talented *person*, who experiences a period of training, is adventurous, and perhaps even is insubordinate; a *domain* or discipline within which the individual works; and a *field* (judges, institutions) that decides the quality of the creations. All three parts of the model appear in Gardner's definition of a creative person:

---

[6]It is easy to confuse the near-synonyms "domain" and "field," which is one reason to think of "the larger field" or even "society."

[7]*Creating Minds* is highly recommend reading, covering many important ideas and developments in the domain of creativity, creative traits of the seven persons, plus Gardner's own remarkable insights and conclusions.

The creative individual is a person who regularly solves problems, fashions products, or defines new questions in a domain in a way that is initially considered novel but that ultimately becomes accepted in a particular cultural setting. (p. 35)

As with Csikszentmihalyi, Gardner's conception of creativity is highly restrictive. Perhaps more so: "Of the many individuals and works that undergo scrutiny by the field, only a few are deemed worthy of sustained attention and evaluation ... And of the works that are appreciated at a given historical moment, only a small subset are ever deemed to be *creative* ... The works (and the workers) so judged actually cause a refashioning of the domain" (p. 38). In his example, he explains how, out of one thousand budding artists at work in Paris, "one or two at most will paint in a manner that becomes so highly valued that their efforts will ultimately exert some effect on the domain—on the structure of knowledge and practice to be mastered by the next generation of painters" (p. 39). The other 998½ are indistinguishable from chopped liver.

Gardner's definition and assumptions are defensible, but only if the reader accepts his eminence definition of *creativity* as obviously and extremely restrictive. To use his figures, Gardner's definition eliminates the possibility of being creative for 99.85 percent of people *who, in fact, are doing creative things*, specifically, his other 998½ Parisian artists. Gardner dismisses the possibility of self-actualized creativeness by arguing that "an individual cannot be creative in the abstract ... but must make his or her contributions in particular domains" (p. 37). Sayonara, ciao, and auf Wiedersehen to all efforts of the Creative Education Foundation, most creativity classes and workshops, your creativity class and this text, and all supporters of the CPS model, brainstorming, Synectics, and every other effort to strengthen a general, self-actualized form of creativeness.

Simonton: Chance-Configuration Theory

Earlier in this chapter we mentioned Simonton's (1988) "fifth *P*," *persuasion,* and in Chapter 1 his suggestion that chance plays a role in both the production of innovative ideas and in their social acceptance. Persuasion and chance fit together in his *chance-configuration theory* (Simonton, 1988). Like Gardner (1993), Simonton accepts the notion that "individuals become 'creative' only insofar as they impress [persuade] others with their creativity" (p. 386). However, Simonton's chance-configuration theory has different roots, one in his background as a social psychologist interested in personal influence, another in Campbell's (1960) Darwin-inspired *blind-variation and selective retention* model of creative thought.

Campbell's three core assumptions, accepted by Simonton, appear in the label of Campbell's model. First, to solve a problem there must be some means of generating ideational variation; second, there must be criteria that select only the adaptively fit ideas; and third, selected idea variations must be preserved and reproduced.

With a seemingly slight alteration of Campbell's basic model, Simonton emphasizes, first, the chance (but not totally random) permutations of manipulable mental elements, such as ideas, concepts, recollections, or other aspects of cognitive schemata. We now have ideas or "potential permutations." Second, only the most stable (coherent, sensible) of the permutations are retained for further processing. Stable permutations, or "configurations," take their shape because of experience, rules and conventions, and sensibility. A configuration (solution) is selected based on its apparent usefulness or suitability to the problem.

Following considerable "intrapsychic" development and polishing of the innovation/configuration, the third and final step is the social one. The person now must take a leadership role. He or she must persuade others of the quality—the creativeness—of the final product. The product must be accepted; it must be viewed as having value to the endeavors of sophisticated others within that domain.[8]

Investment Theory of Creativity

Invest in Creativity: Concepts from Economics

For a short while, economic and investment terms seemed a profitable way to describe creativity. For example, several scholars described how an investment in the creative development of our youth (involving costs) reaps short- and long-term benefits for society (Rubenson, 1991; Rubenson & Runco, 1992; Walberg & Stariha, 1992); or how "investing" in one's own creative research or theory ideas, although risky, can reap greater profits ("buying low, selling high"), compared with buying into well-established and popular ideas (Sternberg & Lubart, 1992, 1995). "Buying low" means pursuing ideas that are unknown or unpopular but have growth potential, and "selling high" means "cashing in" when the ideas (and you) become popular. Sternberg and Lubart (1990) titled one paper "The Creative Mind: An Investment Theory of Creativity." They recently titled another "Investing in Creativity" (Sternberg & Lubart, 1996) to emphasize society's error in underinvesting in the study of creativity relative to its importance in the world. They also summarized their investment theory of creativity.

Walberg's Economics

Walberg's (1988) definition of "human capital" included the motivation, skills, and creativity of the person. Said Walberg, people are "capital assets to themselves and others" (p. 342). Their time is valuable and should be allocated efficiently. Also, young people face choices between working versus investments in enhancing their personal "capital," "which involves risky short- and long-term opportunities, costs, and benefits" (p. 343). The production of talent can involve costs, such as child-rearing expenses, as well as benefits, such as added earnings and psychological satisfaction.

A Capital Idea!

Gardner (1993) found the vocabulary handy, mentioning that potentially creative children who have opportunities to discover and explore "will accumulate invaluable 'capital of creativity,' on which they can draw in later life" (p. 31).

I'll Have a Big Mac, Please

I have always liked analogical models. As insightfully reported in my review of the investment model (Davis, 1992), I have long felt that life is like a hamburger—the more you put into it, the better it is. Life can be a plain dry burger or a zesty Big Mac. Analogical models are marvelous theoretical and teaching devices. They simplify complex topics by summarizing large amounts of information in compact, understandable ways. They help illustrate interrelationships among parts. They provide a language and sometimes a visual illustration to aid understanding and prediction. A popular example is the information processing model, which uses computer flow charts to summarize interactions among environmental input, attentional processes, sensory stores, short-term and long-term memories, rehearsal, response modes, and executive control processes. Not bad for one-fourth page of flow-chart-looking boxes and arrows.

Analogical Models Summarize and Illustrate Information

Does It Work?

Analogical models are neither right nor wrong, valid nor invalid. They either work or do not work in helping us understand point-for-point correspondences. The investment model of creativity plays its simplification and instructional roles nicely. It can lead to new insights about creativity if an investment idea or concept stimulates someone to look for an interesting parallel process in creativity. For example, bad investments—perhaps in the wrong career or in a creative bank heist—can cause personal bankruptcy.

---

[8]In one page I have attempted to summarize an original, thoughtful, and complicated 41 page article. The word *oversimplification* comes to mind. Apologies to Dean Keith Simonton.

Interactionist Model of Creative Behavior

Interaction of Person and Environment Factors

This book tries to present a brief overview of most of the important topics in creativity—self-actualization, barriers, definitions and theories, personality traits, abilities and cognitive styles, stage models of the process, creativity techniques, tests, training, and more. Essentially, everything interacts with everything else. An interactionist model that attempts to tie much of this together in one picture appears in Figure 3.2 (Woodman & Schoenfeldt, 1990). The main emphases are on *person* and *environment*. When you think about it, what else is there? According to the authors, various theories and research focus sometimes on aspects of the person, sometimes on features of the environment, and "sometimes both plus their reciprocal influences are necessary to even begin to understand what is going on" (p. 280). It takes a couple of minutes, but Figure 3.2 almost is self-explanatory. It includes *antecedent conditions* (A), such as one's background, socialization, gender, and other biographical variables; the *"organism"* (O) or person, which includes his or her personality traits (P) as well as abilities, thinking styles, and "openness" (CS); contextual influences (CI), such as the particular task and the organizational

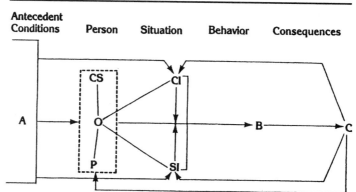

A = Antecedent conditions to current situation. Examples: Past reinforcement history, early socialization, biographical variables—sex, family position, birth order

B = creative behavior

C = consequences

O = "organism" (person)—gestalt of attitudes, values, intentions to behave, motivational orientation, individual differences

CS = cognitive style/abilities—examples: cognitive complexity, divergent thinking, verbal/ideational fluency, problem solving styles/approaches, perceptual openness, field independence/dependence

P = personality dimensions/traits—examples: locus of control dogmatism, autonomy, self-esteem, narcissism, intuition

CI = contextual influences—examples: physical environment, culture, group/organization 'climate,' task & time constraints

SI = social influence—examples: social facilitation, evaluation expectation, rewards/punishments, role modeling

Figure 3.2. An Interactionist Model of Creative Behavior, R.W. Woodman & L.A. Schoenfeldt, *The Journal of Creative Behavior*, 1990, 24(4), pp. 270–290. Reprinted with permission from the copyright holder, the Creative Education Foundation, Buffalo, NY.

climate; social influences (SI), such as expectations and role models; the [solution, creative] behavior (B) itself; and the consequences (C).[9]

Most Approaches to Creativity Can Be Found in the Model

Now the fun part. Cognitive explanations of creativity, which emphasize, for example, abilities and thinking styles, would focus on CS-O-B linkages. Social orientations might be found in SI-O-B (with some interest in CI and A). Developmentalists and gifted education folks would look at A-O-B, A-SI-O-B, and A-CI-O-B sequences. Scholars with an organizational bent would examine the CI-O-B chain. Stage models of creativity (e.g., Wallas and CPS models) focus on O-B-C-O linkages. Skinner and behaviorism fall in the [A, CI, SI]-B-C chain.

Said the authors, "the value of the interactionist perspective is . . . to see how various components, elements, and forces come together to result in the behavior of interest, in this case, creativity" (p. 286). Figure 3.1 seems to illustrate a taxonomic theory, a diagram or illustration of how various pieces of creativity fit together.

Implicit Theories of Creativity: Mark Runco

YOU Have an Implicit Theory of Creativity

The reader will be delighted to discover that what he or she already thinks about creativity has a name: It's an *implicit theory of creativity*. According to Runco (1990), an implicit theory of creativity is just that—a theory or conception of creativity that exists in your mind. It is a prototype that you personally use to decide if a product or a person is creative. In Csikszentmihalyi's (1988, 1990a) and Gardner's (1993) theories, implicit theories are used by the field (or society) to evaluate the creativeness of a contribution.

Runco's research sought to identify implicit theories of creativity used by different groups, for example, artists and nonartists. As a sample of his results, both artists and nonartists agreed that artists were *imaginative* and *expressive*, but artists thought they also were *humorous, open-minded,* and *emotional* while nonartists thought artists were *intelligent, original,* and *"draw well."* Both artists and nonartists agreed that scientists were *intelligent* and *curious.* Both groups also agreed that "everyday creativity" was characterized by being *active,* but artists added *humorous, open-minded,* and *exciting* while nonartists added *imaginative, common-sensical,* and *cooks well.*

Implicit theories or conceptions of creativity exist, as we know, and with Runco's help they are legitimized.

Interdisciplinarity

One recent seemingly "theoretical" thrust is entitled *interdisciplinarity.* This perspective examines the ancient contrast between *art* (and the humanities generally), which focuses on subjectivity and intuition, versus *science* (especially the psychology of cognition), which is rooted in objectivity and quantification. (See, e.g., the entire 1998, Vol 11, No. 1 issue of *Creativity Research Journal,* which consists of 88 pages, two columns, and small print.) One example of a tie between art and science is experimental aesthetics, the effort to understand and measure human experiences elicited by graphic art, music, and literature. Another example is analyzing various relationships among the age and gender of the artist, aesthetic preferences (e.g., representational versus abstract), themes (e.g., an "old age" theme), and the quality (e.g., technical skill, creativeness) of his/her art (Lindauer, 1998). As interpreted by Sawyer (1998), interdisciplinarity includes studies of creativity in *performances,* as in theater, folklore, and ethnomusicology.

---

[9]Only experimental psychologists would refer to people as *organisms,* as though paramecia and lab rats should be included in this discussion of creativity.

The interdisciplinarity movement emphasizes a broader-than-usual focus and a greater depth of understanding by objectively examining creativity in a seemingly boundryless spectrum of artistic and social science activities and contexts.

SUMMARY

Definitions and theories try to clarify complex phenomena. There are many definitions and theories of creativity, due to its complexity. Ninja Secrets was an example of the variety.

Most definitions focus on the creative person, the creative product, the creative process, or the creative press (environment). They interrelate. Simonton suggested a fifth *P*, persuasion.

Person definitions emphasize characteristics of creative people. Lombroso proposed that the creative and the insane have mental degeneration in common. Contrasted with his average man and neurotic man, Rank's creative type seems basically self-actualized.

Jung's visionary type of creative person, who contrasts with his psychological type, is said to draw ideas from primordial archetypes, a collective unconscious. Evidence is thin.

Process approaches include Torrance's definition (sensing problems, forming hypotheses, testing them, communicating results); stage approaches such as Wallas' four-step and the CPS six-step models; plus numerous one-sentence definitions based on combining ideas.

Perkins proposed the generation, selection, and preservation of ideas, with the "combinatorial explosion" of ideas being "mindfully directed" by creative people.

Product definitions emphasize originality ("I am a poached egg"), but usually combined with value, appropriateness, usefulness, or social worth. A convenient circular definition is that "a creative person is someone who does creative things," which emphasizes the product.

Definitions and theories tend not to focus solely on the creative press, but the environment is included in many thoughtful creativity writings. The "press" appears in discussions of barriers, brainstorming, Roger's psychological safety, and the creative climate. Rhodes suggested that creativity stems from social needs, as well as having an appropriate state of technology. Gardner, Simonton, and Csikszentmihalyi stress the role of society in judging what is creative.

Creative people themselves describe mysterious mental happenings that result in creative ideas and products. Lowes argued that Coleridge's drug-induced writing of *Kubla Khan* was a matter of unconscious and colorful combining of ideas and images. Mozart described ideas flowing involuntarily, which later were developed and, when complete, written down quickly. He heard his sequential compositions "all at once."

Freud's psychoanalytic theory focused on an unconscious conflict between the libido (sex drive) and the superego (social conscience), which is resolved in creative fantasies and products. Novels are said to satisfy female erotic fantasies and male egoistic ones. Freud's theory is a negative view of the motivation to create. In the plus column, he stressed regression to childlike thinking (primary process thinking).

Ernst Kris similarly stressed the neurosis-preventing discharge of both libidinal and aggressive energy in creative fantasies. However, Kris emphasized preconscious and conscious mental activity.

Kubie argued that neurotic conflict always is bad for your creative health. Like Kris, he proposed that creative thinking takes place in preconscious mental activity, between conscious and unconscious processes.

Rugg similarly located creative thinking between conscious and unconscious minds, in his transliminal chamber.

Learning theories focus on the reinforcement of correct responses. Skinner claimed that creative acts are explainable via genetics plus one's history of being rewarded for combining pieces into creative wholes. We have no freedom and deserve no dignity, said Skinner.

Maltzman simply proposed that originality, like any other behavior, is strengthened through reinforcement. The view was reinforced by cooperative porpoises.

Staats argued that two stimuli, encountered together for the first time, would elicit a novel (creative) combination of responses.

Mednick suggested that creative people have larger repertoires of mental associations that are available for combination. This capability was said to be measured by their RAT (*Remote Associates Test*), which discriminates against original answers.

Learning theories are criticized for being oversimplifications and reductionistic.

As we saw in Chapter 1, Rogers and Maslow recommend a self-actualization (growth) approach to creativity. Maslow distinguished between self-actualized creativity and special talent creativity. Rogers emphasized psychological safety, internal control, playfulness, and openness to experience.

In the contemporary category, Koestler elaborated on the highly general bisociation of ideas.

Sternberg's three-facet model includes three dimensions of the creative person—intelligence, cognitive style, and personality/motivation. He mentioned an anarchic style of mental self-government.

Amabile's three components were domain-relevant skills, creativity-relevant skills, and task motivation.

Mihalhyi asked "Where is creativity?", leading to a three-part theory including the creative person, the person's domain, and the field of experts who pass judgment. The three must interact.

Gardner used the person, domain, and field theory to elaborate on the apparently highly restrictive group of persons deemed creative. The definition dismisses content-free, self-actualized forms of creativity, which are the focus of many courses, books, and programs.

Simonton combined (non-random) chance variation with his fifth *P*, persuasion, to produce his chance-configuration theory of creativity. The person must persuades sophisticated judges that his or her idea or product (stable permutation, configuration) is creative.

The investment theory of creativity is an analogical model of the creative process. It uses terms from economic theory to explain the value of creativity to society. The analogy seems to work. Is life is like a Big Mac?

The interactionist model focuses on traits of the person and characteristics of the environment. Figure 3.2 demonstrates where cognitive, developmental and gifted, organizational, stage model, and behavioristic approaches to creativity would fit within the diagram.

We all have implicit theories of creativity, studied by Mark Runco.

Interdisciplinarity is a broad-based approach to examining the contrast and connections between art and humanities, on one hand, and objective science, particularly cognitive psychology, on the other.

Definitions and Theories: What Is Creativity?

Self-Test: Key Concepts, Terms, and Names

Briefly define or explain each of these:

The four "*P's*" _____

_____

Simonton's fifth "*P*" _____

Jung's psychological type (of creative person) _____

_____

Jung's visionary type and primordial archetypes _____

_____

Torrance's definition of creativity _____

_____

Perkins' Darwin-influenced model _____

_____

The creative press _____

"Mysterious mental happenings" _____

_____

Freud's psychoanalytic approach _____

_____

Primary process thinking (Freud) _____

_____

Secondary process thinking (Freud) _____

_____

Transliminal chamber (Rugg) _____

_____

Skinner's behavioristic approach _____

_____

Self-actualization approach _____

_____

Koestler's bisociation model of creativity _____

_____

Sternberg's three-facet model of creativity _____

_____

Amabile's three-part model of creativity _____

_____

Csikszentmihalyi's three-part model ("Where is creativity?") _____

_____

Gardner's three-part model, self-actualized creativeness, and chopped liver ___

_____

Simonton's chance-configuration theory (and fifth "P") _____

_____

Investment theory _____

_____

Interactionist model _____

_____

Implicit theories _____

_____

Why are these names important in the creativity field?

Cesare Lombroso _____

Carl Jung _____

Paul Torrance _____

David Perkins _____

Sigmund Freud _____

Ernst Kris _____

Lawrence Kubie _____

Harold Rugg _____

B. F. Skinner _____

Irving Maltzman _____

Arthur Staats _____

Sarnoff Mednick _____

Abraham Maslow _____

Carl Rogers _____

Arthur Koestler _____

Robert Sternberg _____

Theresa M. Amabile _____

Mihalyi Csikszentmihalyi _____

Howard Gardner _____

Dean Keith Simonton _____

Let's Think about It

1. What is your implicit theory of creativity? That is, what is your definition, conception, or beliefs about creativity? Do you emphasize the creative person? The process? The product? The press (environment)? Some combination of these?

   If you don't presently have a theory, make one up.

   _____

   _____

_____

_____

Compare your theory to the psychoanalytic, behavioristic, and self-actualization (humanistic) theories? Any similarities? Main differences?

_____

_____

_____

_____

2. Make up a preposterous, totally unbelievable theory of creativity that explains why some people are highly creative and others are not. (If Freud and Jung can do it, so can you.)

_____

_____

_____

_____

3. What is your reaction to the heavy emphasis on the role of society (sophisticated judges) deciding what is and what is not creative (proposed by Csikszentmihalyi, Gardner, and Simonton)?

_____

_____

_____

_____

Crossword Puzzle 3.1 (Solution at end of book)

ACROSS

1. Creator of "generation, selection, preservation of ideas" theory
5. The first "*P*"
6. Psychoanalytically-oriented theorist who emphasized the role of preconscious (fringe conscious) thinking
9. People with Torrance's first name
10. Not generation or preservation of ideas
11. Rugg's "_____ chamber"
14. The "p" that refers to environmental influences on creativity
17. Flying saucer
19. Sternberg's first "facet"
20. The second step in Torrance's definition, formulating _____
22. Koestler's theory, in one word

DOWN

1. Not person, product, or press
2. Captain of Starship Enterprise
3. The third "*P*"
4. One who creates
5. Wallas' first stage
7. Nickname for a German sausage sandwich or a screaming kid
8. President Clinton
12. Primordial _____
13. Los Angeles
14. Categories of definitions; the four _____
15. The approach of the Wallas model and the CPS model
18. Claimed that creativity stems from an unconscious conflict between the id and the superego
21. Tender loving care (abbr.)

Crossword Puzzle 3.2 (Solution at end of book)

ACROSS

1. Person, domain, and _____
4. Conducted research on implicit theories of creativity, Mark _____
8. Informal American greeting
9. Proposed 3-part theory in 1 across (known as "Smith")
14. _____ Grande river, separating Texas and great beaches
15. Key witness in OJ case, the _____ driver
16. Economics term for the end of the 12 months when money runs out (abbrev.)
17. "Help!" code
19. Claimed creativity stemmed from a conflict between the id and superego
21. New type of music
23. Famous for having a wizard
24. Proposed 3-part person-based theory: intelligence, cognitive style, and personality/motivation
29. Automobile organization
30. Adopted "Smith's" 3-part theory (limiting "creativity" to a minuscule fraction of people). Wrote recent biography of Freud, Einstein, Picasso Stravinsky, etc.
32. Not the ego or superego
33. Simonton's fifth "P"

DOWN

2. Plural of 32 across
3. Proposed "visionary creative type" who finds inspiration from "primordial archetypes"
4. Gin _____
5. Harold Rugg's "Transliminal _____
6. What the world runs on
7. One piece of apparatus used in a sport famous in Colorado, Utah, and Switzerland
10. Ernst _____
12. City parks full of animals
18. Don't walk
20. Person, _____, and field
22. Shakespeare: "To _____"
25. Uncommon
26. Fiddles and fish
27. Singer McIntyre
28. Garfunkel
31. Not fast play (abbrev.)

One More Time . . .
(and it should be easy by now)

Matching. Select the name or names at the right that best go with the concept at the left. Some names must be used more than once.

_____	1. Chance-Configuration Theory	a. Howard Gardner
_____	2. Bisociation Theory	b. David Perkins
_____	3. Implicit theories of creativity	c. Otto Rank
_____	4. Person, Domain, Field (two answers)	d. Sigmund Freud
_____	5. Has alphabet soup name.	e. Harold Rugg
_____	6. Blames unconscious *id* versus *superego* conflict.	f. "Fred" Skinner
_____	7. Emphasized sensing difficulties, formulating hypotheses, testing hypotheses, and communicating The results	g. Arthur Koestler
		h. George Bush
_____	8. Primordial archetypes	i. Milhalyi Csikszentmihalyi
_____	9. The fifth "P," persuasion	j. Dean Keith Simonton
_____	10. Creative type, or "man of will and deed"	k. Mark Runco
_____	11. Three-factor model: Intelligence, cognitive style, and personality/motivation	l. Carl Jung
		m. Paul Torrance
_____	12. Generation, selection, preservation of ideas (two answers)	n. Therese Amabile
_____	13. Reinforcement of appropriate responses	o. Robert Sternberg
_____	14. Transliminal chamber	
_____	15. Argued that if your work does not alter the domain, it is not "creative." (Two main answers)	
_____	16. Three-part model: Domain-relevant skills, creativity relevant skills, and motivation	

Answers at end of book.

4

the creative person
flexible, funny, and full of energy

[*Scene: Living room of eccentric inventor Alexander Graham Schwartz, recent developer of the automatic talking chicken. TV cameramen have set up microphones, cameras and floodlights. ABC News correspondent Barbara Walters enters and sits down, facing Mr. Schwartz. The floodlights are turned on and the director counts "3, 2, 1!" and points to Ms. Walters.*]

Barbara Walters: (*Smiling*) Mr. Schwartz, is it true that you are stark raving mad? A lunatic inventor in the true traditional sense?

Alexander Graham Schwartz: Mad? Not completely. But sometimes I think funny—I play with ideas, turn things upside down and inside out. I push ideas together and take them apart. Sometimes I look at a problem like I was four-years old—maybe from Mars. Right now I'm working on invisible tennis balls for players who keep saying, "I sure didn't see that one!"

Walters: Hmmm, I see. Tell me Mr. Schwartz, what else is it about creative people that makes them different from others?

Schwartz: It takes energy, a sense of adventure, and the confidence to stick your neck out and do something different—maybe wild and crazy. You can make a real fool of yourself, you know. How many people would go on national television to talk about invisible tennis balls and talking chickens?

Walters: I see your point. Tell me, should everyone try to be a little crazier—a little more creative—or is it just for you eccentric inventors?

Schwartz: (*Jumps up, pretends to shoot down Red Barron*) Eccentric? Who's eccentric? Yes, everyone should think about being more creative. Most people have creative talents that never see the light of night!

Walters: That's very interesting. Mr. Schwartz. Now about those chickens, do they really talk or are you just a ventriloquist?

Schwartz: They talk, absolutely! No hanky-panky here. I start them off as chicks with vowels—long "e," short "a," that sort of thing. Then we get to consonants and whole words. For most, their first sentence is "Wake up, you handsome devil you!" These are for people who can't stand all that cock-a-doodle-do stuff at 5 o'clock in the morning.

Walters: And now, Mr. Schwartz, just one more question. Would you tell me and our viewers at home just how you would like to be remembered?

Schwartz: As somebody with a little humor, a little independence, a little imagination, and who isn't afraid to talk to a chicken.

The gift of fantasy has meant more to me than my talent for absorbing positive knowledge. . . . I ask myself childlike questions, then proceed to answer them.

Albert Einstein

What Makes a Creative Person Creative?

They Have Much in Common

Will Help Us Recognize Creative People

Psychologists and educators have taken many long looks at creative people in a continuing effort to understand the sorts of characteristics that underly and contribute to creativeness. The purpose of this chapter is to examine commonalities—characteristics that have recurred again and again in studies of creative people. Dozens of research studies, buttressed by informed opinions, point to one conclusion: *Creative people may be nonconformist, but they certainly have a lot in common.*

An awareness of characteristics of creativity will help us understand creative people and how they think. It also will help us recognize creative children and adults. We will not become perfect in our recognition of creative talent, however. Consider these examples of creative persons who were *not* recognized by their teachers, professors, or supervisors:

Thomas Edison was told by his teachers that he was too stupid to learn anything.

Albert Einstein was four years old before he could speak and seven before he could read.

Pablo Picasso could barely read and write by age 10. His father hired a tutor, who gave up and quit.

Walt Disney was fired by a newspaper editor because he had "no good ideas."

Louisa May Alcott was told by an editor that she could never write anything popular.

Enrico Caruso's music teacher told him, "You can't sing, you have no voice at all!"

Fred Waring once was rejected from high school chorus.

Several acting schools would not admit *David Suchet*, who portrays Hercule Poirot in the Agatha Christie TV series, because he was too short, could not sing, and showed no promise as an actor.

Harrison Ford (Indiana Jones) flunked out of Ripon College in Wisconsin.

Leo Tolstoy also flunked out of college.

Abraham Lincoln entered the Black Hawk War as a Captain and came out a private.

Winston Churchill failed sixth grade. He also was at the bottom of his class in one school, and twice failed the entrance exams for another.

Werner von Braun failed ninth-grade algebra.

Louis Pasteur was rated mediocre in chemistry at the Royal College.

Charles Darwin did poorly in the early grades and failed a university medical course.

F. W. Woolworth worked in a dry goods store when he was 21, but his employers would not let him wait on customers because he "didn't have enough sense."

Charles Dickens, Claude Monet, Isadora Duncan, and *Mark Twain* never finished grade school.

George Gershwin, Will Rogers, both *Wilbur* and *Orville Wright,* and newscaster *Peter Jennings* dropped out of high school.

A 1938 letter found in 1991 said that western movie star *Gene Autry* "needed to improve his acting," that an acting course was "evidently wasted," and that "he needed darker make-up to give him the appearance of virility." Replied 83-year-old Autry, "A lot of that is true."

Creative Talent: Can Be Subtle, Complex

Such facts are amusing. They also emphasize the complexity, subtlety, and sometimes obscurity of creative talent.

PERSONALITY TRAITS, ABILITIES, BIOGRAPHICAL CHARACTERISTICS

Personality, Cognitive Abilities, Biographical Traits

Distinction Sometimes Blurred

Three types of characteristics combine to produce creativeness: *Personality traits* (including motivation), *cognitive abilities* (including information processing styles), and *biographical traits* (experiences). The distinction between affect (personality), cognition (mental abilities), and learning (biographical traits, experiences) is an ancient one. In the creativity area, the three categories of traits interweave tightly, and each will influence the development of the other two. As easy illustrations, *learning* and experiences help determine the development of one's personality, intelligence, and thinking styles. *Intelligence* relates closely to such personality traits such as ethics, confidence, self-esteem, articulateness, and tendencies to be analytical (Davis & Rimm, 1998), as well as to the type of learning experiences one selects—for example, dropping out of high school or attending medical school. The *cognitive style* of internal control—the feeling of mastery over one's environment and destiny—includes such personality traits as high motivation, independence, self-esteem, social sensitivity and warmth, and even likability (Davis & Williams, 1992). Personality traits, mental abilities, and learning/experiences do indeed interrelate and influence each other.

Some traits of creativity could fit into one category as well as another. For example, *humor, independence, originality,* and *perceptiveness* could be viewed as personality traits, cognitive abilities, or both.

Similarities and Differences

Commonalities Across Different Areas

But Also Wide Variation between and within Areas

You Have an Implicit Theory of Creativity

High Creatives May Not Be Well Adjusted

There are then, commonalities among creative persons in different areas. A creative scientific researcher, a creative artist, and a creative business entrepreneur—by virtue of being creative—will have many personality traits and abilities in common. However, as one might guess, there also is wide variation in personality patterns, abilities, and experiences not only between persons in different areas, but among persons within the same area (e.g., two artists). For example, some perceived differences between artistic and scientific creativity appeared in Runco's research on implicit theories mentioned in Chapter 3. Artists were judged as *expressive, imaginative, humorous, original, emotional,* and *exciting* while scientists were seen as *intelligent, logical, curious, perfectionistic, patient,* and *thorough.* In Chapter 1 we saw that some persons with a great creative talent—Maslow's *special talent creativity*—are well-adjusted in the self-actualization sense and some are not. As we will see later, some highly creative people are fair-to middling in neuroses, schizophrenia, or sociopathy.

Creative in Own Area, Not Others

Except for Gifted Few

Most special talent creative people are creative in their own area, but typically not in another. A creative chemist, for example, may be an unimaginative artist, writer, or cook. On the other hand, a few gifted personages have been creative in many areas—Leonardo Da Vinci, Thomas Jefferson, Benjamin Franklin (best known for trying to electrocute himself with a kite), Howard Hughes, and Orson Welles.

For now, the perhaps obvious message is that even among the single category of people judged "creative" there will be large differences in personality, mental traits, experiences, and capabilities.

CREATIVITY AND INTELLIGENCE: THE THRESHOLD CONCEPT

Creativity and Intelligence are Separate

Before turning to personality, cognitive, and biographical traits, let's look at a long-standing issue in creativity: the relationship between creativity and intelligence. On one hand, creativity and intelligence are recognized as two separate constructs. Landmark research by Getzels and Jackson (1962) and Wallach and Kogan (1965) identified and contrasted highly intelligent versus highly creative students, confirming that the two traits are indeed not the same. Further, developers of creativity tests take pride in demonstrating very low correlations between scores on their creativity test and IQ scores on intelligence tests. Their purpose is to argue that their test measures creative potential and not just components of intelligence, such as verbal ability, logical thinking, or decision making.

But Creativity and Intelligence Also Are Related

Research Evidence

On the other hand, it also is known that creativity and intelligence very clearly are related. Some descriptions of creative people that reflect high intelligence appear in Table 4.1. In the creative eminence area, summarized later in this chapter, we will find total agreement that intelligence is needed for high creativity. For example, after reviewing the biographies of creatively eminent men and creatively eminent women, Walberg and Zeiser (1997) concluded that "the most common psychological trait of eminent women . . . was the same as that shown by eminent American and European men of previous centuries—intelligence" (p. 332). Walberg also compared high school students who had won competitive awards in science or art with control students who were not award winners. Said Walberg

---

Table 4.1
Descriptions Reflecting Intelligence

Analytical	Alert to gaps in knowledge
Articulate	Cannot write fast enough to keep up with ideas
Capable	Clear-thinking
Competent	Complicated
Common-sensical	Finds order in chaos
Ingenious	Knowledgeable
Likes complicated ideas	Logical
Precocious	Rational
Skilled in decision making	Well read
Well informed	

(1988, p. 256), "They [the award winners] indicated they were brighter than their friends and quicker to understand."

In Simonton's (1988a; see also Simonton, 1994, 1997) review of factors contributing to creativity he concluded that "creative individuals are noticeably more intelligent than average" (p. 399). He noted that intelligence fills the brain with images, sounds, phrases, and abstract concepts and the highly intelligent person has a greater chance of forming the novel combinations of ideas, images, and symbols that constitute a masterpiece than does someone with just a "starter set." In a *Newsweek* article about genius, Begley (1993) wrote "Ph.D.'s have a vast, complicated neural web, but high-school dropouts only a sparse, inefficient one. (This could explain why geniuses are more adept at bringing together disparate images, thoughts and phrases: Their brains look like Ma Bell's network)."

Your Brain: Like Ma Bell's Network!

Intuitive Evidence

There also is persuasive intuitive evidence of a correlation between creativity and intelligence. No major creative accomplishments of worldwide significance have emerged from the legions of our mentally retarded citizens. Also, as children grow older, they become smarter. They also produce better quality poetry, art work, and science projects, and they score higher on most tests of creativity, especially divergent thinking tests. There is a good argument for a moderate relationship between creativity and intelligence.

Threshold Concept

The increasingly accepted resolution to this apparent inconsistency regarding whether creativity *is* or *is not* related to intelligence lies in the *threshold* concept. The cornerstone research was Donald MacKinnon's (1961, 1978a) studies of creative architects at the University of California at Berkeley. MacKinnon's creative architects scored higher on intelligence tests than did undergraduate students. However, when the architects were rank-ordered according to peer-rated degree of creativity, the correlation between their IQ scores and their rated creativity was nil, zip, nada (-.08). This research illustrated that *a base level of intellectual ability is essential for creative productivity; above that threshold, however, there is virtually no relationship between measured intelligence and creativity.*

Above a Base Level, No Relationship

Moderate Relationship over Wide Range of Intelligence

Over the total range of intelligence, there is a moderate relationship with creativity. Barron (1961), a colleague of MacKinnon, reported correlations of about .40 (so-so) between creativity and IQ scores, based on his own and others' research. From his study of deceased eminent persons, Walberg (1988) also concluded that the linkage between intelligence and creative eminence is by no means tight: "The brightest . . . are not necessarily the best" (p. 355). His research on contemporary writers, scientists, and those adolescents who won art or science awards suggests that outstanding performance does indeed require a base level of moderately superior intelligence. However, higher levels of intelligence are less important than the present of other psychological traits and conditions (Walberg, 1988; Walberg & Herbig, 1991).

Other Traits Important

These other psychological traits, particularly the personality ones, are the focus of this chapter.

In sum, creativity and intelligence are separate constructs. A highly intelligent person may or may not be highly creative. A highly creative person may or may not be highly intelligent. At the same time, over the wide range of intelligence there is a moderate correlation. The threshold concept assumes a minimal required level of intelligence, about IQ = 120, above which there is little correlation between intelligence and creativity.

Threshold: IQ = about 120

PERSONALITY TRAITS

16 Categories of Traits

After a recent search your author sorted over two hundred adjectives and brief descriptions of creative personality traits into 16 categories. These exclude both

Creative people are independent. "I don't care how you sit when you read the paper," said this innovative thinker. (Wisconsin Center for Film and Theater Research.)

negative traits—with seven categories itself—and a group of pathological characteristics, both of which are discussed later. Sources of creative personality traits and descriptions are Barron (1961, 1969, 1978, 1988), MacKinnon (1976, 1978a, 1978b), Torrance (1962, 1979, 1981a, 1984a, 1984b, 1987a, 1987b, 1995; see also Millar, 1995), Walberg (1988; Stariha & Walberg, 1995; Walberg *et al.*, 1996; Walberg & Herbig, 1991; Walberg & Zeiser, 1997), Simonton (1988a, 1988b, 1990, 1994, 1997), Sternberg (1988a), Tardiff and Sternberg (1988), Solomon and Winslow (1988, 1993; Winslow & Solomon, 1989), Davis (1975, 1995; Davis & Bull, 1978; Davis & Subkoviak, 1978), Rimm (Davis & Rimm, 1982; Rimm & Davis, 1980), Runco (1990), Albert (1990), Gardner (1993), and Professor Alphabet Soup (Csikszentmihalyi, 1988, 1990a, 1990b).

A Bunch of References

The interminable list of characteristics extracted from these sources was sorted into 16 categories via the carefully controlled question: "Now where the heck should this go?" A persnickety person with narrower categories could produce many more groupings; one with wider categories would use fewer. The 16 appeared appropriate and seemed to summarize the main, recurrent traits of creative people found in this literature. The 16 categories of traits are:

Intuitive Categorization

1. Aware of creativeness
2. Original
3. Independent
4. Risk taking
5. Energetic
6. Thorough
7. Curious

8. Sense of Humor

9. Capacity for fantasy

10. Attracted to Complexity, Ambiguity

11. Artistic

12. Open minded

13. Needs alone time

14. Perceptive

15. Emotional

16. Ethical

Categories Interrelate

The categories are interrelated because all are part of the creative personality. Such interrelatedness sometimes made it difficult to decide, for example, whether *nonconformity* best fit under *originality* or *independence*, or whether *adventurous* belonged under *risk-taking* or *energetic*.

Not All Traits Apply to All Creative People

At the risk of overkill, the complete list is shown in Table 4.2. Of course, not all traits will apply to all creative persons. There simply are too many forms of creativity and creative people to make such a generalization. Besides, some traits are contradictory, for example, *receptive to new ideas* versus *sarcastic*. Also, there is a subtype of artistic/poetic creative people who are shy and withdrawn—not at all high in the confidence, energy, and humor that characterize the stereotyped creative nut.

While virtually all traits are self-defining, we will comment briefly on each to insure exposure to some sources and to sometimes surprising elaborations and implications.

Awareness of Creativity

Aware of Creativeness. Most highly creative people are quite aware of their creativeness. They are in the habit of doing creative things and they like being creative. Walberg's (1988) high school art and science award winners were consciously interested in creativity and were confident of their own creativity. "The creative groups felt more creative, imaginative, curious, and expressive and . . . felt that it is important to be creative" (p. 356). They attached great importance to money, but when choosing the "best characteristic to develop in life" they selected "creativity" more often than "wealth and power."

Creativity Consciousness: Extremely Important

Creativity consciousness is a common and important trait among creative people. *In improving our own creativity and in teaching creativity to others, it is the number one trait to develop.*

Now Write This One Down!

Originality. In a memorable understatement, Tardiff and Sternberg (1988) noted that originality and a good imagination "are commonly said to be associated with creative individuals" (p. 434). We suspect also that comedians are reputed to be funny and thieves lean toward dishonesty. Originality obviously is a core characteristic, and in dictionaries often is used interchangeably with creativity. We noted earlier that *originality* is both a creative ability and a personality trait, in the sense of being unconventional, flexible, habitually looking for new ways of doing things, and being a "what if?" person.

Independence, Risk-Taking

Independence, Risk-Taking. The creative person must dare to differ, make changes, stand out, challenge traditions, make a few waves, and bend a few rules. Creative people tend to have an internal locus of evaluation, rather than being swayed too easily by external influences and opinions. Because of their independence and innovativeness, creative people expose themselves to (a) failure,

Willingness to Fail

Table 4.2
Recurrent Personality Traits of Creative People

1. Aware of Creativeness

Creativity Conscious	Values originality and creativity
Values own creativity	

2. Original

Adapts, Is adaptable	A dreamer
Alert to novelty	Avoids perceptual sets
Avoids entrenched ways of thinking	Bored by the routine and obvious
Builds and rebuilds	Clever
Constructs	Does things differently
Enjoys pretending	Fantasizes
Flexible in ideas and thought	Full of ideas
Imaginative	Improves
Innovative	Inventive
Is a "What if" person	Manipulates ideas
Modifies (objects, systems, institutions)	Nonconforming
Odd habits	Radical
Resourceful	Sees things in new ways
Selects the more unusual solutions	Unconventional in behavior
Unique	Uses analogies, metaphors
Uses imagery, visualization	Uses wide categories
Versatile	Visionary

3. Independent

Aloof	Assertive
Believes in oneself	Critically examines authoritarian pronouncements
Does not fear being different	
Dissatisfied with the status quo	Dresses differently
Freedom of spirit that rejects limits imposed by others	High self-esteem
	Individualistic
Independent in judgments	Internally controlled, inner directed
Intense independence	May resist societal demands
May not fit environment	Questions norms, conventions, assumptions
May have conflict between self-confidence and self-criticism	
Outspoken	May need to maintain distance from peers
Prefers working alone	Radical and spirited in disagreement
Self-accepting	Self-aware
Self-confident	Self-directed
Self-organized	Self-sufficient
Sets own rules	Strong willed
Unconcerned with impressing others	Uninhibited

4. Risk Taking

Courageous

Not afraid to try something new

Little regard for social conventions, mores, rules, or laws

Rejects limits imposed by others

Willing to cope with failure

Does not mind consequences of being different

Optimistic

Opportunistic

Speculative

Willing to cope with hostility

5. Energetic

Action oriented

Adventurous

Ambitious

Capable of concentrating

Drive for accomplishment and recognition

Enjoys telling about discoveries/inventions

Excitable

Expressive in gestures, body language

Goes beyond assigned tasks

High commitment

High need for competence in meeting challenges

Impulsive

Joy in work

Persevering

Persuasive

Quick

Seeks interesting situations

Serious

Strives for distant goals

Unwilling to give up

Active

Alert

Blazing drive

Devotion to study or work

Drive to produce

Driving absorption

Enthusiastic

Exciting

Gets lost in a problem

Hard working

High intrinsic motivation

Hurried

Industrious

Overactive, hyperactive

Persistent

Problem centered

Restless

Sensation seeking

Spontaneous

Task-oriented

Vitality

6. Thorough

Organized

Disciplined and committed to one's work

Perfectionistic

7. Curious

Asks many questions

Distractible

Experiments

Likes to hear other people's ideas

Seeks interesting situations

Asks "Why?"

Enjoys taking things apart

Inquisitive

Open to the irrational

Wide interests

8. Sense of Humor

Childlike freshness

Plays with ideas

Playful

Sharp-witted

9. Capacity for Fantasy

Animistic and magical thinking

Had imaginary playmate(s) as a child

Mixes truth and fantasy/fiction

Believes in psychical phenomena and flying saucers

Theatrical interests

10. Attracted to Complexity, Ambiguity

Attracted to Novelty

Is a complex person

Tolerant of ambiguity

Tolerant of incongruity

Attracted to the mysterious, asymmetrical

Tolerant of disorder

11. Artistic

Artistic interests

Enjoys art, music, creative dramatics

Good designer

Sensitive to beauty

Aesthetic interests

Expressive

Sensitive to aesthetic characteristics

12. Open-Minded

Liberal

Open to impulses

Receptive to other viewpoints

Open to new experiences and growth

Receptive to new ideas

13. Needs Alone Time

Internally preoccupied

Reflective

Introspective

Reserved

14. Perceptive

Discerning

Insightful

Intuitive

Sees implications

Senses what should follow the solution

Heightened sensitivity to details, patterns, other phenomena

Observant

Sees relationships

Uses all senses in observing

Good at problem finding

15. Emotional

Can express feelings and emotions

Experiences deep emotions

Low frustration tolerance

Sensitive

Impulsive

Introverted

Withdrawn

Desires attention, praise, and support

Experiences soaring highs and deep lows

Moody

Immature

Irresponsible

Selfish

16. Ethical

Altruistic

Helpful

Idealistic

Sensitive to the needs of others

Empathic

Honest and courageousness

Philosophic

(b) criticism, (c) embarrassment, (d) the distinct possibility of making idiots of themselves, or (e) all of the above. In regard to creatively eminent people, Simonton (1997, p. 340) mentioned that "even after notable achievers establish their reputations . . . failures will accompany successes throughout their lives."

High Energy

Driving Absorption

High Energy. Creative people typically have a high energy level—a certain enthusiastic zest and a habit of spontaneous action. The creative person may get caught up in seemingly simple problems, perhaps working well into the night on an exciting project. "Driving absorption," "high commitment," "passionate interest," blazing drive, and "unwilling to give up" are phrases used to describe the energy and motivation of highly creative persons. The creative artist, writer, researcher, business person, engineer, or advertising executive becomes totally immersed in his or her ideas and creations, literally unable to rest until the work is complete. According to Taylor (1988, p. 99), "One fellow scientist described his colleague by saying that the only way one could stop him from working on his problem would be to shoot him."

Author Schawlow, Nobel prize winner in physics, stated that "The labor of love is important. The successful scientists are often not the most talented, but the ones who are just impelled by curiosity—they've got to know what the answer is" (Amabile, 1987, p. 224). Amabile reported that General Motors' most successful locomotive was designed by a small team of scientists and technicians who had been told four times to "cease and desist from building a locomotive" (p. 224).

C'mon Guys, Stop It!

Thrill Seeking

A related motivational trait has been called *sensation seeking, arousal seeking,* or *thrill-seeking* (Farley, 1986), which combines traits of high energy, adventurous-

Is this creative couple carrying the traits of originality, self-confidence, risk-taking and sensation seeking too far? "I do," said the groom. "They both do," added the bridesmaid, "and who's flying this thing, anyway?" (The Museum of Modern Art/Film Stills Archive.) Still from HOLLYWOOD CAVALCADE © 1939 Twentieth Century Fox Film Corporation. All Rights Reserved.

ness, and risk-taking. A personality test called the *Sensation Seeking Scale* (Zuckerman, 1975) is a better measure of creative tendencies than some creativity tests, according to a study by Davis, Peterson, and Farley (1973). In their research with college students, creative individuals were much more likely than the average to say "yes" they would like to:

Take up skiing

Ride motorcycles

Parachute from an airplane

Try mountain climbing

By hypnotized

Work in a foreign country

Explore strange cities without a guide

They preferred:

Camping to a good motel

To jump right into a cold pool instead of dipping a toe first

Bright colors in loud modern art over subdued traditional paintings

They liked:

Phew!   Some body odors

Positive and Negative Thrill-Seeking

Farley (1986) emphasized that, due to favorable or unfavorable social circumstances, the drive for thrill-seeking may be satisfied in constructive creative outlets or in destructive delinquent ways. There is thus a potential for creative achievement among our delinquent population.

Thorough: Must Finish

Thorough.   The common traits of risk-taking and high energy of the creatively productive person do not present a complete picture of work habits. He or she must finish the work, and therefore has been described as thorough, organized, disciplined, committed to the work, and sometimes even perfectionistic.

Curiosity

Wide Interests, Unusual Hobbies

Curiosity.   The creative person also has strong curiosity, a childlike sense of wonder and intrigue. He or she may have a history of taking things apart to see how they work, exploring attics, libraries, or museums, and have a generally strong urge to understand the world about him or her. The curiosity produces wide interests, unusual hobbies, and an experimenting nature. More than one creative person has muddled college graduation requirements by taking intriguing courses that do not meet graduation requirements.

High curiosity is a classic creative trait.

Good Humor Person

Humor.   An especially frequent creative trait is a good sense of humor, which is first cousin to the ability to take a fresh, childlike, and playful approach to a problem. Many discoveries, inventions, problem solutions, and artistic creations are the result of "fooling around" with ideas, playing with strange possibilities, or turning things upside down or backward. A favorite quote is that "The creative adult is essentially a perpetual child—the tragedy is that most of us grow up" (Fabun, 1968, p. 5). Both Sigmund Freud and Carl Rogers (Chapter 3) agreed that

Are you a Perpetual Child?

regression to a more childlike, fanciful, playful state of mind is an important feature of creative thinking and creative thinkers.

Attracted to Complexity, Ambiguity, Fantasy, Novelty, the Mysterious

Attraction to Complexity, Ambiguity, Fantasy, and Novelty. The creative person is attracted to complexity, ambiguity, fantasy, and the mysterious, a proclivity that may reflect the creative person's own complexity. One test, the *Barron-Welsh Art Scale* (Welsh & Barron, 1963; see Chapter 8), has shown repeatedly that creative persons prefer smudgy, complex, asymmetrical drawings over simple and balanced ones (Barron, 1969).

Martindale (1975) made a relevant observation:

> Confronted with novelty, whether in design, music, or ideas, creative people get excited and involved . . . and overlook defects or problems . . . Less creative students do the opposite. They find fault . . . and start analyzing defects rather than exploring potential.

Tolerance for Ambiguity: Necessary in Elaboration, Development of Ideas

Sternberg (1988a) reviewed the critical role of tolerance for ambiguity, dubbing it "almost a *sine qua non* of creative performance" (p. 143), an observation also made by others (e.g., Barron, 1968; MacKinnon, 1978b; Vernon, 1970; Dacey, 1989). Creative ideas normally require some amount of elaboration and development. It follows that the creative person must work with ideas that are incomplete and ambiguous: Relevant facts are missing, rules are unclear, and "correct" procedures do not exist (MacKinnon, 1978b). Whether writing a novel, creating a work of art, or solving an engineering problem, the ideas will evolve from the original insight or "big idea" through a series of modification, approximations, and improvements—which requires coping with uncertainty and ambiguity.

Stronger Believers in ESP, Flying Saucers, Ghosts

An attraction to complexity and fantasy includes a probably surprising twist: Creative persons tend to be stronger believers in such psychical and mysterious matters as extrasensory perception (ESP), mental telepathy, precognition, astral projection (out-of-body experience), flying saucers, and spirits and ghosts (Davis, Peterson, & Farley, 1973; Schuldberg *et al.*, 1988). They also are more likely to have psychical experiences (Torrance, 1962). Many creative persons have reported mystical experiences, for example, Mark Twain. Another example is the late Orson Welles, creator of the 1938 radio show *The War of the Worlds*, which scared the daylights out of millions of Americans, and the movie *Citizen Kane*, sometimes rated the best movie ever made. Welles frequently demonstrated his psychical abilities on TV shows; but he also was an accomplished magician, suspiciously enough.

Livelier Imagination?

Or Slightly Strange?

There are at least two possible explanations for this belief in paranormal happenings. First, such beliefs may simply reflect the creative person's livelier imagination and openness to fantastic possibilities. Another possibility is that such beliefs reflect a slight psychopathology, which will be described in a few pages.[1]

Artistic

Aesthetic Interests

Artistic, Aesthetic Interests. The creative person usually will rate himself or herself high in being "artistic," whether or not he or she can draw. The creative person thus tends to be more conscious of artistic considerations and also has aesthetic interests—interests in music and dance concerts, plays, art galleries, photo exhibits, antique shows, Masterpiece Theatre, a good sunset, scenic views from the freeway, and so forth. On the *How Do You Think* test (Davis, 1991a; Chapter 8), an inventory for assessing creative personality traits, a high self-rating on *artistic* is one of the single best items on the test (Davis & Subkoviak, 1978).

---

[1]Of course, a third possibility is that highly creative people understand mystical things that escape the rest of us.

One obvious reason for above-average artistic and aesthetic interests is that creative people are more likely to be, or to have been, involved in artistic and aesthetic enterprises—music, dance, theatre, art, handicrafts, or others.

Open-Mindedness

Open-Minded.   Open-mindedness is a prime creative attitude. It includes receptiveness to new ideas and a willingness to look at a problem or situation from other points of view. It includes not fearing the new, different, or unknown, and not making up your mind in advance (Dacey, 1989). Open-mindedness includes a dash of adventurousness and leads to personal growth.

The reader is encouraged to look again at von Oech's 10 whack-on-the-side-of-the-head guides in Chapter 2. Barriers to creativity—such as looking for just one right answer, being practical and logical, and avoiding ambiguity, frivolity, mistakes, and foolishness—are quite inconsistent with creative open-mindedness.

Need Some Privacy, Alone Time

Needs for Alone Time.   Creative children and adults need some privacy and alone time. The urge to create demands time for thinking, for reflection, for solving problems, for creating. Creative children and adults may prefer to work alone, which reflects their creative independence.

Perceptive = Intuitive

Perceptive.   As described by the adjectives in Table 4.1, perceptiveness and intuitiveness include a creative person's higher sensitivity to details, pattens, implications, and "what should follow." Creative people are quicker to see relationships and make "mental leaps." Such perceptiveness and intuition relate to the insightfulness and problem-finding ability of creative people.

Emotional.   A literature exists on *emotional giftedness* or *overexcitability* (e.g., Piechowski, 1997). A probably-very-high-IQ person in this category shows high creativity in the sense of "free play of imagination, with vivid imagery, fantasy ... paranormal thinking, metaphorical thought, inventions, and poetic and dramatic perceptions" (Davis & Rimm, 1998). The syndrome includes having deep emotions, experiencing emotional highs and lows, as well as moodiness and emotional sensitivity. Other traits of the emotionally gifted include high psychomotor activity (e.g., high energy, fast talking), a high concern for right-and-wrong (moral thinking), and an aliveness of sensual experiences.

"Overexcitability": Fantasy, Sensitivity, High Activity

This syndrome may be an explanation of why highly intelligent, highly creative people seem to be strong believers in psychical phenomena and flying saucers.

Ethics: Empathy

Ethical.   Another trait related to high mental ability and creativity is a tendency toward idealism, altruism, sensitivity to others' needs, and just plain helpfulness. Perhaps a lively imagination and the ability to see outcomes strengthens one's empathic understanding of others' difficulties and problems.

NEGATIVE CREATIVE TRAITS

Negative Traits Can Be Upsetting

So far, with few exceptions, the creative person looks pretty good—intelligent, independent, energetic, good sense of humor, artistic, open-minded, perceptive, etc. However, creative children and adults are quite capable of showing habits and dispositions that can upset a normal supervisor, parent, teacher, or other students. Table 4.3 lists some not-uncommon characteristics of creative individuals, most of which were found in Torrance (1962, 1981a), Smith (1966), and Domino (1970). The items were intuitively placed into the seven categories of *egotistical, impulsive, argumentative, childish, absentminded, neurotic,* and *hyperactive*. Some may be rooted in a creative students' general unconventionality, independence, persistence, and perhaps curiosity and humor.

Table 4.3
Common "Negative" Traits of Some
Creative Persons Sometimes

1. Egotistical

Claims rest of the parade is out of step	Intolerant
Snobbish	Self-centered
Selfish	

2. Impulsive

Acts without planning	Capricious
Compulsive	Disorderly
Disorganized with unimportant matters	Impatient
Irresponsible	Tactless
Uninterested in details	

3. Argumentative

Autocratic	Cynical
Defiant	Demanding
May refuse to participate in class activities	Rebellious
Resists Domination	Sarcastic
Stubborn	Uncooperative
Questions rules, conventions, law, authority	

4. Childish

Silly	Immature
Sloppy	

5. Absent-Minded

Careless	Forgetful
Mind wanders	Watches windows

6. Neurotic

Aloof	Sociopathic, mildly
Temperamental	Low frustration tolerance
Moody	Uncommunicative
Unable to control emotions	

7. Hyperactive

Overactive physically or mentally

**Egotistical,
Argumentative,
Capricious**

Many are likely to cause personal or social adjustment problems, for example, *egotistical* ("I know more than anyone here"), *argumentativeness* and *sarcasm* ("I'm always right"), and being *capriciousness, disorderly,* and *careless* ("and I'll do what I want").

In discussing business entrepreneurs—who seem like a creative bunch—Solomon and Winslow (1988) described negative traits of being *mildly sociopathic*

Creative people may forget unimportant details. (The Museum of Modern Art/Film Stills Archive.)

Entrepreneurs Mildly Sociopathic

(or being a *social deviate*), partly because they cannot work for someone else; *clannish*, because they seek out people like themselves; and *outspoken, impatient,* and *stubborn.* On the positive side, the authors noted that entrepreneurs are "confident and optimistic . . . [and are] independent and self-reliant" (p. 170).

When Stubborn Sammy or Independent Elissa show some of the upsetting characteristics in Table 4.2, the teacher might consider the possibility that the symptoms are part of a larger picture of energetic creativeness that may need rechanneling into constructive outlets. In the business or professional setting: patience and understanding.

Rechannel Energy

Patience

THE BERKELEY STUDIES

Most Extensive Studies of Creative People

Architects, Writers, Mathematicians

Tests, Inventories, Observations

The single most extensive examination of traits of creative people took place at the University of California, Berkeley, in the 1950s. Psychologists Frank Barron (1969, 1978, 1988), Donald MacKinnon (1976, 1978a), and others studied nationally recognized creative architects, writers, and men and women mathematicians. The names were selected by nominations from faculty in Berkeley's Departments of Architecture, English, and Mathematics. The creative persons were observed informally over a three-day weekend and took intelligence tests and a variety of personality tests and self-descriptive inventories (e.g., the *Minnesota Multiphasic Personality Inventory*, MMPI; *California Psychological Inventory; Adjective Check List; Myers-Briggs Type Indicator*). Barron also went to Ireland to study innovators in business management, using many of the same tests. Many of the personality traits described in this chapter originated from or were confirmed by this research. For example, their creative people tended to be original, imaginative, independent, verbally fluent, flexible, energetic, productive, artistic, emotional, unconventional, nonconforming, and had aesthetic interests and wide interests generally.

CREATIVITY AND MENTAL DISTURBANCE

Self-Centered, Moody

The Berkeley group also uncovered an interesting trend among high-level creative people, reminiscent of Maslow's sometimes-disturbed *special talent* creative persons (Chapter 1). The research indicated that some traits of these very talented people would not be considered mentally healthy. Compared with representative women mathematicians, creative women mathematicians were more likely to be self-centered, rebellious, and have fluctuating moods, and they tended to be undependable, irresponsible, and/or inconsiderate. Looking at successful creative writers, "the *average* creative writer, in fact, is in the upper 15 percent of the general population on *all* measures of psychopathology furnished by this test!" (MMPI; Barron, 1965, p. 62): *hypochondriasis, depression, hysteria,*[2] *psychopathic deviation, paranoia, psychasthenia,*[3] *schizophrenia,* and *hypomania.* Critically, they also scored high on *ego strength,* a measure of mental health and stability. Barron (1969) summed up his findings with, "they are both sicker and healthier psychologically than people in general . . . they are more troubled psychologically, but they also have far greater resources with which to deal with their troubles."

Creative Writers: High in MMPI Psychopathology

Also High in Ego Strength: Sicker and Healthier

This interesting tendency of highly creative people to show mental disorders has a long history (see, e.g., Andreason, 1978; Jamison, 1989; Richards, 1981; Schuldberg *et al.,* 1988). Noted Schuldberg *et al.,* "research has noted affective disorders, schizophrenia, unconventional or antisocial behavior, and alcohol and substance abuse in eminent and creative individuals and sometimes in their relatives" (p. 648). The research of Schuldberg *et al.* showed that normal (?) garden-variety male and female college students who scored high on a creative personality inventory (*How Do You Think,* HDYT; Davis, 1975, 1991a) also scored high on a combined measure of psychopathology: *perceptual aberration* (e.g., ordinary sounds are reported as sometimes uncomfortable) and *magical ideation* (having superstitious and supernatural beliefs). Shields (1988) found that the best group of items in the HDYT creativity test were those that measured belief in paranormal phenomena (ESP, precognition, flying saucers, etc.), which relates closely to Schuldberg's magical ideation.

Creative College Students Higher in Psychopathology

In Walberg's (1988; Walberg & Herbig, 1991) study of historically eminent people, about a quarter to a third showed definite introversion or neuroses. The business manager of Yves St. Laurent said in a TV interview that, despite his fame and success, the genius of fashion design actually is withdrawn and somewhat neurotic.

Walberg: Some Eminent Men Introverted or Neurotic

We noted Solomon and Winslow's (1988) conclusion that their sample of entrepreneurs showed mild sociopathy and/or were social deviates. Characteristics described as "not necessarily mentally ill but aberrant" included *immature, irresponsible, impulsive, selfish, little anxiety or guilt about immediate acts, little ability to control emotions, low frustration tolerance,* and *little regard for societal conventions, mores, rules,* or *laws.* The description seems to qualify as mild sociopathy.

Sociopathic Entrepreneurs

A study by Walker, Koestner, and Hum (1995) explored the personalities of 48 eminent creative achievers (25 men, 23 women), finding that the "creative achievers were rated significantly higher than controls on general neuroticism, as well

---

[2]Excitability, anxiety, uncontrolled behavior.

[3]Neuroses characterized by fear, anxiety, and phobias.

Creative Achievers Higher on Neuroticism, Depression

as on depressive style and impulsivity" (p. 75). They noted that creative artists and writers Sylvia Plath, Jack London, Virginia Woolf, Jackson Pollock, and Vincent Van Gogh experienced sufficient depression to commit suicide. Jamison (1989) asked 47 award-winning British artists and writers about any history of affective disorders, and 38 percent reported psychiatric treatment for depression. Andreason (1987) found that in a sample of creative writers, a full 80 percent had an affective illness at some time and 43 percent had some type of bipolar (manic-depressive) illness.

Manic-Depressives Higher on Creativity

Relatives, Too

Richards *et al.* (1988) turned the usual procedure around. She began with a sample of 33 manic-depressives and cyclothymes[4] and compared their creativity ratings with those of 33 control subjects. Creative productivity was rated higher among the mentally disturbed. The authors concluded that proneness "for manic-depressive illness may carry advantages for creativity, perhaps particularly among those individuals who are relatively better functioning" (p. 281).

Andreason and Canter (1974) found that even relatives of creative writers showed a higher prevalence of mental illness than relatives of control subjects. Perhaps the reader can think of a colorful and imaginative interpretation or application of this breakthrough.

Finally, observed Barron (1965), "mad as a hatter" is a term of high praise when applied to creative people.

BIOGRAPHICAL CHARACTERISTICS

Not-So-Subtle Traits: History of Creative Activities

Recurrent biographical traits of creative people may be of two sorts, *subtle* and *not-so-subtle*. Not-so-subtle biographical factors are simply the person's history of creative activities and creative behaviors. It is hardly surprising that, beginning in childhood, most creative people accumulate a history of building and making things and of literary, artistic, and scientific involvement. One list of "things done on your own," from Torrance (1962), appears in Table 4.4. Another list of behaviors and characteristics that reflect high creativeness appears in Table 4.5.[5]

If the person has been creative in the past, there is a strong likelihood he or she will be creative in the future. Involvement in creative activities can be used as predictors of creative behavior—predictors that may have more validity than some creativity tests.

Subtle Traits: More Surprising

Owning a Cat

Imaginary Playmate

Subtle biographical correlates of creativity include background facts that are a bit more surprising. Schaefer (1969, 1970) found that creative high school students were more likely to have friends younger and older than themselves, rather than the same age. The creatives also were more likely to have lived in more than one state and may have traveled outside the USA. High school girls who were creative writers were more likely to personally own a cat. Definitely subtle. Schaefer, confirmed in studies reviewed by Somers and Yawkey (1984), also found that creative students more often reported having an imaginary childhood playmate. Said Somers and Yawkey, imaginary companions contribute to creativity by developing originality and elaboration and by fostering sensitivity in relationships.

Perfect Predictors of Creativity?

In your author's experience, two biographical traits each are 100 percent accurate as predictive of creativeness: participation in theater or having had an imaginary playmate as a child. Creative secondary students and adults may laughingly concede "I still have an imaginary playmate." Typically, the young child will talk

---

[4]Mild manic-depressive disorder.

[5]More will be said about these and other biographical indicators of creativeness in Chapter 8 on assessing creative potential.

Table 4.4
A Sample of Creative Activities
(Adapted from Torrance, 1962)

Created a collection of wild flowers (leaves, insects, rocks, post marks, stamps, own writings)

Wrote a play (poem, story, song, jingle, musical composition)

Acted in a play (skit, charades)

Directed or organized a play (skit, puppet show)

Designed stage settings for a skit or play

Designed a model airplane

Created a recipe for a food dish (meat, salad, dessert) or drink mixture

Organized (or helped to organize) a club, paper drive, rummage sale

Made up a song (dance, musical composition, new game)

Pantomimed a story

Investigated the history of his or her community or city

Did an oil painting (watercolor, poster, linoleum cut, block printing, wood carving, ornamental basket, plaster molds)

Illustrated a story, drew cartoons, printed photographs

Created a design for jewelry (or cloth)

Explored a cave

Read a science magazine (or book)

Created an electric motor (musical instrument, toy, ink, leaf prints, scale model of a park or farm)

Planned an experiment, dissected an animal

Grafted a plant or rooted one from a cutting

Kept a daily weather record

Was a bird watcher

Designed a way to improve how we do something at home (in school, Scouts, a club)

Created a way to get along with parents or other boys and girls

Investigated how a government agency (post office, court) operates

Drew up plans for (or constructed) an invention or apparatus

to and play with the imaginary companion, have tea parties, blame things on the playmate ("I didn't break it, Yoohoo did!"), and require mom—or the waitress in a restaurant—to set an extra place at the table. Sometimes there are many imaginary friends and sometimes they are animals. Some creative children do a continuous ventriloquist act, talking back and forth with a stuffed animal or doll. The imaginary friend usually, not always, disappears after children enter kindergarten (Somers & Yawkey, 1984). Persons who claim a background in theater or having had an imaginary playmate (or both, which is common) invariably show the typical creative personality traits described in this chapter. They also will report present or past involvement in creative activities.

Table 4.5
Creative Behavior Characteristics
(from Renzulli & Reis, 1991)

A youngster shows high creativity and motivation when he or she:

Goes "above and beyond the call of duty" in completing, for example, an art, writing, or science project that shows superlative quality.

Is obsessed with a particular topic or area of study.

Persists in questioning about a certain topic or area.

Is labeled by others (not always in a nice way) as the "math marvel," "computer whiz kid," "poet in residence," or "mad scientist."

Wants to "get something going"—a class newspaper, money raising project, field trip, or action on a social problem ("Let's write to the Governor about our polluted lake!").

Has extracurricular activities that are more important than regular school work.

Is sought out by others because he or she is an expert in a particular area.

May start a club, interest group, or project (e.g., film making) on his or her own.

Typically is the class clown or lackadaisical, but becomes very serious and immersed in a particular topic area.

Voluntarily visits museums, laboratories, power plants, etc., on his or her own.

Forgets to come back to class or is always late when returning from a particular course or special interest area, for example, the computer, art, or industrial arts room.

Asks for a teacher's help in getting books that are not available in the school library.

Generalizes or extends a topic under discussion to another (for example, in a science lesson on simple machines, the student quickly moves into modern machines or solar energy).

Is a clever humorist—sees whimsical or zany implications of otherwise serious situations.

Has set up a laboratory, photography darkroom, or other special interest area at home on his or her own.

Feels compulsion to begin work on a topic ("I have to write it down before I go nuts").

Continues to work on a project even though he or she is discouraged by lack of progress.

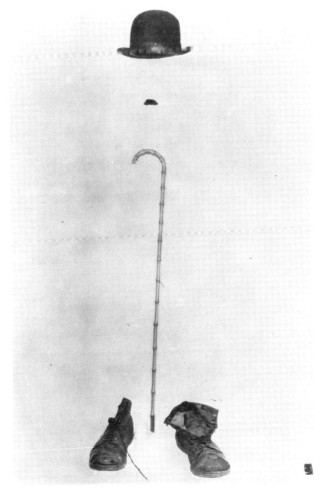

An actual photograph of an imaginary playmate. Can you guess whose playmate he was? (Wisconsin Center for Film and Theater Research.)

THE BUCKETS   **By Scott Stantis**

THE BUCKETS reprinted by permission of United Feature Syndicate, Inc.

Birth Order and Handedness

Birth order and handedness are two traits that occasionally are mentioned as possibly related to creativity.

Birth-Order Effects.   The birth-order effect has been studied for some decades, beginning with Galton's (1876) study of eminent British scientists. There seems little doubt that first-born and only children tend to be more studious, higher achievers, and more likely to be National Merit scholars or even prodigies. They are likely to be better educated and have higher-level careers (Hilgard, Atkinson, & Atkinson, 1979). First-borns predominate among doctors, lawyers, professors, and other professionals (Simonton, 1997). Most U.S. presidents are first or only children (e.g., Schubert, Wagner, & Schubert, 1977), as are about 93 percent of U.S. astronauts.

Speculations on the cause of the birth-order effect border on amusing. Briefly, one view was that first and only children somehow have a more favorable prenatal environment, which produces less "fetal stress." Another explanation proposed that later born children experience repeated and unexpected intrusions by the older sibling, resulting in an altered brain limbic system that makes the younger child more sensitive, anxious, and withdrawn.

Social explanations seem more on target. One argument is simply that first and only children receive more attention, are read to more, and receive more educational encouragement and assistance. Another points out that a new baby requires older children to be more grown-up, responsible, and to depend less on mother for assistance. For example, older children are expected to help with and sometimes care for the new arrival. First borns thus may develop a personality and learning style that aids their informal and formal education and ultimate achievement. For example, in school they tend to work hard, impress teachers, and try hard on IQ tests. This portrait may be compared with the reported tendency of later borns to not work hard in school or on IQ tests, not try to impress the teacher, and not necessarily assume the existence of one right answer (e.g., on an intelligence test; Simonton, 1997). First-born and only children were over-represented in Terman's sample of 1,528 gifted children, most of whom scored above IQ = 140.

While education and achievement favor first and only children, some have argued that later borns generally are more creative. According to Hetherington and Parke (1979), first and only children are more anxious, conforming, passive, and worried about failure—traits that favor academic accomplishment, but not creative thought. Eisenman's (1964) research with 20 art students seemed to confirm that, sure enough, first-borns were less creative than middle or youngest children.

On the other hand, using divergent thinking tests (e.g., listing unusual uses for most anything; see Chapter 8), Lichtenwalner and Maxwell (1969) found that first and only children produced higher, not lower, ideational fluency scores. Runco and Bahleda (1986) found that "only" children, but not first-borns, produced the highest divergent thinking scores. Lichtenwalner and Maxwell and Runco and Bahleda concluded that only-born children develop greater autonomy, which underlies their higher creativity scores.

Simonton (1997) proposed an unusual view—but probably the most sensible one—relating birth order to creativity. Based on a literature review, he concluded that "the overall tendency is for first-borns to achieve eminence in prestigious positions that are well integrated with the Establishment, whereas the later-borns are more likely to succeed as rebellious agents of a new order or even as advocates of disorder" (p. 342). For example, he noted that our scholarly first-borns are more

Only Children and First-Born Higher Achievers

Better Prenatal Environment?

Younger Child More Emotional?

Social Explanations: Attention, Encouragement, Responsibility, Independence

Work Hard, Impress Teachers, Try Hard on IQ Tests

And Vice Versa for Later Borns

First-Borns More Anxious Conforming?

First-Borns More Creative, Independent?

Research Support Here, Too

Simonton: First Borns Achieve within Establishment

Later Borns Artistic,
Conform Less

Highly Credible
Reference!

Birth Order May
Determine Domain,
Not Level, of
Achievement

likely to attain distinction in scientific areas, but the more creative later-borns are likely to distinguish themselves in artistic areas—as artists, writers, or others who conform less to societal expectations. An exception is that classic composers are more aligned with the scientists—they tend to be first or only borns (Schubert, Wagner, & Schubert, 1977). The reference is a real one.

Simonton reached a similar conclusion regarding leadership: "First-borns provide the politicians, while the last-borns populate the revolutionaries" (p. 342). Interestingly, said Simonton, later-borns who do go into science are more apt to become "scientific revolutionaries" who might overthrow established models and standards. Overall, birth order is more likely to determine the domain of achievement (e.g., science versus art), rather than ones eventual level of distinction.

Handedness. While Simonton's conclusions regarding birth order are suggestive, research on the relation of handedness to creativity remains ambiguous.

Left-Handers: Better
Access to Both Halves
of Brain?

There has been speculation that left-handers are more creative. The main—but weak—evidence is that many historically creative people were left-handed, for example, Leonardo Da Vinci, Michelangelo, and Benjamin Franklin. The argument is that left-handed people, most of whom in fact are ambidextrous, have better access to both hemispheres of their brains. That is, with normal right-handed people the left side of the brain controls speech, writing, sequential, and analytical functions; the right side controls spatial, wholistic, intuitive, and creative functions (Al-Sabaty & Davis, 1989; Springer & Deutsch, 1985). The left-handed person's more integrated access to both hemispheres should aid creative thinking and problem solving; at least that's the logic.

Left-Handed Architects

Peterson and Lansky (1980), in fact, discovered that in a sample of 17 architecture faculty, five were left-handed (29.4 percent), and two more were left-handed as children but were "cured," for a total of 7 of 17 (41.2 percent). Dacey (1989) reported that 65 percent of the students in a major art school were left-handed. These figures are substantially above the universe-wide average of 10 percent left-handedness. On the other hand (sorry), with a group of 100 20-year olds Katz (1980) found absolutely no relationship between handedness and scores on three different creativity tests.

Other Research:
No Relationship

Handedness:
Inconclusive

The association of left-handedness with creativity remains inconclusive.

CREATIVE ABILITIES

Cognitive vs. Affective
Traits

In addition to personality (or affective) traits and biographical characteristics, there also are *cognitive* abilities that are important for creative thinking—abilities that are well-developed and often-used by creative people. Such abilities are partly genetic and partly learned. Long-time creativity expert Frank Barron (1988) listed just six "ingredients" of creativity that intermix affective and cognitive traits:

Barron's Six
Ingredients

1. Recognizing patterns
2. Making connections
3. Taking risks
4. Challenging assumptions
5. Taking advantage of chance
6. Seeing in new ways

Barron's six ingredients certainly are central traits of a creative person. However, there are many more intellectual and stylistic abilities that contribute in one

---

Table 4.6
Creative Abilities

Fluency	Able to predict outcomes, consequences
Flexibility	Analysis
Originality	Synthesis
Elaboration	Evaluation
Transformation	Logical Thinking
Sensitivity to Problems	Able to regress
Able to define problems	Intuition
Visualization, imagination	Concentration
Analogical/Metaphorical Thinking	

Probably All Mental Abilities Are Related to Creativity

way or another to creative capability. Actually, it would be difficult to isolate mental abilities that have absolutely *nothing* to do with creativeness. We also noted that the line between "abilities" and "personality characteristics" sometimes is very thin, for example, in the cases of originality, humor, or perceptiveness.

A short list of abilities that seem especially important to creativity appear in Table 4.6. A brief comment on each may be in order.

Fluency is the ability to produce many ideas, verbal or nonverbal, for an open-ended problem or question. Pseudonyms include *associational fluency* and *ideational fluency.*

Flexibility is the ability to take different approaches to a problem, think of ideas in different categories, or view a problem from different perspectives.

Originality is just that—uniqueness, nonconformity in thought and action. Dictionary synonyms include creativity, novelty, rarity, singularity, and innovativeness. Table 4.1 includes 34 personality-related synonyms.

Elaboration is the important ability to add details to an idea, which includes developing, embellishing, improving, and implementing the idea.[6]

Transformation = Perceptual Change

Transformation is a subtle term that could be used interchangeably with *creative thinking* itself. Every creative idea involves a transformation—changing one object or idea into another by modifying, combining, or substituting. Transformation also is "seeing" new meanings, implications, or applications or adopting something to a new use. For nearly four decades J. P. Guilford (e.g., 1986) emphasized the significance of transformation abilities for creative thinking. We will see in Chapter 5 that *perceptual change*—looking at one thing and seeing another—is a creative process which is approximately identical in meaning to *transformation.*

Problem Finding

Sensitivity to problems reflects the ability to find problems, detect difficulties, detect missing information, and ask good questions. As we noted in Chapter 1, many writers, including Albert Einstein, have stressed that creative people generally are excellent "problem finders" (e.g., Getzels & Csikszentmihalyi, 1976; Okuda, Runco, & Berger, 1991; Subotnik, 1988). Creative people can locate problems worth working on, and they always assume their own work can be improved—they find problems with it.

---

[6]Fluency, flexibility, originality, and elaboration are four scores derived from the popular *Torrance Tests of Creative Thinking* (Chapter 8). They are important and well-known creative abilities, but not the only creative abilities.

The related complex ability of *problem defining* includes at least the abilities to (1) identify the "real" problem, (2) isolate important (and unimportant) aspects of a problem, (3) clarify and simplify a problem, (4) identify subproblems, (5) propose alternative problem definitions, and (6) define a problem more broadly. Items 5 and 6 open the door to a wider variety of problem solutions. Note that one's logical thinking ability would be involved throughout "problem defining" as described here.

Note also that both *sensitivity to problems* and *problem defining* seem to require a certain *perceptiveness* and *intuitiveness*, described earlier as personality traits. Once again the distinction between abilities and personality traits is clearly blurred.

Visualization is the ability to fantasize, to see things in the "mind's eye," to mentally manipulate images and ideas. The term is used interchangeably with *imagination* itself and is an essential creative ability. It also is a complex one. Creative writing, for example, has been described as a recursive process of moving back and forth between mental images (based on novel syntheses of memories and current experiences) and the prose itself (Flower & Hayes, 1984). Imagery actually takes place in all senses, not just the visual one, as when Beethoven and Mozart imagined their compositions. Synesthesia is cross-modal imagery, as in "the murmur of gray twilight" and "the sound of coming darkness" (Poe) and "the dawn comes up like thunder" (Kipling; see Daniels-McGhee & Davis, 1994).

Analogical/metaphorical thinking is the ability to borrow ideas from one context and use them in another, borrow a solution from a related problem, or otherwise "see a connection" between one situation and another. Analogical thinking is sufficiently important to justify a relatively substantial chapter in this book (Chapter 7).[7]

Predicting outcomes or consequences is the ability to foresee the results of different solution alternatives and actions. It is related to *evaluation* ability.

Analysis is the ability to separate details, break down a whole into its parts.

Synthesis is the ability to see relationships, to combine parts into a workable, perhaps creative whole.

Evaluation is the important ability to separate the relevant from the irrelevant, to think critically, to evaluate the "goodness" or appropriateness of an idea, product, or solution.[8]

Logical thinking is the ability to make reasonable decisions and deduce reasonable conclusions. It permeates all aspects of creative thinking and problem solving and, logically, would be part of every other ability in this list.

The *ability to regress* includes a facility for "thinking like a child," whose mind is less cluttered by habits, traditions, rules, conformity pressures, etc.—the barriers we explored in Chapter 2. The ability to regress is related to playfulness and humor.

Intuition is a little-understood capability to make "mental leaps" or "intuitive leaps," to see relationships based upon little, perhaps insufficient information, to

Involves Logical Thinking

Perceptiveness, Intuitiveness Involved

Writing: Recursive Process between Imagery and Prose

Imagery in All Senses

Synesthesia: Seeing Sounds

---

[7]While "analogy" and "metaphor" have slightly different meanings, they seem to be used interchangeably in the creativity literature. Typically, creative ideas that stem from "seeing a similarity" or "making a connection" are analogical ("Hey, that bird's nest gives me an idea for a new sandwich!"). A metaphor is the application of a term to describe something to which it does not literally apply, e.g., "the curtain of night" or "God is a fortress." Creative people tend not to worry much about picky distinctions. E.g., was Darwin's use of a branching tree diagram to help explain natural selection a metaphor or an analogy? Does it make any difference? See Gruber and S. N. Davis (1988) for more about metaphorical thinking than you ever wanted to know.

[8]The reader with a background in education might recognize *analysis, synthesis,* and *evaluation* as higher-order thinking skills in Bloom's taxonomy of educational objectives, cognitive domain.

Table 4.7
Information Processing Traits
(Adapted from Tardif & Sternberg, 1988)

Uses existing knowledge as basis for new ideas

Avoids perceptual sets and entrenched ways of thinking

Questions norms and assumptions

Builds new structures, instead of using existing structures

Uses wide categories, sees "forest" instead of "trees"

Thinks metaphorically

Thinks logically

Makes independent judgments

Alert to novelty and gaps in knowledge

Copes well with novelty

Finds order in chaos

Uses internal visualization

May prefer nonverbal communication

Flexible and skilled in decision making

"read between the lines." It relates to *perceptiveness*, described earlier in the personality list.

Concentration is the ability to focus one's attention. It relates to the task-orientation or even "driving absorption" of creatively productive people.

Information Processing Traits

Information Processing Characteristics

A list of dynamic information processing characteristics related to creative thinking, modified from Tardif and Sternberg (1988), and which they extracted from numerous chapters in the Sternberg (1988b) book, appears in Table 4.7. Because these seem self-defining, and in fact overlap with the personality traits and cognitive abilities in Tables 4.2 and 4.6, we will bypass a tedious definition of each.

CREATIVITY AND EMINENCE

Csikszentmihalyi, Gardner: Theories Could Be Here

So Could Simonton's Chance-Configuration Theory

In Chapter 3 we summarized briefly the Csikszentmihalyi (1988; "Smith") and Gardner (1993) theories of creativity, both of which emphasized the components of *person, domain,* and *field* (society). Their restrictive definition of *creative* applied only to persons who were evaluated by the field/society as "creative" and whose ideas permanently altered the domain. Since creative eminence was their focus, both theories could have been included in this section. Simonton's chance-configuration theory, which also noted the importance of outside judges to decide which products are eminently creative, also would fit well in this section.

In recent years many other scholars also have focused on persons who achieve creative excellence or eminence. In this section we will look briefly at contributions by Abraham Tannenbaum, Herbert Walberg, Robert Albert, Benjamin Bloom and Lauren Sosniak, David Feldman, and some additional ideas and traits proposed by Simonton.

Abraham Tannenbaum: The Star Model

As a starting place, Tannenbaum's (1997) five-point star model reviews factors needed to achieve creative excellence. Each factor, or point on the star, includes *static* and *dynamic* dimensions (subfactors). Point 1 of the star is *general ability*, consisting of basic intelligence (static) as well as cognitive and thinking styles such as those in Table 4.7 (dynamic). Point 2 is *special aptitude* in an area such as mathematics, which would include high math ability (static) plus such favorable work styles as problem finding and strategy finding (dynamic). Point 3 is *nonintellective factors*—personality variables such as independence, flexibility, and particularly motivation (static). The dynamic dimension includes overexcitability (described earlier), which includes "inner motivation" plus self-protective aspects of the self-concept such as exerting little effort to protect feelings of superiority. Star point 4 is the *environment*, whose static dimension includes the Csikszentmihalyi/Gardner domain of activity (e.g., movie making) and the field that judges creativeness (e.g., Gene and Roger). The dynamic aspect of Tannenbaum's environment stressed the home climate, with its emphases on achievement motivation, language development, and general learning. Finally, point 5 is *chance* itself, with static factors of the "smile or frown of fortune" (p. 38) and the good/bad luck to be at the right/wrong place at the right/wrong time. Tannenbaum's dynamics of luck included ones tendency to "stir the pot" of random ideas so that a few will connect in productive combinations. Somebody noted that "The harder you work, the luckier you get" (e.g., Davis, 1996b).

In sum, Tannenbaum's five factors were general ability, special aptitude, non-intellective factors (personality, motivation), environment, and chance. All must be present to maximize the likelihood of creative excellence.

Herbert Walberg: Classic Characteristics of Eminence

The research and findings of Walberg have been mentioned several times in conjunction with the threshold concept of intelligence, ones awareness of creativity, and mental disturbance. In his eminence research, Walberg (1988; Walberg & Herbig, 1991; Walberg & Stariha, 1992; Walberg & Zeiser, 1997) reviewed biographical information of 282 historically eminent men, for example, Wolfgang Mozart, Abraham Lincoln, Martin Luther, Johann Wolfgang Goethe, George Washington, Rembrandt, Leonardo Da Vinci, Ludwig Van Beethoven, Charles Dickens, Galileo, and Chuck Darwin. To treat women equally, although he was accused of sexism anyway (I was there; Davis, 1994; Walberg, 1994), he also examined traits of 256 eminent women, for example, Sonia Henie, Ethel Barrymore, Mahalia Jackson, Babe Didrikson Zaharias, Helena Rubinstein, Helen Keller, Grandma Moses, Eleanor Roosevelt, civil rights leader Mary McLeod Bethune, and scientist Rachel Carson.

A central conclusion was that traits of eminent men and of eminent women essentially were identical: All were more intelligent, curious, and expressive than the average, and all were open-minded, self-confident, and versatile. Of relevance, noted Walberg and Zeiser (1997), they were sufficiently inquisitive, original, and imaginative to question current conventions. Further, motivation—in the form of high energy, concentrated effort, and unusual perseverance and ambition—was an essential factor in distinguished accomplishment. Most showed "psychological wholesomeness" in the sense of being ethical, sensitive, solid, magnetic, optimistic, and popular. However, as noted earlier, about a fourth to a third showed introversion or neuroses. Many experienced stimulating family, educational, and cultural conditions during childhood. About seventy percent had clear parental expectations for their conduct, but 90 percent had opportunities for exploration

---

Five Points:
1. General Ability

2. Special Aptitude

3. Nonintellective Factors (Personality, Motivation)

4. Environment

5. Chance

Historically Eminent Men and Women

Identical Traits: Intelligence, Creativity, Confidence, Motivation

"Psychological Wholesomeness"

Or Neuroses

**Encouragement,
Support**

**Exposure to Eminent
Persons**

**Intelligence:
Necessary, but
Not Sufficient**

on their own—emphasizing the importance of autonomy in the development of eminence. More than half were encouraged in their educational and professional development by parents, and a larger majority were encouraged by teachers and other adults at an early age. Most were stimulated by the availability of both cultural materials and teachers in their field of eminence. One surprising finding was that about 60 percent of the eminent males were exposed to eminent persons during childhood.

At least moderately high intelligence was important, but only if you possessed the needed creative personality dispositions. Said Walberg and Herbig (1991, p. 251), "There is no doubt that IQ and eminence are linked. . . . [However] higher levels of intelligence seem less important than other psychological traits and conditions." School grades showed little relation to adult success. Indeed, among eminent women about 70 percent were not particularly successful in school.

Ten percent of the women received a high rating on *beauty*, and "the majority [of eminent men] were judged *handsome*" (Walberg, 1988, p. 355).[9]

Again, the main traits of creatively eminent women and creatively eminent men were identical: Persons in both groups were intelligent, creative, worked hard, persevered, and were thorough (Walberg & Zeiser, 1997). They benefited from encouragement, stimulation, and teaching by parents, teachers, and other adults. Many had tutors and received recognition for early accomplishments. Luck and opportunity also played a part.

Robert S. Albert: Giftedness, Decisions, Knowledge, and Identity

**Knowledge-Based
Decisions, Creativity,
Identity Formation**

Albert (1990) emphasized knowledge-based decisions, the interaction of one's creative personality with one's identity, effort, and one's motivated long-term performances that lead to eminence. Said Albert, for most people creativity, identity formation, and career choices come together in their late teens or early twenties.

Albert described six *guiding lights* that can produce opportunities for high creative achievement:

**Decisions Based on
Knowledge**

1. *Decisions.* Important, life-guiding decisions are based on Albert's second factor—knowledge. To make good knowledge-based decisions one must possess personality traits common to eminent people, which Albert named as openness to experience, opportunism, "intricate involvement with ambiguity, complexity, and intuitiveness" (p. 19), and "intellectual curiosity as a source of self-controlled novelty and change" (p. 19).

2. *Knowledge.* A to-be-eminent person must have a knowledge of his or her needs and a knowledge of his or her world, especially its opportunities. He or she may decide to attend a particular college, for example, in order to become an engineer, design artist, writer, or politician.

**Creativity
Consciousness**

3. *Intentional creative behavior.* One must be creativity conscious, which reflects our first item in Table 4.2.

4. *Emergence of creativity and identity.* Both creativeness and personal identity grow and change.

**Creativity Tied
to Identity**

5. *Creativeness and identity drive one another.* Creativity and identity interact; they each depends on the other's development.

---

[9]If you have questions about the relevance of these two findings, Herbert Walberg can be reached at the University of Illinois, Chicago Circle.

Finally, in an apparent summary statement:

6.   Decisions are based on one's motivational and cognitive needs along with perceived possibilities. Creative behavior is thus highly personal; it highlights individual differences. In fact, career choices define one's identity and relate closely to one's self-esteem and social/interpersonal needs.

Career Choices Define One's Identity

Overall, concluded Albert, giftedness and identity combine in the search for the "best fit" between individuals and their respective educational and occupational environments. Again pointing to motivation, Albert (1990, p. 20) noted that it is "determination and devotion . . . as much as any talents that distinguish the eminent achiever from the less eminent."

Motivation!

Benjamin Bloom and Lauren Sosniak: Parental Support, Individualized Instruction

Bloom and Sosniak (1981; Sosniak, 1997) examined the home environment and early training of accomplished pianists, sculptors, swimmers, tennis players, mathematicians, and research neurologists. Note the three areas of artistic, motoric, and cognitive achievement. They discovered that the person's parents were almost entirely responsible for nurturing early interests and helping develop the child's skills.

Parental Support and Teaching

Typically, one or both parents were interested in the area, and usually were skilled and experienced themselves. In every case the parents encouraged and rewarded the children's interests, talents, and efforts. The parents usually served as a role models; they were living illustrations of the personality and lifestyle of experts in the domain. The children essentially could not resist exploring and participating in the particular talent area—it was expected and accepted as proper.[10]

Professional Instructors

While parents provided the initial training and supervision of practice, at some point each child switched to a professional instructor. Sometimes family support was so strong they would move to another location to be nearer an outstanding teacher or better facilities. The student often would be the single focus of the devoted instructor. During this time the youth's dedication to the talent area grows strong—which explains the willingness to spend about 15 hours per week in lessons and practice.

Importantly, the students learned to handle failures constructively. Failures were learning experiences that pinpointed problems to be solved and skills to be learned. In contrast, according to Bloom (1985), among "talent dropouts failures led to feelings of inadequacy and quitting."

Contrast with Public Schooling

In contrast with today's schooling, Bloom and Sosniak's talent development is totally individualized, highly specialized, more informal (and may resemble play), and has clear purposes and goals.

David Feldman: Precocity, Available Knowledge, and Co-Incidence Theory

Feldman (Morelock & Feldman, 1997) reviewed biographies of such persons as Wolfie Mozart and Bobby Fisher, as well as six more contemporary prodigies who performed at the level of adult professionals before age 10. He attributed such amaz-

---

[10]When watching Olympics on TV, listen for the announcer to comment on how the athlete's parents had excelled in the same sport. Tiger Woods' father had his son hitting golf balls at about age 3. The phenomenon is common.

Co-Incidence of Individual, Environmental, Historical Factors

ing accomplish to a coincidence of *individual, environmental,* and *historical* forces, which he dubbed the *Co-Incidence Theory.*

The *individual* component is the prodigies themselves, who are described as highly intelligent, developmentally advanced, and remarkably "preorganized." A biological propensity toward the talent (imagine a violin player or Sumo wrestler) as well as family support in the area are needed. Physical, social, and emotional development factors—such as manual dexterity and peer influence—determine a prodigy's receptiveness to, for example, violin playing or Sumo wrestling.

Environmental factors emphasize the existence of a highly evolved domain of knowledge that can be taught to the precocious child, for example, sophisticated literatures and instruction in math, chess, or music.

Society Attaches Value to Domain

The main *historical* factor is the value society attaches to a domain, which affects opportunities for learning. Perhaps this is one reason the Jamaican bobsled team did not excel.

Many of the conclusions itemized by Morelock and Feldman (1997) duplicate those of Bloom and Sosniak:

Similar to Conclusions of Bloom and Sosniak

- The children possessed extraordinary ability.
- They were born into families that valued and supported that ability.
- They received instruction from master teachers in ways that engaged interest and commitment.
- The children were passionately committed to their field and found great joy in their achievements.

Personal Inner Strength Can Overcome Unsupportive Environment

Finally, in a recent unpublished report Feldman noted that many theories of creative excellence or eminence, such as that of Tannenbaum (1997) and Simonton (1997; below), assume that *all* of the theorist's important factors must be present. However, Feldman summarized biographies of 17 high-achieving women—all exceptions to this assumption—whose extraordinary "personal inner strength" (perseverance, independence, originality) permitted them to overcome the absence of a supportive environment.

Dean Keith Simonton: Many Factors

0 Times X = ____ ?

Simonton (1997) described a host of factors that contribute to creative eminence. A noteworthy assumption is the *multiplicative* nature of necessary components. All must have an above-threshold value. A too-low value of any one component eliminates the possibility of creative eminence, since zero times anything is zero.

Many of Simonton's components of exceptional achievement can be summarized quickly.

Intelligence, important as usual, sometimes requires a middle rather than a high level, particularly in leadership areas. Noted Simonton, talking over the head of your audience does not persuade listeners of the value of your ideas.

Personality is critical, including traits of high motivation, persistence, and willingness to occasionally fail.

Developmental considerations include ones natural ability plus training and practice: "Genius is not just born; it is also made" (p. 341).

Education is relevant, although many recognized geniuses were miserable scholars. According to Simonton, peak creative eminence is most likely to happen at a middle level of education, at about the bachelor's degree elevation, rather than lower or higher.

A touch of *mental disorder* may stimulate "bizarre thoughts, crazy associations, or offbeat metaphors or analogies" that lead to insights, said Simonton. "Genius level talents probably reside at the delicate boundary between a healthy and an unhealthy personality" (p. 341).

Regarding *birth order*, we have seen Simonton's suggestion that first-born and only children are more likely to realize creative eminence in science, politics, or other socially valued area. Later borns may excel in artistic or other nonconformist areas.

Traumatic events, with accompanying unhappy childhoods, may contribute. Parental loss runs high among distinguished scientists. As possible explanations, Simonton suggested that, first, such events may make it difficult to conform to social expectations, since parents are not there to teach norms and values. Second, a "bereavement reaction"—namely, attaining fame and fortune—may be needed to reduce the emotional stress caused by the traumatic event. Third, the unpleasant event may strengthen ones ability to handle disappointment and frustration.

The matter is complicated, noted Simonton, and includes such matters as bright children who do not realize their potential, late-blooming adults who showed no early promise, gender considerations, "spirit of the times" (*Zeitgeist*) factors, crystallizing experiences, socioeconomic class, religious affiliation, and chance, plus interactions among the variables and non-linear relationships in which a mid-level is most optimal.

"Bereavement Reaction" = High Achievement

CULTIVATING A MORE CREATIVE PERSONALITY

This chapter and Chapter 1 should make it clear that creativity, both general self-actualized creativity and special-talent creativity, is tied closely to personality. Based upon outcomes of creativity training programs and courses (e.g., Davis & Bull, 1978; Edwards, 1968; Torrance, 1987b, 1995), there is every reason to believe that attitudes and personality can be changed to produce a more flexible, creative, and self-actualized person. Simple exposure to the topic of creativity, as in reading this book, can raise *creativity consciousness*—probably the single most important part of becoming a more creative individual.

One source of evidence for environmental (learning) influences on creativity, including both affective and cognitive components, comes from the eminence literature. Many creatively excellent, even eminent persons were exposed to stimulating family, educational, and cultural conditions during childhood. Most important, and common, was a trait of strong drive and perseverance. The harder they worked, the more productive (and luckier) they became.

Many of the traits in this chapter probably can be changed in a more creative direction—if a person is motivated to do so. Increases in creativeness, incidentally, frequently are accompanied by increases in self-confidence and independence (Parnes, 1978), although it is a chicken-egg problem as to which causes which. One might consciously try to strengthen curiosity and wide interests. One also might cultivate artistic and aesthetic interests via exposure to creative domains—attending concerts and plays and visiting art galleries, museums, and scientific exhibits. One' adventurousness can be exercised by exploring new places and trying new activities. Most likely, one's sense of humor can be sharpened.

Of critical importance, becoming involved in creative activities is guaranteed to increase one's creativity consciousness and other creative personality characteristics, as well as strengthen some creative abilities and visibly increase creative productivity.

Courses, Programs Strengthen Creativity

Creativity Consciousness

Eminence: Evidence for Environmental Support

Are You Motivated to Become More Creative?

Most Important: Doing Creative Things!

SUMMARY

Studies of creative people indicate that despite their unconventionality and individualism, they have a lot of traits in common.

Three relevant types of characteristics are personality traits, cognitive abilities (including information processing styles), and biographical characteristics. The distinction between personality traits and cognitive abilities sometimes is blurred.

There are common traits among creative people in different areas, such as art and science, but also differences in characteristics between areas and between individuals within the same general area.

Most special talent creative people are creative in a single area.

Over the wide range of intelligence, creativity and intelligence are moderately related. The threshold concept states that above an IQ of about 120 there is no relationship. Other factors, particularly personality and motivation, determine creative productivity.

Over 200 creative personality traits were reduced to 16 categories: Aware of own creativeness (creativity consciousness), original, independent, risk taking, high energy (even thrill-seeking), thorough, curiosity, humor, attraction to fantasy, attraction to complexity and ambiguity (including a belief in paranormal phenomena), artistic (including having aesthetic interests), open-minded, a need for alone time, perceptive, emotional, and ethical.

Negative traits, likely to disturb others, fell into the seven categories of egotistical, impulsive, argumentative, childish, absentminded, neurotic (including sociopathic), and hyperactive.

Much information on the creative personality came from research by Frank Barron and Donald MacKinnon at Berkeley, where they studied creative architects, writers, and mathematicians.

Many showed neuroses or psychoses, especially the creative writers. However, writers also scored high on MMPI ego strength, indicating they were psychologically "sicker and healthier" than the average. Even relatives of creative people may be disturbed.

Nonsubtle biographical traits include one's background of creative interests, hobbies, and activities, as listed in Torrance's "things done on your own." Subtle biographical traits include traveling, owning a cat, having an imaginary childhood playmate, and participating in theater. The latter two appear to be perfect predictors of creativeness.

First-born and only children are likely to be higher achievers in school and careers, probably because of social reasons—they receive more attention, encouragement, and responsibility. Simonton proposed that first and only children tend to achieve eminence in establishment areas, such as science; later borns tend to achieve eminence in less-conforming artistic areas.

Speculations regarding handedness and creativity remain unconfirmed.

Barron listed "six ingredients" of creativity that mixed personality and cognitive traits: recognizing patterns, making connections, taking risks, challenging assumptions, taking advantage of chance, and seeing in new ways.

Many (or all) abilities can contribute to creativity. Some seemingly important ones include fluency, flexibility, originality, elaboration, transformation, sensitivity to problems, problem defining, visualization, analogical/metaphorical thinking, predicting outcomes, analyses, synthesis, evaluation, logical thinking, ability to regress, intuition, and concentration.

Relevant information processing traits include using existing knowledge as a basis for new ideas, avoiding perceptual sets, questioning norms and assumptions, using wide categories, being alert to novelty and gaps in knowledge, coping well with novelty, "finding order in chaos," using internal visualization, skill in decision making, and others.

The topic of creative eminence would include the theories of Csikszentmihalyi and Gardner, plus Simonton's chance-configuration theory, in Chapter 3. Tannenbaum's star model included the five points of intelligence, special aptitude, nonintellective factors (personality, motivation), environment, and chance.

Walberg reviewed characteristics of eminent men and women, finding common characteristics of high motivation and perseverance, thoroughness, intelligence, open-mindedness, confidence, curiosity, versatility, and supportive environments (parents and tutors). Some showed introversion or neuroses.

Albert's model of eminence included making good decisions based on knowledge of ones needs and knowledge of the world (including its opportunities). Intentional creativity is important. Creativity and identity grow together and drive each other, resulting in a best fit between individuals and their educational/ occupational careers. Central traits were determination and devotion.

Bloom and Sosniak are known for emphasizing the critical early role of parents as both teachers and supporters of talent development. Students later switched to high quality teachers. Individualized, specialized, and informal talent development, with clear purposes and goals, contrasts with typical education.

Feldman's co-incidence theory stemmed from the study of prodigies. He emphasized the three necessary components of the capable individual; his or her environment, which includes a specialized domain of knowledge; and history, which stressed the cultural value placed on a creative skill.

Feldman recently summarized biographies of eminent women whose personal inner strength allowed them to overcome an unsupportive environment.

Simonton itemized a host of factors that contribute to eminence: intelligence, personality, development (ability and training), education, mental disorder, birth order, traumatic events, and more.

Creative attitudes and personality traits can be strengthened. Especially recommended is involvement in creative activities.

The Creative Person:
Flexible, Funny, and Full of Energy

Self-Test: Key Concepts, Terms, and Names

Briefly define or explain each of these:

Threshold concept _____

_____

Sixteen categories of creativity traits _____

_____

Sensation seeking (arousal seeking, thrill seeking) _____

_____

Negative creative traits _____

_____

The Berkeley studies _____

_____

Subtle and not-so-subtle biographical traits _____

_____

Creative abilities _____

_____

Tardiff and Sternberg's (1988) information processing characteristics (Table 4.7) ___

_____

Why does your author think these names are important in relation to creative personality or creative eminence?

Frank Barron _____

_____

Donald MacKinnon _____

_____

Abraham Tannenbaum _____

_____

Herbert Walberg _____

_____

Dean Keith Simonton _____

_____

Benjamin Bloom and Lauren Sosniak _____

_____

David Feldman (Hey, is this a coincidence?) _____

_____

Let's Think about It

1. Summarize in as few words as possible the relationships between creativity and:

    a. Mental disturbance _____

    _____

    b. Birth order _____

    _____

    c. Handedness _____

    _____

    d. Intelligence _____

    _____

2. Why are some people more creative than others? Bring in all the factors you can think of (from this chapter or your own experience and best guesses).

_____

_____

_____

_____

_____

Which factors do you think are most important? _____

_____

Least important? _____

_____

3. What might teachers do to foster the development of the "important" factors? (DO NOT look at the last sentence of this chapter, just before the Summary.)

_____

_____

_____

4. What are some implications of the relation between mental illness and creativity?

_____

_____

5. Imagine that you are a teacher of young elementary school children. List five good ideas for PREVENT-ING them from becoming more flexible, creative thinkers and problem solvers.[11]

a. _____

b. _____

c. _____

d. _____

e. _____

---

[11]In Chapter 7 this strategy is called reverse brainstorming.

6. What can YOU do to become a more creative person?

_____

_____

_____

7. Think of three bizarre ideas for increasing the creativity of high school students—ideas that are guaranteed to get you FIRED.

a. _____

b. _____

c. _____

7. Creative abilities and information processing traits mentioned in this chapter include:

> **Originality   Analysis   Evaluation/Decision Making   Synthesis   Making Connections
> Seeing in New Ways   Elaboration   Fluency   Flexibility   Logical Thinking   Able to Regress
> Able to Predict Outcomes   Transformation   Intuition   Sensitivity to Problems
> Able to Define Problems   Questions Norms   Visualization   Finds Order in Chaos
> Analogical Thinking   Avoiding Perceptual Sets**

a. Draw a circle around the seven you believe are most important.

b. Draw a square around the six you believe are least important.

c. Underline darkly the five you believe YOU are best at.

d. Be sure you understand all of these terms.

Thrill-Seeking Test

Many highly creative people are "thrill seekers" or "sensation seekers." How would you score on this short test of thrill seeking?

Indicate the degree to which each statement applies to you. Use the following scale:

1 = No
2 = To a small degree
3 = Average
4 = More than average
5 = Definitely

_____   1.   I would like to learn mountain-climbing.

_____   2.   I would like to get a pilot's license.

_____   3.   I would like to live and work in a foreign country.

_____   4.   I would like to be hypnotized.

110

_____ 5. I like a cold, brisk day.

_____ 6. I would like to try sky-diving (parachute jumping).

_____ 7. I like the nonsense forms and bright colors of modern art.

_____ 8. I usually jump right in a cold pool, instead of slowly getting used to it.

_____ 9. On vacation, I prefer camping to a good motel.

_____ 10. I would like to take up skiing.

_____ 11. I am a risk taker.

_____ 12. I avoid activities that are a little frightening.

_____ 13. I would take a college course that 50 percent flunk.

_____ 14. I enjoy a job with unforseen difficulties.

_____ 15. I like to explore new cities alone, even if I get lost.

Scoring: Add up your ratings. The following is a guideline for interpretation:

15–27	Low in thrill seeking
28–39	Below average
40–51	Average
52–62	Above average
63–75	High in thrill seeking

5

the creative process
steps and stages,
perceptual changes, and imagery

[*Scene: Office of Marvin J. Mogul, tycoon Hollywood movie producer. Mogul is in a heated debate with creative script writer Woody Allen.*]

Marvin J. Mogul: Look Woody, time is money! We gotta' have that scene written by tomorrow noon—at the latest!

Woody Allen: So I'm writing, I'm writing, I'm writing! I'm not a faucet, you know! You want hot jokes? Cold jokes?

Mogul: If you're workin' so hard, how come every time I see you you're starin' out the window? You're not workin', you're starin'.

Woody: It's called incubating! I'm incubating! If you were a writer, you'd know. You can't write unless you incubate. Every writer incubates!

Mogul: Woody, you're not gettin' paid to hatch baby ducks, you're paid to write. Please pick up your pen and put some words on the paper. Please?

Woody: Didja' ever hear about Muses? Shakespeare had Muses, Hemmingway had Muses, I got Muses! An' I can't rush my Muses! I gotta' stare out the window, incubate, and let my Muses do their work! When my Muses get ready they'll give me some funny stuff—believe me!

Mogul: Muses? Muses? First it's baby ducks and now you're subcontracting to mythical spirits! Please Woody, for me, put the pen in your hand. Now here's some nice clean paper . . .

Woody: OK, OK! Tell you what. I'll do some rough outlines . . . invent a few characters, maybe write a few jokes. You like Jewish jokes? No Jewish jokes. What about mugger jokes or maybe a few Bill Clinton jokes . . .

Mogul: No script?

Woody: No script. This is called preparing. I'm studying the problem, thinking about what we need, kicking around a few possibilities. Writers prepare all the time. It gives the incubator something to work with. It's like an Italian cook fondling his noodles and garlic . . . he prepares, getting ready to attack.

Mogul: What happened to your Muses?

Woody: They don't like Italian food. Now please lemme' alone Marv. I gotta' stare.

To give a fair chance to creativity is a matter of life and death for any society.
Arnold Toynbee

Combining Ideas

Mysterious Mental Happenings

Koestler's Bisociation

What Do Reese, Einstein, and Hillary Have in Common?

Creative Process: Steps and Stages

The topic of the creative process brings us to a core issue in the field of creativity: *Where do ideas come from?* In this book we saw a glimpse of this topic in the *creative process* section of Chapter 3 dealing with combining ideas into new creations. Under *mysterious mental happenings* we found that much about internal creative thinking and problem solving remains a mystery even to creative people. We did learn that artists find ideas while sketching, writers find ideas while writing, and scientists find ideas while doing science, indicating that active involvement stimulates both the recall of relevant experiences and the creation of new possibilities.

Nothing in the theory section of Chapter 3 suggested where ideas actually come from or how they are created, except Koestler's bisociation of ideas notion, which essentially is combining one idea (or elaborate plane of experience) with another to produce a novel intersection. Chocolate plus peanut butter equals *Reese's Peanut Butter Cups.* Or classic laws of the propagation of light plus the Lorentz transformation can produce new light propagation equations compatible with the principle of relativity (Einstein, 1961), if you are well prepared in that sort of thing. Or a cartoonist combines the O. J. Simpson trial with Hillary Clinton's legal problems to produce "More bad news, the bloody glove fits Hillary." Simonton's (1988) chance-configuration theory simply assumed the existence of some means for generating ideational variation, which he described only as "operations on . . . mental elements" (p. 389). Perkins' (1988) "mindful direction" of the "combinatorial explosion" of possibilities takes us little further.

This chapter first will look at the creative process as a sometimes conscious sequence of *steps* or *stages* through which the creative person proceeds in clarifying a problem, working on it, and producing a solution that resolves the difficulty.

© Copyrighted Chicago Tribune Company. All rights reserved.

Perceptual Change

**Imagery and
Visualization**

Techniques

**Later: Analogical
Thinking**

Other Techniques

Second, we will examine the creative process as a mostly involuntary, relatively rapid change in perception. This mental transformation takes place when a new idea, meaning, implication, or solution suddenly is detected. Third, we will look at other aspects of imagery and visualization and their role in creativity.

The topic of the creative process also encompasses the *techniques* and strategies that all creative people use, sometimes consciously and sometimes unconsciously, to produce the new idea combinations, analogical relationships, meanings, and transformations. *Remarkably, the issue of techniques of creative thinking is scrupulously ignored in tomes that present theories of creativity, despite the fact that every creative person uses such techniques.* Chapter 6 will focus on that most common and effective creative thinking technique, *analogical thinking*—seeing a connection between one situation and another, as when cockle burrs inspired engineer George De Mestral to create Velcro, or a cartoonist sees a connection between David and Goliath and steroid testing and writes, "Bad news David, the Philistines want to check you for steroids!" Could the Clinton cartoon result from borrowing a popular historical event and combining it with a 1997 White House problem? Chapter 7 will review other techniques of creative thinking, primarily "standard" techniques such as brainstorming that are used by many creative people and are taught in many creativity courses, texts, and workshops.

One Process or Many?

Same Process?

Many Processes?

Combining Ideas

Analogical Thinking

Common Stages

**Common Global
Processes**

**Idiosyncratic Abilities,
Experiences, Thinking
Styles**

**Different Media,
Different Problems
Require Different
Processes**

In discussing the complexity of creativity in Chapter 1 we noted that intelligent, creative people claim that the creative process is basically the same in art, science, business, and elsewhere. Other intelligent, creative people argue that there is no one creative process, and there may be as many creative processes as there are creative people. The truth depends upon which aspect of the creative process one looks at.

At a fairly global level, most new creations are combinations of previously unrelated ideas, and so one can view the creative process as combining Idea #1 with Idea #2 to produce novel Idea #3. Common creative techniques, particularly analogical thinking and modifying existing products, can be used by creative thinkers in any topic area to produce novel Idea #3.[1] There also is a similarity in the steps or stages through which an artist, scientist, business person, or other problem solver proceeds in defining, clarifying, and solving a problem.

However, despite commonalities in such global processes as combining ideas, using similar idea-finding techniques, and proceeding through similar steps, there still are unique and idiosyncratic experiences, abilities, perceptions, thinking styles, and strategies that influence the creative processes of each creative person. Further, the particular area or media within which one creates—math, chemistry, biology, painting, architecture, poetry, music, theatre, etc.—logically demands thinking with different concepts and with different problem solving techniques. Even within a given media, specific types of problems will require different "processes"—writing comedy will require different processes than writing obituaries, and designing garages requires different processes and considerations than designing shopping centers. Therefore, in some global ways the creative process may indeed "be the same" in different areas and among people with different creative specialities; however, the creative process also must be different according to the media in general, the requirements of the creative task, and the idiosyncrasies of every creative individual.

---

[1]Modifying the important attributes of an existing product is an effective and not uncommon idea-finding technique. In Chapter 7 it is called *attribute listing*.

"Do I think 'chance' plays a role in creativity? No, of course not. It's all hard work. I don't believe in taking chances." (The Museum of Modern Art/Film Stills Archives.)

CREATIVE PROCESS: INSIGHT, CHANCE, OR HARD WORK?

We also mentioned in Chapter 1 that different opinions exist regarding whether creativity is "building on an initial insight" or whether it is the result of systematic planning and hard work—with sudden "insights" and chance discoveries playing no significant role.

These views are not inconsistent. A creative problem solution may be born instantly in an "Aha!" (insight) experience, inspired perhaps by the chance encounter of a needed idea or solution. A creative product also may result from months or years of systematic planning, hard work, and trial-and-error experimentation—perhaps based on an earlier "Aha!" or insight that was a chance occurrence. For example, in Hollywood one busy street passes through a tunnel under a hill. The illusion of height created in the Harold Lloyd movie *Safety Last* was discovered by chance—in a sudden insight—when a fence was trimmed out of a picture taken from that hilltop. The movie scenes themselves, of course, required months of planning, development, hard work, and creative problem solving.

STEPS AND STAGES

Necessary Steps: Clarifying the Problem, Working on It, Finding a Solution

Solving a problem or "doing something creative" necessarily involves the three steps already casually mentioned—clarifying the problem, working on it, and finding a good solution. More formal sets of stages are elaborations of these. For example, Torrance's (1988) definition of creativity that we saw in Chapter 3 describes a stepwise process of:

Torrance Definition

1. Sensing a problem or gap in information
2. Forming ideas or hypotheses
3. Testing and modifying the hypotheses
4. Communicating the results

John Dewey's Two Steps

John Dewey (1933), writing on the nature of thinking, compressed the Torrance steps into just two, with no apparent loss of information. First, there appears a state of doubt, perplexity, or mental difficulty in which the thinking originates; followed by an act of searching, hunting, or inquiring to find material that will resolve the doubt, and settle and dispose of the perplexity.

THE WALLAS MODEL

Since 1926: Graham Wallas

The most traditional analysis of stages in the creative process was originated by Wallas in 1926. The fact that the model has survived three-quarters of a century of scrutiny says something about the appeal of the model. There are four steps.

Preparation

Preparation. *Preparation* includes just that—exploring and clarifying the situation, perhaps looking for the "real" problem, thinking about requirements for a good solution, gathering and reviewing relevant data, becoming acquainted with innuendos, implications and perhaps unsuccessful solutions, itemizing available materials and resources, and so on. *Synectics* (Chapter 6) guru William J. J. Gordon called this "making the strange familiar," an important creative activity. Wallas emphasized its conscious and deliberate nature.

Incubation: Fringe Conscious Activity

Incubation. One entire issue of the *Journal of Creative Behavior* (Issue 1, 1979) was devoted to untangling the mysteries of *incubation*. Success was limited. According to Wallas (1926), and as we saw in the theories of Kubie and Rugg (Chapter 2), incubation may best be viewed as a period of preconscious, fringe-conscious, off-conscious or perhaps even unconscious mental activity that takes place while the thinker is (perhaps deliberately) jogging, watching TV, playing golf, eating pizza, walking along a lakeshore, or even sleeping. In Wallas' own words, "The incubation stage covers two different things, of which the first is the negative fact that during incubation we do not voluntarily or consciously think on a particular problem, and the second is the positive fact that a series of unconscious and involuntary (or foreconscious and forevoluntary) mental events may take place during that period . . . the period of abstention may be spent either in conscious mental work on other problems, or in a relaxation from all conscious mental work."

Guilford: Some People More Reflective Than Others

Guilford (1979) suggested that incubation takes place during reflection, a pause in action, and that some people are simply more reflective than others.

Illumination: "Eureka!"

Illumination. The "Aha!" or "Eureka!" experience. Basically, there is a sudden change in perception, a new idea combination, or a transformation that produces a solution that appears to meet the requirements of the problem. There usually is a good feeling, even excitement.

Verification

Verification. *Verification* is checking the solution (what else), in case your Eureka turns out to be a vacuous idea.

Resemble Scientific Method

Stages Not Invariant

Like other sets of stages, the Wallas stages resemble steps in the scientific method of stating the problem, proposing hypotheses, planning and conducting research, and evaluating the results. Note also that the Wallas stages are not an invariant sequence. Some stages may be skipped or the thinker may backtrack to an earlier stage. For example, the process of defining and clarifying the problem (preparation) often leads directly to a good, illuminating idea. Or if the verification confirms that the idea won't work or is not acceptable, the thinker will recycle back to the preparation or incubation stage. Further, noted Wallas, it is common to be consciously preparing (e.g., acquiring information) for one problem or verifying a solution to another while incubating still others.

An Information Processing Theory of Incubation

Levels of Processing Theory

Developments in cognitive psychology suggest another way to interpret the less-than-conscious incubation process. *Levels of processing theory* focuses on the common human ability to consciously attend to one, and only one, main activity (such as talking, listening, watching, or thinking), yet conduct several other activities at the same time. For example, while talking you also can walk, chew gum, drive a car, or notice leaves rustling in the wind. These other activities are said to be processed at lower levels of consciousness.

Low Level (Fringe Conscious) Activity: Matching Input against Schemas

With No Match, Input Gets Full Attention

More specifically, or more theoretically, the familiar and expected activities and events are said to be "matched" against internal representations (or *schemas*) of these activities and events (e.g., Norman, 1976). If there is a match, these events are "accounted for" and further processing at a higher, conscious level is unnecessary. The events are dealt with completely at a fringe-conscious or even unconscious level. However, if something unexpected or novel occurs—stepping in dog stuff, biting a grain of sand, or seeing a horse in the road or a parrot in a tree—the matter cannot be handled at the lower, unconscious level. That is, the novel event does not match existing schemas; it therefore is passed to higher processing levels where, by definition, it receives one's full attention.

Incubation: with Fringe Conscious Solution—Full Attention

It is conceivable that incubation involves similar information processing activities. "Getting away from the problem" essentially means that one's high-level, conscious attention is directed toward other matters—other problems, watching TV, playing golf, eating pizza, etc. However, perhaps one's fringe-conscious or unconscious processing activities occasionally review a particular problem and possible solutions. When something novel occurs—namely, a good solution—the matter instantly gets passed to higher levels of processing. It gets your full attention. Psychologically, you experience it as a sudden "Eureka!" experience.

Similar to Psychoanalytic Primary, Secondary Processes

This level of processing interpretation of incubation is similar to Kris' psychoanalytic description of creative thinking (Chapter 3): Preconscious primary process fantasy activity is followed by a "Eureka!" and conscious secondary process logical thinking.

THE CREATIVE PROBLEM SOLVING (CPS) MODEL

CPS Model: It Works

It is difficult to say enough about the extremely useful Creative Problem Solving (CPS) model, a remarkable set of six (or five) stages. It is virtually guaranteed to help you solve or find ideas for any type of personal or professional problem. The strategy originally was formulated by Alex Osborn (1963), creator of brainstorming, founder of the Creative Education Foundation (CEF), and co-founder of Batten, Barton, Dursten and Osborn, the highly successful New York advertising agency. Sidney Parnes, a bright and creative person who followed Osborn as President of CEF, invested nearly 40 years teaching creativity workshops, institutes, and college courses—and thinking about the creative process. His best shot at "What is the creative process?" and "How can we teach creativity?" is (you guessed it) the CPS model. Parnes' (1981) inspiring book *Magic of Your Mind* explains how using the CPS model can improve your life (remember the self-actualization emphasis in Chapter 1?). Parnes' book and the CPS model are highly recommended.

Creativity leaders Treffinger, Isaksen, Firestien, and Dorval (Treffinger, Isaksen, & Firestien, 1982; Treffinger, Isaksen, & Dorval, 1994a, 1994b) understand well the remarkable potential of this model as an effective and teachable creative problem solving strategy. They refined the use of the CPS model in some insightful ways that will be described in this section.

The model usually is presented as five steps. However, Parnes and Treffinger and colleagues also note a sixth step, a preliminary one—called *mess-finding*—which involves locating a challenge or problem to which to apply the model (see Inset 5.1). The total six stages are *mess-finding, fact-finding, problem-finding, idea-finding, solution-finding* (idea evaluation), and *acceptance-finding* (idea implementation). Treffinger, Isaksen, and Dorval (1994a) split the six steps into three components: Mess-finding, fact-finding, and problem-finding constitute "Understanding the Problem"; idea-finding by itself is the "Generating Ideas" component; and solution-finding and acceptance-finding are the "Planning for Action" component. They stress flexibility in using the model: If it is helpful, one may move from any component directly to any other. Note that their "Understanding the Problem" component essentially is identical to Wallas' (1926) first stage of preparation.

The steps guide the creative process. They tell you what to do at each immediate step in order to eventually produce one or more creative, workable solutions. A unique feature is that each step first involves a *divergent* thinking phase in which one generates lots of ideas (facts, problem definitions, ideas, evaluation criteria, implementation strategies), and then a *convergent* phase in which only the most promising ideas are selected for further exploration. Figure 5.1 illustrates the divergent/convergent nature of each step.

Mess-finding is elaborated in Inset 5.1. The next step—which would be the first step if you already have selected a problem, or if a problem has selected you—is *fact-finding*, which involves listing what you know about the problem or challenge. It includes "Visualizing . . . in your imagination everything you know about it" (Parnes, 1981, p. 133) or "Examining many details, looking at the Mess from many viewpoints" (Treffinger, Isaksen, & Dorval, 1994a, p. 19). The goal is "to help you explore all the information, impressions, observations, feelings, and questions that you have about a mess on which you've decided to work" (Isaksen & Treffinger, 1985). Parnes recommends *who, what, when, where, why,* and *how* questions:

Who is or should be involved?

What is or is not happening?

When does this or should this happen?

Where does or doesn't this occur?

Why does it or doesn't it happen?

How does it or doesn't it occur?

As an example, let's say the problem is thinking of ways to stimulate creativity in a classroom or business organization. An individual or group first would list

<!-- margin notes -->
Parnes: Magic of Your Mind

CPS Advocates: Treffinger, Firestien, Isaksen, Dorval

Six Steps (or Five) Guide Creative Problem Solving

Divergent Then Convergent Thinking at Each Step

Mess Finding

Fact Finding

Who Did What When, Where, Why, and How?

Inset 5.1
Discovering Problems and Challenges

There is one crucial stage in the CPS model that takes place *before* the five steps of fact-finding, problem-finding, idea-finding, solution-finding, and acceptance-finding: finding a problem, opportunity or challenge to which to apply this dynamite model. Instead of passively waiting for a problem to bang on the door and demand a creative solution, we can take a more active, high-initiative approach to improving our lives by looking for nuisances, challenges, or things that you would like to see happen—difficulties that seem to cry out "Help! Help! Get the CPS model, quick!"

To help you discover challenges and opportunities and generally increase your problem sensitivity, Parnes (1981) itemized a list of prodding questions, some of which are itemized below. Do these suggest topics for one-person CPS sessions?

What would you like to get out of life?

What are your goals, as yet unfilled?

What would you like to accomplish, to achieve?

What would you like to have?

What would you like to do?

What would you like to do better?

What would you like to happen?

In what ways are you inefficient?

What would you like to organize in a better way?

What ideas would you like to get going?

What relationship would you like to improve?

What would you like to get others to do?

What takes too long?

What is wasted?

What barriers or bottlenecks exist?

What do you wish you had more time for?

What do you wish you had more money for?

What makes you angry, tense, or anxious?

What do you complain about?

---

all of the facts they could think of relating to training creative thinking and perhaps to the nature of creativity and creative abilities. The *who, what, when, where, why* and *how* questions aid thinking in this step. The list of ideas is then convergently narrowed to a smaller number of facts that might be especially productive.

Problem-Finding: IWWMW?

The second stage, *problem-finding*, involves listing alternative problem definitions. *One principle of creative problem solving is that the definition of a problem will determine the nature of the solutions.* In this step, it helps to begin each statement with "In what ways might we (or I) . . . " (IWWMW). For example, IWWMW find divergent thinking exercises, find workbooks or other materials, find resource persons or consultants, learn about creativity training methods, have someone else do the creativity training, have the persons involved teach themselves, and so on.

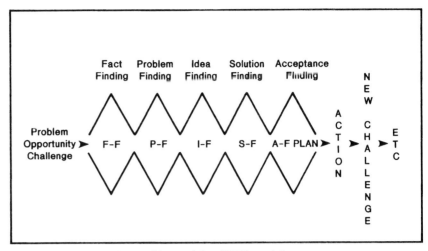

Figure 5.1. The creative problem solving (CPS) model.

What Is the "Real" Problem?

Ask "Why?": Broadens Problem Definition

It may help to ask what the *real* problem is: What is the main objective? What do you really want to accomplish? Also, in most cases asking *"Why* do I want to do this?"* after each problem statement will lead to another statement that is more broad and general. For example, asking "Why do I want to find divergent thinking exercises?" leads to the answer "In order to strengthen creative attitudes and abilities," which suggests the broader problem statement "IWWMW strengthen creative attitudes and abilities?" And asking "Why do I want to strengthen creative attitudes and abilities?" leads to "In order to improve creative potential and self-actualization," leading to the more general "IWWMW improve creative potential and self-actualization."

Idea-Finding: Use Deferred Judgment

One or more of the most fruitful definitions is selected for the third stage, *idea finding*. This is the divergent-thinking, brainstorming stage. Ideas are freely proposed, without criticism or evaluation, for each of the problem definitions accepted in the second stage.

Solution Finding Is Idea Evaluation

The fourth stage, *solution finding*, should have been named *idea evaluation*. In three related steps, (1) criteria for evaluation are listed, (2) the ideas are evaluated, and (3) one or more of the best ideas are selected. In general, evaluation criteria might include:

Common Criteria

Will it work?

Is it legal?

Are the materials and technology available?

Are the costs acceptable?

Will the public accept it?

Will higher-level administrators accept it?

Would grandmother approve?[2]

Criteria: Screen Ideas

Relating specifically to the problem of teaching creativity, some criteria might be: Will the strategy strengthen important creative abilities? Will it teach creative attitudes and awarenesses; that is, will it work? Will it cost too much? Will it take too long? Are materials available? Will others accept the idea? Will the students enjoy the experience? Will they cooperate? The list may be convergently reduced

---

[2]Another list of evaluation criteria appears in Chapter 7.

"I've told you for the last time, Mildred, IWWMW doesn't mean 'I'll wipe my white mitts wherever I want'!" (The Museum of Modern Art/ Film Stills Archive.)

to the most relevant criteria. As Isaksen and Treffinger (1985) point out, the "criteria are used to screen, select, and support options for which you will eventually be developing a plan of action."

Evaluation Matrix

Take Another's Perspective

Sometimes, an evaluation matrix can be helpful, with possible solutions listed on the vertical axis and the criteria across the top (see Figure 5.2). Each idea is rated according to each criteria, perhaps on a 1 to 5 scale, with the ratings entered in the cells. The scores would be totaled to find the "best" idea(s). Parnes (1981) suggested that you also can evaluate ideas by taking the perspective of another

Figure 5.2. Example of an Evaluation Matrix. The problem was, "How can we teach creativity?" Each idea is rated on a 1 (low) to 5 (high) scale according to each criterion. Total scores are then tallied.

person and imagining how the idea looks to them; or else visualizing others' reactions as you tell them about the idea.

List Good and Bad Points

Another evaluation device is to make a list of what is *good* and what is *bad* about each idea. This approach helps prevent prematurely discarding an idea that has some good qualities or prematurely accepting an idea that has some serious faults.

Acceptance-Finding: Action Plan

Finally, *acceptance-finding* (idea implementation) amounts to thinking of "ways to get the best ideas into action" (Parnes, 1981). It may involve creating an action plan, which is a plan containing specific steps to be taken and a timetable for taking them.

Sources of Assistance, Resistance

Treffinger (1995; Treffinger, Isaksen, & Dorval, 1994b) noted that acceptance finding also involves searching for *assisters* and *resisters*. Assisters are people ("key players"), essential resources, and the best times, places, and methods that will support the plan and contribute to successful implementation. One also must identify resisters—obstacles such as contrary people, missing materials, ineffective methods, bad timing, bad locations, or other matters that can interfere with acceptance. One can ask "What are some difficulties that might arise?" and "What is the worst imaginable thing that could happen?" These two questions lead to a list of "Areas of concern" plus ideas for "How to prevent it" and "How to respond if it happens" (Isaksen & Treffinger, 1985). Said Treffinger (1995), one makes the best possible use of assisters, and avoids or overcomes sources of resistance.

Difficulties: Areas of Concern

Convergent Techniques: Treffinger

Treffinger, Isaksen and Firestien (1982) noted that training in creative problem solving always emphasizes *divergent* techniques. They outlined some *convergent* techniques that can be used in any of the five CPS steps to aid in finding "good" facts, problem definitions, ideas, evaluation criteria (and solutions), and implementation strategies for further exploration. Especially interesting are their *hits* and *hot spots*. Hits are ideas that strike the problem solvers as important breakthroughs—directions to be pursued further because they could form the basis for a good problem solution. Groups of related hits are called hot spots. Hot spots are thus "a collection of hits that center around a specific issue or relate to a similar

Hits!

Hot Spots

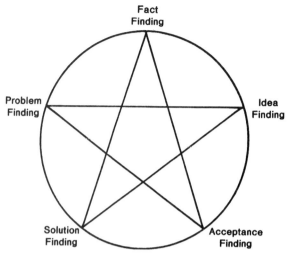

Figure 5.3. An alternative conception of the CPS model emphasizing that one may flexibly move from any stage to any other.

aspect of the problem." The hot spot is given a label that paraphrases the essential meaning of this group of hits and thus "suggests the strongest aspect of the hot spot." In the convergent part of each CPS step, think of hits and hot spots as good leads to good solutions.

Steps Should Be Habitual, Automatic

In his book *The Magic of Your Mind*, Parnes (1981) leads the reader through problem after problem with the goal of making the five steps habitual and automatic. That is, when encountering a problem, challenge, or opportunity one quickly would review relevant facts, identify various interpretations of the problem, generate solutions, evaluate the ideas, and speculate on how the solution(s) might be implemented and accepted.

Useful in Classroom, Corporation

Other Sequences of Steps May Help

In the classroom or corporation. Parnes' CPS stages may be used to guide a creative thinking session that (1) teaches an effective creative problem solving strategy, (2) improves understanding of the creative process, (3) exposes learners to a rousing creative-thinking experience, and (4) solves a problem. Incidentally, while chatting with Parnes over 1½ hot fudge sundaes (yes, Parnes ordered 1½ hot fudge sundaes), he mentioned that people tend to use the five stages too rigidly. On a sticky napkin he diagrammed a star-shaped model enclosed in a circle, emphasizing that—if it helps the creative process—one may flexibly move directly from any one step to any other. Rub a little chocolate on Figure 5.3 and you will get the full flavor of his suggestion. Actually, a little-known fact is that Osborn (1963) had reversed Stages 1 and 2 in the first place, with *problem-finding* preceding *fact-finding*.

A TWO-STAGE ANALYSIS

Two-Stage Model: Big Idea, Elaboration

Stripped to its essentials, creating something in art, science, business, or any other area involves two fairly clear steps: The *big idea* stage and an *elaboration* stage. The big idea stage is a period of fantasy in which the creative person looks for a new, exciting idea or problem solution. After the idea is found, perhaps using analogical thinking or some other creative thinking technique, the elaboration stage requires idea development, elaboration, and implementation. That is, the artist must assemble the materials, do preliminary sketches, and create the final work; the novelist must create characters and plot and write the story; the research scientist or business person must organize the details and carry out the work necessary to implement the big idea. The two stages are similar to the ones mentioned earlier by Dewey, although he more strongly emphasized the motivational aspect—having a state of doubt, perplexity, or difficulty that stimulates the problem solving.

Some (e.g., von Oech, 1983) have assumed that only the first stage requires imaginative, creative activity—idea combining, idea modifying, analogical thinking, projecting future needs, or other imagery and fantasy. When the creative idea is found, logical thinking activities of analyzing and sequential planning are needed to develop and implement the idea. Actually, continued creative thinking and problem solving are needed for the elaboration and development stage as well as the initial fantasy stage. Consider, for example, the elaboration and development of the plot for a novel, a research idea, or building the Panama Canal; much imagination and creative problem solving are needed after the big idea is found.

Von Oech: First Stage Is Right Brain Thinking

Second Stage: Left Brain Thinking

Creativity Also Needed in Second Stage

THE CREATIVE PROCESS AS A CHANGE IN PERCEPTION

The process of creation frequently involves a dramatic and usually instantaneous *change in perception*. There suddenly is a new way of looking at something, a *transformation*, a relationship that was not there before. One perceives new idea combinations, new implications, new meanings, or new applications. This phenomenon occurs whether the illumination is a simple modification of a cookie recipe, perhaps substituting mint candies for chocolate chips, or an unfathomably complex discovery in mathematics, physics, medicine, or astronomy.

One simple way to illustrate this sudden perceptual change is with visual puzzles. For example, look at Figure 5.4. There is one main, meaningful figure that was created, in fact, from a photograph. After you find this figure, try to locate (1) a flying pig, (2) an Al Capp Li'l Abner character with a snaggle lower tooth, (3) a woman with her hair in a bun reclining on a sofa (she is in white). If you can find these easy (?) ones, look for (4) the Road Runner, (5) Harry Belafonte,

New Relationship, Meaning, Transformation, Idea Combination

Visual Puzzles Illustrate Perceptual Change

Figure 5.4. Mysterious picture. Can you find the one main picture? Ten other meaningful pictures? What else can you see? (Sidney J. Parnes, Ruth B. Noller and Angelo Biondi, excerpted from *Guide to Creative Action*. Copyright © 1976 Charles Scribner's Sons. Reprinted with the permission of Charles Scribner's Sons.)

(6) Popeye, (7) Blackbeard the Pirate, (8) a side profile of Jesus, (9) right next to Jesus a lady in a boufant hairdo, and (10) E. T. You will find yourself exclaiming, "Oh, there it is!" or "Now I see it!" The solutions are outlined at the end of this chapter.

We do not understand this sudden perceptual change or transformation very well. It is the mental activity underlying the creative insight itself; it is the very birth of creative inspiration. In some cases the perceptual transformation takes place while viewing or thinking about one or two objects or ideas, and then mentally modifying them, combining them, or otherwise detecting a new meaning or relationship. We already mentioned that one of Harold Lloyd's movie makers experienced an abrupt perceptual change when a hilltop view of a Hollywood street suddenly was seen as an illusion of great height. A sudden transformation in verbal perception and meaning is illustrated by the bumper sticker "My karma ran over my dogma." A writer may "see" an intriguing story take shape as the result of a visit to Kuwait and Baghdad. A product developer may "see" a new product, new use for a material, or new marketing possibilities while flipping through the Yellow Pages. Inventor De Mestral "saw" a new line of fastening devices while plucking cockleburrs from his hunting dog. The perceptual change or transformation process appears to be partly, if not largely, involuntary.

Perceptual Transformation Is Mysterious, Lies at Core of Creative Inspiration

Heavy Karma!

Creativity frequently involves a change in perception. "My perceptions change all the time," agrees Ben. "I think I need an alignment." (The Museum of Modern Art/ Film Stills Archive.)

"Ok, stick 'em up, stick!" said the sheriff, who had just read the book *Playful Perception*. "I know you're the one who did the stick up! Where did you stick the loot! I hope you like stickin' around, 'cause you're gonna' be stuck in our jail for a long time!" (Wisconsin Center for Film and Theater Research.) Copyright by Universal City Studios, Inc. Courtesy of Universal Studios Publishing Rights. All rights reserved.

Playful Perceptions May Aid Perceptual Change Ability

Awareness Plans

One book entitled *Playful Perception* (Leff, 1984) seeks to teach creative thinking by helping the reader to perceive the environment in creative, entertaining, and unusual—make that *weird*—ways. Leff describes the use of *awareness plans*, essentially "mental recipes" that require a person to select items in the environment and perform certain operations on them. Such plans are intended to stimulate insight and curiosity and help us treat things in life in a constructive and enlightened fashion, relate to others in creatively cooperative ways, and generally use our "powers of attention and imagination ... (to open) doorways to expanded awareness on a variety of fronts." Some exercises are designed for fun and fantasy.

Exercises

You probably will not be able to resist trying some of the following exercises (adapted from Leff, 1984):

Try seeing and thinking about everything around you as if it were alive. (Is the light bulb a visitor from space? The trash can a helpless, hungry creature?)

Think of past and future reincarnations of things around you. (In its next life, will that garbage can be a Sears trash compactor?)

Think of alternative meanings and interpretations of common things and events. (Is the clerk's "May I help you?" a religious invocation? A four-word poem? A secret password? Is a volleyball game a new dance?)

Reverse things, events, and causation from what you normally assume they are. (Articles in garbage may be seen as valuable treasures, expensive jewelry as junk. Bicycles cause kids feet to turn in circles.)

View the world from the perspective of an animal or an object. (How does the big dog look to a visiting cat? What if you are the room you are in, and the things in the room are part of you?)

See everything as edible and imagine how it would taste.

Look at objects as the tops of things, and imagine what the underground portion looks like.

Visually search your environment for things that are beautiful or aesthetically interesting.

Look for things you normally would not notice.

Look for boring things, and then think of something interesting about them.

Imagine the likely past and future of different objects.

Think about cultural values implied by things in your environment.

Think about what you can learn from whatever you encounter.

These kinds of exercises should indeed strengthen one's ability to make perceptual changes and transformations.

THE IMAGERY-CREATIVITY CONNECTION

Imagery: Back and Forth Interaction with Activity

It seems evident that creativity takes place in the head or mind via the manipulation of mental images. The word *imagination* is a virtual synonym for *creativity* itself. There often is a back-and-forth interaction of mental activity with physical activity—scribbling, sketching, manipulating, talking, writing equations, sketching flow-charts, plinking a piano, and the like. A few years ago Aristotle wrote "The soul never thinks without a mental picture" (Yates, 1966, p. 32), implying that images supply the continuous connection between perception (input), thought (mental activity), and action (output).

Behaviorism: Imagery Doesn't Count

One article, coincidentally entitled "The Imagery-Creativity Connection" (Daniels-McGhee & Davis, 1994),[3] elaborated on the nature and common use of imagery in creativity. To review some historical notes relating to imagery, early behaviorist John B. Watson, the "father of behaviorism," denied the existence of imagery, calling it "a figment of the psychologist's terminology." To Watson, thinking was subvocal speech—silent motor activity in the throat—which earned his position the suitable name of "Muscle Twitchism." Behaviorist Skinner did not improve matters much, proposing that one's behavior (response) was triggered by the environment (stimulus) and the consequences (reward) strengthens the tendency to act the same way again. During the 1960s transition to cognitive psychology, concessions to mental imagery took the form of implicit verbal responses and verbal associations, which behaviorists could live with. Meanwhile,

---

[3]The article was almost entirely the brain-child of former graduate student and creative person Susan Daniels.

**Fantasy, Imagery =
Primary Process
Thinking**

earlier in the century and in the psychoanalytic ballpark, Freud proposed that *primary process* thinking, which we saw in Chapter 3, would occur during relaxation and includes dreams, reveries, free associations, and fantasies. Definitely closer to human creativity than a rat punching a bar to get fed, or thinking *"navy"* when you hear *"army."*

**Mental Imagery Was
Ostracized**

It is quaint that the author of a major 1964 article, entitled "Imagery: The Return of the Ostracized" and published in the top status *American Psychologist*, felt compelled to argue for the very existence of mental imagery. Holt's (1964) supporting evidence (other than in his own head) stemmed from published reports of hallucinations, neurological research, drug-induced imagery, and creativity studies. More positively, he categorized several types of images, many of which relate closely to creative imagery:

Types of Imagery

Thought images are faint, subjective representations without sensory input. They include memory images and imagination images; they may involve any sensory modality or be totally verbal.

Eidetic images are said to be greatly enhanced thought images of such vividness and clarity as to seem like actual perceptions. The person, particularly a child, may believe the images are real. Too much of this probably would land a person on lithium or in an institution.

Synesthesia, as we mentioned in Chapter 4, is cross-modal imagery, in which, for example, one may hear colors or taste shapes.

Hallucination is imagery related to a person's beliefs. It is perceived as part of reality, but in fact does not exist. The related *paranormal hallucination* is said to be the experience of a ghost or other religious, mystical, or supernatural vision or materialization. In certain circumstances hallucination seems acceptable.

Dream image. Hallucinations during sleep.

Hypnagogic and *hypnopompic images* are images of great clarity which appear in the drowsy state just before sleep (hypnagogic) or in the drowsy state while awakening (hypnopompic). These are times of fantasy and imagination related to those daily problems and challenges.

Useful in Creativity

Highly creative individuals are most likely to cite *dream images, hypnagogic* and *hypnopompic images*, and conscious, purposeful *imagination images* (a subtype of thought images) as sources of creative ideas (Daniels-McGhee & Davis, 1994).

Historic anecdotes are unnecessary to convince readers of the reality of imagery. Nonetheless, the following classic examples illustrate some processes of constructing, taking apart, modifying, combining, and transforming mental imagery—in any sensory mode or across sensory modes (synesthesia)—into new ideas. Said Beethoven:

Ludwig's Synesthesia

I carry my thoughts with me for a long time . . . I shall not forget [a theme] even years later. I change many things, discard others, and try again and again until I am satisfied; then, in my head, I begin to elaborate the work . . . It rises, it grows. I hear and see the image in front of me from every angle" (Hamburger, 1952, p. 194).

Beethoven's sound images had form and color.

We noted that creativity in writing can happen "between the pencil and the paper." William Wordsworth's imagery and writing did indeed interact during the writing process. Said Wordsworth, "A picture is not thought out and settled beforehand. While it is being done it changes as one's thoughts change" (Jeffrey, 1989, p. 83). Wordsworth defined a poet as a person with intensely vivid imagery plus the ability to communicate those images.

Kandinsky's Synesthesia

Artist Wassily Kandinsky expressed his experiences with a touch of synesthesia when he wrote that "the sound of colors is so definite that it would be hard to find anyone who would try to express bright yellow in the bass notes, or [a] dark lake in the treble" (Solso, 1991, p. 20).

Einstein Thought in Images

Despite writing books and articles, Einstein did his thinking almost entirely in images. "The words or the language, as they are written or spoken, do not seem to play any role in my mechanism of thought. The psychical entities which seem to serve as elements in thought are certain signs and more or less clear images which can be voluntarily reproduced and combined" (Einstein, 1952, p. 43).

Woodward: Double-Helix Visualization

Robert Woodward, whose double-helix model of growth and reproduction won him a 1965 Nobel Prize, could visualize complex three-dimensional structures in space, the path of possible reactions within the structure, and possible transformations of that structure. Said Woodward, it is "the sensuous elements which play so large a role in my attraction to chemistry. I love the crystals, the beauty of their form—and their formation; liquids, dormant, distilling, sloshing!; swirling, the fumes; the odors—good and bad; the rainbow of colors; the gleaming vessels of every size, shape, and purpose . . . [chemistry] would not exist for me without these physical, visual, tangible, sensuous things" (C. E. Woodward, 1989, p. 237). He also wrote "chemical synthesis is entirely a creative activity in which art, design, imagination, and inspiration play a predominant role" (p. 233).

Kekule's account of his discovery of the benzine ring is an often-cited and particularly vivid description of the role of mental imagery in creative thinking and problem solving:

Kekule's Snaky Benzine Ring

> I turned my chair to the fire and dozed. Again the atoms were gamboling before my eyes. The smaller groups kept modestly in the background. My mental eye, rendered more acute by visions of this kind, could now distinguish larger structures, of manifold conformation, long rows sometimes more closely fitted together, all twining and twisting in snake-like motion. But look! What was that? One of the snakes had seized hold of its tail and the form whirled mockingly before my eyes. As if by a flash of lightening I awoke. (Koestler, 1964, p. 118)

Imagery and the Creative Process

A key question is: What do creative persons *do* with mental imagery that is different. Note first that involuntary perceptual processes ("I see those McDonald's arches!") promote organization, constancy, and survival. Voluntary processes are less rigid; they can operate deliberately on the mental images stimulated by perceptions and memories ("Forget it, let's pick up some crackers, ham, Gouda, and Grey Poupon"). One possibility then, is that the creative individual has superior voluntary control over such processes as selective attention, recall, manipulation and modification of mental images, generation of novel images ("How do we farm in the year 2050?"), and perhaps even cross-modal representation. The person more easily can modify a single mental image to create several novel possibilities (Flowers & Garbin, 1989).

Involuntary Processes Promote Organization

Voluntary Ones More Flexible

Superior Voluntary Control?

Looseness of Perception

According to Flowers and Garbin, creativity requires a certain "looseness" of perception, rather than tight organization and constancy, and an absence of perceptual rigidity. When one is dozing, dreaming, or on drugs perceptual mechanisms which normally organize the world become "decoupled" from sensory input, providing opportunities for fantasy and innovation.[4] The perceptual mechanisms essentially "run on their own." Note that "decoupling" is indeed more likely to occur during hypnogogic and hypnopompic states, periods of high creativity for many individuals. Said Kosslyn (1983, p. 91), "One can create scenes that never existed or transform the commonplace into the extraordinary . . . [We can] imagine the world not merely as it is, but as it could be."

Of course, during wakeful periods of sobriety the ideas are evaluated, selected, and refined in accord with the second part of this chapter's two-stage theory. Chapters 6 and 7, dealing with creativity techniques, will describe specifically how some creative people successfully manipulate mental images.

SUMMARY

The "creative process" topic deals with where ideas come from, for example, as in Koestler's bisociation (idea combining) notion.

The creative process can refer to sets of stages, the perceptual transformation that occurs during creativity, manipulation of mental imagery, or to techniques and strategies.

Many global processes are common across different areas. However, the creative processes of each person are influenced by experiences, abilities, styles, strategies, and specific problem requirements.

Insight, chance, and hard work are not inconsistent views of creative productivity. All have a role and often are interrelated.

Three intuitively necessary stages are clarifying the problem, working on it, and finding a solution.

Torrance's definition of creativity included steps of sensing a problem, forming hypotheses, testing the hypotheses, and communicating the results.

Dewey reduced problem solving to two steps: a state of perplexity followed by searching for a solution to resolve the difficulty.

The classic Wallas model included preparation, incubation, illumination, and verification. The stages do not necessarily occur in exactly that order.

Guildford suggested that incubation takes place during reflection, and that some people are more reflective than others.

Levels of process theory suggests that incubation may involve fringe-conscious "low level" mental activity. If a good solution is encountered, it is passed to higher, conscious levels of processing.

The CPS model included six steps of mess-finding, fact-finding, problem-finding, idea-finding, solution-finding (idea evaluation), and acceptance-finding (implementation). The first stage sometimes is ignored. Each step involves a divergent then a convergent phase.

Treffinger and colleagues noted three components: understanding the problem (mess-finding, fact-finding, and problem-finding), generating ideas (idea-finding), and planning for action (solution-finding plus acceptance finding).

The CPS model guides the creative process. It represents both a creative process and an effective way to teach creative problem solving.

Mess-finding is locating a problem to which to apply the CPS model.

Fact-finding is aided by asking who, what, when, where, why, and how questions.

Problem-finding involves listing IWWMW questions, looking for the "real" problem, and asking "Why?" after each problem statement.

---

[4]Is Walgreen's America's largest drug dealer? Did you just experience a change in perception?

Idea-finding requires deferred judgment, the main brainstorming principle.

Solution finding includes listing evaluation criteria, evaluating the ideas, and selecting the best idea(s). An evaluation matrix may be used. One also can take another's perspective on the problem, or list what is good and what is bad about each idea.

Acceptance-finding results in an action plan.

Treffinger recommended looking for assisters and resisters. His convergent techniques included finding hits, seemingly important ideas, and hot spots, which are groups of related hits.

Parnes recommends practicing the CPS model until the five steps become habitual and automatic. Said Parnes, the steps can be used in any order, if it helps.

A two-stage analysis of creative problem solving included a big idea stage, followed by an elaboration stage. Creativity is involved in both stages.

Perceptual change or transformation is a mysterious but core process that underlies insight and creative inspiration. It can be demonstrated with visual puzzles, in which new meanings, transformations, and idea combinations suddenly are "seen."

Leff's book *Playful Perception* provides many exercises, or action plans, for perceiving the environment in new and creative ways.

Imagery was ignored in classic behaviorism (Watson, Skinner). Creative imagery relates closely to Freud's primary process thinking.

When imagery was beginning to become legitimate (1960s), Holt differentiated thought images, eidetic images, synesthesia, hallucinations, dream images, and hypnagogic and hypnopompic images. Dream images, hypnagogic and hypnopompic images, and deliberate imagination images (a type of thought image) are the ones most used by creative people.

Imagery was described by Beethoven, Wordsworth, Kandinsky, Einstein, Woodword, and Kekule.

Involuntary perceptual processes promote constancy and organization. Voluntary processes can underlie manipulation and modification of mental images. "Looseness of perception" and "decoupling" of perceptual mechanisms have been suggested.

Solutions to Visual Puzzle

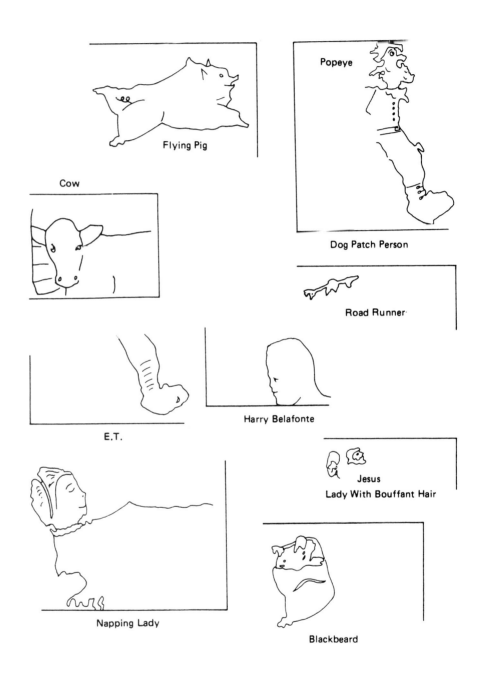

The Creative Process:
Steps and Stages, Perceptual Changes, and Imagery

Self-Test: Key Concepts, Terms, and Names

Briefly define or explain each of these:

Torrance's definition of creativity _____

_____

John Dewey's two-step model _____

_____

Graham Wallas' four-step model _____

_____

Incubation _____

_____

CPS model _____

_____

IWWMW _____

_____

Mess-finding _____

_____

Solution-finding _____

_____

Acceptance-finding _____

_____

Hits _____

_____

Hot spots _____

_____

Two-stage analysis _____

_____

Creative process as a change in perception _____

_____

Playful Perception _____

_____

Imagery in classic behaviorism _____

_____

Hypnogogic, hypnopompic _____

_____

Involuntary, voluntary perceptual processes in imagery _____

_____

Why does your author think these names are important?

Paul Torrance _____

Graham Wallas _____

Alex Osborn _____

Sidney Parnes _____

Donald Treffinger _____

Let's Think about It

1. In your own creative productivity (even if it is just writing term papers), how much of the final product is due to *hard work*, one or more sudden *"insights,"* or some *chance* happenings or discoveries?

   Hard work: _____percent

   Sudden Insights _____percent

   Chance Discoveries _____percent

2. Can you paraphrase the author's resolution to the issue of whether there is just *one* creative process or *many*?

   _____

   _____

   _____

   _____

3. Can you apply Wallas' model—*preparation, incubation, illumination, verification*—to the process of creating either an artistic or literary product?

   Preparation: _____

   Incubation: _____

   Illumination: _____

   Verification: _____

4. Think of an imaginary problem or challenge (e.g., removing a reluctant and fierce possum from your garage; convincing your sister or brother not to run off with a chimney sweep; preventing Martians from controlling your mind; owning a new Porsche by next Monday; etc.)

   Walk yourself through the CPS stages. Make up stupid information as you proceed.

   General Problem: _____

   Fact-finding: What do I know about the problem? What are some important facts?

   _____

   _____

   _____

   _____

Problem-finding: Think of different ways the problem could be defined. Ask "What is the REAL problem?" Begin each statement with "In What Ways Might We . . . ? ("IWWMW . . . ?")

IWWMW _____?

IWWMW _____?

IWWMW _____?

Idea-finding: Use your wildest imagination to think of ideas and solutions.

Idea 1: _____

Idea 2: _____

Idea 3: _____

Idea 4: _____

Solution-finding: Do some super ideas stand out? Should you create an *evaluation matrix* to help select the best idea(s)?

Criteria 1: _____

Criteria 2: _____

Criteria 3: _____

Criteria 4: _____

Rate each idea from "1" (junk!) to "5" (terrific!) according to each criteria. Add up the points. Most points wins.

Acceptance-finding: How can you get your best idea into action?

Action Plan: _____

_____

_____

5. Now think of a REAL problem or challenge you have (e.g., not enough time; raising money for a ski trip to Europe; raising your grade-point average; learning to play the ukelele or speak Russian; job hunting; etc.).

Work through the CPS stages again.

General Problem: _____

Fact-finding: What do I know about the problem? What are some important facts? Ask yourself *who, what, when, where, why,* and *how* questions.

_____ _____

_____

_____

_____

_____

Problem-finding: Think of different problem statements. What are some alternative ways of "framing" the problem? What is the REAL problem? Again, it helps to begin each statement with "IWWMW?".

IWWMW _____?

IWWMW _____?

IWWMW _____?

IWWMW _____?

IWWMW _____?

Idea-finding: Brainstorm ideas for one or two of your best problem statements.

Idea 1: _____

Idea 2: _____

Idea 3: _____

Idea 4: _____

Idea 5: _____

Solution-finding: Are there some good ideas? Do you need to create an evaluation matrix to help select your best idea(s)? Be sure to use good evaluation criteria.

Criteria 1: _____

Criteria 2: _____

Criteria 3: _____

Criteria 4: _____

Criteria 5: _____

Rate each idea from "1" (won't work or not acceptable) to "5" (extremely promising) according to each criteria. Add up the points. Most points wins.

Acceptance-finding: How can you get your best solution(s) into action?

Action Plan: _____

_____

_____

_____

6. *Creative Perception* Exercises.

   a. Carry on an imaginary conversation with your childhood bike.

   b. Try reversing cause-effect relations you see (e.g., your instructor's shoes are dragging him or her around the room; the piece of chalk is forcing your instructor to create those words and illustrations).

   c. Look around and react to the room you are in from the point of view of an ant, duck, starving mouse, or space alien.

   d. Imagine how everything you see would smell; then predict it's future.

7. Mental imagery

   a. Explain "looseness" of perception.

   b. Explain "decoupling" from perception.

8. Word search. Draw a ring around the words listed below. They may appear right to left, left to right, top to bottom, bottom to top; or on a diagonal. The process of solving word-search puzzles is mostly trial-and-error searching.

```
W  S  P  U  Z  Z  L  E  L  O
I  N  C  U  B  A  T  I  O  N
N  I  K  Y  E  W  E  D  O  T
S  R  D  R  P  H  I  T  S  O
I  N  I  E  T  S  N  I  E  P
G  L  S  G  A  M  P  P  N  S
H  C  G  A  Q  B  R  C  E  T
T  Y  O  M  N  R  O  B  S  O
N  W  B  I  G  L  O  O  S  H
```

CPS	Idea
Dewey	Imagery
Einstein	Incubation
Hits	Insight
Hot Spot	Looseness
	Puzzle

6

creative inspiration through analogical thinking

[*Scene: Mountain top cave in eastern country. Rich but simple Americans, John and Mary Simple, are seeking the meaning of life from bearded guru Swami Ci-Alli, seated in lotus position*]

John: Tell me, Swami Ci-Alli, what is the meaning of life?

Swami: (*Somberly*) Life is a hamburger.

John: It is? I mean, what is life all about?

Mary: He's speaking metaphorically, John. He means that the total sandwich is made of what you put into it. Am I right, Swami?

Swami: You see through mist with eyes of magic fog lamp.

John: Oh, okay. But what should I do in this world? What is the best life?

Swami: An arrow can only fly straight.

John: Huh?

Mary: It's metaphorical again, John. I think he means that you should get out more, maybe take up archery.

Swami: Not quite, madam. I mean that a ball can only bounce.

Mary: Well, there's my bowling ball that doesn't . . .

John: Maybe he means that I am what I am and I should do what I do best. Right, Swami?

Swami: Your thoughts are a razor cutting through the beard of reality.

Mary: And what else, Swami Ci-Alli? I mean, this was an expensive trip.

Swami: You must sail the oceans of the unknown and discover islands of truth.

John: Wait a minute. Sir Isaac Newton said that hundreds of years ago!

Swami: If you want originality, you must toss your own metaphorical salad.

Mary: Let's get out of here, my feet are beef in a meat grinder, dough under a rolling pin, blasphemers on the inquisitors' rack, . . .

John: Oh, cut it out!

I am a thief—and I glory in it . . . I steal from the best where it happens to be—Plato, Picasso, Bertram Ross . . . I think I know the value of what I steal and I treasure it for all time—not as a possession but as a heritage and a legacy.

Martha Graham

Most Creative Ideas Stem from Analogical, Metaphorical Thinking

We Make a Connection

One cannot overstate the importance of analogical and metaphorical thinking in creativity.[1] It is simply and absolutely true that many—perhaps the large majority—of our creative ideas and problem solutions are born in analogical and metaphorical thinking. *When we think analogically or metaphorically, we take ideas from one context and apply them in a new context*, producing the new idea combination, new transformation, new theoretical perspective, or more colorful literary passage. We "make a connection" between our current problem and a similar or related situation.

"Was Inspired by"

Analogical and metaphorical thinking is extremely common in all areas of creativity and creative problem solving. The frequent comments "was inspired by" and "is based upon" indicate that ideas for a specific creation were suggested by or borrowed from another source by the particular composer, novelist, movie maker, artist, architect, decorator, designer, scientist, engineer, new product developer, business entrepreneur, or other creative person. Said historian Jacob

Bronowski, Koestler Agree

Bronowski (1961), "The discoveries of science, the works of art, are explorations—more, are explosions—of (seeing) a hidden likeness." Arthur Koestler (1964) observed that the creative thinker finds such metaphoric and analogical connections while ordinary individuals do not.

CATS Inspired by T. S. Eliot Poetry

Perhaps a first example is in order. The brilliantly creative and successful Broadway musical *CATS* was "based on" *Old Possum's Book of Practical Cats*, a book of poems by T. S. Eliot. The *CATS* playbill reads:

> Most of the poems comprising *Old Possum's Book of Practical Cats* have been set to music complete and in their originally published form . . . However, some of our lyrics, notably *The Marching Song of the Pollicle Dogs* and the story of *Grizzabella*, were discovered among the unpublished writings of Eliot. The prologue is based on ideas and incorporates lines from another unpublished poem entitled *Pollicle Dogs and Jellicle Cats*. Growltiger's aria is taken from an Italian translation of *Practical Cats*. *Memory* includes lines from and is suggested by *Rhapsody on a Windy Night*, and other poems of the *Prufrock* period. All other words in the show are taken from the Collected Poems.

Is analogical thinking important in high-level creative accomplishment? Do creative ideas come from nowhere?

May Be Sudden

Sometimes an analogical connection will burst into awareness suddenly and unpredictably. That is, a sudden "insight" may be a matter of instantly "making a connection."

May Take Painstaking Search

Other times the creative person will deliberately and painstakingly search for suitable analogical relationships, as when a professional advertiser looks for a good strategy for promoting a client's product or an architect searches his or her books and magazines for ideas for a creative home or building.

---

[1] As we noted earlier, in the creativity literature the distinction between *analogy* and *metaphor* is blurred to the point where the terms are used nearly (not completely) interchangeably.

Ideas come from somewhere. The design for this automobile was inspired by a door hinge. "Hey fellas," yelled the exasperated inventor, "Could you pull ahead? I gotta' slam my frame!" (Wisconsin Center for Film and Theater Research.)

IS "BORROWING" IDEAS ETHICAL AND VIRTUOUS?

When Is "Borrowing" Actually Stealing?

Analogical Thinking Common, Usually Legitimate

In the following pages of examples, the reader will see that analogical and metaphorical thinking is exceedingly common in creative innovation. It is both an explanatory creative *process*; it also is a learnable creative thinking *technique*.

But where, one might ask, does stealing and plagiarism end and true originality begin? Young and idealistic creative persons may worry about this issue more than experienced and successful ones, who realize that (1) ideas come from somewhere, (2) the analogical use of ideas is common, effective, and usually quite legitimate, and (3) seeing analogical and metaphorical connections is quite a creative thing to do.

Martha Graham's comment after the opening dialogue in this chapter—about the honest, legitimate, and creative stealing of ideas—seems right on target regarding the ethics of "borrowing" ideas. T. S. Eliot is reputed to have stated that "good writers borrow ideas, great writers steal them."

Using analogically related ideas as an idea source usually poses no ethical questions at all, as when:

Chemist Kekule used the circular snake as an analogical inspiration for the benzine ring.

Bohr used the solar system as a model for the structure of the atom.

Darwin found inspiration for his theory of natural selection in selective cattle breeding.

A fourth-grader says, "Hey, let's turn the classroom into a carnival for parents' night!"

A movie maker or writer of Broadway plays uses any number of historical events, Biblical events, or comic book characters for inspiration (e.g., *Jesus Christ Superstar, Evita, Superman, Batman*).

A novelist, mystery writer, or playwright finds inspiration in real events, myths, news stories, or children's stories, as Truman Capote, Ernest Hemingway, Agatha Christie, Shakespeare, and many others have done.

In the business and corporate world, borrowing and modifying other successful (e.g., marketing) strategies generally is good problem solving. We will see many more examples of analogically, and ethically, "borrowing" ideas in later sections.

Of course, if you literally "lift" someone else's work, for example, a scientific theory or a contemporary musical composition, change a few details and then claim it for your own, that quite obviously is unethical, if not illegal as well. To avoid copyright infringement, one publisher of American folk tunes changed the title of *Happy Birthday* to "*Happy Bird Day*" and published exactly the original melody. Lyrics were changed to bird words.

Happy Bird Day?

Grey Areas

There are, however, grey areas, as when a TV movie plot is based directly on, say, an Agatha Christie or other novel without crediting the source; an artist too-closely copies the techniques and ideas of another; or 17 companies create their own version of the *Weed Eater*. One must reach one's own conclusions regarding the originality and ethics of creations that appear too-directly influenced by a successful predecessor.

ANALOGICAL THINKING IN CREATIVE INNOVATION

Two-Stage Model

Before we look at how analogical and metaphorical thinking is used to find new ideas, it is important to recall the two-stage model of the creative process described in Chapter 5. Again, this is not a theory of how creative problem solving takes place, it is a statement of fact. Stage 1 is the *Big Idea* stage in which the main idea for the artistic creation, invention, or problem solution is found. Stage 2 is the *Elaboration* and development stage in which the Big Idea is implemented. In the following examples analogical and metaphorical thinking takes places most clearly in the Big Idea stage—finding that new idea for a creative problem solution, composition, invention, theory, and so on. After the Big Idea is found, of course, it must be developed and implemented, which may or may not involve additional analogical thinking.

Analogical Thinking in Big Idea Stage

MUSIC

Your author would not even hint that all music written by all composers is analogically borrowed from earlier melodies. Some compositions inexplicably pop into the heads of classic and contemporary composers, with roots somewhere in their immense mental store of musical experiences and potential musical combinations. Other compositions are the product of laboriously experimenting with ideas—manipulating, modifying and revising until something good is created. However, there are many instances in which the Big Idea for a composition clearly is borrowed from an earlier piece, consciously and deliberately.

Much Music Based upon Earlier Melodies

Liszt

Franz Liszt composed 15 Hungarian Rhapsodies, cleverly titled "Hungarian Rhapsody Number 1," "Hungarian Rhapsody Number 2," "Hungarian Rhapsody

Tchaikowsky
Cesar Cui

Brahms, Beethoven

Aaron Copland

Broadway Show Based on a Painting

Barry Manilow

Oh Say, Can You Serve Me Another Pint of Ale?

A Common, Creative Composing Strategy

Many Cartoons Analogically Based

Art Buchwald: Master of Humorous Metaphors

Tax Fantasies

Number 3," and so on. All 15 "were built upon traditional songs or dance airs of the romantic gypsies of Hungary" (Thompson, 1942, p. 90). Franz had good company. Peter Tchaikowsky based his *Marche Slav* on a folk tune, the same tune used by Cesar A. Cui for his *Orientale*, which accounts for the "striking similarity between this melody (*Orientale*) and that of *Marche Slav*" (Thompson, 1942, p. 11). And more: "The waltzes of Brahms like those of Beethoven have for their inspiration the old German 'Landler' or peasant dance . . . " (Thompson, 1942, p. 38).

Aaron Copland's *Appalachian Spring* symphony was based upon a Shaker folk tune entitled *Simple Gifts*. His bouncy *Hoe Down* from *Rodeo* seems to be an arrangement of a traditional American hoe down. However, to keep Copland's creative genius in its mystical perspective, in a 1984 television interview Copland mentioned that when music comes alive in his head, he has no choice but to find pencil and paper and start writing.

The Broadway musical *Sunday Afternoon in the Park with George* was inspired by Georges Seurat's famous painting *Sunday Afternoon on the Isle of La Grand Jatte* and Seurat's personal life.

In the popular music category, daughter Sonja Davis was one day playing Chopin's *Prelude in C Minor*. She stopped in mid-melody to announce, "Hey, this is Barry Manilow's '*Could It Be Magic*'!" A check of the Manilow album cover credited these composers, "Barry Manilow, Adrienne Anderson, and F. Chopin." Another long-time hit, Francis Scott Key's *Star Spangled Banner*, is based upon an English drinking song.

The Big Ideas for these and many other popular songs and classical pieces were borrowed from earlier, usually simpler tunes. This is not plagiarism, it is a common analogical creative thinking process used by uncommonly creative people.

CARTOONS

Many newspaper cartoons, both political cartoons and cartoon-strip "'funnies," are good examples of analogical thinking in creativity. While all cartoons are not necessarily inspired by related sources, many of them are. If you watch, the best cartoons usually are analogical in nature, with ideas from an unrelated context combined with a current political event or with regular cartoon-strip characters. To the reader, the resulting combination produces a surprising and comical "Aha!" experience.

Note the several types of idea sources for the cartoons on the following pages—news events, political events and issues, a John Lennon song, and children's stories. It is not unusual to see political and other cartoons based upon, for example: popular TV commercials[2]; movies such as *Jaws*, *Star Wars*, or *Rambo*; mythology such as *Dracula* and *Frankenstein*; or classic literature such as *Robin Hood*, *Dr. Jekyl and Mr. Hyde*, the *Wizard of Oz*, or *Alice in Wonderland*. Cartoon strips such as *Frank and Earnest*, *Zippy*, and *The Wizard of Id* regularly incorporate current news and political events into their cartoon setting. (Where did the title "Wizard of Id" come from?)

Political humorist Art Buchwald has used analogical and metaphorical thinking in his syndicated column to poke fun at political events and politicians. One April 15 column on tax fantasies, inspired by books on sex fantasies, appears in Inset 6.1. Even within the larger tax fantasy metaphor, Buchwald metaphorically borrowed ideas from "fat sheriff" commercials and from *Cinderella*.

---

[2]In two different cartoon strips a child stuck his head out a car window and asked someone in the next car, "Pardon me, do you have any Grey Poupon?"

ALL WE ARE SAY—ING....

....iS GiVe WAR A CHANCe....

© Copyright, Minneapolis Star-Tribune, Reprinted with permission. All rights reserved.

THE FAR SIDE   **By Gary Larson**

Moses as a kid

THE FAR SIDE © FARWORKS, INC. Used by permission of UNIVERSAL PRESS SYNDICATE. All rights reserved.

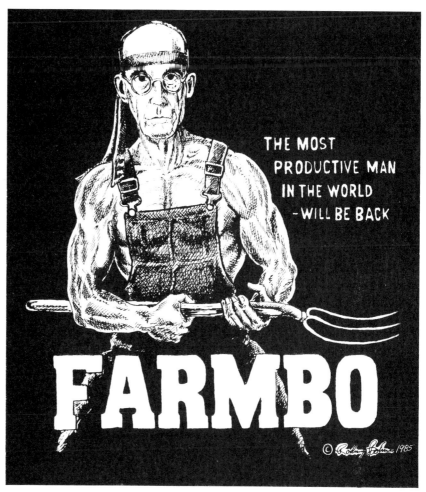

This poster borrowed one idea from RAMBO and another from the classic painting *American Gothic*. (Reprinted by permission of Rodney Bohner.)

© by and permission of News American Syndicate.

By permission of Mike Lukovich and Creators Syndicate.

© Tribune Media Services, Inc. All Rights Reserved. Reprinted with permission.

EVERY FOUR YEARS CINDERELLA IS VISITED BY A COUPLE OF FAIRY GODFATHERS.

AUTH © The Philadelphia Inquirer. Reprinted with permission of UNIVERSAL PRESS SYNDICATE. All rights reserved.

Infantry, with Air Support, Overruns Pork and Beans!

See how it works? Could you write a picnic episode, describing in battlefield terms the difficulties with ants and their allies the bees? Could you describe how to bake cookies using the language of a hospital operating room? Could you use the language of a cat stalking a mouse to describe a clever salesperson trying to sell someone an expensive color TV set? Try it.

Your Turn

If those exercises worked, perhaps you are ready for more. Think about the idea sources in the top section of Inset 6.2. Imagine how some of them might be used in either a political cartoon or a brief written satire involving the topics at the bottom of the page. Go ahead and try a few. You probably will surprise yourself?

SCIENCE AND INVENTION

Gordon: Examples of Analogical Thinking

Gutenberg: Movable Type

William J. J. Gordon (1974b), champion of the analogical basis of creativity, described a number of instances of analogical thinking in science and invention. For example, it seems that Gutenberg (1398–1468), inventor of movable printing type, was not too crazy about hand-engraving an entire page of text on a single slab of smooth wood. The analogy of coin-making, in which plain discs are stamped by a coin punch, suggested separate metal letters that could be arranged and reused again and again. A wine press suggested his printing press.

Bissel's Oil Pump

In the 1850s George B. Bissel grew tired of inefficiently gathering oil out of shallow wells with buckets or else sopping it up with blankets and then wringing them out. He borrowed ideas from a brine pump at a salt plant to design a similar

---

Inset 6.1
Erotica for April 15 May Ease the Pain*

Columnist and political humorist Art Buchwald is a master of deliberate metaphorical thinking—transferring ideas from one situation to another. The outcome is always funny. Well, usually. The two fantasies reproduced here actually are metaphors within a metaphor—within the "tax fantasy" metaphor ideas are borrowed from the 1970s "fat sheriff" Dodge commercial and from the Cinderella fairytale.

By ART BUCHWALD

WASHINGTON—Many magazines have been doing articles on sex fantasies. It's amazing how many men and women will talk about them if their names are not used for publication. But it's rare to have anyone admit that they have tax fantasies. After prying and cajoling, I finally got several people of both sexes to tell me their favorite tax fantasies.

L. D., a 30-year-old car salesman, writes: "I have this tax fantasy, maybe two, three times a week. I'm called down to the IRS office for an audit. The agent tells me to bring down all my receipts and records.

"He looks like a fat sheriff in a TV commercial sitting behind his desk smoking a large cigar. I tell him I have been meticulous about my deductions, and he'll find everything in order.

"He chuckles and says, 'That's what they all say. Why don't you make it easy on both of us and tell us exactly how much you've cheated Uncle Sam out of this time?'

"I say, 'It's all here. Every cent I deducted has been verified and accounted for.'

" 'Okay,' he says, taking out his mini-calculator. 'If you want to play rough, I can play rough.' He starts hitting the calculator with his fat fingers. It takes three hours. He goes over the figures again and again. He can't find one thing wrong with my tax return. His face is red. 'There has to be something here,' he says.

"After the fourth time he realizes that the return is perfect. He looks at me, opens the top drawer of his desk and excuses himself to go to the men's room. I wait in my chair. Suddenly I hear a gunshot from the washroom. An aide says, 'Don't feel bad. For him it was the only honorable way out.' "

T. R. is a 21-year-old career woman who has worked her way up in the stockroom of a very cheap department store. Her boss is known as the "wicked stepmother." Every April there is a ball given by the store before the spring clearance sales.

The stepmother says T. R. can't go to the ball until she counts all the glass slippers that are still unsold from a previous Cinderella promotion which never got off the ground.

As T. R. is counting the boxes, a Fairy Godmother arrives with a new dress from Bergdorf Goodman and a diamond ring borrowed from Elizabeth Taylor. T. F. goes to the ball and meets a handsome prince. He falls in love with her, but at the stroke of midnight she has to leave. She loses her glass slipper. After a futile search he finally finds T. R. in the stockroom and tries the slipper on her foot. It fits.

He confesses he's really not a prince but actually works for H & R Block, the tax consultants. He explains to her that if they get married they could save $345 a year on their income tax. Overcome with the thought of the tax loophole, she says yes, and they live happily ever after.

---

*Reprinted with permission of Art Buchwald.

Inset 6.2
Now Imagine You Are a Cartoonist or Columnist:
Exercise in Analogical Thinking

Look at the "scenarios"—the characters, their vocabulary, the setting, their goals or problems—in the top section below. See if you can create an original cartoon by metaphorically applying the ideas to one of the topics in the bottom section. Sometimes there will be an easy fit, for example, just using the caption "Coke is it!" under a drug scene. Go ahead, sketch your ideas. If you prefer, try a short written spoof like the Art Buchwald column.

ORIGINAL SCENARIO—SOURCE OF CHARACTERS AND IDEAS

Alice in Wonderland (Queen of Hearts, Mad Hatter, March Hare, Mushroom that makes you grow)

Snow White (seven dwarfs, Prince Charming, Wicked Queen with "Mirror, Mirror on the Wall," poisoned apple)

Cinderella (ugly step-sisters, wicked step-mother, magic coach)

Goldilocks and the Three Bears

Three Little Pigs and the Wolf (straw, wood, and brick houses)

Sleeping Beauty (awakened by kiss from handsome prince)

Rapunzel, who let down hair for prince to climb

Little Red Riding Hood, the Wolf, basket of goodies, Grandmother

Kissing a frog, who turns into a prince

Tom Tom the Pipers Son, Stole a Pig and Away He Run

Robin Hood, who steals from the rich to give to the poor

Star Wars Characters (Luke Skywalker, Princess Leia, Darth Vader, Ben Kenobi, Yoda, Ewoks, Walking Machines)

E. T., who wants to phone home and go home

Sasquatch (Yeti, Big Foot); Loch Ness Monster (Nessie)

A McDonalds commercial, with Ronald McDonald

"Coke Is It" commercial

Superman, Batman

Bible (Moses, Noah, Daniel in lion's den, Adam and Eve)

Weather forecast, with weather map showing storms, sunny skies

SITUATIONS IN WHICH TO USE CHARACTERS AND IDEAS

Star Wars space defense system

Summit talks between U.S. President and Russian leader

China becoming more capitalistic, less communistic

Political revolutions in Central American country (pick one)

Revisions in Federal Income Tax that still favor the rich

Smoking, drug, and gang problems in schools

Elementary children carrying guns to school

News about fertility pills leading to multiple births

News about unsafe automobiles or airplanes

News about Japanese car imports

News about federal spending or the national debt

Problems in unified Germany and other former communist countries

Problems with continuing dictatorships in Haiti

News about AIDS continuing to spread

Other current events?

Watt: All Aboard for Tea

pump for raising oil. James Watt's steam engine was inspired by the jangling lid of his mother's tea kettle. The wife of Luigi Galvani placed a steel knife on a tin plate, accidentally touching a frog's leg that suddenly twitched. Galvani deduced that electricity had been created by the joining of two dissimilar metals and promptly invented the battery. His young son deduced that the leg was not yet dead and promptly smacked it with a cleaver.

Galvani's Battery: Hopping Good Idea!

Brunel's Underwater Tunnel

Sir Marc Isambard Brunel was wrestling with the problem of efficiently constructing underwater tunnels. He happened to observe a shipworm constructing a tube for itself as it moved forward through a timber, which suggested a short steel cylinder that could be pushed forward as tunnel work progressed. Were it not for that worm, New York's Holland and Lincoln tunnels would be filled with water today.

Morse: Relay Stations

Samuel Morse's first telegraph messages became weak after just a few miles. Stagecoach relay stations, where fresh horses were added, suggested relay stations at appropriate distances where more power could be added to the fading signal.

Howe's Sewing Machine Needle

The development of Elias Howe's sewing machine was aided when Howe put the eye in the point of the needle, which was suggested by weaving shuttles. Howe's sewing machine principle was applied by the Singer Company to a leather stitching machine for making shoes.

Darwin's Natural Selection

Charles Darwin observed that animal breeders could selectively breed for characteristics that improved the market value of their animals. This observation suggested that a similar process could happen in natural selection in nature.

Whitney's Cotton Gin Based on Unsuccessful Cat

Eli Whitney claimed that he developed his cotton gin after watching a pussycat trying to catch a chicken through a fence. The cat missed, coming up with a pawful of feathers. Hundreds of paws on his cotton gin reach through a tight fence and pull cotton away from the seeds.

Pasteur: Fermenting Flesh?

Wine grapes, which ferment only when crushed, suggested to Louis Pasteur that human flesh would not putrefy unless an open wound allowed putrefying agents to get in. An experiment confirmed this novel idea, which advanced medical understanding of infections and the use of Band-Aids to prevent them.

Westinghouse Air Brake

George Westinghouse, after surviving a head-on train crash, learned of a Swiss rock drill that was powered by an air hose 3,000 feet from the compressor. He immediately designed the Westinghouse air brake. Scotsman Dunlop's first tire was not only inspired by the flexibility of a garden hose, it *was* a piece of garden hose wrapped around a wheel.

Dunlop's Tire First Used on Grass

Cockleburrs = Velcro

One autumn, inventor George De Mestral was walking with his hunting dog through a field that was booby-trapped with cockleburrs, most of which ended up on the dog. During the extraction process he examined the structure of the burrs and determined to replicate its ferocious cling in a commercial product. After hundreds of attempts and dollars, and several years' work, velcro was born.

Duryea's Carburetor

Charles Duryea, looking for a better way to squirt gas into engine cylinders, used the analogy of his wife's perfume atomizer to develop a spray injection carburetor. The Wright brothers needed to be able to turn their plane. The solution came from a buzzard who twisted the back of its wing slightly downward to

Wing Flaps from a Buzzard

Many ideas have their roots in analogical thinking. This person's barber was inspired by a blender. "I think I liked punk better," said Mr. Hunchbach. (The Museum of Modern Art/Film Stills Archive.)

Rapid Fire Razor

increase air pressure in order to turn. Tying a buzzard to each wing did not work, but movable wing flaps did. The Schick injector razor, invented by an army person, was inspired by the loading mechanism of the repeating rifle.

These are a handful of the many discoveries and inventions "inspired by" or "based upon" some analogically related object, process, or idea.

LITERATURE, MOVIE-MAKING, TV, BROADWAY

Shakespeare's Sources

Big Idea Clear, but Elaboration Mysterious

Scholars in university English departments sometimes do source studies to identify the sources of ideas and inspirations underlying the works of noteworthy authors and playwrights. We will go right to the top by examining the idea sources of William Shakespeare. Table 6.1 presents a shortened version of a complete list of Shakespeare's plays and their idea sources that appears in the World Book Encyclopedia. The left column lists some of his better known plays, the right column identifies the source from which he apparently derived the characters, settings, and main plots. While the Big Idea for each play has been traced, the

Table 6.1
Idea Sources of Shakespeare
(Abridged from the World Book Encyclopedia)

Play	Source
Taming of the Shrew	Taming of the Shrew (unknown English playwright)
Romeo and Juliet	Romeo and Juliet (poem by Arthur Brooke)
Merchant of Venice	Il Pecorone (short story by Giovanni Fiorentino)
Julius Caesar	A tragedy from Plutarch's Lives
Much Ado About Nothing	Orlando Fusioso (comedy by Ludovico Ariosto)
Twelfth Night	Farewell to the Military Profession (short story by Barnabe Riche)
Hamlet	Hamlet (play by unknown English author) and Histoires Tragiques (Francois Belleforest)
All's Well that Ends Well	The Palace of Pleasure (short story by unknown author)
Othello	Promos and Cassandra (play by George Whetstone)
King Lear	The Union of Two Noble and Illustrious Families of Lancaster and York (by Edward Hall, historian) and Holinshed's Chronicles (16th century history book)
Macbeth	Holinshed's Chronicles
Antony and Cleopatra	Plutarch's Lives

character development, dramatic conflicts and tension, humor, and so on are creative beyond description. It is the elaboration and development stage of creativity that appears to be the most mysterious and intriguing process, and one that sets Shakespeare apart from mortal bards.[3]

Movies, Novels, Plays Have Metaphorical Sources

Many movies, novels, TV dramas, and broadway plays continue to be inspired by or based upon recognizable events and idea sources. The following is a small sample:

Contemporary Events

From contemporary events: *All the President's Men* (from Watergate), *In Cold Blood* (a midwest murder), *High Noon* (inspired by senate investigations of organized crime in Hollywood), *Killing Fields* (Cambodian holocaust).

History

From history: *The Longest Day, From Here to Eternity, Tora, Tora, Tora, Voyage of the Damned* (all from World War II); *Gone With the Wind, Red Badge of Courage* (Civil War); *I Caludius, Cleopatra, Ben Hur, Salamis* (Roman, Egyptian, Greek history); *Les Misrables; Zulu.*

Biographies

From biographies: *Citizen Kane* (life of San Francisco newspaperman William Randolph Hearst), *El Cid* (legendary Spanish hero), *Edison, the Man, Patton, The Miracle Worker* (Helen Keller), *Elephant Man* (story of John Merrick), *Elvira Madigan* (last woman hanged in England), *Gandhi, Bird Man of Alcatraz, Three Faces of Eve, I'll Cry Tomorrow* (Lillian Roth), *John Paul Jones, When We Were Kings* (athletes), *Evita, Shine* (story of pianist David Helfgott).

---

[3]Example of "seeing a connection" in humor: Did you know that Shakespeare's mother was an Avon lady?

Bible

From the Bible: *Ten Commandments, David the King, Jesus Christ, Superstar, Moses.*

Classic, Contemporary Literature

From classic and contemporary literature: *Dr. Jekyll and Mr. Hyde, Ivanhoe, David Copperfield, Alice in Wonderland, Wizard of Oz, Jane Eyre, For Whom the Bell Tolls, To Kill a Mockingbird, Tale of Two Cities, Superman, Batman.*

Mythology, Legend

From mythology, legend, supernatural: Frankenstein and Dracula movies, including *Love at First Bite, American Werewolf in London,* and *I Was a Teenage Werewolf; Three Musketeers, Harry and the Hendersons* (Sasquatch), *Independence Day.*

Shakespeare Has Been Moonlighting

The 1980s TV show *Moonlighting* based a St. Patrick's day show on a leprechaun looking for a pot of gold; a Christmas show included numerous Christmas themes, including a baby and three detectives named King ("three kings"); Shakespeare inspired at least two *Moonlighting* episodes (e.g., his *Taming of the Shrew*).

What are some other movies, novels, TV shows, or Broadway shows inspired by specific sources?

ACTING

Actors and Actresses must develop their stage and screen personalities which often, perhaps always, are borrowed from character types they know. In a newspaper interview, the star of the 1985 TV detective series *Lady Blue,* Jamie Rose, said "My inspiration for the character is Clint Eastwood's 'Dirty Harry.' In my mind, she (my character, Katy Mahoney) is Dirty Harriet." The article reported, "Ms. Rose, 26, had the prop master furnish her with a fake .357 magnum pistol with a four-inch barrel, then rented a VCR and all four 'Dirty Harry' movies. 'I hooked up the video to my hotel room TV and kind of shot along with Clint—again and again.'"

Lady Blue Is Dirty Harriet

Other actors and actresses will borrow the personalities of, for example, Marilyn Monroe, James Cagney, James Bond, and others. Watch for them on TV.

ARCHITECTURE, CLOTHES DESIGN

These two unrelated topics are lumped together because they both can make use of the same analogical strategy for finding ideas. Want to design a creative home? Ideas for a unique wardrobe? Try thinking about other countries and other times. Visit a museum, look at pictures in history books, or flip through encyclopedias. Do you think you could find a few hundred inspirations from Mexico, the orient, Holland, Greece, Ancient Egypt, Peru, Africa, Switzerland, America's pilgrims, Atlanta in 1855, Disneyland, New Orleans, the roaring 1920s, rural America, other places and times? Of course you could. Professional designers have stacks of books and magazines filled with ideas waiting to be modified and applied. The castles at Disneyland and Disney World were inspired by the Neuschwanstein castle near Fussen, Germany. Frank Lloyd Wright used Viennese, Japanese, and Aztec designs in his architecture. Frank was reasonably successful.

Other Countries, Other Times

Magazines: Sources of Metaphorical Inspiration

ANALOGICAL THINKING IN PROBLEM SOLVING

Unless you have a clearly convergent problem with one and only one correct answer (for example, an arithmetic problem, "Where's my dog?" or "Whose picture is on the fifty?"), creativity can be involved in every step of problem solving. The CPS model in Chapter 5 illustrated how creativity can help clarify a problem (fact-finding stage), define the problem (problem-finding), list solution alternatives (idea-finding), evaluate ideas (solution-finding), and implement the solution(s) (acceptance-finding).

Creativity in All Steps of Problem Solving

Analogical Thinking in Idea Finding

The most obvious use of analogical thinking in the CPS model is in the idea-finding process. Consider a problem such as "How can we get more parents to the school play?" One could find ideas by asking questions that stimulate analogical thinking, such as:

Stimulating Questions

What else is like this?

What have others done?

What could we copy?

What has worked before?

What would professionals do?

Deliberate, Spontaneous Analogical Ideas

Such questions elicit deliberate analogical thinking. Analogical ideas also will occur spontaneously—"Say, Benedict Arnold High School got free newspaper and radio advertising. John Wilkes Booth High held a raffle with the admission ticket—community businesses donated tons of prizes!"

Osborn's Checklist

Incidentally, two of the above five questions appear in Osborn's checklist "73 List Spurring Questions" (Chapter 7). That checklist encourages analogical thinking for finding ideas and problem solutions.

SYNECTICS METHODS

Analogy-Based Techniques Bring Together Different Elements

Gordon: Well-Rounded Person!

The word *synectics* is from the Greek *syn*, meaning "together," along with *-ectics*, which was arbitrarily selected (Prince, 1982). Synectics is "the joining together of different and apparently irrelevant elements" (Gordon & Poze, 1980a, 1980b). The synectics methods are conscious, analogy-based and metaphor-based techniques for bringing together these different elements. The originator of the synectics methods is William J. J. Gordon, former school teacher, horse handler, salvage diver, ambulance driver, ski instructor, sailing schooner master, college lecturer, and pig breeder. The outcome of the pig project was "a lot of bone and not much bacon, but they were the fastest pigs in the East" (Alexander, 1978).

Patents, Creative Writing Awards

Familiar Inventions

Gordon and his colleagues hold more than 200 patents and their creative writing, published in the *New Yorker* and *Atlantic Monthly*, won them an O. Henry Short Story Award and a Science Fiction Award. A few examples of synectics inventions are Pringles Potato Chips, a trash compactor, the electric knife, an early space suit closure device for NASA, a space feeding system, the space-saver Kleenex box, disposable diapers, a disposable baby bottle with formula, an ice cube maker, a jet marine engine, a Ford truck frame suspension system, an accelerated wound-healing system, operating table covers, Sunoco's dial-your-own-octane gas pump, and the presumably similar automatic liquor dispenser.

Made Creativity Techniques Conscious, Teachable

For Adults

For Children

Gordon's early experience with creative thinking groups helped him to identify analogical thinking strategies that creative people use spontaneously. He clarified these strategies, making them conscious and teachable in a form for adults (e.g., Gordon, 1961; Prince, 1968) and for children. Said Gordon (Gordon & Poze, 1980b), "Everyone, to some degree or another, consciously or unconsciously uses analogies to solve problems. The purpose of . . . synectics is to give you a way to use analogies that will make your problem-solving process more effective." In agreement, former synectics colleague George Prince (1968) observed that the procedures "help you think unhabitually." Gordon's workbooks and exercise books *Making It Strange* (Gordon, 1974a), *New Art of the Possible* (Gordon & Poze, 1980b), *Metaphorical Way of Learning and Knowing* (Gordon & Poze, 1971), *Teaching Is Listening* (Gordon & Poze, 1972a), and *Strange and Familiar* (Gordon & Poze, 1972b) give children first-hand experience with the fascinating synectics problem-solving methods of *direct analogy*, *personal analogy*, *fantasy analogy*, and *symbolic analogy*.

Have You Sunflowered Lately?

Gordon's strategies inspired some of the exercises in Stanish's workbooks *Sunflowering* (Stanish, 1977), *Hippogriff Feathers* (Stanish, 1981), and *Hearthstone Traveler* (Stanish, 1988).

Direct Analogy

Direct Analogies from Nature

Gordon: Progress of Civilization Due to Analogical Thinking

Cave Person Makes a Connection

Snakeskin Belt

Raking the Harbor

With the *direct analogy* method, the problem solver is asked to think of ways that related problems have been solved. While analogies of any sort are welcome, those from nature are especially encouraged. How have animals, birds, flowers, insects, worms, snakes, and so on solved similar problems? Gordon and Poze (1980b), for example, speculate that civilization itself progressed when individuals made analogical connections—seeing that this situation is like that situation. Imagine a starving cave person unsuccessfully trying to spear fish with a sharp stick. There are fish all over the place, but cave person cannot stab enough to feed family and friends. Cave person sees a small swarm of flies become entrapped in a spider's web. Aha! Cave person makes an analogical connection, dashes back to the group, dumps the neighbor out of a hammock and uses the hammock to net fish by the dozens. Another primitive has trouble keeping his pants up, and a snake wrapped around a rock suggested the first belt (Gordon & Poze, 1972b). When his socks kept falling down, a little garter snake suggested a similar solution.

Gordon himself was part of an emergency group faced with removing a sunken ship that blocked the Tripoli harbor during WW II. An army colonel imagined his mother vigorously raking away at dirt lumps in her garden, which suggested blasting the offending ship to smithereens and then "raking" it level just as mother did. It worked

Pass the Salted Leaves, Please

In one synectics session the problem was to package potato chips compactly, without breaking them, and to reduce shipping costs. Wet leaves—which pack snugly together without breaking—led to Pringles Potato Chips. Magnesium-impregnated bandages that sped up the healing of wounds came from the analogy of a broken electrical wire—one must restore transmission across the damaged gap (Gordon & Poze, 1980b).

Good for Any Problem

Safe Ideas

Virtually any sort of problem can be attacked with the direct analogy method. For example, in a University of Wisconsin creativity workshop for retired people many expressed concern for their personal safety. With the direct analogy approach the problem became: How do animals, plants, birds, etc., protect themselves, and how can these ideas help the elderly?[4] The idea list included spray cans of skunk scent, slip-on fangs and claws, a compressed air can that screams when activated, a snake-faced mask that scares the bejeebers out of potential muggers, an electronic device that secretly "yells" for the police, traveling only in groups, and camouflage or disguises, for example, wearing a police uniform.

Personal Analogy

What Thoughts Run through Your Bubble Gum Head?

For New Perceptions, Become Part of the Problem

Imagine you are a piece of bubble gum. You are sitting quietly in your box with your bubble gum friends on the shelf of a candy store. A little boy walks in, places five cents on the counter and points at you. How do you feel? What are your thoughts? You notice that the little boy's nose is running and he sniffles a lot. How do you feel about your immediate future?

With the *personal analogy* method the thinker achieves new perspectives on a problem by imaginatively becoming part of that problem. What would you be like if you were a dazzling dinner for important friends? Or a really efficient floor mop? If you were a check book, how could you avoid becoming lost? In one

---

[4]The author is indebted to Jean Romaniuk for suggesting this problem.

"There I was, learning to swim with the personal analogy method. I imagined I was a frog and . . ." (The Museum of Modern Art/Film Stills Archive.)

Oily Example

synectics problem solving session, the group members (intelligent adults) imagined themselves to be rapidly multiplying viruses, tiny and crowded, in order to shed light on the problem of getting an accurate sample of oil-saturated rock from under a reservoir. Said one person, "I feel I am a very successful virus. With the way these other guys feel, I can sit back and relax, enjoy life and play a guitar. One is going to take care of reproducing and one killing. Why should I worry?" Responded another, "I resent his playing his guitar while I'm panicky!" (Gordon, 1961). The eventual solution stemmed from "calming the oil down by stroking it like a cat," which led to freezing the gooey sample with liquid nitrogen so it could be brought to the surface intact.

Einstein Got Personal

As we will see in Chapter 7, Einstein used the personal analogy method when he imagined himself on a speed-of-light trip through space, which contributed to his theory of relativity.

Imagining yourself to be a problem object or process should stimulate an inside view of the situation—and some new ideas while you are there. What would you be like if you were an extremely efficient racing bike? Leaf rake? Flashlight? Ski parka? Snow blower/remover?

Fantasy Analogy

Wild Wish Fulfillment

With the *fantasy analogy* approach the problem solver thinks of fantastic, far-fetched, perhaps ideal solutions that can lead to creative yet practical ideas. Gordon (1961) saw this method as a sort of Freudian wish-fulfillment. In one of his sessions the task was to invent an air-tight zipper for space suits. In response to the question, "How do we in our wildest fantasies desire the closure to operate?"

Space Suit Closure

(Gordon, 1961, p. 49), group members imagined two rows of insects clasping hands on command to draw the closure tight. This fantasy led to a workable device.

Get Fired Technique

An almost tongue-in-cheek strategy that appears to be a variation of the fantasy analogy method was called the *Get Fired Technique*. As described by synectics thinker George Prince (1968, p. 73), "The idea you develop must be so outrageous and such a violation of common sense and company policy that when you present it to your boss he will immediately fire you." In the example accompanying this quote the problem was to "Devise a liquid cake icing that will firm up when released from a can." The get-fired idea was: "I am going to hire out-of-work West Virginia coal miners—very small ones—and put one in each can. When the person presses the valve, the miner goes to work!" The craziness stimulates the playfulness that facilitates creative thinking (Prince, 1968).

Also Solved Miner Unemployment Problem

Problems That Solved Themselves

The fantasy analogy method includes looking for ideal or perfect solutions, such as having the problem solve itself. Years ago some creative people probably asked: How can we make a carriage propel itself? How can we create a magic drain that will make bones and waste disappear? (Prince, 1982). Consider also: How can we make a refrigerator defrost itself? How can we create a fabric that eliminates ironing? How can we make an oven clean itself? How can we make a forgotten iron shut itself off? Plug in engine diagnosers probably came from, "How can we make the motor tell us what's wrong?" Teachers might pose such questions as: "How can we get the School Board to want to give us a new basketball floor? How can we get the hallways to keep themselves free of litter? How can we get delinquents to want to be honest citizens?" People in business can ask: How can we make the product double its own sales? How can we have employees raise their own morale? What will the ideal kitchen (bathroom, family room, garage) be like in the future?

Use in the Corporation

Use in School

Working Backward from an Ideal Goal

This strategy of looking for perfect, fantastic solutions builds upon the time-tested problem solving method of working backward from an ideal goal. Thinking of what you ideally want, then figuring out how to reach that goal is an effective and creative way to solve problems.

Symbolic Analogy

Compressed Conflict

A fourth synectics technique is called *symbolic analogy*; other names are *compressed conflict* and *book titles*. Your dictionary will call them *oxymorons*. The strategy is to think of a two-word phrase or "book title" that seems self-contradictory, such as "careful haste" or "gentle toughness." The compressed conflict would relate to a particular problem and would stimulate ideas. For example, the phrase "careful haste" might be used by educators or fire fighters to stimulate ideas for quickly and safely evacuating a large school building. "Gentle toughness" might stimulate ideas for designing automobile tires, durable fabrics, or long-distance bicycles.

Stimulates Ideas

In one zany synectics session the problem of designing an ice cube maker led to the problem restatement "How [can we] make an ice tray disappear after ice is made." This definition suggested the analogy of a boy breaking a window—after which he disappears (Prince, 1968). Book titles for boy-breaks-window included *healthful destruction, right wrongness, intelligent mistake*, and *rational impetuousness*. Speculating on examples of rational impetuousness led to an electric eel, which rationally defends itself by impetuously shocking enemies, and from the eel to a material that would shrink at about 20 degrees fahrenheit and release the ice cubes.

Window Breaking Is Impetuous Idea

Electric Eel Invents Ice Cube Maker!

Gordon and Poze (1980b) presented some practice problems to help you create and use paradoxes:

Exercises

Imagine you wish to design a new safety pin that cannot stick the user or open accidentally; it also must be removable and reusable and cost under 5 cents. What are some two-word paradoxes? What are examples of these paradoxes? Do the examples suggest some creative problem solutions?

Imagine you have a littering problem in your school or company, even though there are plenty of trash barrels around. What are some book titles? What examples do the book titles suggest? Do the examples suggest some creative solutions?

An exercise from a synectics workbook, *Teaching is Listening* by Gordon and Poze (1972a), includes a direct analogy, a personal analogy, and illustrates how a symbolic analogy can stimulate ideas:

1. What animal typifies your concept of freedom? (Direct analogy)

   _____

2. Put yourself in the place of the animal you have chosen. Be the thing! Describe what makes you feel and act with so much freedom. (Personal analogy)

   _____

   _____

   _____

3. Sum up your description of the animal you chose by listing the "free" and "unfree" parts of your animal life.

   Free: _____

   _____

   Unfree: _____

   _____

4. Express each of these parts of your life in a single word. Put together these two words and refine them into a poetic, compressed conflict phrase.

   _____   _____

   _____   _____

   _____   _____

5. Circle the phrase you like best. Write an essay about freedom. Use any material you may have developed in this exercise.

Gordon's Equation Form of Synectics

In his book *The New Art of the Possible*, Gordon (1987) sought to teach the use of analogies in creative problem solving by using an equation. The four steps take the form of an analogy that one might find in an intelligence test or thinking skills exercises:

$$\frac{\text{Step 1. Paradox}}{\text{Step 4. (Equivalent)}} = \frac{\text{Step 2. Analogue}}{\text{Step 3. Unique Function}}$$

As an example, let's consider a management problem used by Gendrop (1996), who worked with Gordon himself. Step 1, the problem or issue (stated as a *paradox*) was that the more management encouraged product improvement ideas from sales people, the fewer ideas the salespeople submitted. The Step 2 *analogue* was quicksand. The Step 3 *unique function* was stated as "viscous material with a base molds to the body and creates a suction." The Step 4 *equivalent*—the relationship of the analogue to the paradox—was to give sales people a "solid base" that would encourage ideas instead of sales. To change the focus from sales to ideas, a solution was to release one sales person per month to work on product improvement.

Teaching Synectics Thinking

The Synectics Methods: Information on Techniques, Process, Importance of Analogical Thinking

For students and adults, the synectics methods themselves can be material for lessons on (a) creative thinking techniques, (b) the nature of the creative process, and (c) the importance of analogical thinking in creativity. For students of all ages, including professional adults, Gordon and his colleagues have published workbooks and text books filled with exercises aimed at strengthening skills of analogical thinking, and aimed at helping the reader understand the creative power of analogical thinking. The following are similar to exercises in Gordon (1974a), Gordon and Poze (1971, 1972a, 1972b, 1980b), Stanish (1977), and Davis (1996a).

Exercises

What animal is like a bass fiddle? Why?

A hamburger is like a _____ because _____.

How is a jar of paste like a school bell?

Which is stronger, a brick wall or a young tree? Why?

Which is heaviest, a boulder or a sad heart? Why?

What color is sadness? Why?

In what way can coolness be seen?

In what ways can softness be heard?

What is another sound like a dog's bark?

How is life like a flashlight battery?

Which grows faster, your self-confidence or an oak tree?

What could have given a cave dweller the idea for a spear? What was the connection?

A parachute is like what animal? Why?

Why is a calendar like a mirror?

What would it be like to be inside a lemon?

If you were a pencil, how would it feel to get sharpened? To get chewed on? To get worn down to a stub?

When you are happy you are like a _____.

When you are busy you are like a _____.

How is someone who steals like a hungry shark?

How is Shirley-the-Shoplifter like a good case of the measles?

How is vandalizing like sticking your finger in a light socket?

How is a friendly, helpful person like a hot fudge sundae?

How is a good education like a good dream?

How is an iceberg like a creative idea?

If a classroom were a lawn, what would the weeds be? How do the weeds affect the rest of the class?

It Is Important, Convinced?

Analogical and metaphorical thinking lie at the core of much creativity. Further, it may be possible to directly teach analogical thinking strategies, such as the synectics methods, or to indirectly strengthen skills of analogical thinking with practice and exercise.

SUMMARY

Most creative ideas are in some way born in analogical or metaphorical thinking. One sees a similarity or makes a connection between the present problem and a related situation. The credits "was inspired by" and "is based upon" imply an analogical or metaphoric source for the artistic, literary, scientific, or technological innovation.

The analogical connection may appear suddenly, as in an insight, or require a painstaking search.

Borrowing and transferring ideas usually is a genuine and legitimate creative process, not plagiarism. However, there are ambiguous cases.

Analogical and metaphorical thinking appear most obviously in the Big Idea stage of the two-stage model described in Chapter 5.

Many classical and contemporary music composers have used existing tunes as the basis of their compositions (e.g., Tchaikovsky, Copland, Barry Manilow).

The seemingly funniest political cartoons and cartoon strips are analogically based upon popular movies, well-known TV advertisements, children's stories, news events, and other sources.

Examples of analogical thinking in science and invention included Gutenberg's movable type and printing press, the battery, the steam engine, a strategy for building underwater tunnels, the cotton gin, and the air brake.

Shakespeare's Big Ideas apparently came from identifiable sources. Countless movies and TV shows have been "inspired by" contemporary and historical events, biographies, the Bible, classic and contemporary literature, mythology and legend, and in the case of *Moonlighting*, even holidays.

Actors and actresses may analogically pattern their characters after personality types they know.

Ideas for architecture and clothes design may be borrowed from other countries and other times.

In problem solving one can use analogical thinking to stimulate ideas by asking such questions as: What else is like this? What have others done? What could we copy?

Synectics methods are deliberate analogical thinking techniques developed by William J. J. Gordon. He made some spontaneous (unconscious) techniques conscious and teachable.

With direct analogy the thinker looks for ways that related problems have been solved, especially in nature.

With personal analogy one achieves new perspectives by becoming part of the problem.

Fantasy analogy is a wild wish-fulfillment approach, including looking for ideal or perfect solutions. Prince's "get fired" technique seems a variation of fantasy analogy.

Symbolic analogy is using two-word compressed conflicts to stimulate ideas.

In a 1987 book Gordon recommended the use of a four-step equation for using analogical thinking in problem solving: 1. Paradox, 2. Analogue, 3. Unique Function, and 4. Equivalent (the solution).

Teaching the synectics methods themselves helps the learner to understand creative thinking techniques, the nature of the creative process, and the importance of analogical thinking. Exercises may strengthen analogical thinking abilities.

Analogical and metaphorical thinking are extremely important in creativity.

Creative Inspiration through Analogical Thinking

Self-Test: Key Concepts, Terms, and Names

Briefly define or explain each of these.

Analogical thinking _____

_____

Direct analogy _____

_____

Personal analogy _____

_____

Fantasy analogy _____

_____

Symbolic analogy _____

_____

Why does your author think these names are important?

Bill Shakespeare _____

_____

William J. J. Gordon _____

_____

Let's Think about It

1. Imagine that you are chairperson of a civic group, and you need to raise $600 to take 50 poor children on a summer field trip to visit a science museum and a university campus.

   Find ideas by asking yourself: What have others done? What could we copy? What has worked before?

   a. _____

   b. _____

   c. _____

   d. _____

   e. _____

   f. _____

   g. _____

   h. _____

   i. _____

   j. _____

2. Look at the cartoon exercises in Inset 6.2. Use the *Original Scenario* section to find cartoon ideas for at least two CURRENT political or other newsworthy situations. You can draw or just verbally explain your ideas.

   For example, "Tom Tom the Piper's son" could be used to satirize any example of theft or invasion; the "Mirror, mirror on the wall" scene from the Snow White fairy tale could portray any seemingly charming person who turns out to be unpleasant.

   Cartoon a. Situation _____

   Cartoon b. Situation _____

3. Use the *direct analogy* strategy to think of ideas for removing three inches of water from your basement floor. (E.g., ask "How do animals, plants, or other phenomena in nature move water from here to there?)

   _____

   _____

   _____

   _____

4. Use the *personal analogy* method to help you think of ideas for encouraging elementary children to finish their cafeteria lunches, and not waste food. (E.g., ask "What would I be like if I were a lunch that was ALWAYS 100 percent eaten?" Or "What would my attitude or personality be if I were a kid that ALWAYS finished his or her lunch?" Or "What kind of cafeteria would I be if I STRONGLY encouraged kids to finish their lunches?")

_____

_____

_____

_____

5. Use the *fantasy analogy* method to think of ideas for improving school attendance ("What in my wildest imagination would make kids hate to miss school?")

_____

_____

_____

_____

6. How might you use the *symbolic analogy* "cheap luxury" to help you find ideas for taking a trip to Yellowstone Park with equally poor college friends.

_____

_____

_____

_____

7. You work for an advertising agency. Your boss wants you to come up with some GREAT magazine advertising ideas for *Micro-Wizards* computer company, which just produced a new super-fast computer with a gigantic memory.

   a. How would you use analogical thinking to find ideas; that is, how specifically might you borrow, modify, or build on others' successful ideas (without "stealing")?

   _____

   _____

   _____

165

b. What are some of your ideas?

_____

_____

_____

8. a. What Biblical, historical, or contemporary events do you think might make some good movies (perhaps in a year 2010 setting?)

_____

_____

_____

_____

_____

_____

b. Where else might you find inspiration for new movies?

_____

_____

_____

_____

techniques of creative thinking
increasing your idea-finding capability

[*Scene: Tavern on Park Avenue in New York City. Dr. Malaprop is slopping down his fifth mug of Pflatz Light when Sam Straightman approaches.*]

Sam Straightman: Excuse me, aren't you the famous Dr. Malaprop? Can I buy you a beer?

Dr. Malaprop: Why thanks, sonny. I'll have a Pflatz Light, and I appreciate the jester of good will!

Straightman: Say, have you done any interesting traveling lately, like to Panguitch, Utah?

Malaprop: Oh yes, definitely. My wife and I are both expired now and so we travel a great deal—London, Athens, Moscow, Panguitch, Anchorage . . . it just goes on and on *ad mausoleum*. But we do get tired of those hotel signs that say "No Vagrancy." You know, just last week we strolled Shawn's-Easy-Way in Paris. I saw some very poor people there and gave each one about ten cranks.

Straightman: You mean francs?

Malaprop: Of course. That's what I said. Yes, I have a very great affliction for poor people. It's fun to hold them out. I suppose they all suffer from exterminating circumstances.

Straightman: You're famous for your creative writing, Dr. Malaprop. Where does your creativity come from?

Malaprop: I'm glad you asked. Creativity is so impudent! I'm absolutely enameled of the topic.

Straightman: And where do you get your ideas?

Malaprop: Well, for one thing I use lots of analogies and matadors. And I have personal techniques that I use with absolutely deliberate porpoise. All creative writers use personal creative thinking techniques.

Straightman: Tell me about your porpoises. Is your fish bill high?

Dr. Malaprop: (*Sneezes!*) Excuse me! I think I have a defection in my androids. Now, what was your question? I gotta' hurry off to my tax advisor H & R Clock.

167

Straightman: Never mind, Dr. Malaprop. Are you sure you won't have another Pflatz light? You're such a clone!

I maintain that there is a desperate social need for the creative behavior of creative individuals . . . in education . . . the sciences . . . industry . . . individual and family life . . . [and] our leisure time activities.

Carl R. Rogers

Techniques for Creating New Perceptions, New Combinations

In Chapter 5 we examined the creative process in three ways, as a series of steps one may take in solving a problem creatively, as a sudden perceptual change or transformation, and as ideas in mental imagery that are modified and combined. Chapter 6 continued our analysis of the creative process with a look at the most common process, often a deliberate technique, of analogical and metaphorical thinking. This chapter extends the technique orientation of Chapter 6 by reviewing other creative thinking strategies that creative people use to find ideas and problem solutions—strategies that create the new perceptions and idea combinations.

Using Techniques Is a Creative Process

Relative to traditional literature, it is novel to categorize creativity techniques as *processes* of creativity. However, in reading this and the preceding chapter on analogical and metaphorical thinking, it should be obvious that following a conscious procedure that leads to new ideas certainly is a creative process.

This Chapter: Personal, Standard, Techniques

This chapter is divided into two main sections. First, *personal* creative thinking techniques are individual strategies that are developed and used by every creatively productive person. Second, *standard* techniques are strategies that are taught in many creativity books, courses, and workshops. It is important to emphasize that *in every case* the particular standard technique originated as some creative person's personal technique for producing ideas and solving problems. Like the Synectics methods, these strategies were made conscious, knowable, and teachable.

PERSONAL CREATIVE THINKING TECHNIQUES

Used by All Creative People

Personal techniques are methods that are developed and used by all creative people, regardless of the subject or content of his or her creations. The topic lies at the core of such central questions as "Where do ideas come from?" and "What is the nature of internal creative process?" The reader will detect that the majority of personal creative thinking techniques involve analogical thinking—borrowing, transferring, and modifying ideas and problem solutions.

Majority of Personal Techniques Are Analogical

Examples Everywhere

After you become sensitive to this notion of personal creative thinking techniques, you will see them continually. For example, while looking at a movie, TV show, paperback book, political cartoon, or new consumer product or while listening to a new hit tune you may understand where the creative person found the idea. The particular innovation might be recognized as a "spin-off" or modification of an earlier idea, a combination of several familiar ideas, or the innovator may have analogically based the idea on a news event, an historical event, or an earlier melody, book, movie, etc.

Modifications, Combinations

Idea Sources

Einstein: Mental Experiments

As an example in the science area, Einstein used what he called "mental experiments" to stimulate new perspectives and ideas. For example, in what seems to be a personal analogy, Einstein once imagined himself as a tiny being riding through space on a ray of light, which contributed to his general theory of relativity.

In art we find recurrent subjects and styles with every creatively productive artist, reflecting his or her personal creative thinking techniques. Picasso, for

Disassembling Picasso

Degas: Ballerinas

Gauguin: South Pacific

Seurat: Pointillism

Is Lautrec's Technique Too Loose?

Utrillo: On the Street

DaVinci: Faces for Supper

Mythology, Bible, History

example, deliberately disassembled faces and other elements and put them back together in more original arrangements. He also used analogical and metaphorical thinking, most obviously in his African, Harlequin, blue, and pink (rose) periods during which his paintings were "inspired by" particular themes.

Edward Degas borrowed the beauty and grace of ballerinas, and sometimes thoroughbred horses, for his famous painting style. Renoir is noted for his soft, pastel, frilly and flowery female subjects and still lifes. Paul Gauguin found ideas in South Pacific natives and settings, again and again. Georges Seurat used a "dot" painting style (pointillism), usually featuring people, water and sailboats. Van Gogh's style—dashes instead of dots—was admitted to be influenced by his friend George Seurat. The unique style of Toulouse-Lautrec's heavily outlined, tall, and cartoonlike subjects in evening dress also is familiar. Maurice Utrillo used simple street scenes, devoid of humans. Even Leonardo da Vinci reportedly wandered Italian streets, sketchbook in hand, to find interesting faces for his painting *The Last Supper*. Throughout the history of art, ideas for paintings have been taken from mythology, the Bible, or historical events. Ideas come from somewhere, and techniques can be used to pry them loose from that somewhere.

Professional comedians also use personal creative-thinking techniques, both for their unique type of humor and for their original delivery style. As illustrated, more or less, at the outset of this chapter, one technique is to use funny malapropisms, a routine borrowed from comedian Norm Crosby (as were about half

All creative people develop personal styles and idea-finding techniques. This creative chap operates his handle with a distinctive creative flair. "I can do it with my left foot up, too," says Charlie. (The Museum of Modern Art/Film Stills Archive.)

Rickles' Insults

Rivers: Even Ripley Wouldn't Believe It!

Does Dangerfield Have a Poor Self-Concept?

Star Wars Aided by Reading Epics

Horse Opera Formula?

Creative People Use, Are Aware of Techniques

1. Help Students Understand Techniques

Modification, Combination Legitimate Creativity

2. Can Adopt Existing Techniques

Additional Techniques

of the malapropisms). Don Rickles insults people, using the same insults again and again ("Shut up dummy, you're makin' a fool of yourself!").

Joan Rivers and Rodney Dangerfield both continually put themselves down. Rivers claims that when she was a child she was so ugly her father sent a picture of her to Ripley's *Believe it or Not*. They sent it back with a note "We don't believe it!" Dangerfield's most famous line is "I don't get no respect," always accompanied by sweating and straightening his tie. When he was born the doctor told his mother "I did everything I could, but he's gonna' be okay!" Said Dangerfield, "I had to share my sand box with two cats. They kept tryin' to cover me up! Once I called this girl for a date, she said 'Sure, come on over, there's nobody home.' So I went over an' nobody was home! Last week my psychiatrist said I was crazy. I told him I wanted a second opinion an' he said, 'Okay, I think you're ugly too!' "

Early movie comic Charlie Chaplin invented his still-imitated walk, and combined comedy with sympathy and tenderness. Rival W. C. Fields made us laugh with sober surprises—"I love children, if they are properly cooked."

A new generation of women comics use the shock value of brash sex and earthy language for their laughs. Nope, no examples; see cable TV after 9:00 P.M.

The *Star Wars* series, released in the 1970s and again in 1997, are among the most successful Hollywood movies ever. They were based partly upon an effective personal creative thinking technique used by movie maker George Lucas. While writing the script for the original *Star Wars*, Lucas read books on mythology. Said Lucas in a *Time* magazine interview, "I wanted Star Wars to have an epic quality, and so I went back to the epics." Thus we find a young man who must prove his manhood to himself and to his father; he rescues a fair maiden in distress; he has an older and wiser mentor (actually two, Ben Kenobi and Yoda); and he battles with a villain, Darth Vader. Many western movies have been built around the same epic principles.

Examples of personal creative thinking techniques probably are as endless as the number of highly visible creative people. Probably all are aware of most of their idea-finding techniques and their unique, creative styles.

Encouraging Personal Creative Thinking Techniques

The following are three general ways to help students and others develop personal creative thinking techniques. First, as presented mainly in Chapters 5 and 6 and this chapter, we can help students understand deliberate methods and techniques that are used by even extraordinarily creative people to "find" ideas. This helps demystify creativity and helps convince new innovators that they also can build upon, modify, and combine existing ideas without feeling uncreative.

Second, the techniques presented in Chapters 5, 6, and the present chapter can become "personal" creative thinking techniques that a person may adjust to fit his or her personal style of creative thinking. That is, the Creative Problem Solving model (Chapter 5); the Synectics methods of direct analogy, personal analogy, fantasy analogy, symbolic analogy, and Gordon's four-step analogy equation (Chapter 6); along with the standard techniques reviewed in this chapter become "personal" techniques—if they work for an individual— when they are adopted as perhaps habitual ways of creatively finding ideas and solving problems.

The following are additional recurrent, deliberate techniques for finding ideas and viewpoints.

1. Consistent with analogical thinking, we can review successful styles or idea sources used by persons with similar types of problems, for example, in art, music, advertising, journalism, creative writing, speaking, theater, business, or science research.

2. Also analogical in nature, we can look for parallel problems and solutions, for example, in books in one's field, the Internet, history or travel books, encyclopedias, catalogs, the Yellow Pages, and the like.

3. We always can modify, combine, adapt, and improve present ideas.

4. We can prod our imaginations by asking "What would happen if . . . ?"

5. We can start with an "ideal" or "perfect" goal or solution—such as having the problem solve itself—and work backward to deduce what is required to reach that goal.

6. We can ask ourselves how the problem will be approached or solved 25, 100, or 200 years in the future. At present, the Arthur Anderson School of the Future program in Oakland, California, is designing teaching and learning systems partly by speculating on how students will be educated 50 years in the future.

3. Learn from Doing Creativity, and from Instruction

Third, personal creative thinking techniques are acquired in the course of doing creative things or from instruction by people who use such techniques. Therefore, it is important for students to become involved in creative activities. In school these might include art, photography, creative writing, theater, journalism, physics labs, computer projects, or other activities that require creative thinking and problem solving. Two national school programs, *Odyssey of the Mind* (OM) and *Future Problem Solving* (FPS), are designed to stimulate active creative problem solving (see Chapter 9; also Davis & Rimm, 1998).

In the corporation, practicing creativity can take innumerable forms, for example, thinking of and implementing ideas to increase efficiency, employee morale, or production; reducing waste, costs, and overhead; and designing new products, new processes, new methods, new procedures, new marketing techniques, new automation systems, and new uses for computers.

Visiting Professionals

Visitors also can teach personal creative thinking techniques. For example, in the schools a visiting professional program can help students understand the creative processes of a successful artist, writer, scientist, or business entrepreneur. In the corporation it can be very enlightening to hear about creativity and idea-finding techniques either from persons who are themselves creatively productive, or from consultants acquainted with blocks to creativity and techniques for sparking new viewpoints, perceptions, analogies, and idea combinations.

Consultants

Creative Models

A tremendous benefit of visiting creative talent is that these people serve as models—successful examples of creative personalities and creative minds to whom many people are rarely exposed.

STANDARD CREATIVE THINKING TECHNIQUES

Taught in University, Professional Creativity Courses

Learnable by Students

There are several well-known methods for producing new ideas and new idea combinations which, as we mentioned, are taught in most university and professional creativity training courses. The strategies also may be taught to high school students, middle school students, and even elementary students. It is important to emphasize that the techniques are intended to *supplement*—not replace—one's intuitive idea supply. When you have a sticky problem and run out of ideas, one or more of these techniques will help.

As an illustration of the usefulness of deliberate imagination-prodding methods, Davis (1996a, 1996b) used, as teaching devices, the brainstorming and reverse brainstorming procedures presented in this chapter, plus analogies (Chapter 6), visualization (Chapter 11), "What would happen if . . . ?" (Chapter 11), plus other empathy-stimulating activities in two character education books, an idea book for

Creativity Techniques Can Help Teach Values

teachers plus a self-study workbook for students. The goal was to prompt students to think (creatively, futuristically) about and make commitments to positive values; to help them understand both the personal benefits of productive values and the life-damaging consequences of poor values. As some examples:

Brainstorming. "Why should we be honest? List all of the ideas you can think of." "What happens to people when they drop out of high school? Let's think of all the ideas we can." "How many ways can you think of to save electricity at home?" "What rights to ALL of us have—children, parents, teachers, store clerks, and everyone else?"

Reverse Brainstorming. "How many ways can we think of to show that we just are not to be trusted?" "How many ways can we think of to be unfriendly and to hurt the feelings of a new student in class (or in the neighborhood)?" "How many ways can we violate each others' rights?"

Analogical Thinking. "How is being rude to people like a flat tire on a bicycle?" "How is responsibility like a good wrist watch?" "How is a good education like a good dream?"

Visualization. "Imagine that you are a big, dumb, pushy bully . . . you see a smaller child and you yell, 'Hey stupid, is that your face or a pile of garbage?' . . . You laugh because you think you are funny . . . In class you turn to Maggie in the next seat and whisper, 'Hey Lanky, how come you're so tall an' skinny? Weather okay up there? Glad I ain't a toothpick like you!' [etc., etc.]"

What Would Happen If . . . ? "What would happen if everyone were a thief?" "If nobody were friendly to YOU?" "If nobody accepted responsibility for their bad behavior?" "If the school were vandalized every night?"

Intuitive and Forced Creativity

Intuitive vs. Forced Creativity

We should note the distinction between *intuitive* creativity and *forced* creativity. Intuitive creativity, as the name suggests, refers to the unpredictable inspirations that may or may not appear when and where you need them. There is nothing wrong with inspiration, intuition, and spontaneous creative thought; they solve problems and keep the topic of creativity interesting. With forced creativity, a person or group consciously decides to sit down and creatively attack a problem using one or more techniques to clarify the problem and generate creative ideas for it.

BRAINSTORMING

Should We Call It "BSing"?

Corporate Uses Are Unlimited

Anyone interested in creative processes or creative problem solving should try group brainstorming. Newcomers to brainstorming always are impressed by the surprising ideas and perceptions of others—ideas that in the group setting stimulate or "cross-fertilize" further ideas and viewpoints, sometimes called "idea hitch-hikes." Brainstorming undoubtedly is the most popular form of forced creativity, and is used regularly to prod flights of professional imagination. Corporate and business uses of brainstorming are without limit, for example, in developing new products, in improving existing products or processes, or in solving marketing, advertising, or personnel problems. In the classroom a flexible teacher will schedule brainstorming sessions either for practice in creative thinking or for solv-

Classroom: Creativity Exercise or Solving Real Problems

ing real problems, such as high absenteeism, messy school grounds, traffic safety, bicycle thefts, drug use, raising money, or selling play tickets.

Reasons for the popularity of brainstorming are not particularly mysterious:

Reasons, Reasons

It's intuitively appealing.

It's simple.

It's fun.

It's therapeutic.

It works.

Deferred Judgment: High Intuitive Appeal

The high *intuitive* appeal stems from the single hard-and-fast rule, the principle of *deferred judgment*—the seemingly self-evident notion is that criticism and harsh evaluation will interfere with flexible idea production. The originator of brainstorming, Alex Osborn (1963), simply noted that one cannot be critical and creative at the same time. Makes sense. Deferred judgment produces the essential *creative atmosphere* (creative attitudes, psychological safety) that is an essential ingredient for innovative thinking.

Creative Atmosphere

Simple Enough for You Kids

Brainstorming is *simple* because, again, the only strict rule is no criticism or evaluation. No training is needed beyond a few minutes' clarification of the groundrules (below). Even young children can brainstorm real or imaginary problem, thereby exercising their creative abilities, learning attitudes and principles of effective thinking, and learning a creativity technique.

Fun

Regarding *fun*, professionals sometimes feel guilty about being paid for having such a swell time. New idea combinations are often humorous. Note that jokes, like other creative ideas, also are made of surprising idea combinations.

Therapeutic

The *therapy* comes from the enjoyable session itself, from being asked for ideas (which is rare in many organizations), from the chance to speak up, kick around ideas and solve problems, and from satisfying basic and often stifled needs to create and construct.

Effective

And it *works*, whether the goal is to stimulate imagination, flexibility and creative attitudes as a training exercise—for children or professionals—or to solve some elusive corporation problem. For example, a Denver postmaster and eleven staff brainstormed the problem "What can be done to reduce man-hour usage?" Some of the 121 ideas led to a saving of 12,666 man hours (okay, person hours) in the following nine weeks. A Pittsburgh department store, stuck with some chair-covering material, brainstormed "other uses" for the fabric, leading to advertising that sold the entire stock in a week. A brainstorming group at Heinz Foods spent just one hour on the problem "How can we help increase the sales of products made at this factory?" They generated more and better ideas than a special committee had produced in ten ordinary conferences. Reynolds Metals brainstormed some "new and more convenient ways to package a client's cornmeal mix." Some of the ideas were included in a prize-winning and sales-winning package. Finally, the success of the New York advertising agency Batten, Barton, Durstine, and Osborn—the late Alex Osborn's own organization—is good evidence for the effectiveness of brainstorming.

Post Office: Saving Person Hours?

Unusual Uses Problem

Heinz: 57 Varieties of Increased Sales

Corny Solution Wins Award!

And Don't Forget BBD & O

The four groundrules of brainstorming are uncomplicated:

Defer Criticism and Evaluation

1. *Criticism is ruled out.* This is deferred judgment, which means, as delicately stated in *Imagination Express* (Davis & DiPego, 1973), "You don't want some crab knocking down people's ideas before they have a chance." Deferred judgment produces the receptive, encouraging creative atmosphere. The difference is reinforcement, not punishment, for innovative, perhaps even far-fetched ideas.

Wild and Crazy Can Suggest Practical and Useful

2. *Freewheeling is welcomed.* Said Osborn, the wilder the idea the better. Apparently preposterous ideas can suggest imaginative yet workable solutions. You are more likely to find a creative idea by being wild first and "taming down" the idea second, rather than criticising, evaluating, and editing as you go. This rule supplements Rule number 1 and prepares the thinker to try to be imaginative, to look for different and unusual solutions, to view the problem from novel perspectives, to constructively accept the off-the-wall ideas of others, and to use wild ideas as springboards for workable ideas. In one of the your author's classroom brainstorming sessions, it was suggested that a movie theater could be quickly emptied by collapsible seats that slide patrons out the front of the room. This free-wheeler was followed immediately by the more practical idea of seats that fold down so that in an emergency patrons could rapidly exit by walking over them.

It's That Five Percent!

Are wild ideas wasted? Well, yes. It is assumed that about 95 percent of the ideas will not merit further exploration. The other 5 percent may help solve problems in imaginative and effective ways.

With More Ideas, More Good Ideas

3. *Quantity is wanted.* This principle reflects the purpose of the brainstorming session, which is to produce a long list of ideas. The mathematically sensible rationale is that with a larger number of ideas there is a better chance of finding good ideas. Typically, ideas produced later in the session—after the quick-and-easy common ones are out—will be more imaginative.

Hitch-Hiking Is Legal

4. *Combination and improvement are sought.* This lengthens the idea list. Actually, during the session thinkers spontaneously will hitch-hike on each other's ideas, one idea inspiring a bunch more.

Leadership Simple

Use Chalkboard

It is comparatively simple to run a brainstorming session. The leader reviews the four groundrules, along with procedural details. For example, some groups keep a small bell in the center of the table to ding anyone who criticizes or even asks for justification for an idea ("Why did you suggest that?"). Some leaders prefer to go around the table, letting each participant speak in turn, but allowing someone with a pressing idea to interrupt. It is best to write ideas on a chalkboard where they will be available for combination, modification, and non-duplication. Stenographers and tape recorders also have been used.

Leader Organizes, Explains Rules, Is Focal Point

The leader's role is straight-forward. In addition to organizing the session, explaining the groundrules, and reviewing the problem, he or she occasionally asks "Does anyone else have an idea?" Sometimes the leader serves mainly as place for participants to stare and to address their ideas.

Ask for Facts, Alternative Definitions

A more sophisticated leader may take suggestions from the CPS model (Chapter 5) and ask "Well folks, what do we know about the problem?" (fact-finding) or "How else can we define, view, approach, or broaden the problem?" (problem-finding). Helping the group broaden the problem can be especially valuable. For example, instead of redesigning heating elements on an electric range the group can look for innovative ways to "heat food"; instead of building a better mouse trap the group can think of ways to "get ride of mice." We noted in Chapter 5 that asking "Why" after each problem definition produces increasingly more general problem statements.

Group Composition

In addition to the four main groundrules, Osborn (1963) suggested a few more procedures for effective brainstorming. Group size should be about 10 or 12. An ideal panel consists of a leader, an associate leader, about five regular members, and about five guests. Note, however, that one can brainstorm problems *alone* or with a 500-person audience.

Different Experience, but Same Rank

To increase the source and variety of ideas, members should be heterogeneous in training, experience, and gender. In most circumstances, rank should be roughly equal. Imagine the intimidating and stifling effect of Microsoft President Bill Gates sitting in on managerial-level brainstorming session.

48 Hours Before, 48 Hours After

With serious problems (not "What can a clever chipmunk do while blind-folded?"), the problem should be circulated 48 hours in advance so that members can come in with ideas. A follow-up request for ideas may be circulated 48 hours after the session in order to salvage ideas that participants wish they would have thought of at the time.

For Silent Periods

Idea-Spurring Questions

During silent periods, if any, the leader may ask the quieter members for ideas, pull out some shirt-pocket ideas of his or her own that were prepared in advance for such an occasion, or else suggest a new way to look at the problem. The leader also can roll out Osborn's *idea-spurring questions* (below), which Osborn frequently used in brainstorming sessions.

Do You Really Need a Barnstorming Group?

Incidentally, a critical presession consideration is whether to use a group to solve the problem in the first place. Even Osborn (1963) recognized that "Despite the many virtues of group brainstorming, individual ideation is usually more usable and can be just as productive."

Some Ideas Will Look Good

Evaluation Criteria, Evaluation Matrix

Assuming the group produces a nice, long list of ideas—some absurd, some wild and innovative, and others quite serious—what then? This group or another group can evaluate the ideas in any number of ways. Realistically, a few ideas sometimes simply will look darn good, and they probably are. This simplifies idea evaluation. However, if a potential solution may have messy complications or implications, it is possible to brainstorm criteria for evaluation and use a formal evaluation matrix as explained in Chapter 5. Some evaluation criteria can focus directly on those potential complications and implications. Some possible criteria are:

Criteria

Will it work? Will it do the job? Does it improve present methods?

Are the materials available? Are needed personnel available?

Does it reduce costs? Eliminate unnecessary work? Increase production? Improve quality? Improve safety? Improve the use of manpower? Improve working conditions? Improve morale?

Does the idea really "grab" people? Do people ask "Why didn't I think of that?"

Is it timely?

Is it a temporary or permanent solution?

Will it cost too much?

Is it too complicated? Is it simple and direct?

Is it suitable? Will others accept it (higher management, the public, our union, suppliers' unions, parents, the secretary, your mother)?

Is it legal?

Are there patent infringements?

Are we trying to swat a fly with dynamite?

In the classroom or corporation, using objective criteria for the evaluation process serves several purposes:

Purposes for Using Criteria

1. Using criteria helps us evaluate ideas systematically, and therefore to solve a problem in a reasonable, mutually agreed upon way.

2. It helps children and adults learn to evaluate as part of the overall creative problem solving process.

3. It requires people to consider many aspects of a problem, including aspects that did not occur to anyone during the session

4. In some cases it can help a group explore its own value system relative to the problem at hand (e.g., "How can we save money training school bus drivers?")

5. Finally, evaluation can prove that thinking of "silly" and "far-fetched" ideas truly can result in good and practical solutions to problems.

Variations

Stop-and-Go Brainstorming

Variations of brainstorming may be useful in particular circumstances. The first is *stop-and-go brainstorming* in which short, about 10-minute periods of unrestrained free-wheeling are interrupted by brief evaluations. The evaluations help keep the group on target and/or help select profitable directions ("Say, let's think some more about improving traffic safety near the school specifically for joggers and bike riders"). The second is the *Phillips 66* technique for use with large audiences. After the problem is explained, small groups of six will brainstorm for six minutes, after which each group reports either all or its best ideas to the larger group.

Phillips 66 Is a Gas

Reverse Brainstorming

The third variation is an extremely potent one. Fun, too. With *reverse brainstorming* new viewpoints and perceptions are found by turning around the basic problem: How can we increase costs? Increase waste? Run up the light bill? How can we stimulate absenteeism? How can we promote drug use? Increase traffic or factory accidents? Reduce sales? Increase complaints? Suppress creative thinking? With reverse brainstorming the participants usually list what in reality is actually happening.

Brainwriting

Brainwriting is a quieter version of brainstorming that capitalizes on idea hitchhiking. Members of each small group are instructed to write down an idea or problem solution, then pass the paper to person on the right. The next person may:

1. Use the idea to stimulate another idea, and write the new idea on the paper.

2. Modify the idea and write down the modification.

3. Write down a completely new idea.

The process is continued until the sheets circulate back to the original owner. Ideas are discussed further and perhaps informally or formally evaluated.

Whole Brain Approach

Herrmann Is No Half-Wit

Osborn recommended that an effective brainstorming group be composed of persons with different training and experience. William E. Herrmann's "whole brain" approach, brought to you by his Whole Brain Corporation, is a variation on this theme. His underlying theory is that different people are strong in different thought processes. Specifically, a person might be outstanding in *analytical, verbal, intuitive,* or *emotional* abilities, each of which is assumed to be controlled by a different part of the brain. Herrmann devised a questionnaire that identifies the thinking ability dominant in each person. He then organizes creative thinking groups that have each type of thought represented. In essence, the group has a "whole brain" that is strong in all of his identified thought processes (Smith, 1985).

Herrmann's exact strategy might be difficult to implement without hiring Mr. Herrmann himself. However, the apparently successful approach underscores the significance of heterogeneity in brainstorming group composition—in training, experience, gender, and particular thinking gifts.

Electronic Brainstorming

Someone combined the concept of *brainstorming* with *modern electronics* to produce *electronic brainstorming*. It was bound to happen—if Edison did not invent light bulbs, someone else would have. A general term is *Group Support Systems* (GSS), which refers to electronic systems that help work groups solve problems by improving interpersonal communication and structuring the discussion and decision making. According to Siau (1995), GSS typically aids communication in the four areas of (1) generating ideas or plans, (2) making decisions, (3) resolving conflicts (e.g., of viewpoints or power), and (4) seeking consensus (e.g., for executing ideas). Brainstorming falls in category 1. Voice messaging (audio) and email (text/graphics) are two electronic methods that do not require simultaneous participation of members in a single location. Said Siau (1995, p. 211), electronic brainstorming "transcends the time and space constraints that burden groups who meet face-to-face; namely, that all of their members must be at the same place at the same time."

Siau noted the traditional advantage of brainstorming over individual problem solving—the increased number of individuals with diverse backgrounds and experiences who are exposed to the "cross-fertilizing" ideas of others. On the downside, three disadvantages of conventional brainstorming groups are: (1) *production blocking*, which is withholding ideas simply because only one person at a time can talk; (2) *evaluation apprehension*, the reluctance to suggest ideas, perhaps incomplete or poorly developed ones, because they might be criticized; and (3) *social loafing* (free-riding), the tendency to invest less effort in group projects because members can sit back and leave the work to others.

Electronic brainstorming seems to have the advantages but none of the disadvantages of conventional brainstorming groups. Specifically, because many individuals are contributing the diversity of viewpoints and suggestions excites further creativity. Also, with electronic brainstorming production blocking virtually disappears—the ideas are available for consideration at each member's convenience. Since there is no face-to-face interaction, electronic brainstorming reduces the problem of evaluation apprehension. If the input is anonymous, and it can be, evaluation apprehension essentially is eliminated.

Electronic brainstorming groups seem to outperform verbally interacting brainstorming groups, as well as nominal groups (a raggedy bunch of non-interacting individuals), suggesting that social loafing also may not be a problem. Overall, according to Nunamaker, Applegate, and Konsynski (1987), "the automated version of the brainstorming model appears to neutralize many of the group effects that have been responsible for poor performance of group brainstorming in the past."

Note that electronic brainstorming solves the problem of limiting the number of participants to the size of the available room. It also removes the problem of some persons being unavailable at a given time. It even removes the difficulty of inviting eminently qualified persons from distant locations. Space and time constraints are indeed eliminated.

For completeness, we should note that Siau named three types of GSS conferences that solve the space problem, but not the time one ("Gee whiz, can't we have the session at any other time except Monday at 11:00?"). *Synchronous video systems, telephone conferences,* and *interactive computer conferences* allow persons at diverse locations to participate in the same brainstorming session, but all must be available simultaneously.

GSS: Improves Communication, Structures Discussion and Decision Making

Voice Messaging, Email

Production Blocking

Evaluation Apprehension

Social Loafing

No Production Blocking, Reduced Evaluation Apprehension

Reduced Social Loafing

Eliminates Space and Time Problems

Three GSS Types Eliminate Only the Space Problem

Cautions about Brainstorming

In 1963 Osborn offered a number of cautions about brainstorming. His warnings likely apply to electronic brainstorming as well as to traditional 12-person groups in Room 251 at 10:30 A.M. His main admonition was simply that brainstorming is not a cure-all for every person or organization needing effective solutions for difficult problems. Brainstorming may fail to provide the creative breakthroughs that were anticipated. Osborn suggested three reasons for some disappointments. First, the organizers and members may not be following the recommended procedures. Second, they may have unrealistically expected miracles in the first place. Third, some individuals can be more creative alone than when in groups. Again, all forced creativity techniques should supplement, not replace, an individual's intuitive, original thinking.

ATTRIBUTE LISTING

Brainstorming is a general thinking strategy that mainly requires creative attitudes and a creative atmosphere. Attribute listing is a more specific technique for generating new ideas that, in fact, can be used within a brainstorming session.

Inset 7.1
The Attribute Listing Method*

Some breakfast cereals are shaped like tiny little letter O's. Let's invent some new breakfast cereals by thinking of some different *shapes, flavors, colors*, and *sizes*. These are four *qualities* of breakfast cereals, right? Be imaginative.

SHAPES	FLAVORS	COLORS	SIZES
_____	_____	_____	_____
_____	_____	_____	_____
_____	_____	_____	_____
_____	_____	_____	_____
_____	_____	_____	_____
_____	_____	_____	_____
_____	_____	_____	_____
_____	_____	_____	_____

Robert Crawford (1978), the designer of attribute listing, and who in 1931 at the University of Nebraska taught probably the very first creativity course, argued that "Each time we take a [creative] step we do it by changing an attribute or quality of something, or else by applying that same quality or attribute to some other thing." Attribute listing is therefore both a *theory* of the creative process and a practical creative thinking *technique*. Following Crawford's definition, there are two forms of attribute listing: (1) *attribute modifying* and (2) *attribute transferring*. Either strategy may be used individually or in a group.

Attribute Modifying, Attribute Transferring

List Ideas for Each Attribute

Attribute Modifying

With attribute modifying the thinker lists main attributes (characteristics, dimensions, parts) of the problem object or process and then thinks of ideas for improving each attribute. For example, a group might invent new types of candy bars or breakfast cereals by first identifying important attributes (e.g., size, shape, flavor, ingredients, color, texture, packaging, nutritional value, audience, product name) on the blackboard, and then listing specific ideas under each main attribute. Particularly good combinations may be picked out of the lists of ideas. Inset 7.1 includes three exercises from *Imagination Express* (Davis & DiPego, 1973) intended to teach attribute listing to upper elementary and junior high school students.

Suppose you were a toy manufacturer with a warehouse full of unsold skateboards. The problem is to change one (or more) parts or qualities of the skateboards to make them really different so they'll once again sell like crazy and make you another million $$$. List some parts or qualities of the skateboards, and then think of ideas for changing these parts. Be creative.

Part or quality	#1 _____	#2 _____	#3 _____	#4 _____
Changes:	_____	_____	_____	_____
	_____	_____	_____	_____
	_____	_____	_____	_____
	_____	_____	_____	_____
	_____	_____	_____	_____

What are some *qualities* of

a. a doorbell? _____

b. a bicycle basket? _____

c. a Band-Aid? _____

d. a piece of sandpaper? _____

e. a paperweight? _____

f. a rose? _____

g. an umbrella _____

h. a potholder? _____

i. a cocker spaniel? _____

---

*From *Imagination Express*, © 1973 DOK Publishers. Reprinted by permission.

In Engineering, Substitution Method

Attribute listing is taught in design engineering courses under the name *substitution method*; you "substitute" different sizes, shapes, colors, materials, etc.

Characters, Objectives, Obstacles, Outcomes

Do creative people really use this technique? Fran Striker, Professor of English at the University of Buffalo, used attribute listing for a couple of decades to help generate radio and TV plots for his *Lone Ranger* series. Striker used the attributes of *characters, objectives, obstacles,* and *outcomes* in a diagram similar to the first exercise (breakfast cereals) in Inset 7.1. As examples, from his unpublished college text *Creative Writing Workbook* (Striker, undated), in the first column he listed ideas for *characters*—for example, a playboy, scientist, nurse, king, and grave digger. Some *objectives* included obtaining love, wealth, or honor; escaping from captivity, fear, or persecution; or getting revenge against an arsonist, slanderer, or the community. A sample of *obstacles*—needed for dramatic conflict and emotion—included being pitted against beauty, power, or the law; being blind, despised, or stupid; a lack of courage, loyalty, or tact; or being held to a contract, tradition, or promise. Finally, a list of ideas to stimulate possible *outcomes* included espionage,

Let's See, How Many Possibilities Are There?

disguise, persuasion, wits, or the sacrifice of pride, wealth, or life. Even with Striker's paltry sample of 42 ideas per column, the possible story combinations are virtually endless.

Western Books: Experience, Idea Sources

Striker also kept a stack of western paperbacks in the corner of his office, suggesting that (1) he had acquired considerable experience regarding the contents of American western stories, and (2) he mined the books for ideas when additional inspiration was needed. Lest his thinking appear oversimplified, Striker's *Creative Writing Workbook* and college course also included lessons in introducing the preliminary situation (time, place, characters, atmosphere, initial incident), how to

Complex Technical Skills and Creativity

create conflict and emotion,[1] how to develop a central story purpose, 10 insightful and experienced explanations why your story can be rejected, and more.

In sympathy with beginners, he wrote "Take heart! Every great writer was once an amateur" and "The work of great writers which you hold in high esteem is never typical of their overall output, but rather a carefully selected bit from a lifetime of writing. The great bulk of their writing ... is distinctly mediocre in quality—and their early work is generally drivel." The quotes reflect, as we saw in our chapter on creative attitudes, the creative person's enthusiastic drive and

But Keep Trying!

persistence plus the willingness to sometimes fail.[2]

Use with Corporate Problems

Attribute modifying may be used with any sort of problem in which the attributes, dimensions, or parts are identifiable. For example, the problem of reducing absenteeism in the corporation could be reduced to dimensions of "sources of unpleasantness" in the company, "type of employees who frequently stay home," "type of inducements, rewards or punishments, that might reduce absenteeism," and perhaps others. Marketing strategists often convert their problem into attri-

Marketing

butes of "ways to attract new customers," "ways to maintain old customers," and "ways to increase sales to old customers."

New Product Development

Any type of product improvement or new product development problem is a natural for attribute listing. New lines of refrigerators are created by substituting, for example, new colors, new sizes, new shapes, new door arrangements, new shelf designs, more attractive appearances, new materials, new dispensers, new butter and veggie keepers (and maybe a rack to hold chilled wine), or other new modifications, uses, or functions.

---

[1]Consistent with the checklist method described later, Striker included a checklist of 45 emotions that a creative writer might use.

[2]Fran Striker had a subtle sense of humor. In Spanish, his Indian companion's name, *Tonto,* means "stupid." Tonto's name for the Lone Ranger, *Kemo Sabe,* doesn't mean anything. But *quien no sabe* translates "[one] who knows not"—a know-nothing. ("C'mon, Stupid, after 'em!" "I'm coming, you Know-Nothing!") This joke continued for years, right under our monolingual noses.

Attribute Transferring

Attribute Transferring Is Analogical Thinking

Attribute transferring is another name for analogical thinking, which we covered in Chapter 6. When Fran Striker lifted a plot, character, or "new angle" from one of his westerns and modified it to fit a Lone Ranger episode, he was transferring an attribute to a new creation. As described in Chapter 6, to stimulate attribute transferring—or analogical thinking—one can ask: What else is like this? What have others done? Where could we find an idea? What could we copy? What has worked before? What would professionals do? And so on.

Borrow a Theme

For example, in the classroom or the exhibition hall some truly creative and memorable displays could be created by borrowing attributes (ideas) from a carnival, a circus, Disneyland, MacDonald's, a Frankenstein or Star Wars movie, an old west hoedown, and so on.

Barron (1988, p. 83) made a strong statement about the creative process that seems to justify Crawford's enthusiasm for attribute listing as a core creative process:

Barron Emphasizes Significance of Attribute Listing

> . . . the ability to change things . . . is central to the creative process. New forms do not come from nothing, not for us humans at any rate; they come from prior forms, through mutations, whether unsought or invited. In a fundamental sense, there are no theories of creation; there are only accounts of the development of new forms from earlier forms.

Understand Sources of Ideas, Valuable Technique

At any age level or with any learners the two attribute listing strategies provide material for a good lesson in "where ideas come from" and in using an effective creative thinking technique, one used by many—Crawford and Barron might say *all*—creatively productive people.

MORPHOLOGICAL SYNTHESIS

A Matrix Method

Many Combinations Quickly

Morphological Synthesis basically is an extension of the attribute modifying procedure (Allen, 1962, 1968; Davis & DiPego, 1973). Here, specific ideas for one attribute or dimension of a problem are listed along one axis of a matrix. Ideas for a second attribute are listed along the other axis. Lots of new idea combinations are in the cells of the matrix. One sixth-grade Milwaukee class used the technique to invent new sandwich ideas (Figure 7.1). The kids had a swell time designing the new sandwich spreads, many of which are not too revolting. They also learned that they are capable of thinking of clever new ideas and that, if needed, this "checkerboard method" (Davis & DiPego, 1973) can help them find ideas. Note that with a third dimension, for example, 10 types of bread, we would have a three-dimensional cube containing 1,210 ($11 \times 11 \times 10$) idea combinations.

Can Use 2, 3, 6 Dimensions

The morphological synthesis method may be used with a half-dozen or so dimensions by listing ideas in columns and, if you wish, cutting the columns into vertical strips. Each strip would slide up or down and new idea combinations would be created by reading horizontally (Fabun, 1968). With the strategy used by Fran Striker to generate *Lone Ranger* plots, four dimensions were used. If Striker systematically examined each and every one of his hundreds of possible combinations, we would call his method *morphological synthesis*, as Shallcross (1981) did, rather than *attribute listing*. The methods are similar.

Earlier in this chapter we mentioned two books for teaching character and values, both of which use creativity techniques to stimulate students to think about their own character and values. Each section of *Teaching Values: An Idea Book for Teachers (and Parents)* (Davis, 1996a) covered one category of values, namely, Honesty and Trustworthiness, Rights of Others, Manners, School and Work Habits, Energy and the Environment, and "Personal Development" (e.g., responsibility,

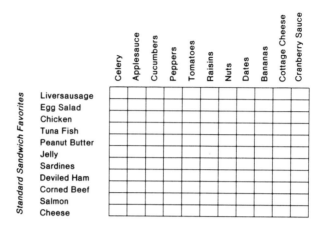

A Morphological Sandwich

A sixth-grade Milwaukee class used the morphological synthesis method to generate 121 zany ideas for creative sandwiches. Can you find a tasty combination? A revolting one?

New Companions to Add Zest

Ratings of Various Spreads

Flavor	Choices				
	1st	2nd	3rd	4th	5th
Super Goober (Peanut Butter/Cranberry)	17	2	1	0	4
Charlie's Aunt (Tuna and Applesauce)	3	16	2	2	1
Irish Eyes are Smiling (Corned Beef and Cottage Cheese)	0	0	16	2	6
Cackleberry Whiz (Hard-Boiled Eggs/Cheese Whiz)	1	3	2	14	4
Hawaiian Eye (Cream Cheese and Pineapple)	3	3	3	6	9

(Six girls had squeamish stomachs and did not participate.)

Figure 7.1.

Ideas for Exercises Aided with Morphological Synthesis Technique

compassion, valuing health, valuing respect, caring for animals). *A separate morphological synthesis chart was used to help generate exercises for each section.* For example, types of honesty and trustworthiness were listed on one axis (not cheating, not stealing, not shop lifting, not lying, returning things, keeping promises, not vandalizing), and idea-finding techniques appeared along the other (brainstorming, reverse brainstorming, analogical thinking, visualization, taking another perspective, "What would happen if . . . ?"). The half-dozen morphological synthesis charts helped generate hundreds of ideas for thought-provoking exercises.

There Was More

Of course, *Teaching Values* included other material, such as introductory chapters, a quick summary of moral education theory, a *Values Bill of Rights,* crossword and word search puzzles, values quizzes, and more. However, ideas for exercises came directly from a series of morphological synthesis charts. The strategy produced more ideas than the author could use; he stopped writing when the book seemed long enough.

Can You Create a Novel Sandwich?

How about a little practice with the morphological synthesis method. Look at the sandwich makings in Figure 7.1. Can you substitute a few more exotic entries into the vertical and horizontal axes, add a "bread" dimension, and create some spit-inducing (or is it "mouth-watering") combinations? You might try using two ideas from the vertical axis with one from the horizontal axis. How about pastrami with green peppers on rye? Sliced turkey with a little deviled ham and celery on

Roof inspector Gilbert Gluefinger used the morphological synthesis technique to find ideas for getting to the building top. "The combination of 'climb' and 'wall' produced this solution," observes the regretful inspector. "Maybe I should have tried 'ride' and 'elevator'." (The Museum of Modern Art/Film Stills Archive.)

cracked wheat? Liversausage with tomatoes and walnuts on pumpernickel? Peanut butter with sardines and ginger root on white? Well, three out of four isn't bad.

IDEA CHECKLISTS

May Directly Suggest Ideas, or Indirectly Stimulate Creativity

Yellow Pages

Sometimes, one can find an idea checklist that suggests solutions for your problem. A checklist may directly suggest ideas and solutions, or else items on the list may indirectly stimulate combinations far beyond what actually appears on the list. As some examples, the Yellow Pages of a phone book may be used as a direct checklist for problems like "Who can fix the TV?" or "Where can I get a haircut?"

**Catalogs,
Advertisements**

**Walk through the
Store**

**Osborn: 73 Idea-
Spurring Questions**

Arnold's Checklist

**Small: Big Ideas from
Checklist**

A high school counselor might use the Yellow Pages for ideas on career counseling—"Look over these 10,000 occupations Chris, maybe you can find a few interesting career possibilities." A department store or cheese store catalog or a jewelry store advertisement can be an idea checklist for a gift-giving problem. Wandering through a grocery store, department store, gift shop, or florist shop also amounts to reviewing "idea checklists" for creative meals, gifts, clothes, or centerpieces. A trip through the Yellow Pages or a department store catalog also might suggest product markets or applications for a new process or material.

Some idea checklists have been designed especially for creative problem solving. These lists indirectly push the imagination into new idea combinations and new analogical solutions. The best known of these is Osborn's (1963) *73 idea-spurring questions* (Table 7.1). Slightly simplified versions of Osborn's checklist have appeared in creativity workbooks for children, for example, *Hippogriff Feathers* (Stanish, 1981) and *The Hearthstone Traveler* (Stanish, 1988). A children's version sometimes is called the SCAMPER technique (e.g., Westberg, 1996), an acronym for *S*ubstitute, *C*ombine, *A*dapt, *M*odify/Magnify/Minify, *P*ut to other uses, *E*liminate, and *R*everse/Rearrange. As you wander through Osborn's list, ask yourself how a hamburger, TV, suitcase, soda pop product, or other object or process could be improved. The ideas will appear almost involuntarily.

In a creative engineering class at MIT John Arnold (Mason, 1960) developed a short list of self-questions aimed at improving critical engineering features of commercial products (Table 7.2). Think about a bicycle or a proper upright vacuum cleaner as you look through his list. Finally, Marvin Small, in a volume modestly titled *How to Make More Money*, created a product-development checklist similar to Osborn's 73 idea-spurring questions (Table 7.3). Pick anything from Band-Aids to children's books to wheel bearings as you peruse Small's idea stimulators.

As with other techniques, using idea checklists can stimulate nonobvious and nonhabitual idea-combinations.

Table 7.1
Osborn's (1963) 73 Idea-Spurring Questions

Put to other uses? New ways to use as is? Other uses if modified?

Adapt? What else is like this? What other idea does this suggest? Does past offer parallel? What could I copy? Whom could I emulate?

Modify? New twist? Change meaning, color, motion, sound, odor, form, shape? Other changes?

Magnify? What to add? More time? Greater frequency? Stronger? Higher? Longer? Thicker? Extra value? Plus ingredient? Duplicate? Multiply? Exaggerate?

Minify? What to subtract? Smaller? Condensed? Miniature? Lower? Shorter? Lighter? Omit? Streamline? Split up? Understate?

Substitute? Who else instead? What else instead? Other ingredient? Other material? Other process? Other power? Other place? Other approach? Other tone of voice?

Rearrange? Interchange components? Other pattern? Other layout? Other sequence? Transpose cause and effect? Change pace? Change schedule?

Reverse? Transpose positive and negative? How about opposites? Turn it backward? Turn it upside down? Reverse roles? Change shoes? Turn tables? Turn other cheek?

Combine? How about a blend, an alloy, an assortment, an ensemble? Combine units? Combine purposes? Combine appeals? Combine ideas?

While Osborn's checklist did not say *Look stupid*, it did say *Reverse, Turn it backward*, and *Put to other uses*. "I just invented the horse-hair beard!" exclaimed Max Harp. (Wisconsin Center for Film and Theater Research.) Copyright by Universal City Studios, Inc. Courtesy of Universal Studios Publishing Rights. All rights reserved.

Table 7.2
Arnold's Checklist for Improving Engineering Features

Can we increase the function? Can we make the product do more things?

Can we get a higher performance level? Make the product longer lived? More reliable? More accurate? Safer? More convenient to use? Easier to repair and maintain?

Can we lower the cost? Eliminate excess parts? Substitute cheaper materials? Design to reduce hand labor or for complete automation?

Can increase the salability? Improve the appearance of the product? Improve the package? Improve its point of sale?

Table 7.3
Small's Checklist for New Product Ideas

Can the dimensions be changed? Larger? Smaller? Longer? Stratify? Converge?

Can the quantity be changed? More? Less? Fractionate? Combine with something else?

Can the order be changed? At the beginning? Assembly or disassembly processes?

Can the time element be changed? Faster? Slower? Longer? Shorter? Chronologized? Renewed?

Can the cause or effect be changed? Energized? Altered? Destroyed? Counteracted?

Can there be a change in character? Stronger? Weaker? Interchanged? Resilient? Uniformity? More expensive?

Can the form be changed? Animated? Speeded? Slowed? Deviated? Repelled? Admitted? Rotated? Agitated?

Can the state or condition be changed? Harden? Soften? Preformed? Disposable? Parted? Vaporized? Pulverized? Lubricated? Drier? Effervesced? Coagulated? Elasticized? Lighter?

Can the use be adapted to a new market? Men? Children? Foreign?

Dictionary Technique: Free Associating

Dictionary Technique. The *dictionary technique* works much like an idea checklist. You flip through the pages, find an interesting word, and start making associations that are at least remotely related to your product or problem. For example, artists and writers at Current, Inc., a Colorado greeting card company, free associated to the word *shrink*, leading to their *Wee Greetings*, a line of greeting cards the size of business cards. Associating to *enlarge* led to cards that contain balloons and confetti (Smith, 1985).

SUMMARY

Using a creative thinking technique is a creative process.

Personal techniques are individual idea-finding strategies that all creative people use. Most personal creative thinking techniques involve analogical thinking.

Einstein used "mental experiments" to stimulate new perceptions and ideas.

Artists develop pet topics and styles that lead to their creative products. Ideas for art have been derived from the Bible, mythology, and historical events.

Comedians also use unique sources for their humor, for example, insults and self-criticism.

To develop personal idea-finding techniques, understand the techniques that others use. Standard procedures and techniques, such as the CPS model, Synectics, analogical thinking, and techniques of this chapter—if they work for you—can become personal techniques.

Additional techniques include asking "What would happen if . . . ?", working backward from the goal, or speculating on how the problem will be solved in the future.

Other recommendations are to become involved in creative activities, and to invite creative professionals and consultants to discuss creativity techniques. Creative persons serve as models.

Standard creative thinking techniques are taught in university and professional creativity courses. They also can be learned by elementary and secondary students. Davis used creativity techniques to prod students to think about their character and values.

Techniques involve forced creativity, which contrasts with intuitive creativity.

Brainstorming, based mainly on the principle of deferred judgment, can be used for any sort of corporate or business problem. Classroom uses include fanciful creativity exercises and solving real problems.

Brainstorming is intuitively appealing, simple, fun, therapeutic, and it works, usually. Osborn's four groundrules included no criticism (deferred judgment), wild freewheeling, quantity is wanted, and combination and improvement are desired.

The leader organizes the session, reviews the groundrules and procedural details, and explains the problem. He or she may ask for problem facts or alternative problem definitions. Group members should vary in backgrounds and training to stimulate different viewpoints; they should be equal in status to reduce inhibitions.

An important decision is whether or not to use a brainstorming group in the first place.

Some ideas simply may stand out, or evaluation criteria and an evaluation matrix may be used. Evaluation teaches people to evaluate as part of the creative process and to look at many problem components. Evaluation may help clarify the group's values, and can prove that silly ideas may suggest productive ones.

Variations include stop-and-go brainstorming, the Phillips 66 technique, and reverse brainstorming.

Brainwriting, used with small groups, involves circulating sheets of paper from person to person, with each person adding modifications or new ideas.

Herrmann's whole brain approach amounted to building a creativity group composed of people each of whom is strong in a particular ability—which agrees with Osborn's emphasis on heterogeneity of brainstorming group membership.

Electronic brainstorming, a form of Group Support System (GSS), is claimed to improve conventional brainstorming because it removes constraints of time and place. Forms such as voice messaging and email reduce or remove production blocking, evaluation apprehension, and social loafing. Three types of GSS solve the space (but not the time) problem: synchronous video systems, telephone conferences, and interactive computer conferences.

Osborn cautioned us that brainstorming is not a miracle cure-all, particularly if recommended procedures are not followed. Some folks are more creative alone.

Crawford's attribute listing included attribute modifying and attribute transferring (analogical thinking). Fran Striker use a form of attribute listing to generate plots for Lone Ranger episodes. Crawford and Barron agreed that modifying existing ideas is a core creative process.

Morphological synthesis amounts to attribute listing in a matrix form. One normally would use two or three dimensions, but six or more are possible. Your author used morphological synthesis charts to help generate hundreds of exercises for a character education book. The technique suggests large numbers of ideas.

The Yellow Pages or catalogs can serve as idea checklists. Osborn's 73 idea-spurring questions was deliberately designed to stimulate creative thinking. Arnold's idea checklist was oriented toward improving engineering features; Small's list toward generating new product ideas.

With the dictionary technique one free associates to relevant words, much like using an idea checklist.

Techniques of Creative Thinking: Increasing Your Idea-Finding Capability

Self-Test: Key Concepts, Terms, and Names

Briefly define or explain each of these:

Personal creative thinking techniques _____

_____

Brainstorming _____

_____

Reverse brainstorming _____

_____

Deferred judgment _____

_____

Stop-and-go brainstorming _____

_____

Phillips 66 technique _____

_____

Brainwriting _____

_____

Whole brain approach _____

_____

Electronic brainstorming _____

_____

Attribute listing technique _____

_____

Attribute modifying _____

_____

Attribute transferring _____

_____

Morphological synthesis _____

_____

Idea checklists _____

_____

Osborn's 73 "idea spurring questions" _____

_____

Why does your author think these names are important?

Alex Osborn (especially!) _____

Robert Crawford _____

William Herrmann _____

Let's Think about It

1. Brainstorming. You are an executive for Tombstone Pizza, Inc. You just brought home a Mexican Pizza, and the wheels started spinning. "Mexico isn't the only place with unique groceries," you think to yourself. Think of other countries (or locations, such as western U.S.) that might suggest new and exciting pizza combinations, and then suggest some of the ingredients that would represent that country.

    Name of your first pizza invention (include country or area) _____

    Possible ingredients _____

    _____

    Second pizza _____

    Possible ingredients _____

    _____

Third pizza _____

Possible ingredients _____

_____

Fourth pizza _____

Possible ingredients _____

2. Let's try REVERSE brainstorming. Imagine there is a burglary problem in your neighborhood. Think of all the ideas you can to make the problem WORSE. That is, what can you do to attract burglars and make it easy for them to break in and steal your stuff?

_____

_____

_____

_____

_____

Do these ideas give you a few suggestions for reducing break-ins?

_____

_____

_____

3. Imagine you are a short-story writer, perhaps aspiring to write TV scripts. Let's use attribute listing to generate story ideas. Be imaginative.

In the first column list interesting *characters*. They can be real characters in today's news; mythological or Biblical characters; characters with magical abilities; perhaps stereotyped characters from mysteries, romances, adventure stories, westerns, science fiction; etc. Include some important *objects* (powerful, valuable, magical) in this list and, if you wish, an *animal* or two.

In the second column list some *goals* (objectives)—things that story characters might want to possess, achieve, become, prevent, have happen, get revenge against, cure, etc.

In the third column list some *obstacles*, such as being blind, poor, or gullible; personality weaknesses; bureaucratic barriers; lack of power; traditions; weather; isolation; etc.

Finally, list some *outcomes* (solutions), perhaps stemming from cunning, courage, espionage, persistence, prayer, wits, changing one's mind, or sacrificing something one values.

Characters	Goals	Obstacles	Outcomes
_____	_____	_____	_____
_____	_____	_____	_____
_____	_____	_____	_____
_____	_____	_____	_____
_____	_____	_____	_____
_____	_____	_____	_____
_____	_____	_____	_____
_____	_____	_____	_____

Now pick three or four ideas from the *Characters* column and one or two ideas each from the *Goals*, *Obstacles*, and *Outcomes* columns, and sketch an outline of your creative TV episode.

_____

_____

_____

_____

_____

4. Look at Osborn's "73 idea-spurring questions" in Table 7.1 (p. 184). Look around the room or in your pocket, purse, or back pack for some relatively simple consumer product (perhaps the backpack itself). Use the "questions" in the list to think of ways the product might be changed or improved.

Object: _____

Ideas for improvement:

_____

_____

_____

_____

_____

_____

_____

_____

_____

_____

5. What's "good" about the concept of "creativity techniques"?

    _____

    _____

    _____

    _____

    What's "bad" about "creativity techniques"?

    _____

    _____

    _____

    _____

6. Think about recent movies, books, breakfast cereals, Broadway shows, inventions, political cartoons, or new consumer products you have seen lately. Where do you think the idea might have come from? That is, can you think of a technique or source of inspiration the innovator might have used to create the idea?

    Innovation 1: _____

    Likely Source or Technique: _____

    Innovation 2: _____

    Likely Source or Technique: _____

    Innovation 3: _____

    Likely Source or Technique: _____

7. What might be an OPPOSING view of "where ideas come from" which contrasts with the conscious or unconscious use of "techniques." (Hint: Does anything in Chapter 3, on theories and definitions, suggest opposing or inconsistent views of the source of creative inspiration?)

    _____

    _____

_____

_____

Can you think of situations in which no apparent "technique" was used for inspiration?

_____

_____

_____

For Study and Review

Be sure you understand the meaning of "personal" techniques and how they might be acquired, and the mechanics of every "standard" technique. Know the four groundrules of brainstorming, and the variations of brainstorming (reverse brainstorming, stop-and-go brainstorming, Phillips 66, brainwriting, and electronic brainstorming).

assessing creative potential
issues, biographical information, tests

[*Scene: Laboratory of Dr. Frankenstein. The Frankenstein monster is strapped to his table as Kool-Aid bubbles mysteriously over bunsen burners. Dr. Frankenstein is discussing the future of his creation with assistant Igor.*]

Dr. Frankenstein: Well Igor, he looks great! Those insightful eyes and that creative intellect! He's ready for Paramount Pictures anytime!

Igor: I don't know, boss. He's got eyes, but I think I'd worry about his intelligence and creativity.

Dr. Frankenstein: What's this? Do I detect a hint of doubt? Very well, we'll give him a test of creativity!

Igor: What kind of creativity test? There's two kinds, divergent thinking tests and personality-biographical inventories.

Dr. Frankenstein: Both, of course! He'll pass with flying colors! Now, Monster, give my doubting friend here some unusual uses for a brick!

Monster: (*Violently*) GRRAWL!! GRRAWL!!

Dr. Frankenstein: Excellent, Monster! Did you hear that Igor? He said "gravel." You chop up the brick and use it for gravel! Another idea Monster?

Monster: (*Less violently*) GRRAWL!! GRRAWL!!

Dr. Frankenstein: Another creative insight! "Gavel"—for bringing the court to order, obviously. Excellent! Excellent! Well Igor, what do you say to that?

Igor: But boss, I don't think he. . .

Monster: (*Beginning to grin*) GRRAWL! GRRAWL!!

Dr. Frankenstein: A "girl doll"! Of course! An inspired answer! Slip some doll clothes on the brick and there you have it! The score is Monster 3, Igor zip!

Igor: But boss, he. . . .

Dr. Frankenstein: Now Monster, what unusual or creative hobbies have you had?

Monster: (*Grinning from electrode to electrode*) ARGHUNH!! ARGHUNH!!

195

Dr. Frankenstein: Art, huh? VERY good. Anything else?

Monster: ARGHUNH!! ARGHUNH!!

Dr. Frankenstein: Aardvark? You had a pet aardvark? Brilliant! That's a very creative trait indeed!

Igor: But boss, he's just. . .

Dr. Frankenstein: I'm surprised at you Igor. A better man would admit he's wrong! I'm calling the studio right away. He can shuffle and growl with the best of them!

Igor: If you say so boss.

Men occasionally stumble across the truth, but most of them pick themselves up and hurry off as if nothing had happened.

Winston Churchill

Bad News: Can't Predict Adult Creative Eminence

Let's begin with a realistic, bad-news/good-news appraisal of the challenge of identifying creative potential, particularly in school-age children and youth. The bad news is that achieving a truly high level of accuracy in predicting who has great creative potential and definitely will become a creative celebrity cannot be done. It has not been done yet.

Good News: Lots of Ways to Identify Creative Personality, Abilities, Talent

The good news is that, within limits, there are *lots* of ways to identify creative personality dispositions, creative abilities, and creative talent in elementary and secondary students and adults. In this chapter we will look at contemporary uses of creativity tests, informal and formal ways to assess creative potential, some reasons for pessimism about measuring creativity, and the use of high IQ as suggestive of creative capability. We will review informal biographical and behavior indicators of creativity, along with instruments and methods for tabulating them, and then turn to two main types of formal, published creativity tests: personality/ biographical inventories and divergent thinking tests.

True Goal: To Identify Creative Potential

Note at the outset that there are many ways to *identify* students with above-average creative potential. Using tests and inventories to objectively *measure* creative abilities and creative personality and motivational characteristics is just one way to identify creative potential, and in some circumstances may not be the best way.

USES OF CREATIVITY TESTS

There are three main uses of creativity tests: for identifying creatively gifted children for gifted programs, for research, and for counseling.

Identifying Creatively Gifted Children. The predominant use of creativity tests is for selecting creatively gifted students for participation in programs for the gifted and talented. State directors, district G/T teacher-coordinators, and other program planners (school board members, parents) are becoming more and more aware that high intelligence is just one type of giftedness. Eventually, students who are creatively gifted probably will make the most valuable contributions to society, and certainly deserve the frog-kissing, prince-becoming benefits of G/T programs.

Selecting Kids for G/T Programs

Selecting creative children requires some index of creativeness, which often means creativity test scores, hopefully supplemented with teacher, parent, peer, or self-ratings of creativeness plus enthusiasm for the program, along with other information.

Research.   A second important use of creativity tests is for research into the nature of creativity and creative people. Creativity tests typically are used in two ways. First, researchers may need to identify creative children or adults in order to compare them, their backgrounds, or their task performance with "regular" (control) children or adults. If the researcher wishes to explore whether creative persons are more likely to have certain personality traits, motivations, abilities, cognitive styles, behavior patterns, career choices, histories, low anxiety, a cat, an imaginary playmate, or a belief in flying saucers, the experimenter first must locate the creative subjects. The second research use of creativity tests is to evaluate any beneficial effect of some educational or creativity training experience, for example, a gifted program that focuses on training problem solving and creativity.

Incidentally, sometimes the most effective way to evaluate creativity training effects is not with a published creativity test—which may not measure what was taught—but with an original questionnaire that asks: Was the experience worthwhile? Do you believe you are more creative as a result of the program? Did you enjoy the experience? Are you more likely to engage in creative activities as a result of the experience? Such an inventory usually will produce more direct, relevant results than a published test that asks participants, for example, to list unusual uses for a tin bucket.

Counseling.   The third use of creativity testing is in counseling and guidance. A counselor or school psychologist in the elementary or secondary school may want more information about a student who is referred because of apathy, underachievement, uncooperativeness, disruptiveness, or other personal or education problems. For example, a creative child who is independent, curious, artistic, risk-taking, and who has high energy and a good sense of humor may not be "well-rounded" and may have few friends (Millar, 1995; Torrance, 1981a). Further, he or she may have an aversion to routine, rigid, authoritarian classrooms—resulting in a refusal to complete work, becoming aggressive or a class clown, feigning illness to stay home, or other maladaptive behavior. Information regarding creativeness will help the counselor diagnose the problems.

FORMAL AND INFORMAL EVALUATION OF CREATIVITY

For convenience we may categorize creativity identification methods as *formal* or *informal*, depending upon whether the method uses creativity test scores or the subjective opinions of teachers, parents, or students themselves. Sometimes, informal methods are disguised as formal tests, as when rating-scales are used to record informal impressions of students' creative abilities, personality traits, or past creative activities.

Sometimes It's Easy

The informal identification of creative students may be easy. Many highly creative children, adolescents, and adults are quite visible. They are bright, active, energetic, and have a terrific sense of humor. They are quick with novel ideas and they probably relish their highly visible involvement in art, writing, dance, musical composition, theater, social action, science entrepreneurship, unusual hobbies, or at the microcomputer.

As one easy way to identify at least some creative people, consider these two questions: (1) Did you have an imaginary playmate as a child? (2) Have you been involved in theater—children's theater, high school productions, community theater, either as an actor or in props or costumes? As we noted in Chapter 4, in your author's experience adults who had an imaginary playmate or have a background in theater always show other characteristics of creativity—they have creative attitudes and personality traits and they virtually always have a background of doing creative things. It is common for people who had an imaginary playmate also to have been active in theater. Note that you could identify perhaps two dozen creative high school students simply by telephoning the theater teacher and asking for a list of theater kids. A similar search could locate elementary or secondary students who have produced outstanding, perhaps award-winning projects for art, creative writing, or science fairs.

The challenge is to identify the less visible creative children, those whose creative capabilities are not asked for and therefore not seen.

PESSIMISM ABOUT MEASURING CREATIVITY AND CREATIVITY TESTING

Measuring Traits and Abilities versus Predicting Creative Eminence

Attitudes regarding our ability to evaluate creativity differ dramatically. On one hand, educators committed to fostering creativity and giftedness agree that students with creative potential can and should be *identified*. On the other hand, critics hold the opinion that true creativity cannot be *measured* with currently available creativity tests.

One reason for pessimism, as we saw in Chapter 1, lies in the complexity and many forms of creativity—for example, the many kinds of needed personality traits, motivations, and intellectual abilities; the distinction between self-actualized and special talent creativity; the required combination of training, experience, available knowledge, and an environment that rewards a particular type of creative thinking; the role of non-rational factors such as fantasy, illogical thinking, and sometimes a touch of psychopathology; and the two biggest "ifs" of all, chance and opportunity. As a sample of mystery in creativity thinking, we noted in Chapter 5 that composers hear symphonies in their heads. A comparable process happens with writers—as Ernest Hemingway once said, "The stuff comes alive and turns crazy on ya'" (Bass, 1968). The reader also may recall remarkable speculations on the roles of Muses, psychical capabilities, the libido, primordial archetypes, and accessing a universal mind.

We review this sample of complexity and mystery to remind ourselves that trying to measure "creativity" with paper-and-pencil tests oversimplifies highly complicated phenomena. Such complexities (and more) limit the ability of creativity tests to measure creative capability or productivity.

A second reason for pessimism is partly semantic, centered on whether we define *creativity* as (1) possessing personality traits, relevant abilities, or experience in creative thinking versus (2) having achieved creative eminence. With the first definition there seems little doubt that children and adolescents identified by teachers, parents, or creativity tests as possessing strong creative cognitive and affective traits will—on average—behave more creatively than a random sample of students. For example, their products and achievements will be evaluated as more creative and they will pursue more creative interests, careers, and hobbies (e.g., Davis, 1975, 1989a; Davis & Rimm, 1982; Okuda, Runco, & Berger, 1991; Torrance, 1981a, 1988; Torrance & Safter, 1989).

But can we predict great creative eminence? As we conceded at the beginning of this chapter, it has not been done yet. Consider the odds. The combination of high-level personal and environmental factors that lead a handful of people to

---

Sidebar notes (left margin):

Ask Theater Teacher

Ask about Creative Project Awards

Attitudes Differ on Measuring Creativity

Due to Complexity and Other Factors

Can Predict Creative Potential

Cannot Predict Creative Eminence

creative eminence extends many miles beyond the scores produced by creativity tests and inventories.[1]

By way of comparison, our esteemed intelligence tests do not predict professional eminence one whit better. Among Lewis Terman's 1,528 gifted children, nearly all of whom scored above IQ 140 (some above 180), not even one reached the eminence of an Einstein, Picasso, or Howard Hughes (Golman, 1980). In fact, one person who was tested and did not qualify in Terman's screening was William Schockley, who went on to co-invent the transistor and earn a Nobel Prize—he out-achieved all 1,528 people who met Terman's IQ criterion of genius. To quote Dean Keith Simonton (1997, p. 340), "Rather than become a gifted child, he became a famous scientist instead."

Hey, We Can't Predict Eminence from IQ Scores Either!

Reliability and Validity Issues

There also are measurement reasons for pessimism regarding our ability to develop valid tests of creative potential. Creativity tests have built-in statistical difficulties. Because of the kinds of complexities we have reviewed, efforts to build an omnibus, sweeping test of "creativity quotients" (CQs) simply cannot produce an instrument with enormous validity coefficients nor high reliability coefficients of some types.[2]

Built-In Statistical Difficulties

Let's consider validity. Validity coefficients are correlation coefficients that reflect the degree of relatedness (or similarity) of two sets of scores, in the present case, scores from a creativity test and scores from some other measure of creativity. If a creativity test is valid, its scores will correlate well with the other measure of creativity. Apart from complexity problems, validity coefficients cannot be extremely high because of differences between the content of the test and the content of the validating criterion. For example, *construct* validity often takes the form of a correlation between creativity test scores and measures of other mental constructs, particularly personality traits related to creativeness, such as confidence, humor, intuitive orientation, sensation seeking (adventurousness), or social anxiety. There is no reason to expect a high correlation between a test of creativity and, say, a test of social anxiety. They are different animals.

Validity = Relatedness

Test and Criterion Are Different

One common form of *criterion-related* validity is a correlation between scores on one creativity test and scores on another creativity test—which compounds the reliability and validity problems of each test. "So-so" times another "so-so" equals an even worse "so-so." Another type of criterion-related validity is a correlation between creative test scores and an outside validating criterion such as teacher ratings of student creativity, ratings of creative products (Davis & Rimm, 1982), or with adults, number of patent applications or supervisor ratings (e.g., Taylor, 1963), ratings of the creativeness of art, writing, and invention samples (Davis, 1975; Davis & Subkoviak, 1978), number of high school creative achievements, number of post-high school creative achievements, scores on a creative lifestyle checklist, ratings of one's highest creative achievements, and ratings of the creativeness of one's future career image (Torrance & Safter, 1989). Once again, differences between test content and criterion content will prevent high validity coefficients.

Correlation between Two Tests Compounds Problems

With criterion-related validity, developers of creativity tests find themselves in a no-win situation. If validity coefficients are high, chances are excellent that the

---

[1]We described many traits, experiences, environmental conditions, and theories of creative eminence in Chapters 3 and 4.

[2]Interrater and internal consistency reliabilities can be very high, often in the .90s (e.g., Davis, 1975; Torrance, 1990a, 1990b). However, test-retest and alternate forms reliabilities typically are a more modest .50 to .75, often lower.

Validity Coefficients Must Not Be Too High or Too Low

content of the test and the content of the criterion are just too similar, probably in a trivial way—for example, using scores on an "unusual uses for bricks" test to validate scores on an "unusual uses for boxes" test. One has good reason to be suspicious of creativity tests that claim validity coefficients higher than about .6, which approaches the ozone level. On the other hand, if the creativity test and the creativity criterion are quite different, such as scores on an unusual tests and supervisor ratings 10 years later, the validity coefficients almost certainly will be low. If validity coefficients are below about .30, predictive ability and usefulness of the test are in question. Too high and you lose; too low and you lose again.

Optimism about Identifying Creative Persons

Based upon my own experience in developing creativity tests (Davis, 1975; Davis & Rimm, 1982), Torrance's 22-year longitudinal study of his divergent thinking tests (e.g., Torrance & Safter, 1989), and a host of other studies that validate the use of personality inventories, divergent thinking tests, and biographical information (reviewed later in this chapter)—and despite complexity problems, critic's pessimism, and measurement problems—many creativity tests are on-target, moderately valid, and helpful within certain limitations.

False Negatives: Test Failure
False Positives: Cheating

One limitation is *false negatives*—the failure of a test to identify a truly creative person due to a Grand Canyon of difference between test content and the individual's particular form of creativeness. *False positives*, the identification of an uncreative person as highly creative, are not likely, although some (perhaps many) tests can be faked by shrewd and unprincipled test takers. For example, when instructed to do so college students deliberately can produce high scores on an inventory assessing creative personality characteristics (Ironson & Davis, 1979); they also can deliberately list "wild" ideas on divergent thinking tests, thereby inflating their originality scores.

Typically, a high creativity test score means that the student probably has good creative potential and/or creative experience, which may have been invisible due to student reticence or to a classroom that did not ask for creative ideas.

Solution: Two Criteria of Creativity

Because of limitations in reliability and validity, creativity test results must be used cautiously and preferably in combination with other information regarding students' creativeness. If creativity tests, rating scales, or nominations are used, it is best to use at least *two* such criteria. For example, scores on a divergent thinking test may be used along with scores on a personality/biographical inventory; or else scores on either type of creativity test may be used together with teacher (or parent) ratings of creativeness. If a student scores high on two criteria, we can be comfortable about naming that student as having creative potential. In contrast, if a student scores average or below average on a *single* criterion, such as one creativity test, it could be (and often is) a great error to accept that mediocre score as a true measure of creative capability.

Two Criteria Increase Confidence

It is common in the field of gifted education to recommend a multidimensional approach to identification, that is, to use many selection criteria. Within the creativity area, we also should use several identification criteria.

HIGH IQ AS AN INDICATOR OF CREATIVE POTENTIAL

Early research by Barron (1969), MacKinnon (1961, 1978a, 1978b), Getzels and Jackson (1962), and Wallach and Kogan (1965) confirmed our common sense sus-

**Creativity and
Intelligence
Are Related**

picion that creativity and intelligence are different, yet related. One visible difference lies in the role of personality and motivation characteristics. No one claims that a person's level of intelligence level depends heavily on personality and motivational traits, but many know that creative productivity does. You may recall Sternberg's (1988; Chapter 4) three-facet model of creativity in which two factors included a mix of thinking styles, personality traits, and motivation and the third factor was intelligence.

Getzels and Jackson (1962) made the important observation that their high-intelligence students were capable of thinking creatively—but they were not disposed to do so. Perhaps they were conventional by habit, insecure about being different, or just not motivated to think creatively because creativity was not encouraged or rewarded. The Getzels and Jackson conclusion underscores the key role of attitudinal, personality, and motivational characteristics, with *creativity consciousness* at the forefront.

**Personality,
Motivation Important**

We already have seen the Barron and MacKinnon *threshold* concept (MacKinnon, 1978a; Chapter 4), which states that a minimum IQ of about 120 is needed for noteworthy creative accomplishment.

There is little question that intelligence and creativity are different, but important to the present argument, they also are related. We know from research by Catharine Cox (1926), the Goertzels (Goertzel, Goertzel, & Goertzel, 1978), Walberg and Herbig (1991), and Simonton (1997)—again, along with our intuitions—that high intelligence is a requisite trait among creatively eminent men and women.

**High Intelligence
Suggests Creative
Potential**

An implication is that young people with high intelligence have a unique potential for creative productivity. Therefore, high intelligence is a good clue for identifying creative potential.

INFORMAL IDENTIFICATION: BIOGRAPHICAL INFORMATION

Creative Activities, Creative Behavior

**Use Self-Reports for
Identification?**

Developers of creativity tests sometimes use self-reported creative activities as a criterion for validating creativity tests (e.g., Okuda, Runco, & Berger, 1991; Torrance & Safter, 1989). One wonders: Could we not use the self-reports of creative activities to identify creative persons in the first place?

Tests Are Incomplete

Creativity tests are incomplete. Personality inventories measure just personality/motivational dispositions and divergent thinking tests measure a sample of divergent thinking abilities. We have a serious case of truth in advertising. However, biographical information—details about students' actual creative activities and behaviors—reflects traits underlying both types of tests plus whatever other cognitive abilities and styles, experiences, environments, and the like have contributed to their real creative behavior.

**Biographical
Information
More Valid**

**Background of
Creative Activities?**

A seemingly self-evident way to locate creative students or adults is to look for a background of creative activities. Does the person constantly make or build things? Does he or she have wide interests, unusual hobbies, unique collections? Perhaps dinosaurs, magic, Egyptology, Charlie Chaplin impressions, or a collection of animal bones? Does the person have unusual experience or talent in art, poetry, creative writing, decorating, handicrafts, music, dance, computer programming, or a science area? Perhaps you have met a "dinosaur kid," a "photography kid," or a youngster who knows more about Picasso, Gandhi, Russian cosmonauts, DNA, or the history of computers than do the teachers.

**Theater, Imaginary
Playmate**

If a student or adult happens to be a "theater kid," one need look no further. The other powerful indicator mentioned earlier and in Chapter 4 was having had an imaginary playmate as a child. Students with a background in theater or who had an imaginary playmate always show other personality and background traits of creativity.

Action Information: Renzulli

Renzulli's Action Information.   Renzulli's concept of *Action Information* is used to help select energetic, creative students for participation in gifted education programs (Renzulli, 1994; Renzulli & Reis, 1985, 1997). Action information reflects creative behaviors and creative personality traits—energy, imagination, resourcefulness, high interest, the works—which teachers can use to help identify creative students. Renzulli and Reis assembled many examples of the kinds of behaviors exhibited by creative children and adolescents. Part of their list appears back in Chapter 4, Table 4.5. Students who show these or similar behaviors are good candidates for having potential for present and future creative work.

Consensual Assessment: Amabile

Consensual Assessment Method.   With Amabile's (1983) *consensual assessment* strategy teachers deliberately elicit samples of creative work from students. Groups of teachers then informally evaluate the creativeness of the products. In one study (Hennessey & Amabile, 1988), 5- to 10-year-old children made up a story, in about 10 minutes, to fit a wordless picture book adventure of a boy and his dog at a pond. Three teachers rated the stories on *creativity, how well they liked the story, novelty, imagination, logic, emotion, grammar, detail, vocabulary,* and "*straightforwardness.*" Interrater reliability was remarkably high, indicating that the teachers' implicit theories of creativity were quite in agreement.

Detroit Creativity Scales

Detroit Public Schools Creativity Scales.   The *Detroit Public Schools Creativity Scales* (Parke & Byrnes, 1984) use a process similar to Amabile's consensual assessment. In this case, however, community experts in a subject area evaluate the creativeness of music compositions, music performances, dance, art, short story and novel writing, drama, poetry, or speeches. One problem might be locating and recruiting experts in each area.

Note that evaluating actual creative products and behaviors, as in the informal methods described by Renzulli, Amabile, and Parke and Byrnes, reflects the way talent and capability are recognized in the real world (Borland, 1997).

Creative Activities Inventories

Research confirms that self-reported involvement in creative activities is a solid indicator of present and probably future creativeness (e.g., Bull & Davis, 1980; Holland, 1961; Richards *et al.*, 1988; Runco, 1987). Certainly, the face validity of such information is high.[3] Holland (1961), for example, found that high school students who were creatively talented in art or science could be identified by assessing their history of creative activities. He concluded that past creative achievement is the *single best predictor* of future creative achievement.

History of Creative Activities

CACL: Five Domains

Creative Activities Check List.   Okuda, Runco, and Berger (1991) used the *Creative Activities Check List* (CACL), adapted from Hocevar (1980), as a criterion for evaluating the predictive ability of problem-finding tests. Their version of the CACL included 50 creative activities in five domains. Each item began with "How many times have you . . . ?" and upper elementary students were asked to respond (1) never, (2) once or twice, (3) three to five times, or (4) six or more times. The five domains were *art* (e.g., painted an original picture), *crafts* (designed a craft out of wood), *literature* (written a poem or short story), *mathematics* (applied math

---

[3]Translation: It looks like it should work.

in an original way to solve a practical problem), and *public performance* (choreographed a dance). Students were instructed to think only of activities outside of school—not class projects or homework. Scores were the average rating (1 to 4) in each domain plus the overall average rating. Subscale internal reliabilities ranged from .71 to .91 and for the total scale, .91. Problem-finding scores correlated between .38 and .58 with CACL subscores and total score. Concluded Runco (1987), creative activities questionnaires such as CACL have "more than adequate psychometric properties" (p. 121).

<table>
<tr><td>Society for the Prevention of Cruelty to Animals</td><td>

SPCA.   With their *Statement of Past Creative Activities* (SPCA) inventory, Bull and Davis (1980) asked college students to "List any creative activities (artistic, literary, technical, or scientific) in which you are or have been engaged in the past 2-3 years." The creativity scores derived from the SPCA showed moderately good correlations with other criteria of creativity, for example, .41 with scores on the *How Do You Think?* inventory (Davis, 1975; discussed later) and .40 with an original measure of "internal sensation seeking" (which evaluated, e.g., desire for fantasy/daydreaming and vividness of imagery), created by Bull.</td></tr>
<tr><td>Creative Behavior Inventory: Lees-Haley</td><td>

Creative Behavior Inventory.   Lees-Haley's (1978) *Creative Behavior Inventory* includes a checklist of creative behaviors along with an open-ended question which, together, assess past creative performance. Higher scores would reflect, for example, having written a play, choreographed a dance, published a poem, acted in a movie, or created a scientific theory. The inventory has been used successfully with both middle school (Lees-Haley & Swords, 1981) and elementary students (Lees-Haley & Sutton, 1982).</td></tr>
<tr><td>Torrance's Things Done on Your Own: 100 Possibilities</td><td>

Things Done on Your Own.   Over thirty years ago, in the last three pages of *Guiding Creative Talent*, Torrance (1962) presented a checklist of 100 creative activities entitled *Things Done on Your Own*. The checklist evaluates children's creative activities in "language arts, science, social studies, art, and other fields" (p. 251). Students were asked to "Indicate which ones you have done during this school term . . . Include only the things you have done on your own, not the things you have been assigned or made to do" (p. 251). Look again at Table 4.4 in Chapter 4, which includes a sample of Torrance's 100 creative biographical activities.</td></tr>
<tr><td>Create Your Own</td><td>

Original Self-Report Inventories and Checklists.   In addition to published checklists and open-ended assessments of creative activities, it would not be difficult to create an original self-report inventory for either students or parents to complete. As an example, the following simply asks about a student's past or present strong interests or hobbies:</td></tr>
</table>

> Describe any hobbies, collections, or strong interests that you [your child may] have had. For example, have you [has your child] been really interested in reptiles, writing poetry or stories, magic tricks, theater, computers, Ancient Athens or Rome, dinosaurs, unusual collections, art, creating or building things, handicrafts, music, or space travel or other science area? Other hobbies or strong interests? If so, list them.

Most likely, a few statements reflecting outstanding creative involvement and creative potential will float to the top.

<table>
<tr><td>Biographical Information Valid, Useful</td><td>

A relationship between past, present, and future creativity is not surprising. Therefore, reports of past and current creative activities—determined with open-ended questions or structured checklists—should be highly valid and useful ways to identify creative children and youth.</td></tr>
</table>

FORMAL IDENTIFICATION: INVENTORIES AND TESTS

Two Categories: Personality, Divergent Thinking

There are two main categories of creativity tests, *personality inventories* and *divergent thinking tests*. We mentioned earlier that personality inventories evaluate the kinds of attitudes, personality dispositions, motivational characteristics, and sometimes interests and biographical information described in the previous sections and in Chapter 4—but such inventories do not assess cognitive creative abilities. Divergent thinking tests evaluate a sample of cognitive abilities, but ignore personality traits and background information, except as these may affect test performance. Most divergent thinking tests ask students to respond with as many answers as they can to an open-ended problem or question, such as the 90-year old "List unusual uses for a brick" problem. The tests typically are scored

Fluency and Originality, at Least

at least for ideational *fluency*, the total number of relevant ideas, and *originality*, the uniqueness or statistical rarity of each idea.

CREATIVE PERSONALITY INVENTORIES

Scales for Rating the Behavioral Characteristics of Superior Students

SRBCSS Used by Teachers

A shining example of on-target efficiency is Renzulli's (1983) 10-item creativity rating scale from his *Scales for Rating the Behavioral Characteristics of Superior Students* (Table 8.1). A teacher who knows an elementary or secondary student well can use the scale to rate the student's creativeness. The scale evaluates important, intuitively appealing, and empirically sound traits of creative children, adolescents, and adults. Its contents square well with other descriptions of the creative personality.

How Do You Think?

Pronounced "Hide It"?

The *How Do You Think?* (HDYT) test (Davis, 1975, 1991a; Davis & Subkoviak, 1978) evaluates such traits as independence, confidence, risk-taking, energy, adventurousness, curiosity, reflectiveness, humor, playfulness, liking for complexity, artistic interests, creative interests and activities, as well as belief in ESP and flying saucers.[4] HDYT includes 100 items in a 5-point rating-scale, "No," "To a small extend," "Average," More than average," and "Definitely."

High Internal Reliability

Good Concurrent Validity
Construct Validity

HDYT has shown reasonably good psychometric properties (e.g., Runco, Okuda, & Thurston, 1988; Schuldberg, 1993). Internal reliability, for example, virtually always is above .90. The inventory originally was validated against actual creative products (art, writing, inventions) required for a college creativity class ($r = .42$; Davis, 1975). With an experimental and a control group, Davis and Bull (1978) demonstrated that HDYT scores were significantly higher as a result of taking a college creativity course, which is evidence of construct validity. Moss (1991) found a correlation of .53 between HDYT scores and the *Myers-Briggs Type Inventory* measure of *intuition*.

Used as a Criterion of Creativity

Runco, Okuda, and Thurston (1988) used HDYT scores as a criterion for validating nine divergent thinking measures. Correlations ranged from .14 to .45 between HDYT scores and the divergent thinking scores. Runco, Okuda, and Hwang (1987) found that HDYT scores were correlated with success in a math and science program for gifted and talented high school students, even when ability scores (PSAT-Math) were controlled. Runco *et al.* (1987) concluded that the HDYT, along with PSAT-Math, could be used to select students for gifted programs.

---

[4]HDYT is available from the author.

Table 8.1
Scale for Rating Characteristics of Creative Students

	1	2	3	4
1. Displays a great deal of curiosity about many things; is constantly asking questions about anything and everything.	___	___	___	___
2. Generates a large number of ideas or solutions to problems and questions; often offers unusual ("way out"), unique, clever responses.	___	___	___	___
3. Is uninhibited in expressions of opinion; is sometimes radical and spirited in disagreement; is tenacious.	___	___	___	___
4. Is a high risk taker; is adventurous and speculative.				
5. Displays a good deal of intellectual playfulness; fantasizes; imagines ("I wonder what would happen if. . . . "); manipulates ideas (i.e., changes, elaborates upon them); is often concerned with adapting, improving and modifying institutions, objects, and systems.	___	___	___	___
6. Displays a keen sense of humor and sees humor in situations that may not appear to be humorous to others.	___	___	___	___
7. Is usually aware of his impulses and more open to the irrational in himself (freer expression of feminine interest for boys, greater than usual amount of independence for girls); shows emotional sensitivity.	___	___	___	___
8. Is sensitive to beauty; attends to aesthetic characteristics of things.	___	___	___	___
9. Is nonconforming; accepts disorder; is not interested in details; is individualistic; does not fear being different.	___	___	___	___
10. Criticizes constructively; is unwilling to accept authoritarian pronouncements without critical examination.	___	___	___	___

Reproduced by permission of Joseph Renzulli.

High School, Middle School, Gifted Elementary Kids

HDYT seems to work well with high school and middle school students, although middle school students may need a word or two defined (Lees-Haley & Swords, 1981). One study successfully used HDYT with 61 gifted 9 to 12-year-old children, showing correlations of .42 and .59 with their *Creative Behavior Inventory* (Lees-Haley & Sutton, 1982), a checklist of creative activities mentioned earlier. Lees-Haley and Sutton recommended the HDYT for identifying creative elementary children because it worked and because the children found it "interesting, engaging, and stimulating."

Based on 25 years of observing HDYT performance, your author's conclusion is this: It works surprisingly well!

Group Inventory for Finding Talent: The GIFFI Tests

GIFFI II

There have been several spin-offs from HDYT. The *Group Inventory for Finding Interests II* (GIFFI II; Davis & Rimm, 1980, 1982) is a high school inventory built of 60 items from the HDYT, again in a 5-point rating scale format. GIFFI II has been validated with urban, suburban, and rural students of many ethnic groups and at all socio-economic levels. The original validity criterion was teacher ratings of student creativity plus ratings of the creativeness of students' short stories. The median validity coefficient was .45. Sample items from GIFFI II, and therefore HDYT, appear in Table 8.2. GIFFI II produces a total creativity score plus five

Subscales Available

subscale scores, *confidence, challenge-inventiveness, imagination, creative arts and writing,* and *many interests*.

GIFFI I

The *Group Inventory for Finding Interests I* (GIFFI I) for middle school students is a combination of (simplified) items from HDYT plus items from Rimm's ele-

Table 8.2
Sample Items from GIFFI II

Item	Trait
I have a very good sense of humor.	Humor
I have done a lot of creative writing.	Creative Activity
I enjoy thinking of new and better ways of doing things.	Originality
I tend to become childishly involved with simple things.	Playfulness, Curiosity
I am quite original and imaginative.	Self-rating of Creativity
I am very curious.	Curiosity
I have had many hobbies.	Wide Interests, Many Hobbies
I have been active in photography or film making.	Creative Activity
I am able to work intensely on a project for many hours.	Energy, Commitment
I would like to learn mountain climbing.	Adventurousness, Risk-Taking
I have a great many interests.	Wide Interests
I have participated in theatrical productions.	Creative Activity
I am artistic.	Artistic
I am a risk-taker.	Risk-Taking

mentary level *Group Inventory for Finding (Creative) Talent* (GIFT; Davis & Rimm, 1982; Rimm & Davis, 1979, 1983). As with GIFFI II, GIFFI I also includes 60 items with 5-point rating scales, and it also produces a total creativity score plus scores on the same five subscales.

Group Inventory for Finding (Creative) Talent: GIFT

GIFT
Creative Traits Appear in Elementary School

The *Group Inventory For Finding* (Creative) *Talent* (GIFT; Rimm, 1976; Rimm & Davis, 1980) includes three forms, *Primary* for grades 1 and 2, *Elementary* for grades 3 and 4, and *Upper Elementary* for grades 5 and 6. The inventories are relatively brief, just 32, 34 and 33 yes-no items in length, with 25 items common to all three levels. The main difference between forms is the size of the print.

The GIFT inventories primarily assess independence, flexibility, curiosity, perseverance (energy), breadth of interests, and past creative activities (e.g., "I ask a lot of questions," "I like to paint pictures"). Along with a total score, three subscale scores are *imagination, independence*, and *many interests*.

Valid with Many Groups, Many Nationalities

The GIFT tests have been used with children who are white, black, Spanish surnamed, high SES, low SES, urban, suburban, rural, immigrant, learning disabled, gifted, Israeli, French, Australian, and Chinese (Rimm & Davis, 1976, 1980). Internal reliability figures, using data from several studies, for the primary, elementary and upper elementary forms were .80, .86, and .88, respectively. Frequently, the validation research conducted by others was more favorable than our own, which testifies not only to the value and virtues of GIFT but to our unquestionable honesty as well. Validity coefficients usually range from about .25 to .45, sometimes lower and sometimes higher.

Preschool and Kindergarten Interest Descriptor

PRIDE

Preschool? Yes indeed, the creative traits are there and can be evaluated (by parents) with high reliability and good validity. PRIDE is the *Preschool and Kindergarten Interest Descriptor*. (The acronym PRIDE does not fit its title too well, but it sounds better than PKID.) PRIDE may be used with children age 3–6. It consists of 50 five-point rating scale items ("No" to "Definitely") and it measures the same kinds of traits assessed by GIFT, the two GIFFI tests, HDYT, and other creativity inventories—"many interests, curiosity, independence, perseverance, imagination, playfulness, humor, and originality" (Rimm, 1983).

Filled Out by Parents

Unlike the others, parents fill out the questionnaire, requiring about 20–35 minutes. Rimm (1983) noted that "Since a student self-report inventory tends to be unreliable for children who are ages 3–5, PRIDE was developed for use by parents based on their observation of their children."

Subscales

An internal consistency reliability of .92 was reported. Like GIFT, validity was established by correlating PRIDE scores with scores derived by combining (preschool) teacher ratings of creativeness with experimenter ratings of the creativeness of children's pictures and short stories. With three samples of children, three validity coefficients were .38, .50, and .32. As with GIFT and the GIFFI tests, there are subscale scores (*many interests, independence-perseverance, imagination-playfulness, originality*) that may prove useful.

Exercise in Divergent Feeling

CAP: Assesses Divergent Thinking and Personality Traits

Frank Williams (1980) did not have the decency to consider the tidy organization of this chapter when he devised his *Creativity Assessment Packet* (CAP). What he did consider was that a sensible evaluation of children's creative potential should include one divergent thinking test along with two inventories for assessing creative personality traits. His CAP tests awkwardly must be described in two places.

Exercise in Divergent Feeling

Williams' *Exercise in Divergent Feeling* is built of 50 items in a 4-point rating-scale format. It produces a total creativity score plus the four subscale scores of *curiosity, imagination, complexity,* and *risk-taking.*

Unclear Validity Criteria

Ten-month test-retest reliabilities for all three CAP instruments for 256 students in grades 3 through 12 were said to be "in the sixties." Williams claimed validity coefficients for CAP between .59 and .76, which in creativity test development are extremely high. Unfortunately, the specifics of which CAP test scores were correlated with what validity criteria were not clear. Fekken (1985), another perceptive test reviewer, soundly criticized the CAP tests for poor norming samples and unclear and inadequate reliability and validity data.

The Williams Scale

Williams Scale: Parents Fill Out

The Williams Scale is not a skin disorder, but another personality-oriented CAP inventory, this one used by a parent or teacher to evaluate student creativeness. It consists of 48 3-point ("Often," "Sometimes," "Seldom") rating-scale items. Eight sections assess factors of *fluency, flexibility, originality, elaboration* (which normally are considered divergent thinking abilities), *curiosity, imagination, complexity,* and *risk-taking,* with six questions per section. Only a total creativity score is used.

Yea Sayer Gets High Score

Open-Ended Questions

A potential problem is that all 48 items are positively related to creativity, which means that a busy "yea sayer" parent or teacher could quickly check the "Often" column, with just a sketchy reading of the actual questions, and dramatically inflate creativity scores. A unique and positive feature of *The Williams Scale* is the set of four open-ended qualitative questions on the back page. These ask parents to explain *why* they believe their child is intelligent or creative, and what they expect of a school program for creative students.

Creativity Attitude Survey

Creative Attitudes, Personality: CAS

Schaefer (1971) developed a creativity inventory for grades 4 to 6 entitled the *Creativity Attitude Survey* (CAS). The CAS includes 32 yes-no items and seems to measure many of the same traits evaluated by GIFT and the GIFFIs: confidence in one's own ideas and imagination, appreciation of fantasy and wild ideas, humor, an interest in art and writing, a desire for novelty, and an attraction to the abstract and magical. The manual reported internal consistency reliabilities of .75 and .81 and a five-week test-retest reliability of .61. Adequate.

Sensitive to Training Effects

Evidence for validity was provided by research with 31 fifth-grade children who participated in a creativity training program for one hour per week for 14 weeks. Their CAS scores improved significantly from pretest to post-test while the scores of students in two control groups did not. Twenty months later, children who received the creativity training still scored higher on the CAS than did the others.

A second validity study in primarily African American and Puerto Rican American schools with 321 experimental and 366 control children replicated the earlier project: Post-test CAS scores for the trained children were significantly higher than for control children. Finally, 17 students who were nominated by a fifth-grade language arts teacher as having shown "concrete evidence of creativity" scored higher on the CAS than 18 other students who were judged equally bright. One reviewer (McKee, 1985) noted that although the CAS has not been widely adopted, it could be used for evaluating the success of programs designed to teach creative thinking in elementary age children.

**Creativity Training
Influences Attitudes**

Test author Schaefer (1970) concluded that "Favorable changes in attitudes toward creativity seem to be a primary effect of creativity training programs, and these attitudinal changes seem to be relatively resistant to extinction over time." Read this statement again. The quote mirrors one main point of this entire volume.

Creativity Self-Report Scale

**Feldhusen Used 67
Torrance Descriptors**

Feldhusen, Denny and Condon (1965) created an unpublished inventory, the *Creativity Self-Report Scale*, consisting of 67 phrases considered by Torrance (1965) to describe the "behaviors and attributes" of creative persons. If you can find Torrance's book, the test is available. Junior or senior high school students simply check which of the phrases "is true of you." A sample of the 67 items appears in Table 8.3. As with *The Williams Scale*, a danger is that a "yea sayer" can unjustifiably earn a top score.

Adjective Check List

**ACL: Absent-Minded
to Zany**

**Domino: 59 Adjectives
Are Indicators**

George Domino Version.   The *Adjective Check List* (ACL; Gough & Heilbrun, 1965) contains 300 adjectives from *absent-minded* to *zany*. The test taker takes the test by marking those adjectives that apply to him or her. The ACL manual does not include a scoring key for creativity. However, Domino (1970) devised a creativity key which includes 59 of the 300 adjectives. In scoring the ACL for creativity it is necessary to control for the number of adjectives checked, since an enthusiastic chimpanzee could endorse all 300 items and earn a perfect creativity score. Domino's scoring system therefore includes a table in which the raw score

---

Table 8.3
A Sample of Creativity Self-Report Scale Items
(Feldhusen, Denny & Condon, 1965)

Not bothered by mess or disorder	Sometimes stubborn
Like adventure	Persistent
Like things which are mysterious	Willing to take risks
Full of energy	Sometimes sloppy
Like working with ideas	Sometimes act without planning
Full of curiosity	Question authority and rules
Like to be independent	Open-minded
Have some odd habits	Enjoy taking things apart
Get lost in a problem	Cannot write fast enough to keep up with thoughts
Like complicated ideas	
Ask many questions	Sometimes question or disagree with statements made by the teacher
Like to hear other people's ideas	
Act childish or silly sometimes	Stick with a project to completion
A self-starter	Seen by some students as being different
Self-confident	Look for new ways of doing things
Good sense of humor	Not afraid of being thought to be "different"
See beauty in some things	

Table 8.4
Gough's (1979) Scoring Key for
the *Adjective Check List*

Positive Items		*Negative Items*	
Capable	Interests wide	Affected	Honest
Clever	Inventive	Cautious	Interests Narrow
Confident	Original	Commonplace	Mannerly
Egotistical	Reflective	Conservative	Sincere
Humorous	Resourceful	Conventional	Submissive
Individualistic	Self-confident	Dissatisfied	Suspicious
Informal	Sexy		
Insightful	Snobbish		
Intelligent	Unconventional		

Score: 18 (positive items) minus 12 (negative items). (No correction for number of items checked.)

(number of the 59 items checked) is converted to a standard score, based on the total number of adjectives checked.

The ACL, with the Domino scoring systems, appears to be a good adult creativity test. In one study with college students (Davis & Bull, 1978), the ACL showed high internal consistency reliability and good validity in predicting the rated creativeness of students' art and writing projects. Further, the ACL was sensitive to creativity training effects: Students who had taken a creativity class scored higher than students who had not yet taken the class. ACL scores reflected changes in personality and self-concept as a result of exposure to concepts in creativity.

At the end of this chapter, the 59 adjectives in Domino's scoring key appear in Table A and his guide for converting raw scores to standard scores appears in Table B.

Harrison Gough Version.   Gough (1979) himself validated a 30-item creativity scale for the ACL that he believes is superior to Domino's creative scale, even though it is shorter (Table 8.4). Gough's scale is more easily scored because there is no correction for the total number of adjectives checked. One simply subtracts the number of negative indicators endorsed from the number of positive indicators endorsed.

Barron-Welsh Art Scale

Many lists of characteristics of creative people will include "attraction to complexity" or "preference for complexity and asymmetry," characteristics that in part were born in the research of George Welsh and Frank Barron with their *Barron-Welsh Art Scale* (Welsh & Barron, 1963). The test is unlike other creative personality inventories. In fact, it's not an inventory at all, but it does evaluate attraction to complexity, asymmetry, and ambiguity. The test is a set of 80 abstract line drawings, some simple and balanced and others complex and asymmetrical. Test takers simply mark (+ or -) which of the drawings they like and which they

Margin notes:

Reliable, Valid, Sensitive to Training

Gough: 30 Adjectives Are Indicators

B-W Art Scale: Preference for Complexity

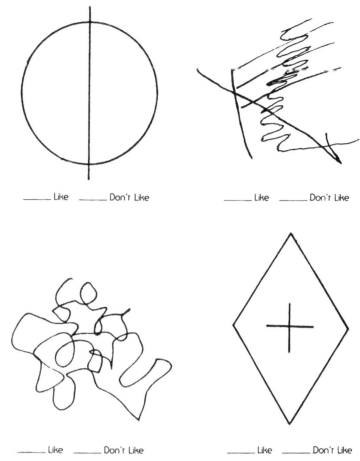

Figure 8.1 Patterns similar to those in the *Barron-Welsh Art Scale*. Are you simple and balanced? Or complex and smudgy?

do not like. Artists and people who are more creative tend to like the complex and asymmetrical drawings and to not like the simple and balanced ones. Some patterns similar to those in the Art Scale appear in Figure 8.1.

There is a correct answer for each of the items—"like" or "don't like"—although 20 of the 80 items are "fillers" which are not scored. One's creativity score is the total number of correct answers (0-60). With adults the test is quite good, but it has not been widely used in the schools.[5] The *Barron-Welsh Art Scale* may or may not be useful below college level.

Kirton Adaptation-Innovation Inventory

KAI: Adaptors and Innovators

A final personality-related inventory is the British *Kirton Adaptation-Innovation Inventory* (KAI; Kirton, 1987). It differs from other creativity inventories in that it measures *style* of creative problem solving, not *level*. The KAI evaluates two styles that are assumed to be ends of a continuum. *Adaptors* tend to accept the problem as defined and generate creative ideas designed to "do things better" (Mudd, 1995). They are more likely to use conventional solutions. Adaptors are described as resourceful, efficient, organized, and dependable, but also closed-minded and dogmatic. At the other end of the continuum, *innovators* solve problems by trying

---

[5]Translation: Your author does not know of any studies using this test with elementary or secondary students.

new approaches. They may redefine the problem and break previously perceived restraints in order to "do things differently." Innovators are described as original, energetic, individualistic, spontaneous, and insightful, but sometimes impractical, abrasive, and creators of confusion. According to Kirton (1976), innovators access a larger cognitive domain than do adaptors.

Good Theory

Puccio, Treffinger, and Talbot (1995) administered a slight modification of the KAI to 59 British workers from an iron foundry and 81 from a research and development organization. Sure enough, a more adaptive style was related to products "that fulfilled their intended purposes or functions . . . followed accepted and understood rules associated with the job . . . and had clear practical applications" (p. 167). The products were "logical, adequate, well-crafted, and useful" (p. 157). An innovative style was highly related to products described as "new or unusual . . . caught the attention of others . . . [and] helped others view their work in new and different ways" (p. 167). These products were said to be "original, attractive, transformational, and expressive" (p. 157).

They Don't Get Along Well

Mudd (1995, p. 242) noted that "Adaptors and innovators do not readily get on, especially if they are extreme scorers. Middle scorers . . . do not easily reach the heights of adaptation or innovation as do extreme scorers . . . but they more easily act as 'bridges,' forming the consensus group and getting the best out of clashing extreme scorers."

According to Hammerschmidt (1996), extreme adaptors and innovators just don't speak the same language. KAI scores range from 32 to 160, with an American mean of 95—and an average organizational work group difference of just 5 KAI points will cause communication problems. As validity evidence, Hammerschmidt compared 4-person organization *planning* groups (more rule-bound and requiring more conventional thinking) versus *implementation* groups (less structured and requiring less conformity). When adaptors and innovators were assigned to work groups consistent with their KAI preference, the group was more successful.

Innovators: Higher Divergent Thinking Scores

The KAI showed an internal consistency reliability of .86—indicating that all test items generally measure the same thing, namely, adaptation-innovation concepts—and validities that relate KAI scores to several organizational performance measures (e.g., organizational fit, job tenure, and productivity; Mudd, 1995). Comparing KAI scores with divergent thinking scores, Gelade (1995) confirmed that, sure enough, innovators produced more original ideas and a greater number of ideas.

While the KAI seems designed for adults—for example, in business, administration, and management—it apparently can be used with middle-school students (Selby, Treffinger, Isaksen, & Powers, 1993).

Cautions in Using Personality Information to Identify Creative Students

Students Differ (Surprise!)

As perhaps an obvious caution, despite recurring commonalities in personality traits, not all creative students will show all traits. Creative students differ dramatically from each other. Some are high achievers whose creativity takes socially valued artistic and scientific forms. Other creative students will be more unconventional in appearance and behavior, and even may be rebellious and antiestablishment—unwilling to tolerate a bureaucracy perceived as inflexible and irrelevant to their problems or to world problems. Many creative students will be energetic, outgoing, confident, and comical—our classic theater types. Others, perhaps artistic, poetic, or scientific-minded students, will be introverted, anxious, and socially withdrawn.

Teacher Pleasers

In rating or nominating students as creative, some teachers will not recognize characteristics of creativity. They might favor the dutiful and conforming "teacher pleasers" over the sometimes unconventional, over-active students who may think oddly, dress oddly, ignore rules and conventions, ask too many questions, do poor work when not interested, or be radical or defiant.

ADHD

Some energetic creative students will be perceived by teachers as having attention deficit hyperactivity disorder (ADHD). Because of the similarity of symptoms of ADHD and the creative personality (Cramond, 1994), some teachers are more likely to recommend consulting a physician about medication than to nominate an active child as creative.

Are You a Pseudo-Creative?

A minor caution in identifying creative secondary school students is the existence of a few *pseudo-creatives*, pretentious students who feign creativeness by dressing and acting the way they believe eccentric creative people are supposed to dress and act.

Nonetheless, a teacher, counselor, school psychologist, or parent who is aware of personality and biographical indicators of creativeness can capitalize on the information to formally or informally identify creative potential in children and adolescents.

DIVERGENT THINKING TESTS

Torrance Tests of Creative Thinking

By far the most popular creativity tests of any kind are the *Torrance Tests of Creative Thinking* (Torrance, 1966a). Torrance inadvertently may have led others to believe that his tests measure creativity, all creativity, and nothing but creativity, but he did not delude himself. In his original technical manual, Torrance (1966b) wrote:

Torrance Was Not Trying to Kid Anyone

> Since a person can behave creatively in an almost infinite number of ways, in the opinion of the author it would be ridiculous even to try to develop a comprehensive battery of tests of creative thinking that would sample any kind of universe of creative thinking abilities. The author does not believe that anyone can now specify the number and range of test tasks necessary to give a complete or even an adequate assessment of a person's potentialities for creative behavior. He does believe that the sets of test tasks assembled in the [Torrance Tests] sample a rather wide range of the abilities in such a universe (p. 23).

Careful Development, Validation, Scoring Guides

The Torrance Tests were 10 years in development, have the most complete administration and scoring guides and norms, have a longitudinal validation history (e.g., Torrance, 1984a, 1988; Torrance & Goff, 1989; Torrance & Safter, 1989; Yamada & Tam, 1996), have been translated into 34 languages, and have recent scoring guides and norms (Torrance 1990a, 1990b).[6] They have generated well over 1,000 published research studies. About 150,000 children and adults take the Torrance Tests each year (Torrance, 1984a). Because the tests are so well known and widely used, we will describe this battery in more detail than others.

The Torrance Tests originated in the 1950s and 1960s from Torrance's *Minnesota Tests of Creative Thinking*, which themselves were based upon Guilford's Structure of Intellect creativity tests (described later). During their 10 years of development

---

[6]The American publisher, Scholastic Testing Service, distributes only an English Language version of the Torrance Tests.

**Verbal A and B;
Figural A and B**

**Verbal Test:
7 "Activities"**

1. **List Questions**

2. **List Causes**

3. **List Consequences**

4. **List Product
Improvements**

5. **Unusual Uses**
6. **Unusual Questions**

7. **What Would
Happen If?**

**Figural Test:
3 "Activities"
All: Complete a
Drawing**
1. **Picture
Construction**
2. **Picture Completion**
3. **Circles**

**Scores of Fluency,
Flexibility, Originality,
Elaboration: Creative
Abilities**

**Fluency: Number
of Ideas**
**Originality: Statistical
Infrequency**

**Originality Scoring
Can Be Ambiguous**

Torrance firmed up administration and scoring procedures, assembled normative data, gathered reliability and validity data, and put it all into four test booklets, four administration and scoring manuals for the Verbal Forms A and B and Figural Forms A and B, and a norms and technical manual. All subtests are timed, with either a 5- or 10-minute limit.

The verbal test, *Thinking Creatively With Words*, is built of seven subtests or "activities." The first three subtests evolve around a curious picture (imagine an elf with pointed ears and pointed shoes looking at his or her reflection in a stream). Torrance feels that the ability to ask questions (sense problems, detect gaps in information) is an important creative ability. In fact, it is part of his definition of creativity (Torrance, 1977, 1988; see Chapter 3). Therefore, the first activity, *Asking*, requires the test taker to list all of the questions he or she can think of about the events in the picture, questions that cannot be answered by simply looking at the picture (e.g., are the ears pointed?). The second subtest, *Guessing Causes*, asks the test taker to list possible causes of the events shown in the picture. The third activity, *Guessing Consequences*, asks for a list of consequences of the events taking place in the drawing.

The fourth verbal subtest, *Product Improvement*, includes a sketch of a stuffed monkey (or elephant). The examinee lists all of the improvements he or she can which would make the stuffed animal more fun to play with. A fifth subtest, *Unusual Uses*, asks the taker to list uses for cardboard boxes (or tin cans). The related sixth subtest, *Unusual Questions*, again focuses upon question asking: List all of the questions you can about cardboard boxes (or tin cans).

The final, seventh verbal subtest, *Just Suppose*, is an old creativity favorite—the "what would happen if . . . ?" question. In this case, the unlikely event is clouds with strings attached to them, or in the other test form, clouds so low you could only see people's feet. What would happen? Would you wear anything but shoes?

There are just three nonverbal or figural subtests in *Thinking Creatively With Pictures*. In all three cases, an incomplete or abstract sketch is presented and the examinee is asked to complete the drawing—making the picture into something meaningful and imaginative. The first subtest, *Picture Construction*, presents a sausage-shaped (or egg-shaped) form which is used as the basis for an imaginative drawing. The second subtest, *Picture Completion*, presents the test taker with ten simple, abstract shapes similar to those in Figure 8.2 which he or she completes and labels. Finally, the third figural activity, *Circles*, includes two pages of circles (or parallel lines) which again are incorporated into complete, meaningful, and perhaps clever drawings.

The subtests of the Torrance Tests, verbal and figural, are scored for *fluency, flexibility, originality,* and *elaboration*. These are considered basic creative abilities, as well as dimensions of the scoring. A newer, streamlined scoring scheme for the Figural Forms A and B, which produces 18 creativity scores, will be described later.

The fluency score is simply a count of ideas listed or drawings completed, after duplications and irrelevant entries (e.g., recopying instructions, writing one's name 20 times, or reciting Mary Had a Little Lamb) are excluded. Originality scores are based upon *statistical infrequency* norms. That is, each idea is listed in a table in the scoring guide where it is awarded 0, 1, or 2 points depending upon how infrequently (rarely) that idea was listed by subjects on whom the test was normed. Scoring for originality is not as simple as scoring for fluency. Because some ideas will be ambiguous or not in the scoring guide, the test scorer must make a judgment as to the degree of "creative strength" shown by the ambiguous idea, and therefore the number of points to award. For example, using a cardboard box for a dog house is not original, but what about using it for a house for a pet anteater, pet Martian, or politician?

Torrance Tests of Creative Thinking

The *Torrance Tests of Creative Thinking* (Torrance, 1966) measure creative abilities of *fluency* (number of ideas), *flexibility* (number of different types or categories of ideas), *originality* (uniqueness) and *elaboration* (number of embellishments). Exercises similar to Torrance's subtests are presented below. Spend a few minutes on each one. Are you fluent? Flexible? Original? Are you elaborate?

Directions: Make a meaningful picture out of each of the nonsense forms below. Try to be original. Give each one a name.

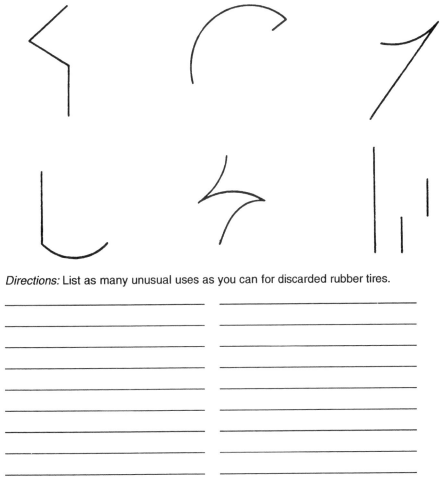

Directions: List as many unusual uses as you can for discarded rubber tires.

_____	_____
_____	_____
_____	_____
_____	_____
_____	_____
_____	_____
_____	_____
_____	_____

(For additional space use inside back cover of book.)

Figure 8.2 Torrance Tests of Creative Thinking

Flexibility: Different Approaches, Categories of Ideas

Flexibility refers to the number of different categories of ideas or the number of different approaches one takes to a problem. For example, if Roberta Rutt's list of tin can uses includes "put buttons in it, put pennies in it, put bottle caps in it, put nails in it, put washers in it, put feather in it, etc.," Roberta would have a very low flexibility score. In scoring the Torrance Tests, as the scorer looks up the originality weight he or she also will find a number indicating the flexibility category. The number of different flexibility category numbers is the flexibility score for that subtest. Read that sentence fast.

Elaboration: Number of Details beyond the Basic Pictures

Title Originality

The figural tests may be scored for elaboration by counting the number of details beyond the basic picture. These are details that are added to the figure itself, its boundaries, and/or to the surrounding space (e.g., additional ideas, decorations, emotional expressions, color, shading). *Title originality*, on a 0 to 3 scale, is an optional *verbal* score that may be derived from figural Activity 1, *Picture*

Test of originality: How many explanations can you think of for the action, or lack of it, in this photo? (The Museum of Modern Art/Film Stills Archive.)

Bonus Points

Construction, and Activity 2, *Picture Completion*. Bonus points (2 to 25) are awarded for Activity 3, *Circles* (or *Parallel Lines*), if the clever person combines two or more circles into a single picture. These points are added to the figural originality score.

Verbal Tests: Elaboration Optional

The verbal tests typically are not scored for elaboration, although directions for this optional scoring are available. One would count the number of additional details in each response beyond what is needed to communicate the basic idea. This could be useful if one were specifically interested in a person's or group's elaboration abilities.

High Interscorer Reliability

Good Test-Retest Reliability

The norms and technical manuals (Torrance, 1974, 1990b) report interscorer reliabilities (the correlation between scores produced by two independent scorers) as high as .99 (for fluency) and almost always above .90. Test-retest reliabilities are in the satisfactory .60 to .80 range, with a few lower and many higher. The test-retest reliability figures are undoubtedly depressed by Torrance's peculiar procedure of using Form A for the first administration and Form B for the later administration, which muddles test-retest reliability with alternate forms reliability.

Construct Validity

Wild Reputations, Original Drawings, High Humor, Ink Blot Creativity

Lower Rigidity

Creative Activities, Hobbies, Career Preferences

Torrance's Landmark Longitudinal Studies

High Scorers: Greater Quantity and Quality of Creative Achievements and High Creative Aspirations

Validating creativity tests is not an easy chore, for reasons cited earlier. Much of Torrance's validation work, in fact, has been of the construct validity type—demonstrating that high scorers on the Torrance Tests show characteristics commonly associated with creativity. One study indicated that high scorers on the Torrance Tests had reputations for producing wild or silly ideas; their drawings were described as highly original, and they tended to be humorous and playful (Torrance, 1974). Another study showed that high scorers were rated high in humor and gave ink blot responses traditionally associated with imagination and creativity—responses were unconventional, fanciful, and included human movement and color (Weisberg & Springer, 1961). Fleming and Weintraub (1962) found a significant inverse relationship between creativity scores and rigidity scores. Still other studies showed Torrance Test scores to be significantly correlated with the originality of imaginative stories (Yamamoto, 1963); involvement in creative activities and hobbies (art, drama, literature, music; Cropley, 1971, 1972); preferences for creative and unconventional careers (Torrance & Dauw, 1965); and teacher nominations of, for example, "Who thinks of the most unusual, wild or fantastic ideas?" (Torrance, 1974).

Research which provides the best evidence of a relationship between Torrance Test scores and real-life creative achievement comes from two longitudinal studies, one involving high school students tested in 1959 and followed up 7 and 12 years later (i.e., in 1966 and 1971); and another involving elementary school students tested in 1958 (and for 5 subsequent years) and followed up 22 years later (i.e., in 1980; Torrance, 1988). The results of these landmark research projects should increase the confidence of Torrance Test users. Compared with low Torrance Test scorers, high scorers reported a larger *quantity* of creative achievements, higher *quality* of their creative achievements, and a higher level of *creative motivation* (career aspirations). For example, the "quantity of publicly recognized and acknowledged creative achievements" included such items as patents and inventions; plays or music compositions that were performed publicly; art work awards; founding a business, journal, or professional organization; developing an innovative technique in medicine, science, business, teaching, etc. The quality criterion was ratings of the "three most creative achievements" of each person. Creativeness of aspirations was primarily assess via answers to two direct questions: (1) "What are your career ambitions? For example, what position, responsibility, or reward do you wish to attain? What do you hope to accomplish?" (2) "If you could do or be whatever you choose in the next 10 years, what would it be?" (Torrance, 1988, p. 58).

Torrance (1984a, p. 4) reported that after 22 years, as young adults

Compared with a High IQ Group

> ... the creatively gifted group excelled a high IQ group on the quality of their highest creative achievements, their high school creative achievements, the number of creative lifestyle achievements, and the creativity of their future career images. They also tended to excel the IQ gifted group on number of post-high school creative achievements but the difference fell short of statistical significance. The doubly gifted group [high creativity, high IQ] equalled but did not excel the creatively gifted group on all five of the criteria of young adult creative achievement.

Over Time, Highs Got Higher, Lows Did Not

Interestingly, the difference in creative achievements and motivations between high and low creatives increased over time—while the highs got higher, the lows did not change.

Given the complexity problems described earlier, validity data, including data from the 22-year longitudinal study, seem reasonable despite criticisms (for sum-

Verbal Tests: Individual Administration in Grades 1–3

maries of pros and cons on the Torrance Tests, see, e.g., Callahan, 1991; Chase, 1985; Torrance, 1990a, 1990b; Treffinger, 1985). The verbal tests may be group administered from fourth grade through graduate school, and individually administered from kindergarten through the third grade. The figural tests may be group administered from kindergarten through graduate school. According to Torrance (1977) the figural tests are more culture-fair.

Scoring Is Time Consuming: Only Divergent Abilities Measured

Streamlined Scoring.   Torrance confessed that, despite generally satisfactory reliability and validity evidence and proven usefulness in education, "many users have made two major criticism: The scoring is too time-consuming and the tests assess only the divergent production abilities and do not tap the essence of creativity" (Torrance & Ball, 1984, p. 5).

Streamlined Scoring: Fluency, Originality, Elaboration, Abstractness of Titles, Resistance to Premature Closure, 13 Creative Strengths

Torrance's (Torrance & Ball, 1984) *streamlined* scoring system, for the figural tests only, was designed to (1) streamline the scoring (surprise!), and (2) assess other dimensions of creativity beyond the divergent thinking abilities of fluency, flexibility, originality, and elaboration. The new system, nine years in development, maintains the *fluency* measure essentially "as is" (which was easy to score in the first place), expedites the scoring of *originality* and *elaboration,* and adds two easily-scored dimensions called *abstractness of titles* and *resistance to premature closure.* Also added were no less than 13 "creative strengths."

Five Norm-Referenced Scores

To be as brief as possible, the five scoring dimensions of fluency, originality, elaboration, abstractness of titles, and resistance to premature closure are considered *norm-referenced,* which means that the number of points earned are relative to the norm group. (Strictly speaking, fluency is not scored relative to a norm group.) The other 13 creative strengths are *criterion referenced,* which means that the criterion (the creative strength) either appears in the person's test or it does not.

13 Criterion-Referenced Scores

Fluency, as in the original scoring guides, is a count of relevant, nonduplicated ideas. If two or more figures are combined, credit still is given for the number of figures used.

Originality is the number of original ideas. That is, non-original ideas, listed in tables, are eliminated.

One *elaboration* point is given for adding: decorations, color, shading, each major variation of design, and each elaboration of the title beyond minimal labeling.

Abstractness of titles is scored from 0 to 3 points according to degree of abstractness, for example, a 3-point idea involves "the ability to capture the essence of the information involved, to know what is important . . . [and] enables the viewer to see the picture more deeply and richly" (Torrance & Ball, 1984, p. 19).

Resistance to premature closure earns 0 to 2 points depending upon the degree to which the test taker (prematurely) closes the incomplete figure, "cutting off chances for more powerful original images" (p. 22).

"+" and "++"

Turning to the list of 13 creative strengths, in general one plus sign ("+") is awarded if 1 or 2 instances of the creative strength occur (in the entire test booklet); two plus signs ("++") are given if 3 or more instances occur.

Emotional expressiveness is the communication of feelings or emotions (sad, happy, angry, scared, lost) in either the drawing or the title.

Storytelling articulateness is including enough detail to put the picture in context and tell a story.

Movement or action is scored if it appears in the title or the picture (e.g., running, flying, dancing, swimming).

Expressiveness of titles is scored if emotion and feeling are shown in the title (e.g., "lonely," "ambitious").

Synthesis of incomplete figures, a rare occurrence, is the combination of two or more figures in the Picture Completion subtest.

"Okay, okay! I'll take a look at the new streamlined scoring system!" (The Museum of Modern Art/Film Stills Archive.)

Synthesis of lines or circles is the tendency to combine two or more circles or sets of lines, which is "an important indicator of a creative disposition or thinking ability" (Torrance & Ball, 1984, p. 34).

Unusual visualization is the tendency to present ideas or objects in usual visual perspective, for example, from underneath, on top, or a cutaway view.

Internal visualization is the tendency to visualize the internal workings of things, for example, body parts seen through clothing, the internal parts of a machine, or ants in an anthill.

Extending or breaking boundaries may occur by lengthening some lines in the Parallel Lines activity (e.g., to make a table), dividing a pair of lines for different aspects of a picture, or by adding depth perception with circles.

Humor—puns, word play, exaggeration, absurdity—may appear in the figures or in the titles.

Richness of imagery is scored if the drawing "shows variety, vividness, liveliness, and intensity . . . has freshness . . . and provides delight for the tired scorer" (p. 44), for example, a pair of cat eyes, an alligator, or a surfer.

Colorfulness of imagery "is defined as exciting in its appeal to the sense of taste, touch, smell, feel, sight, etc." (p. 44), for example, a whale ride, banana store, ghost, or toothache.

Finally, *Fantasy* is reflected in fairy tale episodes or characters from fables, science fiction, or other fantasy literature; also original fantasy, such as talking rain drops or a parachute hat creation.

High Agreement
between Original and
Streamlined Scoring

All 18 Streamlined
Measures Validated

Is 18 Scores Really
"Streamlining"?
Rich Information

A comparison of the original scoring of fluency, originality, and elaboration with the new streamlined scoring showed very high agreement (correlation coefficients of .92, .94, and .92, respectively; Torrance & Ball, 1984). The streamlined scoring test manual presents extensive validity coefficients (correlations between scores and criteria of creativity) for all 18 measures for students in grades 3 through 12, derived from the longitudinal data mentioned earlier plus other research, that range mostly between .30 and .60.

On one hand, changing the scoring system from four to 18 scores somehow loses the flavor of "streamlining." On the other hand, the new scoring system, with practice, is indeed expedient and includes rich information that could be useful in understanding a person's creative tendencies and talents. The reader interested in further details regarding scoring and validation should see Torrance and Ball (1984) and Torrance (1974, 1990a, 1990b).

Research Suggestions for Program Evaluation. As a first suggestion, if a research design for evaluating a training program includes both a *before* and an *after* measure of creativeness using two different test forms, such as Form A and Form B of the Torrance Tests, give half of the subjects Form A and half Form B as a pretest. Each subject would take the other form as the post-test This strategy controls for the possibility that the two test forms may not be exactly equivalent. That is, average scores on Form A (or Form B) might tend to run higher, regardless of intervening training. It would not be sensible or accurate to provide objective test evidence that (1) the gifted and talented program depressed student creativity (because students happened to take the difficult form as a post-test) or (2) the program was wildly successful in teaching creativity (because students took the easy form as a post-test).

Half Take Form A,
Half Take Form B
as Pretest

Use Control Group

As a second suggestion, in evaluating program success a control group (comparable subjects who do not receive the training) is recommended so that a logical person can conclude that improvement from pretest to post-test truly is due to the creativity training, and not due to having taken the creative test once before. Both errors are common.

Creativity and School Achievement. Creative traits such as unconventionality and independence, sometimes mixed with a little resistance to domination and indifference to rules and conventions, surely can work against school achievement. However, other traits and abilities of creative students are definite assets in school: flexibility, curiosity and inquisitiveness, perceptiveness and the ability to see relationships, resourcefulness, high energy and enthusiasm, confidence, inner-directedness, an experimental attitude, intuitive thinking, open-mindedness—and verbal creativity generally. Torrance (1974) reported correlations roughly in the range of .35 to .45 between verbal creativity scores and scores on standardized achievement tests (reading, language, arithmetic), with intelligence held constant. Figural creativity scores showed lower correlations (.16 to .25) with achievement. Torrance noted that correlations between creativity scores and achievement will

Bad for School Success

Good for School
Success

Especially When
Children Taught
in Creative Ways

be lower when children are taught by authority, higher when taught in creative ways such as using discovery, experimentation, and the like.

Low Correlations with IQ Scores

Importantly, summarizing the results of many studies, Torrance reported the median correlation between figural creativity and intelligence as .06 and between verbal creativity and intelligence as .21. These figures indicate that creative abilities and abilities measured by intelligence tests are not the same, especially with nonverbal creativity.

Test for Creative Thinking-Drawing Production

Another instrument has been around for a while, but is just recently being promoted in the U.S. It could be useful. About 1986 Klaus Urban and Hans Jellen in Hannover, Germany, first published a few articles describing their *Test for Creative Thinking—Drawing Production* (TCT-DP). A more recent manual is dated 1993 (Urban & Jellen, 1993). The TCT-DP resembles Torrance's figural tests, but the description and scoring are unique. The test appears to evaluate a combination of creative abilities and creative personality dispositions. According to the authors, in comparison with divergent thinking tests the TCT-DP "may be seen as an attempt to apply a more holistic and gestalt-oriented approach to diagnostics of creativity" (Urban & Jellen, 1993).

TCT-DP: Evaluates Abilities, Personality

Figural, Two Forms

Form A is comprised of a single 6-inch square frame within which are five so-called "figural fragments": a 90-degree angle, a half-circle, a squiggly line, a dot, and a short dotted line. Outside the square frame lies a sixth fragment, a small square with one open side. Form B is identical except the figural fragments are arranged differently. The test can be used with single subjects or groups "between 5 and 95 years of age." Administration requires 15 minutes or less. After considerable practice, scoring is said to require 1 to 2 minutes.

One 1990 evaluation of the factor structure and other psychometric features of the TCT-DP led the highly impressed Polish researchers to recommend that the test be normed and used as an official screening instrument in Poland for identifying gifted and creative students (Urban, 1993).

As for instructions, the administrator reads (says) clearly and slowly:

Untimed, Draw What You Wish

> In front of you is an incomplete drawing. The artist who started it was interrupted before he or she actually knew what should become of it. You are asked to continue with this incomplete drawing. *You are allowed to draw whatever you wish!* You can't draw anything wrong. Everything you put on the paper is correct. When you finish your drawing, please, give me a sign, so that I can take it. . . . Just begin your drawing and don't worry about the time, . . . But we don't have a whole hour to complete this drawing.

As each student finishes the administrator records the time, which is one of 11 scoring dimensions:

1. *Continuations*: Any use, continuation, or extension of the six given figural fragments.

2. *Completion*: Any additions, completions, complements, or supplements made to the used, continued, or extended figural fragments.

3. *New elements*: Any new figure, symbol, or element.

4. *Connections made with a line*: Any connection between one figural fragment or figure and another.

5. *Connections made to produce a theme*: Any figure contributing to a compositional theme or "gestalt."

6. *Boundary breaking that is fragment dependent*: Any use, continuation, or extension of the "small open square" located outside the square frame.

7. *Boundary breaking that is fragment independent*: Drawing extensions, figures, and/or elements that break the boundary or lie outside the large square frame, but are independent from the small open square.

8. *Perspective*: Any breaking away from two-dimensionality.

9. *Humor and affectivity*: Any drawing that elicits a humorous response or shows affection, emotion, or strong expressive power.

10. *Unconventionality*: (a) Any manipulation of the material; (b) any surrealistic, fictional, and/or abstract elements or drawings; (c) any usage of symbols or signs; or (d) unconventional figures.

11. *Speed*: If the drawing accumulates at least 25 points from the first 10 categories, up to 6 more points are awarded for speed. For example, 6 points are awarded if one finishes under 2 minutes, but no points if one takes longer than 12 minutes.

Each dimension earns 0 to 6 points, except *Unconventionality*, which earns 0 to 12 points. The possible total score is thus 0 to 72 points. Points are added together to produce a total score, with no transformations.

Similar to Torrance Streamlined Scoring Dimensions

The authors' claim that the TCT-DP is different and superior to existing divergent thinking tests. However, there is a great similarity to several aspects of the streamlined scoring of the Torrance Tests—of which the authors may have been unaware when they built the TCT-DP. Specifically, both tests award points for unconventionality and fantasy (Torrance's originality), humor and affectivity (Torrance's emotional expressiveness), producing a theme (Torrance's story telling articulateness), and boundary breaking (same in both).

The TCT-DP is a new, carefully developed, and possibly useful creativity test. Some people are impressed with its potential for identifying creatively gifted children. It is difficult to determine whether it will do more than existing American creativity tests.

The Guilford Tests

Guilford's SOI Model

Original Model: 120 Cells

Some problem-sensitive readers may have wondered why Guilford's (1967, 1977) *Structure of Intellect* (SOI) model did not appear in Chapter 3 with other theories of creativity.[7] Answer: It was saved until now. Guilford created a three-dimensional cube—a theory of intelligence—which was intended to describe anything anyone could ever do with his or her brain. Figure 8.3 presents the 1988 (and final) edition of the SOI cube, with its three dimensions of *contents, products,* and *operations.* This newest version is known only to the readers of his five-page 1988 article or this chapter. In its original form (Guilford, 1967), four types of contents combined with six products and five operations to produce 120 cells ($4 \times 6 \times 5 = 120$). Most people who write about Guilford's model stopped here—with "120 SOI abilities" forever ossified in their frontal lobes. In fact, Guilford (1977) extended the model by subdividing the "figural" content into *visual content* and *auditory content,* creating 150 cells. Shortly before his death he also subdivided the "memory" operation into *memory retention* (long-term memory)

Latest and Final Model: 180 Cells

---

[7]Have you wondered why Joy Paul Guilford never used his first name?

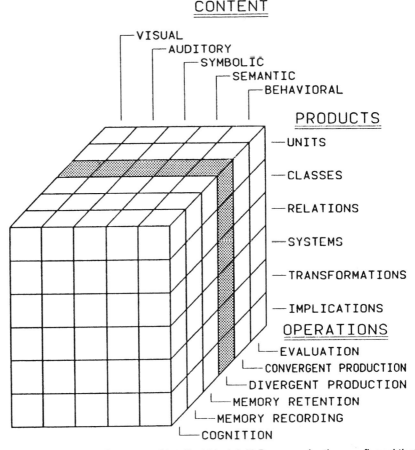

Figure 8.3 The Revised Structure of Intellect Model. X-Ray examination confirmed that Guilford's cerebral cortex looked exactly like this. Reprinted by permission of *Educational and Psychological Measurement.*

and *memory recording* (short-term memory)—producing no fewer than 180 cells (Guilford, 1988).

Each Cell Equals a Cognitive Ability

Our limited space will not permit a complete description of the SOI model (which makes tedious reading anyway). Briefly, each of the 180 cells of the model is interpreted to be a unique cognitive ability. This approach stands in sharp contrast to the two IQ scores of the WISC-III or the four scores of the *Stanford-Binet Intelligence Scale, Fourth Edition.* J. Paul Guilford invested about three decades creating tests that measure each one of those 180 abilities.

Creativity: Divergent Thinking Abilities

The darkened slab of the model in Figure 8.3 includes the operations of *divergent production.* Tests that measure a few of these 30 abilities (6 products × 5 contents) are marketed as tests of creativity. For example, *Word Fluency* is a 4 minute test that requires the examinee to produce a list of words containing a specified letter or letters (e.g., R____ M). In the SOI cube this is divergent production of symbolic units, or DSU. The *Expressional Fluency* test, divergent production of semantic systems (DMS), allows 8 minutes to verbally express an idea using a given first letter for each word (e.g., E ____ R ____ L ____ P ____). Other fluency tests include *Ideational Fluency* and *Associational Fluency*; there also are *Consequences* ("What would happen if . . .?") and *Alternate Uses* tests.

Published SOI Tests

Transformations: Also Creative Abilities

In addition to the divergent production abilities (the darkened slab), Guilford (1986) explained how *transformations* (a *product*; can you find the transformations slab in Figure 8.3?) also are important creative abilities. For example, a scientist

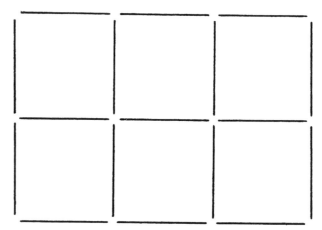

Figure 8.4 Matchstick problem measuring the divergent production of figural transformations (DFT). Try removing three matches to leave four squares; four matches to leave three squares. Do not leave excess, dangling matches.

might be strong in cognition of visual transformations (CVT); a cartoonist strong in cognition of semantic transformations (CMT); and the creativity of scientists, inventors, and decorators will involve the evaluation of visual or semantic transformations (EVT, EMT; Guilford, 1986).

This Puzzle Ignites Thinking

One cell in the 1967 SOI model is the divergent production of figural transformations (DFT)—combining the divergent production operation with the transformation product. One test of DFT may be familiar—matchstick problems. For example, given the six squares in Figure 8.4, one problem is to remove three matchsticks and leave four squares; another problem is to remove four matchsticks and leave three squares. See Guilford (1967, 1977, 1986) for descriptions of the many, many other specific SOI tests.

Supportive Validity Studies

Regarding validity, Guilford's 1967 book reviewed some elderly research showing that, for example, artists scored higher on divergent production of figural systems (DFS) tests than did unselected college students (Welch, 1946); creative writing samples of sixth-grade students correlated .46 and .58 with verbal divergent production composite scores, while their creative drawing samples correlated .50 and .54 with figural test composite scores (Jones, 1960); originality ratings of Air Force captains correlated .30, .36, and .32 with scores on the three divergent production tests Alternate Uses, Consequences, and Plot Titles (creating titles for simple story plots).

Meeker: Diagnostic-Remediation Approach with SOI-LA Test

Incidentally, for some years Meeker (1969, 1978; Meeker & Meeker, 1986) has used groups of the Guilford tests in a diagnostic-remediation (medical model) approach to teaching reading, math, writing, and creativity. Specific weaknesses are diagnosed with the *SOI-Learning Abilities* test, which then are remediated with equally specific exercises (Meeker, Meeker, & Roid, 1985). More recently, Meeker created SOI Model Schools, which include an SOI curriculum (Staff, 1995).

Exercise in Divergent Thinking

Third CAP Test

We mentioned earlier in this chapter that Frank Williams' (1980) *Creativity Assessment Packet* (CAP) included the personality-oriented *Exercise in Divergent Feeling* and *The Williams Scale*. The third part of his CAP battery is his *Exercise in Divergent Thinking*.

Picture Completion: Figural and Verbal Scores

Williams' *Exercise in Divergent Thinking* is almost identical to Torrance's figural subtest *Picture Completion*, although Williams considers it both a figural and a

Fluency, Flexibility, Originality, Elaboration

One Total Creativity Score

verbal test because the title of each artistic creation is assigned a verbal creativity score. The test includes 12 incomplete drawings, similar to those in Figure 8.1, which students have a generous 25 minutes (grades 3–5) or 20 minutes (grades 6–12) to complete, producing fluency, flexibility, originality, and elaboration scores. Instructions encourage students to "Try to draw a creative picture that no one else would think of . . . think of a clever title for your picture . . . Draw as many pictures as you can in the time given." Each title is awarded 0 to 3 points, based largely on length, complexity, creativeness, and humor. Williams adds the five scores together for a total creativity score (which some would say is adding apples and sheep). We earlier noted reliability and validity peculiarities of the CAP manual (Williams, 1980).

Wallach and Kogan Tests

Freebies

The Wallach and Kogan (1965) creativity tests are not published in the sense that you could buy a box of 25 for 20 or 30 dollars. The deal is much better. The tests appear in their entirety in *Modes of Thinking in Young Children*, complete with administration and scoring directions. Educators or researchers can use the tests without charge.

Gamelike Atmosphere

No Time Limits

Removes Influence of IQ

Fluency, Uniqueness

The Wallach and Kogan test administration procedure is unique and well known on two counts. First, a relaxed, game-like atmosphere is established. Second, the tests are untimed. The purpose of these two manipulations is to remove the pressured, test-like atmosphere that characterizes intelligence testing. According to Wallach and Kogan, these game-like and untimed conditions reduce the influence of intelligence upon the creativity scores to about zero.

There are five tests. Each test is scored for *fluency*, the total number of ideas listed, and *uniqueness*, the number of ideas that are not given by any other person in the testing group. Obviously, the uniqueness score will depend upon group size—with only 5 or 10 test takers, uniqueness scores will be much higher than with 100 or 500 students. The Wallach and Kogan sample consisted of 151 fifth-grade children.

Valid for College Students

This is not to say it is a children's test battery. The tests worked very well with a group of 37 college students (Bartlett & Davis, 1974). Fluency and uniqueness scores correlated .33 and .35 with overall ratings of the creativeness of art and writing products and ideas for inventions and creative teaching methods.

Instances

With the *Instances Test*, students list instances or examples of each of four class concepts. For example, "Name all of the *round* things you can think of." Ditto for "things . . . that will make a noise," "square things," and "things . . . that move on wheels."

Alternate Uses

Similarities

Alternate uses is, of course, our old friend the unusual uses test. In eight questions subjects were to "Tell me the different ways you could use a newspaper (knife, automobile tire, cork, shoe, button, key, and chair)." The *Similarities* test asks the person to "Tell me all the ways in which a potato and a carrot (cat and mouse, train and tractor, milk and meat, grocery store and a restaurant, etc.) are alike."

Pattern Meanings

Line Meanings

Two similar tests use visual materials. With *Pattern Meanings* subjects list possible meanings or interpretations of eight abstract visual designs: "Tell me all of the things you think this could be." With *Line Meanings*, instead of neat symmetrical patterns subjects list interpretations of line drawings, some squiggly and abstract, others simple. One, in fact, is a straight line. "Here is another line. You can turn it any way you want to. Tell me all the things you can about it. What does it make you think of?" Drawings similar to those in *Pattern Meanings* and *Line Meanings* appear in Figure 8.5.

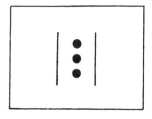   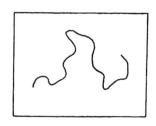

Pattern   Line

Figure 8.5 Items similar to those in the Wallach and Kogan (1965) Pattern Meanings and Line Meanings tests.

Getzels and Jackson Tests

As with the Wallach and Kogan tests, the Getzels and Jackson (1962) tests are published only in the authors' book, *Creativity and Intelligence.* Four of the subsets appear in their entirety, complete with administration and scoring directions. The fifth is copyrighted by others. The four tests again appear to be available for general use without charge.

**Word Association:
List Meanings
Scoring: Number of
Different Meanings**

The *Word Association Test* presents the person with a list of 25 words, each of which has multiple meanings (e.g., *arm, duck, bolt, punch,* and *tender*). Fifteen minutes are allowed to list as many meanings as possible. The creativity score is the total number of *different* meanings listed (e.g., *arm of chair* and *arm of sofa* would receive just 1 point, not 2).

**Uses Test
Scoring: Different
Uses, Unique Uses**

**Different + Unique =
Total**

The *Uses Test* asks the person to—what else—list as many different uses as he or she can for five objects (bricks, pencils, paper clips, toothpicks, a sheet of paper). Again, 15 minutes are allowed. The test is scored for the *number of different uses* for an object and for the relative *uniqueness* of the uses. The test taker receives a uniqueness point for each idea listed by less than one-fifth of the group of responders. The number of different uses is added to the number of unique uses to produce a total *Uses Test* score.

**Hidden Shapes
Scoring: Number
Correct**

Hidden Shapes, the copyrighted test, consists of 18 simple geometric figures, each of which is accompanied by four complex figures. The problem is to identify which complex figure contains the simple figure. The test is supposed to measure "critical exactness" or "critical practicality," which is "predictive of individual and creative work thoroughly done" (Cattell, 1955). A full 3½ minutes are allowed.

**Analytic vs. Global
Thinking**

We should note that some versions of this type of test are called *hidden figures* or *embedded figures* tests, and are interpreted to reflect a cognitive style of *analytic* (or *field independent*) versus *global* (or *field dependent*) thinking (see Witkin, Moore, Goodenough, & Cox, 1977).

**Fables Test: Moralistic,
Humorous,
Sad Endings**

The Fables Test consists of four fables whose last lines are missing. The test taker is allowed 30 minutes to supply (a) a moralistic, (b) a humorous, and (c) a sad ending for each fable. For example:

Starving Grasshopper

A grasshopper, that had merrily sung all summer, was almost perishing with hunger in the winter, so she went to see some ants that lived near, and asked them to lend her a little of the food they had put by.

"You shall certainly be paid before this time of year comes again," she said.

"What did you do all the summer?" asked they.

"Why, all day long, and all night long too, I sang, if you please," answered the grasshopper.

"Oh, you sang, did you?" said the ants. . . .

The answers are scored for *appropriateness* (is it really moralistic, humorous, or sad?) and *relatedness* (does the ending logically follow from the given material?). Appropriateness and relatedness scores are added together for a total *Fables* score.

Finally, with the *Make-up Problems* test students are given four paragraphs, each of which contains numerical statements about (1) building a swimming pool, (2) doing a science experiment, (3) earning money at odd jobs, or (4) conducting a survey of apartment rental rates. Students are allowed approximately 30 minutes to make up as many mathematical problems as they can with the given information. Each problem is scored for the number of *elements* (pieces of numerical information) and number of *operations* (addition, subtraction, multiplication, division). Again, the two scores are added together for a total *Make-Up Problems* score.

Getzel's and Jackson's *Make-Up Problems* test has been used as a test of mathematical creativity.

Thinking Creatively in Action and Movement

Torrance's (1981b) *Thinking Creatively in Action and Movement* (TCAM) is a preschool measure of creative potential. The tests grew out of Torrance's observations of the ways in which preschool children in day-care centers expressed their creativeness. Said Torrance, these tests of creativity in movement are developmentally appropriate to preschoolers and "sample the kinds of creativity that are important in the lives of such children . . . [and the tests] . . . make sense to them." Torrance conceded that his *Torrance Tests of Creative Thinking* "proved to be only marginally successful with five-year olds and were unsuitable with three and four-year olds . . . [because] children at these ages . . . have only marginal skills for expressing their ideas in words and drawings."

The first subtest, *How Many Ways?*, asks children to "think up as many ways as you can to walk or run" between tape markers on each side of the room. The experimenter records the ideas, which are later scored for *fluency* (number of ideas) and *originality* (according to a scoring guide and influenced by judgments of creative strength, with 0 to 3 points per idea). The second activity is *Can You Move Like?*, for example, a tree in the wind and assorted animals, totaling six situations. It is scored in one category, *imagination*, which is rated as the student performs each of the six movements. Activity 3, *What Other Ways?*, requires a large supply of paper cups and one waste basket. The test administrator asks the child how many ways he or she can put a paper cup in the wastebasket. A little known fact is that Michael Jordan got his start by taking this test. The fourth and final subtest is *What Can You Do With A Paper Cup?*, a children's form of the unusual uses test. Both Activities 3 and 4 are scored for fluency and originality, as with Activity 1. Extra credit (up to 4 points) is given for "unusual flourishes and choreographing executed by some children." The student winds up with a total fluency, total originality, and an imagination score.

The tests are basically untimed, although the tester is urged to record the time required for each subtest. Students usually need between 10 and 30 minutes. Scores on the tests appear to have no racial, gender, or socioeconomic bias and are relatively unrelated to previous preschool attendance or measures of intelligence. They can be used with handicapped groups such as emotionally disturbed students and deaf students (Torrance, 1981b).

Torrance (1981b) reported interscorer reliabilities of .99 for fluency and around .96 for originality. He also reported a high test-retest reliability coefficient of .84 for the overall test, with subtest test-retest reliabilities from .58 to .79.

Regarding validity, Torrance again notes the difficulty of finding a suitable criterion against which to validate the tests. Several studies were cited that produced significant correlations between TCAM scores and criteria associated with creativeness. For example, TCAM fluency and originality scores were correlated .44 and .42, respectively, with children's Knock-Knock joke humor. Knock Knock. (Who's There?) Ithsmus. (Ithsmus who?) Ithsmus be about the best data Torrance could find, under the circumstances. Another study showed that 5-year old children trained in problem-solving sociodrama scored higher on the TCAM test than control children without the training.

Who's There?

However, on the negative and eyebrow-raising side, Tegano, Moran, and Godwin (1986) found significant correlations between TCAM fluency scores and IQ scores, suggesting that TCAM performance is not independent of intelligence.

No Support Here

Incidentally, the users' comments reported in the TCAM manual suggest that the test helps improve teachers' creativity consciousness and helps them recognize specific creative children: "What a splendid tool this is. . . . The staff . . . were so awakened, saying such things as 'Why I never saw that in (name) before!' or 'Why I never paid attention to that before!' or 'Oh! Look what I have missed!' or 'I'm going to have a whole new way of teaching now!' "

Helps Creativity Consciousness

Sounds and Images, Onomatopoeia and Images

Thinking Creatively With Sounds and Words (Torrance, Khatena, & Cunnington, 1973) takes the form of two long-playing records that include the two tests *Sounds and Images* and *Onomatopoeia and Images*. They are not "divergent thinking tests" in the strict sense that a test taker will brashly list every idea he or she can think of. However, the test taker does think up and write down ideas that are scored for originality. The tests are clearly performance tests rather than self-estimates of one's creative personality, and they fit best in this divergent thinking category.

2 LP Records

Different Than Other Divergent Thinking Tests

The *Sounds and Images* test presents four abstract sounds. After each sound the test taker is given a few seconds to describe on the score sheet the mental images stimulated by that sound. The set of four sounds is presented three times under the assumption that the associations will become more and more original with repetition. They usually do. Each of the 12 responses receives between 0 and 4 originality points, based upon the norms in the scoring guide. We saw this *statistical infrequency* scoring procedure in our discussion of the Torrance Tests.

Abstract Sounds Stimulate Creative Images

Sounds Repeated: More Originality

Statistical Infrequency Scoring

The *Onomatopoeia and Images* test is similar, except that 10 image-stimulating onomatopoeic words (e.g., *zoom, boom, fizzy,* and *moan*) are used instead of four sounds. Again, the 10 words are presented three times, and 0 to 4 points are awarded for each answer according to tabled norms.

Onomatopoeia and Images: Same Procedures

As with the *Torrance Tests of Creative Thinking*, there are two forms of *Sounds and Images* and two forms of *Onomatopoeia and Images*. The forms differ only in the specific abstract sounds or onomatopoeic words used. Also, the tests are available in an adult form and a children's form. The introductory narratives of the children's forms are simpler.

Two Forms

Adult, Children's Versions

The authors present extensive reliability and validity information for the two tests. Considering both tests, interscorer reliabilities ranged from .88 to .99. Alternate forms reliability, the correlation between scores on Form A with scores on Form B, ranged from a disturbingly low .36, reflecting poor consistency and low accuracy, to .92. Validity criteria varied and so did the validity coefficients, usually between .13 and .45. Correlations between *Onomatopoeia and Images* and measures of intelligence were close to zero.

Apart from its use as a test, *Sounds and Images* makes a good imagination-stimulating creativity exercise, which is what it was created for in the first place (Torrance, Khatena, & Cunnington, 1973).

Useful as Exercises, Too

Other Creativity Tests

Many Unpublished
Tests Available for
Specific Purposes

Lots of Creativity
Tests

If one wished to scour the literature for old, unpublished, or obscure tests—perhaps for a particular subject area or purpose—some lists that include an astonishing variety of instruments appear in Dacey (1989), Davis (1971, 1973, 1989b), Kaltsoonis (1971, 1972), and Kaltsoonis and Honeywell (1980).

As some examples, one unique unpublished creativity test is the *Percept Generic Test*. The administrator repeatedly presents a picture at ever-shorter exposure times until the original is quite unrecognizable (Smith & Carlsson, 1987). We are advised that creative people more quickly break away from the dominant ("correct") perception and construct an imaginative, subjective interpretation. The *Judging Criteria Instrument* (Eichenberger, 1978) is used by peers or oneself to evaluate creativity in a physics class, using rating scales that evaluate fluency, flexibility, originality, elaboration, usefulness, social acceptance, and worth to science. A *Test of Musical Divergent Production* evaluates fluency, flexibility, originality, and elaboration, along with quality, with instrumental music students (Gorder, 1980). A *Life Experience Inventory* is said to identify creative electrical engineers (Michael & Colson, 1979). The *Creative Processes Rating Scales* is an apparently easy-to-use instrument for evaluating sixth-grade children's creativity in the visual arts (Kulp & Tarter, 1986). Torrance worked on the inventories *What Kind of Person Are You?* and *Something About Myself* (Khatena & Torrance, 1976). In addition, still other creativity tests measure empathy with story characters, creative writing, preference for polygons, and motor creativity. There are many math creativity tests, a chemistry creativity test, an "experiential curiosity measure," a pun test, an ingenuity test, and more

A survey of recent literature—particularly in the *Journal of Creative Behavior*, the *Creativity Research Journal*, and computer searches of ERIC and PsychLit—will turn up a large supply of creativity tests. Speaking from experience, it seems that many newcomers to the creativity field experience an overwhelming urge to develop a creativity test.

RECOMMENDATIONS

Your author's first recommendation would be, when possible, to evaluate students' backgrounds of creative activities and current demonstrations of creative motivation and interest. Several evaluation forms and strategies were mentioned earlier; especially noteworthy were Torrance's (1965) 100-item *Things Done on your Own* checklist and Renzulli's (1994; Renzulli & Reis, 1985, 1997) concept of *action information*. With a little imagination the reader can create an original form, perhaps with inspiration from the Torrance and Renzulli methods. A person's record of creative activities and behavior seems logically and empirically the most reliable and valid indicator of future creative behavior.

Information on
Creative Activities
Seems Reliable, Valid

Personality, Divergent
Thinking Tests Work
Reasonably Well

Regarding divergent thinking and personality/biographical types of creativity tests, both work reasonably well—given such built-in limitations as the inherent complexity of creativity and evaluating just part of human creativity (a sample of creative personality traits or a handful of creative abilities). As a practical matter, personality/biographical inventories usually can be administered and scored more quickly and efficiently than divergent thinking tests, although the Jellen and Urban *Test of Creative Thinking-Drawing Production* claims 1–2 minute scoring.

Among personality/biographical inventories, Renzulli's creativity rating scale, the *How Do You Think, GIFT, GIFFI I and II*, and Schaefer's *Creativity Attitude Survey* show high internal reliability and good track records for predicting student creativeness.

"Between you and me, it's the Torrance Tests or GIFT and GIFFI." (The Museum of Modern Art/Film Stills Archive.)

As for divergent thinking tests, the Torrance Tests must remain at the top of the list, due to their careful 10-year development, longitudinal validation studies, and recently revised norms. The more efficient newcomer, Jellen and Urban's *Test for Creative Thinking-Divergent Production,* seems promising. If cost is an issue, the Getzels and Jackson and Wallach and Kogan tests are available in their respective books, have good development histories, and seem available without charge.

Challenge Is to Identify Creative Persons

As a final reminder, the challenge is to *identify* creative children and youth. Tests and inventories that attempt to *measure* creative abilities and personality dispositions are just one way to identify creative youngsters. An awareness of creative characteristics, creative abilities, and especially students' backgrounds of creative activities can help teachers and others identify creative students with accuracy and validity—perhaps without using tests or inventories at all.

SUMMARY

We cannot predict adult creative eminence, due in part to the complexity and mystery of creativity. We can identify creative personality dispositions, some creative abilities, and strong backgrounds of creative activities.

Using creativity tests is just one way to identify creative potential; perhaps not the best way.

Creativity tests are used for selecting creative children for gifted programs; in research for identifying creative subjects and evaluating creativity programs; and in counseling to better understand troubled students.

Identification methods include formal tests and informal ratings and evaluations.

Identification is easy when persons visibly demonstrate creative traits and activities. Having had an imaginary playmate or a background in theater are remarkably good indicators.

We can identify students who, on average, will behave more creatively by measuring creative personality traits and abilities and assessing backgrounds of creative activities. We cannot beat the very long odds of predicting creative eminence, but neither can intelligence tests.

Apart from the complexity problem, creativity test validity cannot be high because test content usually differs from criterion content. Using another test as the criterion compounds the reliability and validity problems.

Validity coefficients cannot be (suspiciously) too high nor disappointingly low.

One problem is false negatives, when a test misses a creative person. False positives refers mainly to faking an undeserved high creativity score.

For accurate identification, two criteria of creativity are recommended, for example, a creativity test plus teacher or parent nominations.

Creativity is related to intelligence. Therefore, high IQ suggests creative potential.

Self-reports of creative activities seem a self-evident and valid way to locate creative students or adults.

Renzulli's action information reflects creative behaviors and personality traits and may be used for identification.

With Amabile's consensual assessment method, teachers elicit and then evaluate samples of creative work.

The Detroit Public Schools Creativity Scales uses community experts to evaluate creative products and performances.

Runco and friends used a Creative Activities Check List, 50 activities in the five domains of art, crafts, literature, math, and public performance, as a creativity validating criterion.

The Statement of Past Creative Activities by Bull and Davis also evaluated creative involvement.

Lees-Haley devised a checklist, the Creative Behavior Inventory, to evaluate students' past creative activities.

Torrance's Things Done on Your Own is another checklist of 100 creative activities.

One also can create an original self-report inventory to assess students' past or present strong creative interests and hobbies.

Personality inventories and divergent thinking tests are the two main categories of creativity tests. Divergent thinking tests are scored at least for fluency and originality.

Renzulli's 10-item creativity scale from his Scales for Rating the Behavioral Characteristics of Superior Students has high face and empirical validity.

Davis's 100-item How Do You Think? test shows high reliability and good validity as a general creative personality/motivation inventory. Spin-offs from HDYT include GIFFI I and II. The elementary level GIFT and the preschool PRIDE also evaluate creative personality traits and behaviors.

Williams CAP battery includes two creative personality inventories. His Exercise in Divergent Feeling, taken by children, evaluates curiosity, imagination, complexity, and risk-taking. The Williams Scale, filled in (or out) by parents or teachers, measures the same four traits plus fluency, flexibility, originality, and elaboration.

Schaefer's Creativity Attitude Survey resembles the GIFT and GIFFI creative attitude/personality inventories. Schaefer concluded that training results in favorable attitudes toward creativity. Amen.

Feldhusen and others devised the Creativity Self-Report Scale—67 descriptive phrases prepared by Torrance—as a checklist of creative behaviors and characteristics.

Both Domino and Gough built creativity scales for the Gough and Heilbrun Adjective Check List.

With the Barron-Welsh Art Scale one indicates which of 80 abstract drawings one likes or does not like. It evaluates preference for complexity and asymmetry.

The Kirton Adaptation-Innovation Inventory identifies adaptors and innovators. The latter seem to fit current conceptions of highly creative personalities—original and individualistic, but sometimes impractical and abrasive.

One caution is that not all creative students will show all creative personality traits, which is not surprising. Also, teachers may favor dutiful "teacher pleasers," or else suspect ADHD and recommend medical treatment for energetic creative children.

The Torrance Tests of Creative Thinking are the best known and most carefully developed and evaluated (over 22 years) divergent thinking battery. They stem from his earlier Minnesota Tests of Creative thinking and include Verbal Forms A and B (seven subtests) and Figural Forms A and B (three subtests). They traditionally are scored for fluency, flexibility, originality, and, for the figural tests, elaboration. Torrance and Ball in 1984 created the streamlined scoring system for the figural tests, which expedites scoring and produces 18 scores.

The German-born Test for Creative Thinking-Drawing Production is a figural test consisting of a 6-inch frame plus six "figural fragments." The TCT-DP evaluates 11 creative abilities and personality dispositions, is administered in about 15 minutes, and may be scored in under 2 minutes (maybe).

The 1988 version of Guilford's Structure of Intellect includes 180 cells. His creativity tests stem from the divergent thinking (operation) part of the model, and to a lesser degree from the transformation (product) slab. Meeker uses the SOI model and her SOI-Learning Abilities tests in a diagnostic-remediation fashion.

Williams CAP includes his Exercise in Divergent Thinking, which is similar to Torrance's Picture Completion test. Williams' test is scored for fluency, flexibility, originality, and elaboration plus a verbal score based on title originality.

Wallach and Kogan administered their tests in an untimed and game-like atmosphere. The battery includes verbal and non-verbal subtests that are scored for fluency and uniqueness.

The Getzels and Jackson tests also include verbal and non-verbal subtests. Their unique Fables Test requires a moralistic, humorous, and sad ending for each of four fables. Their Make-Up Problems test has been used to measure mathematical creativity.

Torrance's Thinking Creatively in Action and Movement is a preschool measure of creative potential. Three subtests ask for different kinds of movements, actions, or pantomimes; a fourth asks for unusual uses for paper cups.

Thinking Creatively With Sounds and Words Includes the two tests Sounds and Images and Onomatopoeia and Images. With Sounds and Images, test-takers write down mental images stimulated by four abstract sounds. Onomatopoeia and Images is similar, except that the stimuli are words.

With searching, a reader could locate many additional creativity tests, perhaps for specific purposes such as evaluating creative potential in math, art, music, physics, or writing.

The author recommends evaluating students' past and present creative activities. Divergent thinking and personality tests also work reasonably well.

The challenge is to identify creative potential. Tests and inventories represent just one avenue.

Table A
Creativity Scale for the Adjective Check List
Developed by George Domino

absentminded	disorderly	logical
active	dissatisfied	moody
adaptable	distractible	original
adventurous	egotistical	outspoken
alert	energetic	quick
aloof	enthusiastic	rational
ambitious	humorous	rebellious
argumentative	hurried	reflective
artistic	idealistic	reserved
assertive	imaginative	resourceful
autocratic	impulsive	restless
capable	independent	sarcastic
careless	individualistic	self-centered
clear-thinking	industrious	sensitive
clever	ingenious	serious
complicated	insightful	sharp-witted
confident	intelligent	spontaneous
curious	interests wide	tactless
cynical	intolerant	unconventional
demanding	inventive	

The 300 item *Adjective Check List* is available from Consulting Psychologists Press, 577 College Avenue, Palo Alto, California. It is an adult personality test which can be scored for creativity by counting (a) the number of the above 59 adjectives checked and (b) the total number of adjectives checked. These numbers are used in Table B to find the standard (T) scores for creativity.

Table B
Conversion of ACL Raw Scores to T Scores

Total # of Adjectives Checked	Males				Females			
	1–75	76–95	96–121	122–300	1–78	79–98	99–119	120–300
Raw Score								
59	116	108	102	87	126	116	105	83
58	115	106	100	86	124	115	103	82
57	113	105	99	84	123	113	101	80
56	111	103	97	82	121	111	99	79
55	110	101	95	81	119	109	98	77
54	108	100	93	79	117	107	96	76
53	107	98	91	77	115	105	94	74
52	105	96	89	76	113	103	92	73
51	103	94	88	74	112	101	90	71
50	102	93	86	72	110	99	89	70
49	100	91	84	71	108	98	87	68
48	99	89	82	69	106	96	85	67
47	97	87	80	67	104	94	83	65
46	95	86	79	66	102	92	82	64
45	94	84	77	64	101	90	80	62
44	92	82	75	62	99	88	78	61
43	91	80	73	60	97	86	76	59
42	89	79	71	59	95	84	75	58
41	87	77	69	57	93	82	73	56
40	86	75	68	55	91	80	71	55
39	84	73	66	54	90	79	69	53
38	83	72	64	52	88	77	68	52
37	81	70	62	50	86	75	66	50
36	79	68	60	49	84	73	64	49
35	78	66	59	47	82	71	62	47
34	76	65	57	45	80	69	60	46
33	75	63	55	44	78	67	59	44
32	73	61	53	42	77	65	57	43
31	72	60	51	40	75	63	55	41
30	70	58	50	39	73	62	53	40

Table B (*continued*)
Conversion of ACL Raw Scores to T Scores

Total # of Adjectives Checked	Males				Females			
	1–75	76–95	96–121	122–300	1–78	79–98	99–119	120–300
Raw Score								
29	68	56	48	37	71	60	52	38
28	67	54	46	35	69	58	50	37
27	65	53	44	34	67	56	48	35
26	64	51	42	32	66	54	46	34
25	62	49	40	30	64	52	45	32
24	60	47	39	29	62	50	43	31
23	59	46	37	27	60	48	41	29
22	57	44	35	25	58	46	39	28
21	56	42	33	24	56	44	38	26
20	54	40	31	22	55	43	36	25
19	52	39	30	20	53	41	34	23
18	51	37	28	19	51	39	32	22
17	49	35	26	17	49	37	30	20
16	48	33	24	15	47	35	29	19
15	46	32	22	14	45	33	27	17
14	44	30	20	12	44	31	25	16
13	43	28	19	10	42	29	23	14
12	41	26	17	9	40	27	22	13
11	40	25	15	7	38	25	20	11
10	38	23	13	5	36	24	18	10
9	36	21	11	3	34	22	16	8
8	35	20	10	2	33	20	15	7
7	33	18	8	1	31	18	13	5
6	32	16	6		29	16	11	4
5	30	14	4		27	14	9	2
4	28	13	2		25	12	8	1
3	27	11	1		23	10	6	
2	25	9			21	8	4	
1	24	7			20	7	2	

Assessing Creative Potential:
Issues, Biographical Information, Tests

Self-Test: Key Concepts, Terms, and Names

Briefly define or explain each of these:

Three current uses for creativity tests _____

_____

Formal and informal creativity evaluations _____

_____

Predicting creative eminence _____

_____

Creativity test validity problems _____

_____

Creative activities checklists _____

_____

Action information _____

_____

Consensual assessment method _____

_____

Divergent thinking tests _____

_____

Personality/biographical inventories _____

_____

Ten-item creative personality test from SRBCSS _____

_____

Creativity scales for Adjective Check List _____

_____

Adaptors and innovators _____

_____

Torrance Tests of Creative Thinking _____

_____

Fluency _____

Flexibility _____

Originality _____

Elaboration _____

Streamlined scoring of the Torrance Tests _____

_____

Test for Creative Thinking-Drawing Production _____

_____

Structure of Intellect Model _____

_____

Creativity Assessment Packet _____

_____

Wallach and Kogan tests _____

_____

Getzels and Jackson tests _____

_____

Thinking Creatively in Action and Movement _____

_____

Why does your author think these names are important?

E. Paul Torrance _____

J. Paul Guilford _____

Wallach and Kogan _____

Welsh and Barron _____

Joseph Renzulli _____

Teresa Amabile _____

Frank Williams _____

George Domino _____

Harrison Gough _____

Which is which?

A. Let's classify each of the following tests, test batteries, or procedures according to whether they are classified in this book as a (1) divergent thinking test, (2) creative personality/motivation inventory, or (3) biographical evaluation of actual creative activities.
    Place a "D" in the space before each test of *divergent thinking.*
    Place a "P" in the space before each inventory that primarily measures creative *personality/motivation* traits.
    Place an "B" in the space before each procedure that primarily evaluates *biographical* information.
B. Also, can you identify which tests were created (at least partly) by creativity leader Paul Torrance? Place a "T" after the name of each test that Paul Torrance developed or helped develop.

_____ *Exercise in Divergent Thinking* (part of *Creativity Assessment Packet*)

_____ *How Do You Think?*

_____ *Things Done on Your Own*

_____ Wallach and Kogan tests

_____ *Exercise in Divergent Feeling* (part of *Creativity Assessment Packet*)

_____ *Kirton Adaptation-Innovation Inventory*

_____ Action information

_____ *The Williams Scale*

_____ *GIFFI I* and *II, GIFT, PRIDE*

_____ *Torrance Tests of Creative Thinking*

_____ *Adjective Check List*

_____ Getzels and Jackson tests

_____ *Thinking Creatively in Action and Movement*

_____ *Thinking Creatively with Sounds and Words (Sounds and Images, Onomatopoeia and Images)*

_____ Guilford tests

_____ *Scales for Rating the Behavioral Characteristics of Superior Students*

_____ *Barron-Welsh Art Scale*

_____ *Creativity Attitude Survey*

Let's Think about It

1. According to the text, why is testing for creative potential a difficult challenge?

_____

_____

_____

Can you add to these ideas—why do YOU think it is difficult to measure a person's creative capability?

_____

_____

_____

2. Do you think "divergent thinking tests" and "personality/biographical inventories" will identify the same creative students? Yes? No? Partly? Sometimes? Explain or comment.

_____

_____

_____

3. Imagine that the Gifted and Talented Committee of a local school district has asked YOU to help them identify creative *elementary* school children for their gifted program. Based on what you have read in this chapter and Chapter 4 (creative personality, abilities, biographical traits), what would you recommend?

_____

_____

_____

4. Imagine that Megacorporation wishes to award $1,000 scholarships to the 10 most creative persons in your previous *high school*. How would you help your old high school identify strong candidates? What would you recommend? (Creativity tests? Accomplishments? Activities? Awards won? Teacher nominations? Some combination?)

_____

_____

5. Now imagine that the local Chapter of *Americans Against Change and Progress* wants to give *Rigidity Awards* to the 10 most unimaginative, rigid thinking, tradition-oriented, and conforming students in your former high school. How might these students be identified? (Under no circumstances should you give humorous answers to this question!!)

_____

_____

One More Time . . .
(and it won't be easy)

Matching. Select the name or names at the right that belong to the creativity tests, inventories, or procedures described at the left. Some names must be used more than once. (Answers at end of book.)

_____	1. _____ Tests of Creative Thinking	a. Guilford
_____	2. Action information	b. Kirton
_____	3. Things Done on Your Own	c. Gough
_____	4. Creativity scale from SRBCSS	d. Michael Jordan
_____	5. Creativity Assessment Packet (3 tests)	e. Wallach & Kogan
_____	6. _____ Art Scale	f. Renzulli
_____	7. Creativity scale(s) for Adjective Check List (two answers)	g. Barron & Welsh
		h. Amabile
_____	8. Adaptation-Innovation Inventory	i. Torrance
_____	9. Test for Creative Thinking-Drawing Production (TCT-DP)	j. Williams
_____	10. Structure of Intellect (SOI) tests	k. Domino
_____	11. Divergent thinking tests included untimed, game-like atmosphere	l. Urban & Jellen
_____	12. Thinking Creatively in Action and Movement	
_____	13. Consensual assessment method	

241

Be acquainted with reasons creativity testing is problematic; the uses of creativity tests; the two general types of creativity tests; benefits of assessing past creative activities; the nature of specific creativity tests described, particularly the well-known Torrance Tests.

9

creativity in gifted education

[*Scene*: *Hell. Devil with short horns, pointed tail, and dressed in red long johns sits behind desk in office cluttered with fat record books and an old typewriter. A flickering Hellish fire illuminates the room. A sign on the desk reads "GIFTED DEMON PROGRAM." A portly applicant is just entering.*]

Devil: (*Impatiently*) Well c'mon sonny, we haven't got all eternity you know! What's your problem?

King Henry VIII: Sonny? Sonny? My good sir, I'm Henry the Eighth, former King of all England! I'm interested in your Gifted Demon Program. I assure you I've had plenty of experience in heinous torture and corrupt leadership. Besides, I've been boiling in fish oil for 450 years and I'm becoming an extraordinarily smelly prune! A change, good sir, would be most welcome.

Devil: Hmmmm. Look Hank, we've got too many kings, kaisers, caliphs, commissars, and you-name-it in the program now. How about a transfer to Flogging and Eye Gouging?

Henry: Not really.

Devil: Well Hank, what we really need are creative troublemakers—how did you do on the *Evil and Skulduggery Test*?

Henry: 87 out of 100.

Devil: Not bad, not bad! Any special accomplishments? Evidence of sinister gifts? Villainous talents? Awards for diabolical evil-doing? How are you on debauchery and depravity? Can you make college students come up one credit short for graduation?

Henry: Well, I've had six wives, beheaded two of them, and I tossed the Catholic Church right out of England.

Devil: (*Smiling*). Not bad at all! Actually Hank, I like your style. Beheading's okay, but what you did to the Pope just tickles my tail! You're in! On your way out, would you send in the next applicant?

Henry: My pleasure, sir, and thank you so much. You'll never regret this.
      (Henry VIII leaves; Cinderella's stepmother Rubella enters)

243

Devil: Well, hello Rubella! How are things down on Brimstone IV?

Rubella: (*Noticeably upset*) Oh, it just couldn't be worse, your Rogueful Royalty! All the time burn, burn, burn! My mascara is a mess and look at my hands!

Devil: Glad to hear things are so infernal! Now, you're interested in our Gifted Demon Program. Wicked Stepmothers' Division I assume?

Rubella: Oh yes, your Sinful Sovereignty! I'm good at beating step-children, dressing them in rags, and making them stay home to sweep up cinders. And I can be very cruel to Walt Disney's mice!

Devil: Not much imagination, I'm afraid. What about glitching computers? Causing accidents and fires? Starting wars? Promoting social diseases?

Rubella: Sir! I have my morals!

Devil: That's what I was afraid of, Rubella—it's back to Brimstone IV. Nobody ever said I was a nice guy!

Rubella: (*Sobbing*) But my eye shadow is streaking, your Heinous Highness, and . . .

Devil: Now would you send in Rasputin and tell the Wicked Witch of the West it'll be just a few minutes.

Demanding that our fast and creative learners do the same work at the same speed as average students is like dragging a Volkswagen in a 100-yard dash.

Gareth Indiana

Gifted Kids, Have Special Needs, Require Differentiated Services

G/T Education Growing Worldwide

The education of students who are gifted and talented is a highly visible education reform movement. At present, every state in the USA has enacted legislation which (a) recognizes that gifted students exist, (b) acknowledges that they have special needs, which usually are not met in regular educational programs, and (c) recommends or requires differentiated educational services for them. Gifted programs also have been created across Canada and in such exotic spots as mainland China, People's Republic of China, Hong Kong, Manila, South Africa, Egypt, Saudi Arabia, India, Australia, Mexico, Dominican Republic, Guam, Brazil, Russia, and Iraq.

Creativity Plays Core Role

Creativity plays a key role in all aspects of gifted education—defining "giftedness," formulating goals and objectives of a program, identifying gifted and talented students, and planning acceleration and enrichment activities that enhance students' creative potential.

Two Aims of Gifted Education

The two fundamental aims of G/T programs are to help individual students develop their high potential, and to provide society with educated professionals who are creative leaders and problem solvers (Davis & Rimm, 1998).

DEFINITIONS OF GIFTEDNESS

Definition of "Gifted" Determines Who Gets Service

Defining *gifted and talented* is important because the definition adopted by a school district will determine who is selected for the special services and training. Also, there is continual danger that one's definition, and consequent identification methods, will discriminate against such special populations as poor, minority, handicapped, underachieving, and even female gifted students.

Terms Sometimes Used Interchangeably

There is no great consensus on the distinction between "gifted" and "talented," even among experts. For example, it is common and acceptable to use the terms interchangeably—we can speak of a "gifted artist" or a "talented artist." In contrast, based on our common use of the terms, the general public and some scholars

Or on a Continuum

see *talent* and *giftedness* on a continuum, as when we speak of "talented" musicians, writers, and scientists, only a few of whom are truly "gifted." But we never reverse this usage.

No Term for Extremely Gifted

As another definitional consideration, every G/T program includes students who barely meet admission criteria, along with one or two others who are extraordinarily gifted. We have no special term to designate such students, although "extremely gifted" and "low-incidence gifted" are used, as are "child prodigies" and the tongue-in-cheek terms "severely gifted" and "profoundly gifted."

Five Categories of Definitions

As an introduction to the definition problem, Stankowski (1978) outlined five categories of definitions of "gifts" and "talents." All but the first currently are used in various programs to guide the identification process.

Outstanding Achievements

First, *after-the-fact* definitions emphasize established prominence in one of the professions. The "gifted" are those who have shown consistently outstanding achievements, usually creative ones.

IQ Cutoff

Second, *IQ* definitions set a cutoff point on the IQ scale. "Gifted" students are those scoring at or above the cutoff, for example, an IQ score of 120 or 130.

Percentage Cutoff

Third, *percentage* definitions set a fixed proportion of the school (or district) as "gifted," based on IQ scores, grades, or teacher recommendations. The percentage may be a restrictive 3 to 5 percent or a more generous 15 to 20 percent, as in Renzulli's (1994) Schoolwide Enrichment Model (described later).

Talent Area Focus

Fourth, *talent* definitions focus on students who are outstanding in art, music, math, science, or other specific aesthetic or academic area.

Creativity (Right on!)

Finally, *creativity* definitions emphasize creative abilities and talents, as reflected in creativity test scores, teachers nominations, or ratings of creative products.

U.S. Office of Education Definition

The sun rises and sets with the 1978 U.S. Office of Education definition of "gifts and talents," which was modified from an earlier statement (Marland, 1972). The definition reads:

U.S.O.E. Definition: Five Categories

> [The gifted and talented are] children and, whenever applicable, youth who are identified at the pre-school, elementary, or secondary level as possessing demonstrated or potential abilities that give evidence of high performance capability in areas such as *intellectual, creative, specific academic* or *leadership* ability or in the *performing and visual arts*, and who by reason thereof require services or activities not ordinarily provided by the school (U.S. Congress, Educational Amendment of 1978 [P.L. 95-561, IX (A)]).

A Multiple Talent Definition

Note that the definition recognizes not only high general intelligence, but gifts in specific academic areas, creativity, leadership, and the arts. It is considered a "multiple-talent" definition. Note also that by including "demonstrated or *potential* abilities" the definition includes underachievers, whose abilities may not be demonstrated in actual high-quality performances.

Curious Inconsistency

As an ironic fact, most states and individual school districts accept the U.S.O.E definition in their formal legislation and in written program plans. But many base actual identification on intellectual criteria—ability scores, grades, teacher nominations for academic excellence—and ignore the other categories. This is called "paying lip service" (can you say "paying lip service"?).

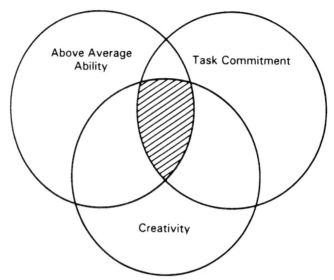

Figure 9.1 Renzulli's three-ring model. Reprinted by permission of J. S. Renzulli.

Renzulli's Three-Ring Definition

High Creativity, High Motivation, Above-Average Ability

Joseph Renzulli's *three-ring definition* of giftedness also is well-known and widely accepted. Renzulli (1977; Renzulli & Reis, 1997) has argued that people who truly make creative contributions to society—that is, truly gifted and talented persons—possess three characteristics: They have high *creativity*, high *task commitment* (motivation), and at least above average (though not necessarily outstanding) *ability* (intelligence; Figure 9.1). It has been a common mistake among people who endorse Renzulli's three-ring definition to *select* for gifted and talented programs only those children who appear to be strong in all three characteristics—creativity, motivation, and intelligence. In fact, say Renzulli and Reis (1991), schools should use various—and flexible—criteria to select students, including both objective test scores and subjective non-test criteria. Students should

Creativity and Motivation: "Developmental Objectives"

display or have the potential to display above average ability in one or more academic areas, or in special aptitudes such as music, art, drama, leadership, or interpersonal skills. The other two rings [motivation, creativity] are considered *developmental objectives* that we attempt to promote in the target population.

That is, as we will see in the discussion of Renzulli's Schoolwide Enrichment Model later, students who show or develop the creativity and motivation will volunteer to work on individual projects with a resource room G/T teacher.

Taylor's Multiple-Talent Totem Poles

Most or All Students Are Above Average (or Gifted) in Something

Thinking Talents

Talents for Getting Ideas Implemented

Calvin Taylor's (1986, 1988) *multiple-talent totem poles* concept does not define "gifts and talents." Rather, it raises our awareness that virtually all students possess special skills and talents of some variety. One version of Taylor's totem poles appears in Figure 9.2. The second through sixth talents (productive thinking, communicating, forecasting, decision-making, planning) were called *thinking talents* that contribute to creativity and problem solving. The final three (implementing,

"I'm above average in ability and high in creativity," said Sleazy Sam, "but motivation was always a problem!" (The Museum of Modern Art/Film Stills Archive.)

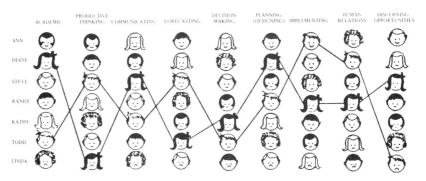

Figure 9.2 Taylor's multiple-talent totem poles, 1984 extended version. Copyright © 1984, Calvin W. Taylor. Reprinted by permission.

"I don't know about academic talent, productive thinking, or communicating, but she has terrific sleeping talent," said Captain Calvin Taylor. (The Museum of Modern Art/Film Stills Archive.)

human relations, discerning opportunities) are essential for getting ideas into action.

The multiple-talent totem poles concept complicates the question: Who should be selected to participate in the G/T program? Different children would be chosen depending upon which talent is emphasized. Said Taylor (1986, p. 317), "Everyone has both strengths and weaknesses all the way across the totem poles." Further, "The more talents that students have activated in schooling, the more chance that the students will find one or more talents in which they are above average or even highly talented" (p. 320).

CHARACTERISTICS OF STUDENTS WHO ARE GIFTED

While high creativity is one characteristic that is important in selecting students for G/T programs, intellectual giftedness typically is valued even more. Apart from its appearance in high IQ scores and high grades, intellectual giftedness also can be seen informally in precocious language skills, including an advanced vocabulary, superior comprehension, and very logical thinking processes. Also common among the intellectually gifted are early reading, writing, math, music, and art skills, along with advanced interests and very wide interests. There also are many common affective traits, such as high motivation and persistence; confidence, low anxiety, better self-concepts, and an internal locus of evaluation; plus higher levels of moral thinking, due to a strong empathy ability and good sense. Superior humor also is common.

Motivation, Confidence, High Moral Thinking, Humor

Prefer Independent Study, Projects

Due to their ability, creativity, independence, and motivation, gifted students prefer to learn in less-structured, more flexible ways—independent study and projects, for example (Griggs & Dunn, 1984).

Terman's Termites

We should mention the Terman studies, since so many lists of characteristics of gifted and talented students are based on his and his colleagues' long-term research (e.g., Terman & Oden, 1947). In the 1920s Lewis Terman (1925) and others used the *Stanford-Binet Intelligence Scale*, which Terman developed, to identify 1,528 boys and girls with IQ scores of 140 and above—the top 1 percent. The personal and professional activities of these people were studied and followed-up in a series of interviews and mailings for the next 60 years. (Many are now in their graves—the only escape from Terman's project.)

Recall test: In Chapter 4 we saw the 1895 claim of Cesare Lombroso that "men of (creative) genius" were:

    a. Sickly and generally emaciated.

    b. hunched-back, lame, or club-footed, due to rickets.

    c. short, bald, and forgetful.

    d. sterile and stuttering.

    e. all of the above.

Terman: Lombroso Wrong:

Yes, "e" is correct. In sharp contrast, Terman actually found that "the average member of our group is a slightly better physical specimen than the average child." They were superior in all academic areas. They also were more trust-worthy, better adjusted, and emotionally stable in their youth and adulthood, as evidenced by lower rates of mental illness and suicide.

IDENTIFICATION OF STUDENTS WHO ARE GIFTED

Identification: Related to Definitions, Program Goals

Space will not permit a detailed discussion of test scores, nomination forms, and matrix systems used in identification nor the problems and delicate issues of deciding who is and who is not "gifted and talented" (see Davis & Rimm, 1998). Identification methods are, or should be, related to program definitions of gift-edness and program content and goals. Selection should include both objective scores (tests, grades) and subjective nominations and ratings.

Use Two Creativity Criteria

Creative talent is one criteria for selection, based on teacher ratings of creativeness, creativity test scores, and perhaps ratings of creative products. For accurate identification, as we noted in Chapter 8 teachers should use two criteria of creativity. A student who scores high on both is extremely likely to be identified correctly as creative.

Regrettably, many state governments and school districts ignore creativity altogether in favor of "real" academic ability, as shown in high grades and IQ scores plus teacher ratings of academic potential—despite the fact that motivated creative students are the most likely to make innovative contributions to society. As one too-common occurrence, an unimaginative and unmotivated student with an IQ score of 130 (the cutoff score) may be stamped *gifted* and admitted automatically to a G/T program, but an enthusiastic and creative youth with an IQ of only 129 will be stamped "not gifted" and excluded. Said Torrance (1984a), "The use of intelligence tests to identify gifted students misses about 70 percent of those who are equally gifted on creativity criteria." Bureaucracies are not particularly famous for flexibility, fairness, or agreeing with your author's totally sensible concern for creative talent.

Results of Using Criteria Rigidly

Torrance: Using Only IQ Scores Misses 70% of the Most Creative

The following is an unelaborated list of identification methods, which are used by school screening committees singly and in every conceivable combination.

Methods

Intelligence test scores

Achievement test scores

Overall Grades or grades in specific areas

Teacher nominations (informal or using rating scales)

Creativity test scores

Nominations by parents, peers, or self

Product evaluations

Talent Pool Approach More Reasonable

As we saw in the section on percentage definitions of giftedness, some programs will select a restrictive 3 to 5 percent, while others will use a talent pool approach—"cast a wide net"—and identify 15 to 20 percent. The philosophy is: When in doubt, admit.

Renzulli and Reis: Five Steps in Identification

Within a wide net approach, Renzulli and Reis (1991) outlined a five-step selection strategy using *all* of the above criteria. First, students who score above the 92nd percentile on intelligence or achievement tests are admitted automatically. Second, teachers nominate additional students who display creativity, motivation, unusual interest or talents, or areas of superior performance. Third, "alternate pathways" such as parent nominations, peer nominations, self-nominations, or creativity test scores are brought to the screening committee for review. Fourth, to avoid biases of current teachers, nominations by past teachers are solicited. Finally, *action information* (remember action information?) reflecting high enthu-

Product and performance evaluations are one way to identify creative talent. "It would be easier if you didn't keep time on my nose," said the budding pianist. (The Museum of Modern Art/Film Stills Archive.)

siasm about a project is used by teachers or students themselves for nomination and selection into the program.

GOALS AND CURRICULA OF PROGRAMS FOR THE GIFTED

Many lists itemize the *needs* of students who are gifted and talented. These logically translate into the *goals* and *curricula* of G/T programs (see Davis & Rimm, 1998). An abbreviated overview of curriculum for the gifted includes:

G/T Program Goals

1. *Maximum achievement in basic skills*, including learning at an appropriate level and pace, and based on needs rather than grade-level appropriateness.

2. *Content beyond the prescribed curriculum*, related to broad-based issues, abstract ideas, theories, and problems that stimulate reflective, evaluative, critical and creative thinking. These may require materials and resources beyond the designated grade-level.

3. *Exposure to a variety of fields of study*, including new disciplines and new occupations.

4. *Student-selected content* based on interests and needs, including in-depth studies of self-selected topics.

5. *Experience in creative thinking and problem solving*, including futuristic thinking.

6. *Development of thinking skills*, such as independent and self-directed study skills, library skills, and research/scientific skills; critical thinking in the sense of evaluating biases, credibility, logic, and consistency; decision-making, planning, organizing, analyzing, synthesizing, and evaluating.

7. *Development of self-awareness and self-understanding* regarding one's capabilities, interests, and needs; appreciating individual differences; and relating to other gifted students.

8. *Development of motivation*, including independent and self-directed thinking and work, plus increased achievement motivation that includes high-level educational and career aspirations.

Avoid "Fun and Games," Busywork

All acceleration and enrichment activities should be planned with these types of objectives in mind. Although it is essential for learning experiences to be enjoyable, they should not be "fun and games" or busywork designed to keep students occupied.

ACCELERATION AND ENRICHMENT ALTERNATIVES

Acceleration

Acceleration: Results in Advanced Placement

Enrichment: All Else

A handy way to differentiate *acceleration* from *enrichment* in gifted education programs is to define *acceleration* as any strategy that results in advanced placement or credit. *Enrichment* includes strategies that extend beyond standard grade-level work, but do not result in advanced placement or credit (that is, anything else).

Some popular acceleration strategies are:

Acceleration Strategies

1. Early admission to kindergarten or first grade

2. Grade skipping ("full acceleration")

3. Subject skipping ("partial acceleration")

4. Early admission to junior or senior high school

5. Credit by examination

6. College courses while in high school

7. College correspondence courses in high school

8. Early admission to college (early high school graduation)

9. Telescoping, for example, four years of high school into three.

Julian Stanley's SMPY

Top SAT-M Seventh Graders

The best-known example of accelerating bright secondary students into college level mathematics courses is the Study of Mathematically Precocious Youth (SMPY) program. SMPY was born at Johns Hopkins University in 1971, brainchild of Julian Stanley. Primarily seventh-grade boys and girls were identified as mathematically precocious (top 1 percent) based on their *Scholastic Aptitude Test-Mathematics* scores (Benbow & Lubinski, 1997). The students participated in fast-paced summer math programs at Johns Hopkins, usually covering one to two years of high school algebra and geometry in three weeks, because, said Stanley, they are working, not sleeping. In addition, they are counseled regarding the suitability of a smorgasbord of acceleration options: They may attend college part-time, earn college credit by taking Advanced Placement classes, skip a grade, collapse two or more years of math into one, or enter college early, perhaps by skipping high school graduation. The results, said Stanley and Benbow (1986), are an increased zest for learning, enhanced feelings of self-worth, reduced egotism due to the humbling effects of working with intellectual peers, far better preparation for college, better fellowship opportunities, and the opportunity to enter a professional career at an earlier age.

Do SMPY Students Get No Sleep?

Smorgasbord of Opportunities

Many Benefits

Talent Search: Based on High SAT-M or SAT-V

Elementary Talent Search

The SMPY model has evolved into the *talent search* concept, which uses both the SAT-Math and the SAT-Verbal to identify and provide advanced (summer) course work for both mathematically and verbally talented predominantly seventh-grade students (Benbow & Lubinski, 1997). Recently, an elementary talent search was initiated to locate (who else) academically precocious elementary students (Assouline & Lupkowski-Shoplik, 1997). Instead of the SAT, the elementary talent search uses, for example, the Educational Testing Service *PLUS Academic Abilities Assessment* and the American College Testing *EXPLORE*. A variety of acceleration and enrichment opportunities are made available, for example, grade skipping, testing out of future classes, taking advanced classes, individualized instruction, academic contests and Olympiads, independent projects, and enrichment classes.

Acceleration Indirectly Fosters Creative Productivity

Most acceleration strategies do not "teach creativity" directly in the same sense that this book teaches creative attitudes, techniques, and an understanding of the topic of creativity. However, by advancing students' knowledge in a subject matter field we indirectly enable them to think creativity in that area and prepare them to make creative discoveries and innovations. They have advanced information with which to be creative.

Enrichment: Grouping Plans

The Old Pull-Out Plan

Many school districts offer enrichment activities within some type of *grouping* structure. For example, the most common grouping plan is the *pull-out* program. Elementary students are "pulled out" of their regular classes two or three hours per week to participate in enrichment activities guided by a G/T teacher-coordinator. If the students must be transported to a resource room elsewhere in the district to work with a resource teacher, the plan is called a *resource room plan,* which is extremely similar in operation to a pull-out plan. The recurrent criticism of pull-out programs is that they are a part-time solution to a full-time problem.

Cluster Grouping

With *cluster grouping*, usually five to ten gifted, say, fourth-graders are "clustered" together in one class, along with other students. They work on independent research projects or advanced academic subjects individually or in small groups.

Special Classes

Some schools will create *special classes* for gifted students within a particular grade level or age range. In addition to covering prescribed grade-level objectives, a variety of enrichment, personal development, and skill development experiences—including creative skills—are planned.

Mainstreaming

Many schools *mainstream* their gifted students, allowing each teacher to provide appropriate activities of the one or more G/T students in his or her class. In some cases mainstreaming is a default plan—the school has made no other provisions to meet the special needs of its children with gifts and talents. In other cases, such as in the Pyramid Model described later, mainstreaming the majority of G/T students is a carefully considered plan.

Special Elementary Schools

Magnet Schools Are Attractive

Some large cities have *special elementary schools* for the gifted, to which students from throughout the school district are bused daily. A similar large-city option is *magnet high school* in which an entire high school attracts students interested or gifted in, for example, math and science, the performing arts, business, or technical and trade skills.

School-within-a-School

With the *school-within-a-school* plan, gifted students from around the district attend some classes with regular students (e.g., physical education, study hall, manual arts, home economics), but also attend special classes taught by special teachers.

Enrichment: Activities

The following are enrichment activities that may be planned within most or all of the grouping options described above.

Library Research Projects

With *library research projects* students pursue answers to a specific problem, such as "Why and how was the Great Wall of China built?" The final product need not be a neatly written report. It could be a more creative demonstration of some activity or skill, a student-made movie or slide show, a TV news report, a mini-play, or a newspaper column.

Art Projects, Science Projects

Learning Centers

There are virtually limitless types of art, theater, and scientific research projects, all of which require creative thinking and problem solving.

Some teachers effectively use *learning centers*, either teacher-made or commercial, to engage gifted students in art, math, science, social studies, creative writing, music, or language-learning projects.

Field Trips

Field trips acquaint students with cultural or scientific topics and with career possibilities. Field trips are valuable for all students; gifted students should have specific problems to solve or questions to be answered.

Saturday and Summer Programs: Mini-Courses

A few colleges and universities sponsor *Saturday programs* and *summer programs*. These typically take the form of mini-courses in art, theater, biology, TV production, limnology, and so forth, and are taught by college graduate students or faculty. There is much creative involvement.

Mentorships

A *mentorship* traditionally involves an extended relationship between a student and a community professional. The student learns the activities, responsibilities, problems, attitudes, and life style associated with the career. While normally a high school plan, mentorships are becoming a popular elementary level enrichment alternative for gifted students (Clasen & Clasen, 1997).

Future Problem Solving

Many schools use the *Future Problem Solving* program as an enrichment activity. A team of five students (in an upper elementary, middle school, or high school division) is registered with the National Future Problem Solving Program at St.

Gifted and regular students benefit from mentorships. This student is learning the skill of boat chimney repair from Captain Sally Sailorsuit. "Just don't forget your lantern," reminded the captain. (The Museum of Modern Art/Film Stills Archive.)

Andrews College in Laurinburg, North Carolina.[1] The team is sent three future-oriented practice problems which deal with such matters as poverty, genetic engineering, robotics, lasers, UFOs, nuclear waste, medical advances, the greenhouse effect, crime, prisons, drunk driving, education, and the militarization and industrialization of space. Each problem is solved with the following model. Note that the model duplicates almost exactly the CPS model described in Chapter 5.

Follows CPS Steps

1. Students research information related to the general future-oriented topic. Specific articles are provided; students also search out books, magazines, or other sources, and perhaps visit agencies and interview experts (Crabbe, 1985).

2. They brainstorm 20 possible problems related to the situation and select one underlying problem they feel is central to the situation.

3. They brainstorm solutions for this problem.

4. They brainstorm evaluation criteria and then, using their five best criteria, evaluate ideas using an evaluation matrix of the type described in Chapter 5. Their ten most promising solutions are rank-ordered.

5. Finally, their best solution is described carefully in a few paragraphs.

The team's work for steps 2–5 is sent to the state Future Problem Solving office for evaluation and feedback. Based on the quality of the third problem, the top

---

[1]A non-competitive Primary Division for children in grades K–3, designed to instruct children in the problem-solving process, began in the Fall of 1984. An Advanced Division, consisting of the most competent teenage problem-solving teams, began in 1982. They work on real business and government problems.

Odyssey of the Mind always includes an excellent creativity-stimulating theater activity. "Just watch your hands," said Cleopatra. "This ain't 'The Best Little Pyramid in Egypt'." (Wisconsin Center for Film and Theater Research.)

State, National FPS Bowls

Good Skill Development

OM

Long-Term Problems

Short-Term Problems

10 percent of the teams are invited to participate in a state FPS bowl, the winner of which is sent to the National FPS competition.

Overall, the FPS experience develops creativity, analytical and critical thinking, research skills, speaking and writing skills, and teamwork and interpersonal skills.

Like Future Problem Solving, *Odyssey of the Mind* (OM; formerly Olympics of the Mind) is a national program designed to foster creative development. A team of seven (five players, two alternates) registers with the state OM committee in an elementary, middle school, or high school division. The OM Association provides each team with detailed directions for preparing *long-term problems* that they will work on usually in weekly meetings throughout the school year. For example, the *Atlantis* problem requires students to construct the illusion of a deep-sea expedition to explore the lost city of Atlantis. The team constructs and operates a submersible vessel that maneuvers two remote arms from inside. The *Straddle Structure* problem requires students to build a specified balsa wood and glue structure that supports as much weight as possible. With *It's Show Time* students develop a musical scene based on a play (for example, *The Emperor's New Clothes, Much Ado About Nothing*); they also prepare a Playbill and an oral summary of the play.

In addition to long-term problems, students also solve on-the-spot *short-term* problems, both in practice and in competition (e.g., "List all of the giants you can think of"). Creative, sometimes off-the-wall answers received three points (e.g., "Eddie Murphy is a giant of comedy," "Cheerios are giant wheels to an ant"), common answers receive one point. Within each state there are regional competitions, the winners of which participate in annual state competitions. State winners compete in an annual world OM competition.

Many Other Creativity-Stimulating Competitions

In addition to the Future Problem Solving and Odyssey of the Minds programs, there are other national programs and competitions that stimulate creative thinking, academic excellence, or both, for example, the Junior Great Books program, Academic Decathlon, Mock Court, and National Forensics League.

PROGRAM MODELS

Program models provide the theoretical structure within which specific enrichment activities, including creativity training, are planned.

Enrichment Triad Model

Triad Model: Renzulli

Probably the best known curriculum guide is the *Enrichment Triad Model* (Renzulli, 1977). It can be implemented with students of any age and in any grouping arrangement. There are three more-or-less sequential but interactive stages (Figure 9.3). With Type I enrichment, General Exploratory Activities, students are exposed to topics that are not a normal part of the school curriculum. While Type I (and Type II) enrichment are recommended for all students, one purpose of Type I exploratory activities is to help students find a later independent project (Type III enrichment). Type I enrichment may involve a well-stocked resource center (books, magazines, other media) and field trips to meet dynamic, creative and productive professionals.

Type I: General Exploratory Activities

Type II: Thinking and Feeling Processes

The purpose of Type II enrichment, Group Training Activities, is to "promote the development of a broad range of thinking and feeling processes" (Renzulli

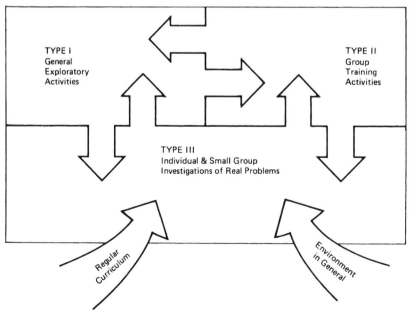

Figure 9.3 Renzulli's Enrichment Triad Model. From J. S. Renzulli, *The Enrichment Triad Model: A Guide for Developing Defensible Programs for the Gifted and Talented.* Mansfield Center, Conn.: Creative Learning Press, 1977. Reprinted by permission.

& Reis, 1985). Renzulli and Reis (1991) recommended developing general and specific skills in the four categories of:

Four Categories of Type II Enrichment

1. *Cognitive and affective thinking*, including creative thinking, problem solving, decision making, critical and logical thinking, and affective processes such as appreciating and valuing.

2. *How-to-learn skills*, such as listening, observing, perceiving, reading, note-taking, outlining, interviewing and surveying, and analyzing and organizing data.

3. *Advanced research skills and reference materials* that prepare the students for Type III investigations, including using the library, information retrieval systems, and community resources.

4. *Written, oral, and visual communication skills* that will be directed toward maximizing the impact of students' products.

Type III: Investigations of Real Problems

Type III enrichment, Individual and Small Group Investigations of Real Problems, is exactly that. The young person becomes an actual researcher or artist dealing with a real problem in an artistic, scientific, literary, business, or other area. Students should be producers of knowledge, not merely consumers or reproducers.

Product, Audience

It is important for students to (a) produce a product and (b) have an audience for their products. The teacher may need a lively imagination to help locate or create audiences for students' Type III products.

Schoolwide Enrichment Model

SEM

The Enrichment Triad Model is incorporated into Renzulli's broader *Schoolwide Enrichment Model* (SEM; Renzulli, 1994; Renzulli & Reis, 1985, 1997). There are a few central characteristics of the SEM plus an even one billion minor details. First, unlike traditional G/T plans that identify about 5 percent of the students for participation, the SEM identifies 15 to 20 percent of the school population for a *talent pool*. Identification is flexible and designed to include students, not exclude them.

Talent Pool Concept

With High Creativity, Motivation: Revolve into Resource Room

Second, talent pool students, and occasionally non-talent pool students, who show or develop high creativity and motivation (that is, they display *action information*) revolve into a resource room to carry out their projects under the direction of a resource teacher. When the projects are completed, students revolve back out.

Enrichment Types I and II in Regular Classes

Third, it is called the *Schoolwide Enrichment Model* because it is intended to be "schoolwide." Both regular teachers and resource teachers bring Type I exploratory activities plus Type II creativity, thinking, research, learning-to-learn, and communication skills into the regular classroom for all children. The SEM thus tries to help all students, as well as those with gifts and talents. It also reduces criticisms of elitism.

Details, Details

To reduce bad guessing about how to implement and run a SEM, Renzulli (1994; Renzulli & Reis, 1985, 1997) has elaborated on the other 999,999,999 details pertaining to the history of SEM, underlying theory, issues, supportive research, identification forms and strategies, parent communications, planning forms for everything (some of which insure that the staff work gets done), learning style assessments, ideas for implementing Types I, II, and III enrichment, lists of specific art, science, language, etc., topics, lists of specific thinking skills to be fostered, strategies for curriculum compacting (to "buy time"), suggestions for project evaluation, and much more.

Feldhusen's Three-Stage Enrichment Model

Emphasizes Creative Thinking

Creativity (and Other) Exercises

Feldhusen's *three-stage enrichment model* (Feldhusen & Kolloff, 1986; Kolloff & Feldman, 1984) centers on three types or stages of instructional activities that primarily are intended to foster creative development.

Stage I focuses upon *basic divergent and convergent thinking abilities.* Corresponding instructional activities include relatively short-term, teacher-led exercises mainly in creative thinking, but also in logical and critical thinking. For example, creativity exercises include unusual uses, product improvement, and "What would happen if . . . ?" problems.

Stage 2 requires *more complex creative and problem-solving activities* that may extend over a longer period of time and, importantly, require less teacher direction and more student initiative. Students learn and practice creative thinking techniques such as brainstorming and the synectics methods; work through systematic problem-solving models such as the CPS and FPS models; or solve detective mysteries in the *Productive Thinking Program* (Covington, Crutchfield, Olton & Davies, 1972).

Techniques, CPS, FPS

Projects

Stage 3 activities aim at strengthening *independent learning abilities.* Said Feldhusen and Kolloff (1981), "Stage 3 projects should challenge gifted youngsters to define and clarify a problem, gather data from books and other resources, interpret findings, and develop creative ways to communicate their results."

Other Curriculum Models

Pyramid Project

Your Mummy Will Like It

The three models summarized above focus on creative development as a main program goal. There are many more models that guide G/T program and curriculum planning. All of these include creative development either directly, as in group creativity exercises, or indirectly, as when students work on independent projects. For example, the *Pyramid Project* (Figure 9.4) is a wide-scale organizational plan that prescribes different services for different levels of giftedness (Cox, Daniel & Boston, 1985). The largest number of "able learners" (the base of the pyramid) receives advanced material in the regular classroom, for example, using learning centers, cluster grouping, and resource room projects. A smaller number of more superior students are placed in full-time special classes for advanced material and skill development. The few at the top of the pyramid attend special schools for the gifted.

ALM: 5 Steps

The *Autonomous Learner Model* (ALM; Betts, 1985, 1991), like Renzulli's School-wide Enrichment Model, is an overall program plan. The ALM includes five steps of (1) orienting students and parents to giftedness and program opportunities, (2) individual development of learning skills and interpersonal skills, (3) enrichment activities, including investigations of high-interest problems and "adventure trips" (e.g., studying geology in the Grand Canyon), (4) seminars in which students research and present topics, and (5) in-depth long-term research projects. These five steps are slightly elaborated in Figure 9.5.

Taylor's Totem Poles Guide Curriculum Planning

(Popular in the Northwest)

Taylor's *multiple-talent totem pole* model (Figure 9.2) also may be used as the basis for curriculum planning. That is, activities may be planned in the areas of *academic, productive thinking, communicating, forecasting, decision-making, planning, implementing, human relations,* and *discerning opportunities.* Schlichter's (1997) *Talents Unlimited* in-service training model acquaints teachers with Taylor's model, describes exercises for strengthening the totem pole talents, and includes practice in planning and teaching the totem pole talents.

Gifted Education Also Is Creativity Conscious

In gifted education, most teachers and program planners are creativity conscious. The goal of developing student creativity therefore runs throughout defi-

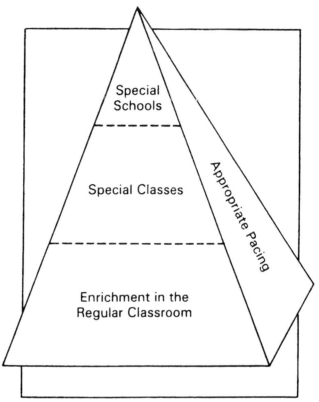

Figure 9.4 The pyramid model. Reprinted from *Educating Able Learners: Programs and Promising Practices*, by June Cox, Neil Daniel, and Bruce O. Boston, copyright © 1985. Reprinted by permission of J. Cox, Gifted Students Institute, and the University of Texas Press.

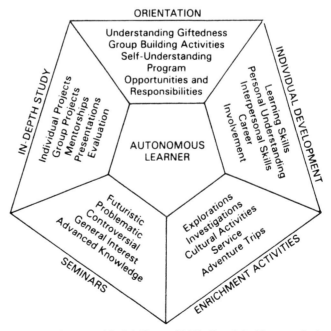

Figure 9.5 Autonomous Learner Model (Betts, 1985). Reprinted by permission of the author and Autonomous Learning Publications.

nitions of giftedness, statements of program goals, selection criteria, acceleration and enrichment curriculum plans, and program evaluation.

SUMMARY

Creativity is central to all aspects of gifted education—definitions, goals and objectives, identification, and acceleration and enrichment activities.

One's definition of giftedness determines who gets the special services. There is no consensus in defining "gifted" vs. "talented"; some use the terms interchangeably, others do not. There is no special term for the extremely gifted child.

Stankowski suggested five categories of definitions: after-the-fact, IQ, percentage, talent, and creativity definitions.

The widely-endorsed U.S.O.E. (multiple talent) definition includes the five categories of general intellectual ability, specific academic talent, creativity, leadership, and ability in the performing and visual arts.

Renzulli's three-ring definition includes high creativity, high motivation (task commitment), and at least above-average ability—characteristics of people who make creative contributions to society.

Taylor's multiple-talent totem pole model raises our awareness that almost everyone can be above average or even outstanding, if we look at many types of talents. His totem pole subdivides into one intellectual talent, five thinking (creativity) talents, and three talents important for implementing ideas.

Intellectually gifted students are developmentally advanced in many areas. They also tend to show high motivation, confidence, humor, and higher moral thinking. These traits appeared in Terman's classic research.

Identification methods should be related to both definitions and characteristics of giftedness. Both objective and subjective information should be used. The overuse of IQ scores discriminates against creative students. There are many identification methods: Ability scores, achievement scores, teacher nominations, creativity test scores, parent nominations, peer nominations, self-nominations, and product evaluations.

Goals of G/T education include: maximum achievement, content beyond the regular curriculum, exposure to a variety of fields, student-selected content, creative thinking and problem solving, thinking skills, self-awareness and self-understanding, and the development of motivation and self-directedness.

Acceleration strategies, as defined here, result in advanced placement or credit.

In Julian Stanley's SMPY, mathematically precocious seventh-grade students participate in fast-paced summer math programs. Talent search programs accommodate both mathematically and verbally precocious students. An elementary-level talent search recently was begun.

Enrichment plans include pull-out (resource room) programs, cluster grouping, special classes, mainstreaming, special elementary schools, magnet high schools, and school-within-a-school plans.

Enrichment activities can include library, art, theatre, or science projects, learning centers, field trips, Saturday and summer programs, mentorships, or participation in Future Problem Solving, Odyssey of the Mind, or other competitive programs.

Program models structure the enrichment activities.

Renzulli's Enrichment Triad Model includes general exploratory activities (Type I enrichment), group training activities (Type II), and individual or small group research projects (Type III).

The Triad model expands into the Schoolwide Enrichment Model, which includes the talent pool concept—identifying 15 to 20 percent of the school for participation. When a student shows or develops high motivation and creativity, the student revolves into a resource room to work on an independent (Type III) project. Regular and G/T teachers do Types I and II activities in the regular classroom.

Feldhusen's three-stage enrichment outlines three levels of creativity training: basic exercises to strengthen divergent and convergent thinking abilities, more complex creative activities such as learning creativity techniques, and involvement in independent projects.

The Pyramid Project is an organizational plan that prescribes mainstreaming for the largest number of "able learners," full-time special classes for more superior students, and special schools for the few most gifted children.

Betts' Autonomous Learner Model is an overall program plan that includes the five steps of orientation, individual development of learning and interpersonal skills, enrichment activities, seminars, and in-depth long-term research projects.

Taylor's Multiple-Talent Totem Pole model also has guided curriculum planning in each of his totem-pole areas.

Creativity in Gifted Education

Self-Test: Key Concepts, Terms, and Names

Briefly define or explain each of these:

After-the-fact definitions _____

_____

IQ definitions _____

_____

Percentage definitions _____

_____

Talent definitions _____

_____

Creativity definitions _____

_____

U.S.O.E. definition _____

_____

Three ring definition (Renzulli) _____

_____

Multiple Talent Totem Poles (Taylor) _____

_____

Talent pool _____

_____

Acceleration _____

_____

Telescoping _____

_____

SMPY _____

_____

SAT-M _____

_____

Talent search _____

_____

Enrichment _____

_____

Pull-out programs _____

_____

Cluster grouping _____

_____

Mainstreaming _____

_____

School-within-a-School _____

_____

Mentorships _____

_____

FPS _____

_____

Odyssey of the Mind _____

_____

Enrichment Triad Model _____

_____

Schoolwide Enrichment Model _____

_____

Types I, II, and III Enrichment _____

_____

Feldhusen's Three-Stage Model _____

_____

Pyramid project _____

_____

Autonomous Learner Model (Betts) _____

_____

Why does your author think these names are important?

Joseph Renzulli _____

Calvin Taylor _____

Lewis Terman _____

Julian Stanley _____

John Feldhusen _____

June Cox _____

George Betts _____

Let's Think about It

1. How do you think the topic of creativity relates to the two main goals of gifted education (described at the beginning of this chapter).

_____

_____

_____

2. Which definition of "giftedness" do you think is the most useful?

_____

Why? _____

_____

_____

3. Think about Taylor's Multiple-Talent Totem Pole model.

   a. In which of TAYLOR'S talents are you above average or outstanding?

   _____

   _____

   b. What OTHER specific strong talent(s) or skills do you have, other than those in Taylor's totem poles (e.g., music, athletics, languages, academics, art, bridge, a particular hobby, street survival, sailing)?

   _____

   _____

   _____

4. Look over the eight "Goals and Curricula" in this chapter. Rank order them according to which you feel should be most important, second most important, etc., in the education of gifted and talented students.

   First in importance: _____

   Second: _____

   Third: _____

   Fourth: _____

   Fifth: _____

   Sixth: _____

   Seventh: _____

   Eighth: _____

5. Let's think like a cranky, negativistic person who is critical of everything—including gifted education. Think of one thing WRONG (e.g., somehow unfair, troublesome, inconvenient, expensive, bad for the student's social life, bad for his or her education) related to each of these *acceleration* methods.

a. Early admission to kindergarten or first grade.

_____

b. Grade skipping

_____

c. Subject skipping

_____

d. Early admission to junior or senior high school

_____

e. Credit by examination

_____

f. College courses while in high school

_____

g. Early admission to college

_____

h. Telescoping

_____

6. Describe the relationship among these concepts: *Enrichment Triad Model*, *Talent Pool*, and *Schoolwide Enrichment Model*.

_____

_____

_____

_____

Crossword Puzzle 9.1

ACROSS

2. Definitions that emphasize already-established excellence and distinction
3. The three-_____ model
4. _____-Talent Totem Poles
6. Accommodating the needs of gifted children in the regular classroom
9. When a parent or peer identifies a child for a gifted program

DOWN

1. Strategies that result in advanced credit or placement
3. Creator of the three-ring definition and the Enrichment Triad Model
5. Multiple-_____ Totem Poles
7. Julian Stanley's famous mathematics acceleration program
8. _____ Problem Solving program

Crossword Puzzle 9.2

ACROSS

2. For example, condensing three years of Spanish into two years
4. Former name of "Odyssey" of the Mind
5. Plan in which students leave the regular classroom for enrichment activities, for example, for two hours on Wednesday afternoon
8. Not acceleration
9. Three-_____ identification model
10. Model in which the largest group of "able" learners are taught in the regular classroom, a smaller number in full-time special classes, the fewest "most able" students attend special schools
14. George Betts' _____ Learner Model

DOWN

1. _____ Enrichment Model (Renzulli)
3. School-Within-a-_____ programs
6. Enrichment _____ Model (Renzilli)
7. Creator of SMPY
11. When a student works with a community professional
12. Government agency that formulated a definition that includes five categories of giftedness
13. Creator of model described in 10 across
15. Test used to identify students for 7 down in Crossword Puzzle 9.1

For Study and Review

This chapter is loaded with information. Be sure you know the meaning of every item in the *"Briefly define or explain"* section above, how G/T students are identified, curricula for the gifted, acceleration and enrichment alternatives, and the different program models.

10

let's be a cuckoo clock
creative dramatics

[*Scene: Principal's Office of the Wonderland Elementary School. Principal Alice is interviewing a prospective creative dramatics teacher.*]

Principal Alice: Well now, what is your name?

Interviewee: Hearts, Queen of Hearts. You may call me 'Your Majesty.' I wonder, don't I know you from somewhere?

Principal: Oh I don't think so. I've been the Wonderland principal for some time. Now, Ms. Hearts. . . .

Interviewee: That's 'Your Majesty.'

Principal: Now . . . Your Majesty . . . have you any experience in teaching creative dramatics? Have you done movement exercises? Awareness exercises? Pantomime? Playmaking? Theater games?

Interviewee: Well . . . in a way. I formerly played a great deal of croquet with flamingos and hedgehogs. That certainly takes movement! Hmmm, you still seem very familiar.

Principal: Any pantomime or playmaking?

Interviewee: Well, I used to help out with tea parties—pretending to pour make-believe tea and that sort of thing. And I always played the part of an irate queen. Would you like to hear my "Off with their heads!"? It's very inspiring.

Principal: Actually, I think I've heard it. Do you, by any chance, remember playing croquet with a little girl who was looking for a White Rabbit wearing a red vest? He was always two days late.

Interviewee: Alice? Is it really you? Imagine, all grown up and running your own school! Do I get the job?

Principal: I can't say for sure yet, although it is nice to see you. At present, the choice has narrowed to you, a Mr. March Hare, and a very strange Hatter fellow.

271

Creative imagination is worth more than mere book knowledge.
Education and intelligence are merely the means by which we facilitate the liberation
of this creative evergy.

R. Simpson, 1922

CD: Unusual Subject

Compared with most academic topics, creative dramatics is a strange subject. There is no standard course content, no achievement tests, and no behavioral objectives. However, creative dramatics does things that no traditional classwork can accomplish.

Imagination, Problem Solving, Concentration, Physical Self, Sensory Awareness, Emotions, Pride, Self-Confidence, Empathy

Like many of the exercises in this book, especially those in Chapter 11, creative dramatics stimulates thinking, imagination, and problem solving. It also uniquely works on increasing awareness and concentration, developing control of the physical self, sharpening the senses, learning to discover and control emotions, developing pride in individuality, strengthening self-confidence in speaking and performing, fostering a sense of humor, and increasing an empathic understanding of others (Davis, Helfert, & Shapiro, 1971; Way, 1967). Yes, creative dramatics makes ambitious claims.

CD Is Not Children's Theater

Creative dramatics is not children's theater. With children's theater a published or original play is obtained, the best actors and actresses are selected (after all, we must impress the principal and the parents), and everyone else paints scenery, operates the lights and tape player, sells tickets, and hands out programs. Creative dramatics is for everyone, not just the few gifted actors and actresses. An audience is not needed or desired, since it would only interfere with the imaginative, concentrated, and sensitive involvement necessary for successful creative drama.

The Leader: Humor and Energy

The leader of creative dramatics should have two personality qualifications: a sense of humor and lots of energy. He or she will need them to survive swinging through the jungle like a monkey, wading across a field of fly-paper, being anchor person for an imaginary tug-of-war, or turning the crank to wind up a giant people machine.

Adults Need It, Love It

Your author taught undergraduate and graduate college courses in creative thinking and problem solving. One highlight always was the creative dramatics session. As a totally new experience, these adults (some in their 30's and older) bend and twist their bodies into dozens of shapes and forms. As a warm-up they shrink into the "smallest thing" they can, then pick themselves up as rag-doll puppets with strings fixed on noses and elbows. They stare at a fellow student, almost a total stranger, mimicking his or her every move in the mirror exercise. They beep, chug, hum, and scrub a fellow student who rolls along on all fours—a Volkswagen in a people-machine car wash. In groups of about eight, each person in turn lifts the lid on an invisible trunk, takes out an invisible thing—a basketball, can of beer, make-up kit, hoola-hoop, saxophone, or inflatable horse—and pantomimes the appropriate action. They listen in silence to sounds that are near and sounds that are far. Then as 1-inch Lilliputians they relax, shut their eyes, and explore the inside of a coffee pot.

It is a time of creative regression, one they do not soon forget.

The remainder of this chapter is divided into six parts: warm-up exercises, movement exercises, sensory and body awareness exercises, pantomime, play-making, and two theater games.

WARM-UP EXERCISES

It always is best to begin a session with some sort of stretching, loosening-up activity—to get the blood flowing and to clear the cobwebs from the cortex. Three suggestions for this are:

Warm-Up Exercises

1. *Holding Up the Roof.* All participants strain to hold up the roof; slowly let it down (to one knee), then push it back up. It is quite strenuous, if done properly.

2. *Biggest Thing.* Everyone stretches his or her body into the biggest thing he or she possibly can. Can you guess what the second part of this exercise is?

3. *Stretching.* Beginning at their heads and working down, students stretch the various parts of their bodies.

MOVEMENT EXERCISES

1. *Circles.* Students stand in large circle. Each person, in turn, thinks of a way to make a circle by using his or her body. All others make the same circle. The circle can be made with part of the body or all of the body; it can be a fixed circle (e.g., a halo) or a moving circle (e.g., a circular motion of the foot or rolling on the floor). Names add to the fun, for example, "This is a halo circle," "This is an eyeball circle," "This is a chicken circle." "This is a Groucho Marx circle."

2. *Tug-of-War.* Pick two five-person teams. The leader narrates: "Now this side seems to be winning. Now the other side is recovering and getting strong. Oh, look out! The rope broke!" Students will fall into two heaps without coaching. Be sure they hear the last six words.

3. *Mirrors.* Everyone needs a partner. One person becomes a mirror that mimics the movements of the partner, who might be brushing teeth, pulling faces, or putting on clown makeup. Reverse roles in two or three minutes.

4. *Toe Tips.* This might be a good follow-up to the mirrors exercise. The pairs of students face each other with toe tips stuck together. They explore moving sideways, forward (or is it backward), hopping, bowling, skating, and anything else they can think of.

5. *Puppets.* There are several variations. The leader can narrate as rag-doll marionettes are lifted from the floor by strings attached to nose and elbow—then dropped! With children in pairs, one is the marionette and the other is the string-pulling puppeteer. The marionette, not the puppeteer, initiates the action which the puppeteer tries to follow.

6. *People Machines.* This is everyone's favorite. There are two main approaches. Students can form groups of 6–12 people and take 10 minutes or so to design and practice their machine. When everyone is ready, each machine in turn is performed for the class. Alternatively, the "add on" strategy can be used: One student begins creating, for example, a cat-petting machine, and others add themselves. Beeps, boops, hums, buzzes, and dings are important. You can slow it down, speed it up. One of the best "add ons" is a pinball machine, with as many as 50 people adding themselves to the growing game!

7. *Ice Cubes.* Everyone is an ice cube that melts. The effects are different if melted by the sun or a stove. A variation is to be (standing-up) sand bags that slowly leak.

8. *Statues.* According to "Go" and "Stop" signals, or the beginning and ending of leader's drum beat, students freeze in ugliest positions imaginable.

Student observers or the statues themselves describe what they are, as soon as they figure it out.

9. *Ridiculous Poses.* On a signal, students strike the most ridiculous pose they can.

10. *Biggest Thing, Smallest Thing Variations.* The biggest/smallest exercise was described above. This can be extended to the lightest/heaviest, stiffest/most rubbery, angriest/happiest, bravest/most frightened, etc. Transitions from one form to its opposite may be in slow motion.

11. *Circus.* Each child becomes a different circus performer or animal. Variations include the leader directing what everyone should be, for example, tightrope walkers, trained elephants, lion tamers, jugglers, etc.; or the performers can create a circus parade, each selecting his or her own character.

12. *Obstacles.* With chalk, draw "start" and "finish" lines about eight feet apart on the floor. One at a time, each student makes up an imaginary obstacle which he must climb over, dodge past, wade through, overcome, etc., to get from start to finish. Observers guess the obstacle. It works best with small groups.

13. *Gym Work-Out.* Participants pantomime activities as if they were in an imaginary gym. They run in place, lift weights, do sit-ups, climb a rope, etc.

14. *Leader Game.* Students form a large circle. One person goes outside the room until called. Another person is selected to start some motion which the other children follow. The first person is brought back into the center of the circle and tries to guess who the leader is. The leader changes the motion when the observer is not watching. When found, it is the leader's turn to leave the room.

15. *Robot Walk.* Each person is a robot with movement and a sound. Whenever one robot touches another robot, both stop, sit down, and begin again to rise, with a new sound and a new walk.

16. *Balloon Burst.* All students are on the floor as *one* deflated balloon. The leader begins to blow the balloon up and the students work together to expand. Variations of balloon bursting: Let the air out slowly, pop with a pin, or blow it up until it bursts. With the individual variation, each person is a balloon that gets blown up and bursts, or else is released and flies with predictable craziness about the room.

17. *Making Letters.* Have two people at a time make any alphabet letter with their bodies. Others guess the letter. Or have larger groups spell ENVIRONMENT or words of their choice.

18. *Nature's Shapes.* Children shape their bodies to become a tree, stone, leaf, growing flower, rain, sun, etc.

19. *Sticky Floor.* Have students glue a portion of their bodies (e.g., elbow) to the floor. Discover movements they can make while glued.

20. *Creative Locomotion.* Have children walk like the Crooked Man, Jolly Green Giant, Raggedy Ann, or a robot; run like a mouse, a duck, Miss Muffet frightened by a spider, or a stiff and arthritic person trying to catch a bus; jump like a kangaroo, popcorn, plow horse, or squirrel. Have them walk on the moon, which has very light gravity, or on another planet whose gravity is twice as strong as on Earth.

SENSORY AND BODY AWARENESS

1. *Body Movement.* Children discover their moving parts when the teacher asks them to move their fingers, then hands, wrists, elbows, shoulders, neck, head, face (chew, make faces, bat eyelashes), back, hips, legs, ankles, feet, and toes. Variations: Ask students for more ideas (e.g., eyeballs, tongue, stomach muscles); ask students to keep *all* parts moving as more are added.

2. *Waking Up the Body.* Have the children lie on the floor in any position with their eyes closed and body relaxed. With slow, quiet music have the children begin waking up the various parts of their bodies one at a time until they are on their feet.

3. *Ordering by Height.* With eyes closed and no talking, a group of 8 or 10 students line themselves up according to height.

4. *Swinging.* Let the group discover all the ways a body can be made to swing—head, arms, legs, waist, etc.

5. *Warm-Up at Different Speeds.* Have children run in place in slow motion, then speed up until children are moving very fast. Variations include jumping, skipping, hopping.

6. *Rag Doll-Tin Soldier.* Have children walk as a limp rag doll, then as a stiffened tin soldier. Ask how their movements changed.

7. *Paper Exploration.* Give each child a piece of paper. Have them balance the paper on different parts of the body (especially the foot); run with the paper on the palms of their hands. Discover what sound effects can be made with the paper.

8. *Exploring an Orange.* Give everyone an orange to examine closely. How does it look, feel, smell, taste? What is unique about *your* orange? Could you pick it out from a crowd of oranges? Have groups of 5–6 students put their oranges in a paper bag; then identify them by touch. Take the orange apart and look at it; taste, touch, and smell the inside. Eat it.

9. *Blind Walk.* An absolute awareness favorite. Divide participants into pairs. The member with eyes shut (or blindfolded) is led under tables and chairs and allowed to identify objects by touch, smell, or sound. Get a drink of water, read names and numbers on doors (such as "boys" or "girls"). Go outside and explore trees, the sun, shade, a flower, etc. Ask students about experiences and discoveries. This exercise can lead to a discussion of blindness and replacement senses.

10. *Empathic Vision.* Ask students to inspect the room through the eyes of an artist, fire inspector, lighting engineer, a termite. Look at today's weather from the point of view of a duck, a skier, a field mouse, smoke jumpers, kite flyers. Who else?

11. *Invisible Balls.* An invisible ball is passed from person to person around a circle or up and down rows. As each person receives the ball, it changes size, shape, weight, smell, etc.

12. *Face Touching.* About 6 to 8 volunteers form a line with eyes shut. Another set of 6 to 8 quietly selected volunteers become partners. Each new partner places one or both hands of the "blind" person on his or her face. The blind partner feels hair, noses, cheekbones, whiskers, earrings, collars, glasses and so forth, gathering information which will allow him or her to identify the partner (who return to his or her previous spot before eyes

are opened). Accuracy is very high, and so the game becomes more sporting when the partner tries to fool the blind person by removing earrings or glasses, standing on a chair, or quickly changing hairdos or sweaters.

13. *Listening.* Have students sit (or lie) silently, listening for whatever they can hear. Encourage concentration, letting sounds evoke associated images and memories. Variations: Listen only for close sounds or far sounds. With eyes shut, have students describe the source of the sounds with their hands, communicating without words.

14. *Imaginary Sounds.* Ask students to suggest and imagine sounds found in particular places—a factory, zoo, railroad station, department store, gas station, police station, etc.

15. *Touching.* Have students touch many surfaces, concentrating fully on the feel. Use strange things (e.g., a piece of coral) and familiar things. A paper sack or a box may be used to hide the objects from sight.

16. *Imaginary Touching.* Have children imagine the feel of different objects and surfaces, for example, warm sand between the toes, a hot sidewalk, a wet paw and a lick on the face, ice cream, a Twinkie, mud, etc.

17. *Body Contacts.* Have participants concentrate on contacts of body places with, for example, soles of shoes, shirt collars, chair seats, contacts between fingers. Can they feel the shirt or blouse in the middle of the back? Can they feel heart beats, stomach, lungs?

18. *Texture Walk.* Have the group walk through imaginary substances, for example, Jell-O, flypaper, deep sand, chocolate pudding, tacks, swamp, etc., with leader and students calling out new substances and surfaces.

19. *Smelling.* Small bottles are prepared in advance with familiar scents in them—Vicks Vaporub, vanilla extract, peanut butter, used coffee grounds, lilac perfume, cinnamon, cloves, rubbing alcohol, antifreeze, face cream, lipstick, and so on. In small groups the scents are passed around one at a time and students discuss the memories that are stimulated by each smell.

20. *Imaginary Smells.* Have students imagine good smells. What are they? Can everyone imagine them? Have them imagine the smell of, for example, tulips, his or her mother, a bus, barn, bakery, hamburger, etc. Ask for suggestions.

21. *Tasting.* Encourage students to be aware of and to concentrate upon different tastes of food. Imaginary tastes can be suggested; perhaps some new taste experiences can be shared, with reasonable sanitary precautions.

PANTOMIME ACTIVITIES

Pantomime involves acting out a story, a scene, or other activity or event without speaking. When a child is asked to pantomime an action, full attention is given to the elements that compose the activity. The student creates the proper shape and movements of his or her body and even intently fixes eyes upon objects in the imaginary environment. With encouragement, students will use face, hands, and body to display such emotions as sadness, glee, surprise, love, anger, or fear. If the same persons were allowed to speak, they might ignore bodily and facial expressions and let only words convey the message. With pantomime students are encouraged to "show me, don't tell me."

This creative dramatics student is pantomiming a cannonball. Will the result knock his socks off? (The Museum of Modern Art/Film Stills Archive.)

Note that many of the exercises described earlier also can serve as pantomime activities. Some candidates are Holding Up the Roof, Tug-of-War, Mirrors, Puppets, People Machines, Circus, Obstacles, Gym Work-Out, Sticky Floor, Creative Locomotion, Rag Doll-Tin Soldier, and Invisible Balls.

Additional pantomime activities include:

1. *Animal Pantomimes.* Have the children imitate the way a particular animal moves. Each child can come into the center of the circle to pantomime his or her animal. The rest of the group can guess the animal, perhaps by moving into the center to feed it. For variety, two or three animals can act out a simple plot, for example: (a) a cat sneaking up on a mouse, (b) a bear looking for honey, but finding bees, (c) a bloodhound tracking down a possum, (d) a bull spotting some picnickers, or (e) a fox stalking a chicken.

2. *Toy Shop.* Each student purchases a toy from a make-believe toy shop clerk, then plays with the toy.

3. *Invisible Trunk.* Students form a circle of 6 to 8 persons. In the center is an invisible trunk (or box). In turn, each person lifts the lid, takes something out, does something with it, then puts it back in the box and shuts the lid.

4. *Hats.* Create a hat shop, real or imagined, in which various kinds of workers come in to select a hat fitting their job, for example, baseball player, policeperson, fireperson, clown, cowboy, movie star, nurse, miner, railroad engineer, etc. With hat in place, each child pantomimes the behavior matching the hat.

5. *Inside Out.* Many pantomimic activities can be explored from the inside out. Children become fish in a tank and others look in. Zoo animals in cages are good possibilities for this activity.

6. *Creating an Environment.* This exercise is much like an add-on people machine. The students think of and create an environment. For example, with a bowling alley environment one child begins rolling a bowling ball down a lane. Others become the ball, pins, the scorecard, a drinking fountain, and whatever else they can think of until the picture is complete. If available, sound effects records are helpful. Other worthwhile subjects or environments are fishing, croquet, baseball, a playground, hanging clothes on the line, a circus, an orchestra, marine fish and animals (octopi, star fish, crabs, lobsters), zoo animals, farm animals, an assembly line processing fish, and so on. Your people will think of more.

7. *Miscellaneous Pantomime.* Many brief sketches may teach characterization, for example, a jolly ice cream shop person making an ice cream soda, a fussy lady trying on hats, a scared mountain climber scaling a cliff, a tired pirate digging for treasure, giggly kids watching a funny movie, a grouchy cab driver fighting five o'clock traffic, a nervous, sneaky thief entering a candy store, an awkward cook flipping pancakes, a burglar surprised by the homeowners. Again, you and your students can think of additional possibilities.

PLAYMAKING

Give Scene, Characterization

Playmaking as a type of creative drama can take many forms. With one straightforward strategy, students are given a simple scene or plot, characterization, and then are turned loose to improvise the action and dialogue. In some examples from Way (1967), one group of three students could be the three stooges robbing a bank. They are so half-witted they do everything wrong, backwards, or both. Other groups of the same idiots can act as a surgery team performing a heart transplant ("Gimme a knife and a blood bucket!"); perform as a musical quartet for trombone, drum, nose harp, and garbage can; erect a tent on a windy, rocky hill; or paint and wallpaper a kitchen.

This Is No Chair, This Is My Wife

The *Chair Smuggling* exercise requires problem solving and on-the-spot improvising. Chairs are illegal in this imaginary country. Each of about 10 students will try to smuggle a chair past a border guard—whose job it is to keep chairs out of the country. The border guard normally is played by the creative dramatics leader who, after some improvised suspicion, allows each student and his or her nonchair to enter. Each student must improvise a story about, and demonstrate, what it is that he or she is trying to bring across the border—certainly not a chair! Real or imaginary chairs may be used.

Reduces Self-Consciousness, Strengthens Confidence, Risk-Taking, Humor

Note that by giving students a perfectly logical reason for being silly, they are helped to overcome feelings of self-consciousness. Fear of failure is reduced and such creative traits as confidence, risk-taking, and humor are strengthened.

Serious Playmaking

Mini-plays need not always be silly. Way (1967) suggested that groups can be miners working against time to reinforce a mine about to cave in; slow-moving astronauts assembling something on the moon; toy store toys (or museum displays) coming alive at the stroke of midnight; or witches cooking up a magic brew. Historical events also present possibilities: Columbus discovering America, the Boston Tea Party, Pilgrims landing at Plymouth Rock, and so forth.

Making a Play

A more involved playmaking strategy runs as follows. After a few warm-up exercises, the leader tells a story. Then the leader and students review the sequence

**Events,
Characterization**

of events—what happened first? Second? The group then discusses characterization, considering physical, emotional, and intellectual qualities (nervous, calm, slow-witted, happy, angry, excited, scientific-minded, attractive, quick-stepping, limping, stuck-up, etc.). The play typically is broken into scenes and worked out

**Without and with
Dialogue**

scene by scene. The group may first act out a scene without dialogue to explore the physical possibilities, believability of the characters, and the overall effect. After the group thinks of ways to make the scene better, it is replayed with improvised dialogue. A scene may be played many times with different students experiencing various roles. This general strategy may be adapted for use with

**Use Fairy Tales,
Myths, History, Stories**

such familiar tales as Goldilocks or Peter Cottontail for small children, Cinderella for third graders, and Pandora's Box for the upper grades. Generally, fairy tales, nursery rhymes, myths, folklore, historical material, and animal stories are good sources for ideas.

**Ask Questions:
Affective, Empathic
Understanding**

Direct questioning may add to the educational experience. For example "Was Goldilocks a burglar?" "Did Cinderella's stepmother hate her?" "Could you hate your mother?" "Why were Cinderella's ugly sisters so mean?" Questions such as "How would you feel if . . . ?" and "What would happen if . . . ?" also will stretch creative, empathic imaginations.

THEATER GAMES: IMPROVISATION

The following two theater games originally were intended to help acting students learn on-the-spot improvisation.[1] They appear to be usable with civilian students, helping them learn to quickly think and create.

**Think Fast: Tossable
Object**

Think Fast! Think Fast! requires one tossable object such as a ball of yarn, stuffed animal, or foam rubber "nerf" ball. Six to 25 students can participate.

Players sit or stand in a circle. The leader uses the tossable object as a prop and begins to act out a character from a fairy tale or nursery rhyme. Words and actions are allowed. The actor must not give out the name of the character or the story.

**Portrays Character to
Be Guessed**

For example, the leader might hold the object as if by a handle and say, "Well, I need to take this basket of goodies to Grandma's house; I think I'll just cut through these woods . . . ." Other players begin guessing the character and the story as soon as they can. When the leader hears the correct answer, he or she names that person ("Lystra got it!") and then quickly tosses the object to someone else, saying

Tosses Object

"Think fast!" The object cannot be tossed to the person who gives the correct answer nor to oneself.

The new person has about 10 seconds, which students silently count down, to begin improvising a new character. The same character as the previous leaders cannot be repeated, but other characters from the same story may be used. Most players will be ready in advance, but if the new person cannot think of a character

**New Person Might
Panic!**

and story, the person will call out "Panic!" and pass the object to the person next to him or her. With the second panic it is customary to pass the object to the person on the other side. Rules are flexible, but a person who panics twice during a game normally is eliminated.

Variations

Think Fast! works fine as is, with or without the elimination feature. However, several options make it more difficult. For example, a shorter time limit (count down) may be used; a particular story or rhyme may be used no more than twice; speech may be prohibited; or for greater difficulty, genders may be reversed—males must portray female characters and vice versa.

---

[1]The author is indebted to Lin Seagren, whose (graduate) creativity class paper is the source of both games.

Be a Number, Any Number

Think Fast! can be adapted to math. Instead of playing a character, children can portray a number. For example, if they are learning multiplication tables the person catching the object may say "I am equal to 6 × 7." More complex clues may be encouraged: "I am more than 5 × 5 but less than 3 × 9." If there is more than one possible answer (e.g., "more than 6 × 7 but less than 5 × 9") the student must have one "correct" number in mind.

What Are You Doing? What Are You Doing? requires no props at all and can be played with groups up to class size. It encourages actors to think of more than one thing at a time.

I Am Not Doing What It Looks Like!

Players form a circle. The first player begins silently miming a common action—brushing teeth, tying shoe laces, picking a sweater, etc. The action must continue until the next player starts acting. The next person, usually on the right, asks "What are you doing?" The answer can be any action *other than* the one actually being performed. The first player continues acting until the new player (who asked) begins acting out whatever the previous player said he or she was doing. The acting continues—soberly, logically, and believably—while the next person asks "What are you doing?" Once again, the answer may not reflect what the actor really is doing. Actions already used may not be repeated, although players may agree to accept a limited number of close variations, such as just three types of eating (pizza, ice cream, rocks).

Variations

There are several variations. For example, a theme may be set, such as the Olympics or activities at school. Because young children have difficulty doing two different things at once, the game can be simplified by allowing the student to stop acting to answer "What are you doing?" But the child still must not answer the question correctly. If students get stuck in an area (feeding my cat, feeding my dog, feeding my snake, feeding the birds, . . .) it may be necessary to ask that children find "other" areas of activities. Young children probably need to be warned to use only "polite" tasks, not toilet ones. Older students also may need to be reminded to use only socially proper answers (use your imagination).

Keep It Clean

Competitive Variation

In competitive versions, a player is ruled "out" if he or she repeats an action already named; stops acting before the next actor begins acting; answers the question by saying what he or she really is doing; takes too long to get started (8 to 10 seconds is a common deadline); or somehow is unable to convey the assigned task.

SUMMARY

Creative dramatics is a unique educational experience aimed at strengthening problem solving, imagination, physical control, sensory awareness, self-confidence, humor, and empathic awareness and understanding of others.

Creative dramatics is not children's theatre; creative dramatics involves everyone.

The leader should have energy and a sense of humor.

Sessions begin with a stretching, warm-up activity or two.

The next activities may include movement exercises, for example, mirrors and people machines; sensory and body awareness exercises, such as the blind walk and exploring an orange; pantomiming, as in animal pantomimes or creating an environment; playmaking; or theater games.

Playmaking can be simple, as when students are merely given a scene and characterization before jumping in. Playmaking also can be extensively and carefully developed, including a discussion of events and characterization, exploration of different possibilities, rehearsing first without dialogue, continual modification and improvement, and rotating parts.

Discussion of roles, characters, dilemmas, etc., adds to the experience by increasing empathy and understanding.

Think Fast! is a theater game that requires one student at a time to portray a character in a common fairy tale or nursery rhyme, which is then guessed by others. With *What Are You Doing?*, a student pantomimes a common activity, but tells the next performer that he or she is doing something different, which the next person must pantomime.

Let's Be a Cuckoo Clock: Creative Dramatics

Self-Test: Key Concepts, Terms, and Names

Briefly define or explain each of these:

Warm-up exercises _____

_____

Movement exercises _____

_____

Sensory and body awareness exercises _____

_____

Pantomime _____

_____

Playmaking _____

_____

Theater games _____

_____

Why does your author think these names are important?

Thomas Jefferson _____

Whitney Houston _____

Paul McCartney _____

Howard Hughes _____

Let's Think about It

1. What are the claimed benefits of creative dramatics?

_____

_____

_____

2. Classify each of the below creative dramatics exercises into its proper category, with:

      WU = Warm-ups
    M/P = Movement Exercises or Pantomime
      SA = Sensory and Body Awareness Exercises
      PL = Playmaking
      TG = Theater Games

_____ Having children imitate the movement of animals

_____ Having students imagine different smells or tastes

_____ Having children walk like a robot, the Jolly Green Giant, or Raggedy Ann

_____ Invisible Trunk exercise

_____ Chair Smuggling exercise

_____ Waking up the Body exercise

_____ Asking the (pantomiming) person "What are you doing?"

_____ Blind Walk exercise

_____ Acting out the Cinderella story

_____ Having students stretch their bodies into the biggest thing (then the smallest thing) they can

_____ Having students pretend they are toy store toys coming alive at midnight

_____ Think Fast! exercise

_____ Holding Up the Roof exercise

3. Let's use *analogical thinking* (Chapter 6) to create some creative dramatics exercises. Look at specific exercises in this chapter in each of the first four categories. Use them as "inspiration"; that is, modify them to produce new exercises.

"Warm-Up" Exercises:

_____

_____

_____

Movement Exercises:

_____

_____

_____

Sensory and Body Awareness Exercises:

_____

_____

_____

_____

Pantomime Activities:

_____

_____

_____

_____

4. *Brainstorm* a dozen ideas for people machines.

_____

_____

_____

_____

_____

_____

_____

_____

_____

_____

_____

11

teaching for creative growth

[**Scene:** *Cottage of Cinderella, her stepmother, and her two ugly stepsisters Drisella and Esmerelda. Stepmother and stepsisters are about to begin brainstorming ideas for harassing Cinderella.*]

Stepmother: Come now girls, we've got to find new ways to make you-know-who as miserable as we can!

Esmerelda: Yes, mama. I'm so tired of her pretty hair, gorgeous face and sweet disposition—why can't she be like the rest of us?

Drisella: OH SHUT UP, ESMERELDA! WE'RE JUST AS DAMN CHARMING AS SHE IS!

Stepmother: Girls! Girls! Don't let the little twit upset you like that! Now, you both know the brainstorming rules.

Esmerelda: Yes, mama. We don't criticize or evaluate, we. . . .

Drisella: You nitwit! Everybody knows that! Well, go on . . . let's hear the rest!

Esmerelda: We suggest whatever wild ideas occur to us, we list lots of ideas, and we modify and combine ideas in order to produce even more ideas. Let's hide her socks.

Drisella: That's a dumb idea. If we're going to hide something, let's be more creative. Let's hide her broom—and then demand that she sweep up the whole house and the front walk!

Stepmother: That's the WORST idea I ever heard, you nincompoop! She's just find another broom and have everything spiffy in a few minutes! What about strangling her cat?

Esmerelda: That's really a stupid one, mama! The cat would put up a big fuss and Cinderella would hear us. Let's put cracker crumbs in her bed, milk in her shoes, vinegar in her yogurt, break the teeth of her comb, cut the strings on her vest, burn her sewing basket, send her to the next kingdom for some salt, and make her clean the chimney—from the inside.

Drisella: You ignorant big-nosed toad, we did all those last week! Look, let's have her take some hot soup over to Tom Tom, the piper's son. Tom Tom has the plague!

Stepmother: She'd just bring it home, you fool! I've got it! Let's stop her from going to the Prince's ball!

Esmerelda: Oh mother, that's a super idea! Isn't it wonderful how a warm, receptive, and encouraging atmosphere can stimulate creative thinking!

Can you teach creativity? You can raise the curiosity and interest of your young masters. You can help them look beyond what is given, look beyond what commonly is the answer. You can guide them in ways to think and find ideas. You can prime the creative use of their abilities. Yes, you can.

Yoda

1. Issues

2. Earlier Chapters

3. Infants, Young Children

4. Five Core Goals

This chapter includes four main parts. We first will look at some issues and considerations that relate to strengthening skills, abilities, and predispositions for creative thinking—beginning with the core questions "Can creativity be taught?". The matter is not simple nor does it elicit quick agreement. Second, we will review concepts, ideas, and assumptions related to teaching for creative growth that appeared in every previous chapter. Third, we will take a broad-based approach to cultivating creative potential by forwarding some uncomplicated developmental suggestions for increasing intellectual growth and problem-solving skills of infants and young children. Finally, we will describe five core goals of creativity training plus strategies for achieving them.

ISSUES IN CREATIVITY TRAINING

Issues

This section will look at these issues:

Can creativity be taught?

Individual differences in responsiveness to creativity training

Individual differences in motivation to create

The importance of a creative climate

Must creativity be taught within a content area?

Can Creativity Be Taught?

The most frequent question your author is asked is, "Can creativity be taught? Or are you born with it?" Sometimes the issue is raised in a more negative form—"I don't think you can teach creativity," followed by the inevitable rationale, "You either have it or you don't!"

Individual Differences

Of course, there are tremendous individual differences in innate creative abilities and in affective dispositions toward creativity, just as there are wide variations in every other mental and physical characteristic. Realistically, no amount of the most carefully orchestrated creativity training can mold an average person into a Leonardo DaVinci, Marie Curie, Thomas Edison, William Shakespeare, Booker T. Washington, or Orson Welles. Such people are born with a special combination of high intelligence, creative ability, extraordinary drive, and a strong sense of vision and destiny. Their drive leads them to acquire a great depth of knowledge and experience in their chosen fields.

Learning: Yes

However, it also is absolutely true that every individual can raise his or her creative skill, creative productivity, and creative living to a higher level. An irrefutable argument for the trainability of creativity is simply that, with interest and effort, all of us can make better use of the creative abilities we were born with.

Creativity Can Be Taught: Torrance

What does creativity guru Paul Torrance (1995) say about whether creativity can be taught?

I know that it is possible to teach children to think creatively and that it can be done in a variety of ways. I have done it. I have seen my wife do it; I have seen other excellent teachers do it. I have seen children who had seemed previously to be "non thinkers" learn to think creatively, and I have seen them continuing for years thereafter to think creatively. I have seen, heard, and otherwise experienced their creativity. Their parents have told me that they saw it happening. Many of the children, now adults, say that it happened. I also know that these things would not have happened by chance because I have seen them not happen to multitudes of their peers. (p. 269)

Torrance itemized 142 studies describing efforts to "teach creativity" with divergent thinking exercises, training in the Creative Problem Solving (CPS) model, training in creative art or writing, establishing a creative climate, or using various creativity training workbooks or programs. Success rates (Torrance Test scores,

Creative thinking and your creative development are important in any career. "I'm sure glad my dental school taught me to use my imagination!" said Dr. Goldcap. "Do I get a lollypop?" asked his nervous patient. (The Museum of Modern Art/Film Stills Archives.)

Massive Evidence

creative products, creative self-perceptions) were good. "Massive evidence" was the phrase Torrance (1987b) used to describe the overall results of these efforts to teach creative thinking. CPS, FPS, and OM especially were recommended.

Individual Differences in Responsiveness to Creativity Training

Differences in Receptiveness to Training

Just as there are immense individual differences in cognitive abilities and affective predispositions for creativity, there also are individual differences in *receptiveness* to creativity training. That is, receptiveness to adopting the required creativity consciousness and other attitudinal predispositions toward thinking creatively and doing things creatively. Some children and adults respond quickly and positively to such training. They learn that, yes indeed, they can imagine, visualize, create, and solve problems better than they expected—the capability was there all along, they just never tried to use it. Others seem impervious to creativity training, due to some combinations of disinterest, rigidity, insecurity, conformity, or other traits and barriers that are incompatible with creative thinking and behavior.

No Sir! You Can't Make Me More Creative!

College Course: Improved Affective Components

Your author taught undergraduate and graduate courses in creative thinking that had two purposes. First was the academic goal of transmitting a body of knowledge about issues, theories, characteristics, processes, tests, and techniques of creativity, along with strategies for teaching for creative growth. The second purpose was to help students become more creatively productive by raising their creativity consciousness, explaining how others use creativity techniques, and motivating them to use their creative abilities. One of our studies showed that, *on average*, students who completed the course improved in their affective creative traits—creative attitudes, predispositions, and self-ratings of creativity—significantly more than students who had registered for but had not yet taken the course (Davis & Bull, 1978).

Memorize the Stuff, Take the Tests

However, there always were substantial differences in the degree to which students' creative potential was affected by the exposure. Some students registered for the course, met the requirements, but remained untouched by the potentially life-changing principles and concepts. Other students experienced changes in their self-perceptions of creativeness and their actual creative output; they discovered capabilities they did not know they had. As a few examples, one person wrote her first and potentially publishable children's book as a direct result of the class; another invented an educational game that was sold to Fisher Price Toys; and another began writing poetry, and lots of it, for the very first time. Two memorable testimonials were "Now I understand my own creativity better" and "Now I do weird things."

Some Are Influenced Profoundly

Be Ready for Differences in Responsiveness

There are wide differences then, in responsiveness to creativity training. Teachers of creativity should be prepared for these differences, and perhaps ready to work a little harder with low-receptivity students.

Individual Differences in Motivation to Create

Motivation Differences

There also are large differences in motivation for creativity. As we saw in Chapter 3, a high energy level is a common characteristic of creative people. Related traits are high levels of curiosity, adventurousness, spontaneity, and risk-taking, plus wide and perhaps novel interests and hobbies. For creative eminence, Torrance's (1987a) "blazing drive" seems to energize the creative productivity.

RAS Theory

Motivation theorists Berlyne (1961) and Farley (1986) assume that the high "arousal-seeking" common among creative people is governed by the reticular activating system (RAS) in the brain stem. According to this theory, creative and adventurous activities are sought out in order to raise an uncomfortably low level of RAS activity to a higher, more optimal state.

Raise Interest, Involve Students

There is not much we can do about students' reticular activating systems. However, the RAS hypothesis does not prevent a teacher from working to elevate students' interest in creative thinking, while concurrently exercising creative skills and abilities and engaging students in artistic, scientific, and other entrepreneurial work.

Creative Atmosphere

Psychological Safety

Deferred Judgment

We do not need a long discussion of the focal importance of a receptive and reinforcing creative atmosphere. Carl Rogers (1962) called it *psychological safety*; in brainstorming it is *deferred judgment*. We saw in Chapter 2 that if creative ideas are not reinforced—or worse, if they are blocked, criticized, or squelched—normal children and adults simply will not produce creative ideas in those unreceptive circumstances. One of our five main goals of creativity training will be fostering creativity consciousness and creative attitudes.

Must Creativity Be Taught within a Content Area?

SA and ST Creativity

We decided in Chapter 1 that creativity need not be taught within a subject area. Effective creativity training may be content free or it may be embedded within a content area. Maslow's (1954) *self-actualized creativity* includes the mentally healthy tendency to approach all aspects of one's life—personal, profession, avocational—in a creative fashion. It is a general, content free form of creative thinking. As we noted earlier, many successful creativity courses, programs, workshops, and educational workbooks try to teach a general creativeness by strengthening creativity consciousness and other creative attitudes, as well as by exercising creative abilities and teaching creativity techniques, perhaps including the CPS model. These efforts help the learner to understand creativity and to approach personal, academic, and professional problems in a more creative fashion. The approach is sensible, common, and effective. It is not tied to a particular subject or content.

Can Teach General, Content-Free Creativity

FPS, OM

For elementary and secondary students, the Future Problem Solving and Odyssey of the Mind programs (Chapter 9) are two excellent examples of successful efforts to teach a general, self-actualized type of creativeness. A highly recommended program for adults is the one-week Creative Problem Solving Institute held in Buffalo, New York, each June. Most participants return home as different, more creative, and more self-actualized persons.[1]

CPS

Special Talent Creativity

On the other hand, Maslow's *special talent creativity* refers to an obviously outstanding creative talent or gift in art, literature, music, theater, science, business, or other area. Special talent creativity presumes some mastery of that area, and the greater the sophistication the more likely are creative contributions. Snow (1986), for example, wrote that "Creativity . . . is an accomplishment born of intensive study, long reflection, persistence, and interest . . . A rich store of knowledge in a field is required as a base for idea production" (p. 1033).

Goals: Strengthening Creative Thinking Skills, Mastering Content and Technical Skills

As for teaching special talent creativity, the two goals are strengthening creative thinking and problem solving attitudes and skills while concurrently guiding students in mastering content and technical skills in the particular area. With the typical independent projects approach, students are given (or find) a high-interest project or problem. They proceed to clarify it, consider various approaches, find

Independent Projects

---

[1]For information write to: Creative Education Foundation, 1050 Union Road, Buffalo, NY 14224.

a main solution or resolution, and then create or prepare the project or problem for presentation. Throughout, students identify and resolve numerous subproblems; they evaluate their methods and results; they acquire content knowledge and develop technical skills; and they develop content-related creative problem solving skills and abilities. The independent projects strategy nicely fits Maslow's category of special talent creativity.

As the reader might guess, special talent creativity may be strengthened while teaching a general, self-actualized type of creativeness, and vice versa. For example, within a primarily content-free creativity session students might brainstorm a science-, history- or math-related problem or they might do creative writing, creative dramatics, or art activities. Conversely, creative projects in a subject area (special talent creativity) are very likely to help develop general creative abilities and attitudes (self-actualized creativity) that extend beyond the specific topic at hand.

A Common G/T Strategy
SA and ST Creativity Overlap

THIS BOOK SO FAR

In our first 10 chapters we have seen many concepts and principles related to becoming a more imaginative, flexible, creative thinker. It will be worth a little paper and ink to review them.

Chapter 1

Creativity Consciousness

Self-Actualization

Chapter 1 sought mainly to increase your creativity consciousness by stressing the importance of creativity both to yourself as a self-actualizing person and to society. Nothing can be more important to life satisfaction—your life satisfaction—than becoming self-actualized: becoming what you are capable of becoming, being an independent, forward-growing, fully-functioning, democratic-minded, and mentally healthy individual.

Chapter 2

Blocks and Barriers

A Few Whacks and Squelchers

Chapter 2 looks at creativity training not from a how-to-do-it view, but from the what-stops-it perspective—blocks and barriers that prevent us from thinking and behaving more creatively. We reviewed the effects of habit and learning, rules and traditions, perceptual blocks, cultural blocks (especially conformity and the cultural mores themselves), emotional blocks, and even resource barriers. We noted that creativity expert von Oech recommended a "whack on the side of the head" to jolt us out of our mental blocks—habits and attitudes relating to finding one right answer; being logical, practical, and correct; avoiding ambiguity, play, and foolishness; and assuming "I'm not creative!" The chapter ended with a list of statements that squelch creative thinking—the idea squelchers.

Chapter 3

Definitions, Theories Increase Our Understanding, Awareness

Reinforce Creativity

The definitions and theories in Chapter 3 increase our understanding of creativity and creative ideas, which indirectly contributes to creativity consciousness. The emphasis of many definitions on *combining* ideas implicitly justifies the use of deliberate creativity techniques that basically force new idea combinations. The ancient learning theory concept of strengthening behavior through reinforcement definitely applies to creativity: Children (and adults) will do what they are rewarded for doing, including thinking creatively instead of convergently. In Plato's words, "What is valued in one's country is what will be cultivated."

Chapter 4

Reinforce Traits of Creativity

Chapter 4 described personality and biographical characteristics of creative people. We normally do not speak of "teaching personality traits." However, it may be sensible to recommend rewarding and encouraging, and cultivating in oneself, these (positive) kinds of creative traits, habits, and behaviors: confidence, independence, willingness to take a creative risk, enthusiasm, adventurousness, curiosity and wide interests, humor and playfulness, attraction to the complex and mysterious, and setting aside some alone time—time to incubate and create. The number one trait to encourage is, of course, a creativity consciousness. Teach-

Encourage Involvement

ers also should encourage aesthetic interests and involvement in creative activities.

As we noted in Chapter 4, the main difference between people who *have* creative abilities and those who *use* their creative potential lies in affective traits that predispose some people to think and behave in creative ways.

Motivation

Research in creative eminence reinforced the importance of high motiva-

Parents

tion—Torrance's "blazing drive." The Bloom-Sosniak (Sosniak, 1997) study stressed the critical role of parents in the early development of talent in artistic, athletic, and academic areas.

Chapter 5

Use Visual Puzzles

Chapter 5 looked at the creative process as a change in perception—"seeing" new meanings, relationships, combinations, and transformations—and described stage analyses of creativity. A teacher can use optical illusions and visual puzzles to illustrate how, with a little effort, one always can "see different things" and find more ideas. The BIG contribution of Chapter 5, of course, is the remarkable

CPS Models: Yes

CPS model—whose five steps almost always produce good, creative problem solutions. A relevant book is *CPS For Kids* (Eberle & Stanish, 1985). A third section explored how creatively eminent persons have used mental imagery, including cross-modal imagery, in their unique creations.

Chapter 6

Analogical Thinking: Pervasive Technique

The crowning creative thinking technique is analogical thinking. Most of the personal creative thinking techniques described in Chapter 7 involve "seeing a connection" between the problem at hand and the solution to another situation, or transferring ideas from one situation to another. Try the analogical thinking exercises in Chapter 6 (Inset 6.2). Show students how it works. Practice the clever synectics variations (direct analogy, personal analogy, fantasy analogy, compressed conflicts) and the analogical thinking exercises at the end of Chapter 6.

Also Enlightening

Combined with the techniques of Chapter 7, you and your students will feel that you better understand how creative people think, and are better able to produce new idea combinations and problem solutions on demand.

Chapter 7

Techniques

When it comes to "teaching creativity," the techniques described in Chapter 7 represent teachable ways that real, honest-to-goodness creative people find creative idea combinations. Brainstorming, attribute listing, morphological synthesis, idea checklists, and others all were derived from creatively productive people. Most of these adult/professional techniques are finding their way into elementary and secondary classrooms via workbooks (Davis & DiPego, 1973; Stanish, 1981, 1988) and teachers who have done their homework on "teaching creativity."

By permission of Mike Lukovich and Creators Syndicate.

Chapter 8

Testing

Chapter 8 on assessing creative potential presented precious little related to improving creativeness. An examination of the underlying assumptions regarding what is being evaluated—usually personality traits, divergent thinking abilities, or experience with creative activities—should help one's understanding of creativity. Guilford (1967, 1986) suggested that to strengthen creative abilities, we might give students exercises similar to the tests that measure the particular abilities. Meeker (Meeker & Meeker, 1986; Staff, 1995) uses approximately this strategy not only to teach creativity, but reading, writing, and math as well. The same strategy would apply to teaching the content of attitude/personality inventories (Chapters 4 and 8).

Can Use Test Content as Exercises

Chapter 9

Gifted Education Aims at Fostering Creative Development

Chapter 9 was the G/T chapter. A main goal of most program models and enrichment and acceleration strategies is strengthening creative thinking and problem solving skills and abilities. For example, the Future Problem Solving

Renzulli

Feldhusen & Kolloff

and Odyssey of the Mind programs were designed entirely to foster creative development. Renzulli's Type II Enrichment includes creativity training (exercises, techniques), and his Type III Enrichment highlights creative involvement in individual research projects. The Feldhusen and Kolloff three-stage model explains that creativity training should begin with basic divergent thinking exercises, progress to more advanced creativity techniques and problem solving strategies, and finally include independent problems and projects.

Chapter 10

**Creative Dramatics;
for Kids of All Ages**

The creative dramatics exercises in Chapter 10 all aim at loosening up the creative juices. If the reader is a proper adult and a non-teacher, you may feel this stuff is not for you. Possibly true. However, some corporate creativity techniques described by Smith (1985) included the following—designed to shake up a few neurons and stimulate some regression: "Now let's have the 'chicken cheer'... A dozen managers shed their jackets and stand up ... The leader starts. One by one, others join in. They flap their arms and scratch at the floor with their feet. Finally, the room fills with crowing sounds a rooster would envy."

Is creative dramatics only for teachers and kids?

This Chapter

In the remaining two sections we first will examine some recommendations for strengthening cognitive growth, problem solving skills, and perhaps creative development of infants and young children.

Turning to school age children, adolescents, adults, and you, the rest of this chapter is built around five main affective and cognitive objectives related to becoming a more creative person and teaching others to become more creative thinkers and producers. The points will review and extend ideas from earlier chapters. The objectives are not complicated and the list is short. We will look at:

Five Goals

1. Fostering creativity consciousness and creative attitudes
2. Improving students' metacognitive understanding of creativity
3. Exercising creative abilities
4. Teaching creative thinking techniques
5. Involving students in creative activities

HELPING MENTAL GROWTH, THINKING, PROBLEM SOLVING, AND CREATIVITY AT EARLY AGES

Social Skills, Mental Development

Should we try to help infants and young children grow up with stronger mental development? Better school readiness skills? More acquainted with thinking, problem solving, and creativity? Or should they find themselves in a college course thinking: "Oh wow! I gotta' think of something original! What do I do now?"

Developmental psychologists have plenty of suggestions for improving young children's intelligence, thinking capability, and social skills which, directly or indirectly, aid their creative growth. The following recommendations can affect virtually all aspects of children's lives. Some suggestions— particularly sharing and taking turns—focus on critical early social skills. Others aid mental development by enhancing infants' and toddlers' experiences and by giving them early practice in thinking and solving problems.

Early Stimulating Environments

**Stimulating
Surroundings**

Everything written about the mental development of babies recommends giving them a stimulating, interesting environment. All sorts of sensory input should be included—mobiles, pictures, noise-makers, button-pushers, grabbers, squeezers, cuddlers, talkers, chewers, balls, Raggedy Anns, and some wonderful measuring spoons. Babies can be carried around the house and outdoors and allowed to look through windows. They need to see, hear, feel, and smell, and when you are not watching they also will taste. The little grey cells will grow and interrelate.

Taking Turns and Sharing

**Taking Turns, Sharing:
Broad Implications**

Early childhood psychologists emphasize two disarmingly simple social skills that can be taught at an early age and that children *will* carry with them into elementary school and beyond. *Taking turns* and *sharing* are early forms of respecting others' rights. They intrinsically include the concepts of right and wrong, fairness, justice, altruism, reciprocity, and "Do unto others" (Santrock, 1996). They are a step toward self-actualization. Imagine little Roberta:

> *Five-year old Roberta will not allow others in her kindergarten class to be first.
> She must be first. She will not share building blocks, crayons, dinosaur models,
> or anything else. Roberta does not understand "taking turns" nor "sharing."
> Roberta's parents need a good spanking.*

Taking Turns

Taking turns is sufficiently simple that parents can begin teaching this value during their child's first year and continue through the pre-kindergarten years as well. The frequent reminder "Now let's take turns" should become a basic value. The game of *peek-a-boo*, which most parents play with their baby anyway, introduces the infant to the principle of taking turns. As you may recall, mom or dad plays the game by covering the baby's face with a light blanket, which soon is removed with great surprise and a big "PEEK-A-BOO!" Then the parent can cover his/her own face, remove the blanket, and again "PEEK-A-BOO!" And it's baby's turn again.

As the children grow, parents have other opportunities to emphasize turn-taking. For example, parent and baby can take turns:

Oh Yuk!

Feeding the poor kid strained spinach.

Rolling a ball back and forth with a verbal "Your turn! . . . My turn! . . . Your turn!"

Pulling the string on the talking toy . . . "It's your turn . . . Now it's my turn . . . Thank you Mr. Talking Toy!"

Hugging the doll or stuffed animal. "It's Daddy's turn to hug Teddy Bear . . . Now it's your turn . . . Thank you! Isn't it fun to take turns?"

Research shows that children who learn the concept of taking turns at an early age are more likely to take turns when they later play with other children.

Sharing

Sharing is the other simple and central social skill (or value) that parents can teach very early. Like taking turns, the idea of sharing can begin during the first year and continue throughout early childhood. As with turn-taking, the way to teach sharing is to give the child lots of examples of sharing:

"Let's share the blocks. Here's some for you, and here's some for me!"

"Here's some apple for you. Here's some for Teddy Bear. Here's some for me. Isn't it fun to share the apple?"

"Let's share the balls. Here's a ball for you. Here's a ball for big sister. And here's a ball for Daddy."

Need Experience, Not Abstract Words

The words *share* and *take turns* are relatively abstract. With toddlers, their meanings can be taught only by experience in sharing and taking turns. Be sure to verbalize "let's share" and "let's take turns." Your child will need to know these meanings—and to possess these values related to right and wrong, fairness, and reciprocity—the minute he or she stumbles into nursery school or kindergarten.

Other Early Adjustment and Thinking Considerations

Other simple forms of manners that will aid school adjustment, and indirectly learning, thinking, and problem solving—and which many adults never master—include:

Social Skills

Asking (e.g., to borrow things).

Waiting and patience.

Being courteous, pleasant, and respectful.

Behaving oneself in public (which means respecting other people's rights).

Being considerate with the elderly and with persons with disabilities.

Being helpful and doing favors.[2]

The following are additional suggestions from developmentalists.

Chores

Give Age-Appropriate Chores.   Feelings of pride and responsibility can be taught by giving young children chores that are suitable for their age. Helping with dishes and straightening one's room are a good start.

Structure

Provide Structure and Predictability.   Young children need the security and good study habits that are born in predictable times for meals, homework, and going to bed.

Value School

Value Schoolwork.   Parents who expressly value schoolwork convey to their child that education is a top priority. Parents who volunteer at school—for tutoring, helping score papers, or assisting with field trips—tell their child with even more emphasis that education is essential.

Reward Effort

Reward School Effort.   Praise your child as he or she masters math or history or participates in school events. Let the child know you support his or her school efforts one hundred percent, or more.

Stimulating Discussions

Stimulate Thoughtful Discussion.   Intellects can be stimulated with discussions of hobbies, movies, current events, school and after-school activities, and so on. You can show interest in your child's activities and you can ask for thought-stimulating ideas: "Everything OK at school? What are you learning?" "What are some ways to make your collection better?" "How come you liked *101 Dalmatians* better than *Star Wars*?" "Tobacco companies are in trouble. Do you think smoking

---

[2]For elaborations, see Davis (1996a, 1996b).

is a good idea?" "Who has a better life, college graduates or people in prison?" Dinner is a good time.

Field Trips

Take Field Trips. Schools take field trips to enrich children's minds and experiences, and families can do the same. Libraries, museums, planetariums, zoos, age-appropriate musicals and plays, and even construction sites and shopping malls are possibilities.

Role Model

Be a Good Role Model. Parents are role models, and what you say and do will be remembered. Statements showing bigotry, intolerance, bad grammar, laziness, or anti-school attitudes will make a lasting impression.

Career Goals

Discuss Educational and Career Goals. Talking with your child about the virtues of education and productive careers is suitable for any age. Many young people do not learn—until it is too late—that gangs, drugs, dropping out, crime, and prison were not their best life choices, despite the attractions and peer pressures at the time. Constructive goal-setting is critical. Although career goals will change from running a candy store to fighting fires to being a forest ranger to becoming an electrician, doctor, or business entrepreneur, parents should help kids become aware of the possibilities and the required preparation.

Stimulating Creative Thinking and Problem Solving

Some suggestions aim specifically at stimulating problem solving capability and creativity in infants and young children.[3]

Infants and Toddlers. Put a toy slightly out of reach so the infant has to think of how to get it. Hide a toy under a see-through scarf or mesh bag—"Where's the ball?"

Encourage Exploration, Solving Problems

Toddlers can be encouraged to explore objects, which may mean a lot of shaking, banging, bending, and squeezing. Have them solve simple problems, such as fitting little things into bigger things, putting toys away in proper places, helping set the table, or retrieving your car keys from a drawer.

Simple Building Materials

Parents can supply handy building stuff such as egg cartons, cans, margarine tubs, shampoo bottles, boxes, plus little things to put in the containers. Other materials that promote creation and expression include paper and crayons, paints, play dough, sand and water, building-type blocks and toys, and simple "dress-up" clothes such as hats and purses.

Pretending

Preschoolers. You can stimulate young imaginations by helping preschoolers pretend to be other things—farm or wild animals, people in various occupations, or even a train, plane, helicopter, or dump truck. You probably could be an excellent cuckoo clock.

Creative dramatics (Chapter 10) suggests many kinds of movement activities and people machines that will loosen the imaginations of preschoolers as well as graduate students.

Following the unusual uses strategy, you can ask children "How else can we use that toy (or material)?"

Planning

Planning may be stimulated by asking, for example, "What are you going to do after dinner, before bed time?" or "What should we do next Saturday?" Ask how we could build something, or how a problem might be worked out.

---

[3]Many suggestions in this section are modified from an unpublished document provided by Kay S. Bull, Oklahoma State University.

Examples of Creativity

Examples of creativity in writing may be demonstrated with stories and poems that use words and pictures in creative ways. Dr. Suess is the king, particularly if you like green eggs and ham.

Combine, Modify

Familiar creative materials may be explored in new ways. Building blocks of different kinds can be used together. Children can paint on paper, cardboard, wood, or fabric. A slab of patio or garage concrete can be the base for sculpting with water, sand, rocks, and mud. Potatoes and soap bars are classic sculpting materials (use a very dull knife). Water, soap bubbles, and food coloring can be mixed. Paper may be folded, rolled up, torn, or cut in different ways. Water, funnels, pieces of hose or tubing, and jars always can exercise young minds.

Weaving can be explored with paper, a hole punch, and yarn. Pipe cleaners are great for . . . well, make up something. Paper and magic markers help drawing and story telling.

More Advanced Building

Building materials and tools for preschoolers may include wood, nails, and a small hammer, along with fabric scraps, string, elastic bands, cardboard boxes, bottle caps, little wheels, and whatever.

Pretending

Dress-up clothes for role-playing and imagination can be more complicated—neckties, shoes, gloves, shirts, pants, dresses, and coats, along with toddlers' hats and purses.

Making Music

Musical instruments can be created—drums from pots, pans, boxes, and plastic bottles; shakers from plastic bottles and beans; tooters from pop bottles and water; and a guitar string from a rubber band stretched between two nails.

CREATIVITY CONSCIOUSNESS AND CREATIVE ATTITUDES

We turn now to the first of five recommendations for "teaching creativity." A focus on raising creativity consciousness and teaching creative attitudes will be followed by suggestions for developing a metacognitive understanding of creativity, strengthening creative abilities, teaching creativity techniques, and involving students in creative activities.

Creativity Consciousness

Increasing creativity consciousness and creative attitudes is the single most important component of teaching for creative growth. Every creative person is aware of creativity and his or her own creativeness. The single best item on adult creativity inventories is the question "Are you creative?" Creative people make conscious decisions: "Today I'm going to think creatively and do some creative work!"

Very Important, Easy to Teach

Ironically, creativity consciousness is both the most important aspect of becoming more creatively productive, yet also the easiest to teach. Creativity consciousness will be a natural outgrowth of virtually any type of creativity exercises and activities, such as reading this book.

Creativity consciousness and creative attitudes includes:

Awareness

An awareness of the importance of creativity for personal development (self-actualization), and for solving personal and professional problems.

An appreciation of the role of creative ideas and creative people in the history of civilization—which may be seen as a history of creative innovation in every field.

Barriers

An awareness of barriers to creativity—habits, traditions, rules, policies, and particularly social expectations and conformity pressures.

Receptiveness

A receptiveness to the novel, unconventional, even zany and farfetched ideas of others.

Involvement	A predisposition to think creatively, play with ideas, and become involved in creative activities.
Risk-Taking	A willingness to take creative risks, make mistakes, and even fail.

Courses Stimulate People to Use Their Abilities
Every college course in creativity and every professional workshop stresses creativity consciousness, appropriate creative attitudes, and removing barriers to creative thinking and behavior. Regardless of whether innate abilities can be changed, by changing attitudes and awareness in a more creative direction we stimulate people to use the creative abilities that they already have.

Creative Atmosphere
Note that the concept of a creative atmosphere, mentioned earlier, fits in exactly here. A creative atmosphere rewards creative thinking and helps it become habitual. It includes Rogers' concept of psychological safety, the deferred judgment concept of brainstorming, and good old-fashioned reinforcement theory.

The reader may wish to look again at the *idea squelchers* in Chapter 2. This is what a creative atmosphere and a creative person are not.

Creativity Consciousness Important
Increasing creativity consciousness and fostering favorable attitudes toward creative thinking is truly item number 1 in becoming a more creative person and helping others to develop and use their creative potential.

METACOGNITIVE UNDERSTANDING OF CREATIVITY

Thinking about Thinking
Metacognition is thinking about thinking—or in this case, thinking about *creative* thinking. The predisposition to think creatively will take a giant step forward if a person knows more about the topic. In fact, a major purpose of this book is to expand the reader's metacognitive understanding of creative thinking. An increased understanding of creativity will help raise creativity consciousness, demystify creativity, and convince readers that given their present abilities they are perfectly capable—with interest and effort—of hatching creative ideas and producing creative things.

Possible Topics
Lessons on creativity can include such topics as:

- The importance of creativity to self and society.
- Social pressures that block or squelch creativity.
- The nature of creative ideas as modifications of existing ideas, new combinations of ideas, and products of analogical thinking.
- Biographies, personality characteristics, and cognitive abilities and styles of creative people.
- How creative people use deliberate techniques, especially analogical thinking, to extend their intuition and spontaneous imaginations.
- What is measured by creativity tests, such as the *Torrance Tests of Creative Thinking*, for example, the meaning of fluency, flexibility, originality, elaboration, resistance to premature closure, breaking boundaries, fantasy, emotional expressiveness, movement, synthesis of figures, and internal visualization.
- The nature of the creative process, as represented in the Wallas (1926) stages or the CPS model. The creative process also can be viewed as a "change in perception" or mental transformation. Visual puzzles, optical illusions, and even *Far Side* cartoons illustrate this sudden "seeing" of new ideas, new meanings, new combinations, and new modifications. Creativity techniques also illustrate conscious idea-finding processes.
- Definitions and theories of creativity.

Creativity lessons also should emphasize relevant principles and points, including:

- Creative thinking and problem solving is important for everyone—it can help you live a more interesting, enjoyable, and successful life.
- Creative ideas usually are modifications and combinations of other ideas.
- Creative people are not rigid. They look at things from different points of view and are aware of pressures to conform.
- Creative people take risks, play with possibilities—and make mistakes.
- They consider lots of ideas, use idea-finding techniques, and look for analogically related ideas.
- They use their talents, not waste them.

EXERCISING CREATIVE ABILITIES

Strengthening Creative Abilities through Exercise

This section will take a little longer.

In Chapter 4 we itemized abilities that logically underlie creativity, each with a brief definition. It is a common and reasonable strategy to try to strengthen creative abilities through practice and exercise, the same way we strengthen skills of reading, typing, solving chemistry problems, and shooting baskets. We will look at some of these abilities (see Table 11.1), noting strategies, exercises, or materials that aim at strengthening that ability.

Fluency, Flexibility, Originality, Elaboration

Divergent Thinking Exercises

Fluency, Flexibility, Originality, and Elaboration.   You should recognize these as the original four abilities measured by the *Torrance Tests of Creative Thinking* (Chapter 8). Many exercises and workbooks use open-ended, think-of-all-you-can divergent thinking problems to try to improve these abilities. Note that such exercises intrinsically raise creativity consciousness and teach creative atti-

---

Table 11.1
Some Creative Abilities That Can Be Exercised

General Creative Abilities

Fluency	Analogical Thinking
Flexibility	Analysis
Originality	Synthesis
Elaboration	Evaluation
Problem Defining	Predicting Outcomes
Visualization	Resisting Premature Closure
Imagination	Logical Thinking

Creative Abilities Particularly Relevant to Art and Writing

Extending Boundaries	Emotional Expressiveness
Movement and Action	Internal or Unusual Perspective
Fantasy	Humor
Colorfulness in Imagery	

Use to Teach Values

tudes—valuing creativity, thinking creatively, and being receptive to innovative ideas of others. Variations can be used to teach constructive values—honesty, manners, promptness, valuing education, neatness, energy conservation, and so on—while strengthening creative abilities (Davis, 1996a, 1996b).

**What Would
Happen If?**

The *"What would happen if . . . ?"* divergent thinking exercise is an old standby. It appears in workbooks for children (e.g., Stanish, 1977) and books for teaching creativity and futuristic thinking (e.g., Shallcross, 1981; Torrance, Williams, Torrance, & Horng, 1978). You can create problems that relate to classroom content, character education, or aspects of business. As some examples, "What would happen . . . ?":

If we did not have arithmetic?

If we had no books?

If people were suddenly unable to write a comprehendable sentence?

If all the pens and pencils in the world disappeared?

If the British had won the Revolutionary War?

If people with blond hair were not allowed in hotels or restaurants and could not vote?

If the only musical instruments were drums?

If people could not solve problems and create?

If Edison had become a plumber and did not invent lightbulbs?

If the Wright brothers stuck to bicycles?

If the computer chip were not invented?

If there were no corn crop in the Midwest this year?

If Miami Beach became the North Pole?

If everyone looked exactly alike?

If no one ever smiled?

If union wages were doubled?

If our main raw material (wood, steel, corn, nylon) became unavailable?

If a totally new product made our biggest seller obsolete?

If company management were decentralized, and 25 vice presidents and supervisors were asked to relocate?

If the company were taken over by IBM?

If parts could not be made in Taiwan?

If there were no McDonald's? No peanut butter? No candy? No cars? No electricity? No nuclear bombs?

If there were no gravity in this room?

If you had an eye in the back of your head?

If no one told the truth?

If everyone were dishonest?

If everyone were a litterbug?

If everyone were rude to everybody else?

If everyone wasted school supplies?

If the school building were vandalized three nights per week and twice on Saturday?

Unusual Uses

Another traditional divergent thinking problem is asking learners to think of *unusual uses* for any common object, for example, discarded tires, ping pong balls, a tea cup, a tennis racquet, a chair, a piece of chalk, a clothes pin, a wink, a new material, a new product, or a new process. Again, it's easy to make up additional problems.

Product Improvements

Product improvement problems ask students to think of ways to change or improve a familiar object, such as a bath tub, Cracker Jacks, Jell-O, a drinking fountain, a bicycle, or a TV set. With character education problems one asks how to improve student helpfulness, honesty, courtesy, promptness, or pro-school attitudes. Product improvement exercises can deal with business matters, such as thinking of ways to improve efficiency, sales, hiring practices, morale, or product quality.

Design Problems

Design problems are similar to product improvement problems. For example, designing a bathtub is about the same as thinking of improvements for a bathtub. Other design problems can ask students to design a dog walking machine, a new trash collection procedure, a safer traffic intersection, a cat petter, an airplane for animals, a burglary-prevention system, a theft proof computer, or children who are never late.

There are virtually unlimited numbers of open-ended questions and problems that would exercise the learner's fluency, flexibility, originality, and elaboration abilities. Some exercises try to focus on just one or another of these four abilities.

Fluency Exercises

For example, *fluency* is exercised by asking students to list things that are round, square, sweet, sour, blue, white, made of metal, made of wood, long and slender, short and stubby, smell good, taste bad, or have sharp edges. Some *flexibility* exercises try to have students look at things from different perspectives, for example:

How does this room look to a tidy housekeeper? A hungry mouse? An alien from outer space?

Flexibility Exercises

How does an old wooden chair look to a tired person? A termite? An antique collector?

How does a train station look to a train? To a duck flying overhead? To a passenger arriving too late for the train?

How does a highway look to a tire? To a crow? To a lost pilot?

How does our health food line look to a nine-year old? A teenager? A college student? A health nut? A jogger? A middle-aged person (who has the cash)? The elderly?

Elaboration Exercises

Elaboration exercises require the learner to build upon a basic idea, for example, developing the dog walking or cat petting machine or the new bathtub in specific detail—measurements, materials, costs. Or writing a story built upon a specified theme, for example, a fish who cannot swim, a child with no hair, or a town with no rules or laws. Or developing the marketing or morale-improvement plan to the last detail.

Some Problems Ask for Solutions

Fluency, flexibility, originality and elaboration abilities also can be exercised with relatively complex brainstorming-type problems. Some problems ask for *solutions*, for example:

How can we make school more interesting?

How can the lunch menu be improved?

How can bicycle theft be eliminated?

How can the school (or home or business) electric bill be reduced?

How can we prevent the best teachers from quitting?

What can we do for a parent on his or her birthday for under ten dollars?

How can our company benefit from the increasing numbers of retired persons and help them at the same time?

Others Ask for Explanations

Other problems ask for *explanations*, for example:

The grass behind a Wyoming billboard is extra lush and green. Why?

The principal unexpectedly cancels gym classes for two weeks. What are some explanations?

Ten paintings were discovered missing from the art gallery on Monday morning, but there was no sign of a break-in. How could they have disappeared?

Sales suddenly dropped 30 percent. What are some explanations?

Ambiguities, Paradoxes Stimulate Creativity

Note that these latter exercises involve presenting students with incompleteness, ambiguities, and paradoxes, all of which raise tension and motivate students to look for new combinations and relationships and to "synthesize relatively unrelated elements into coherent wholes" (Torrance, 1987b).

We have mentioned that it is possible to teach constructive attitudes and values while strengthening fluency, flexibility, originality, and elaboration. Some attitude-related exercises appeared in the "What would happen if. . . ?" and product improvement sections above. Students also can work on such *brainstorming* problems as:

Teaching Values with Brainstorming

Why is it good to be honest?

Think of ways to show respect to the elderly.

Think of ways to show friendliness in the classroom.

How many different safety rules can you think of?

And Reverse Brainstorming

Or with *reverse brainstorming*:

Think of ways to be unpleasant to new students.

How can we create more work for the school custodian? For production workers? Managers? Secretaries?

How might we waste lots and lots of electricity in our school building or company?

How can we avoid thinking creatively?

Exercises for strengthening fluency, flexibility, originality, and elaboration were created by Stanish (1979) and others before the development of Torrance's 18 "streamlined" creativity scores and Urban and Jellen's 13 test scores, both of which represent creative abilities. Both scoring systems also suggest drawing or writing activities that could strengthen underlying creative abilities while teaching elementary principles of creative thinking.

Abilities Suggested by Creativity Tests

In Torrance's *Picture Completion* test, *resistance to premature closure* is the too-early closing of an "open" part of a figure, which prevents one from using the figure in more unique ways. This test itself, or a similar activity, could serve as a creative drawing exercise in which students are expressly advised "Now don't close the figure with another line, because closing the figure can stop you from finding unusual ideas for the figure." The general principle is: Don't grab the first

This enthusiastic teacher is trying to convince his principal of the pressing need for more creativity training in the curriculum. "Okay, Okay! We'll add art! We'll brainstorm! We'll do 'What would happen if?' " agrees principal Florence Flathead. (The Museum of Modern Art/Film Stills Archive.)

idea that comes along; don't jump to conclusions; keep your mind open to more possibilities.

Emotional expressiveness, which Jellen and Urban called *affectivity*, also can be encouraged in the *Picture Completion* test or in creative writing assignments. Many students will not think of adding features of gaiety, gloom, or disappointment to a picture, short story, or poem.

Movement and action can be encouraged in drawing or writing as a route to greater originality and interest.

Synthesis of incomplete figures and *synthesis of lines and circles* also are legitimate rule-breakers that rarely occur to test takers. Students can be urged to: "Go ahead and combine two or three figures (circles, pairs of line) if you wish. Nobody said you had to make a single picture out of each little drawing. Your picture probably will show more imagination if you combine some of the figures. Think of lots of possibilities." Students should try to look at any challenge from a broad perspective, one with more possibilities than originally assumed. Can they think about bending or breaking drawing or writing rules? Samples of Salvadore Dali's art work will convey the idea.

Internal visualization, unusual visualization, and *unusual perspective* are the tendencies to visualize something from the inside, top, bottom, or other unusual perspective, or to imagine a two-dimensional picture as three-dimensional. Such visualization and perspective-taking can be encouraged, just as with other suggestions. "You could draw (or write about) something as if you were inside, as if you were looking at it from underneath or on top, or from some other viewpoint. How would it look to a high-flying duck or to a curious mouse? Can you find some different ideas for strange ways to see something?"

How Does It Look Inside?

Extending or breaking boundaries can be encouraged. "The pair of lines don't have to belong together—you can split them into different parts of the picture." "Sure, you can draw beyond the frame. Nobody said you had to draw only on the inside of the frame." "You don't have to write about normal people. Give them strange powers. Invent some new kinds of people. Turn something upside down or backwards. Maybe Gwendolyn guinea pig can talk or go for a bike ride." Looking at things differently is a solid principle of creative thinking.

Humor also may be encouraged. To anticipate "But how do I draw something funny?" the teacher can suggest that students draw something absurd (like a combination animal) or exaggerate something, like the size of ears, teeth, a chin, a nose, or a smile. Add ideas from *Star Wars* or *Snow White*. Cartoonists do these things regularly.

Colorfulness of imagery refers to drawings that appeal to other senses. "Can you make your drawing (or writing assignment) appeal to our sense of taste? Touch? Smell? Feel? What would be some ideas?"

Fantasy is just that. "If you can't think of an idea, how about including characters from a fairy tale, fable, *101 Dalmatians* or *E.T.*? Or what about other imaginary features—can you put arms and legs on something? Make things in your picture talk or sing? It's your drawing, your sailboat can sing a song or dance on the lake if you want it to." Although students may follow the teacher's suggestions too closely (and draw a dancing sailboat), they at least are learning to look for possibilities beyond the givens and the assumptions.

Strengthening Other Creative Abilities

Sensitivity to Problems, Problem Finding. Exercises aimed at strengthening problem sensitivity should have the learners find problems, detect difficulties, or detect missing information. One type of exercise aimed at increasing problem sensitivity has students *ask questions* about an ambiguous situation or even a common object. What questions could you ask about clouds? Computers? The sun? The ocean? Weather? The competitor's products? Increasing creative thinking? A variation would begin with "What don't we know about . . . ?" Question asking also may be placed in a fictitious TV interview context (Myers & Torrance, 1964): What three questions might you ask a Latin American dictator who has been driven from office? The mother of eight children just named "Mother of the Year"? A bus driver who refused to stop working after winning a five million dollar lottery?

Problem Defining	*Problem Defining.* Problem defining exercises would evolve around:
Identifying the Real Problem	1. Identifying the *real* problem and simplifying and clarifying the problem, for example: "What is the real problem here?" "What are we trying to do?" "What is it that really needs attention?"
Important Aspects	2. Isolating important aspects of a problem, for example: "What are the important parts of this problem?" "What should we focus on?"
Identify Subproblems	3. Identifying subproblems, for example: "What problems are related to this main problem?" "What problems will follow from each solution?"
Alternative Definitions	4. Proposing alternative problem definitions, for example: "How else can we define the problem?" Remember the "In What Ways Might We . . . ?" strategy in Chapter 5?
Broaden Problem	5. Defining a problem more broadly to open new possibilities, perhaps by asking "Why?" after each problem definition.

Visualization, Imagination

Visualization and Imagination.   Many exercises stimulate visualization and imagination. Two books, *Put Your Mother on the Ceiling* (DeMille, 1973) and *Scamper* (Eberle, 1995), are built upon the principle that imagination can be strengthened with exercise. Both ask the listeners to relax, shut their eyes, and visualize the substance of some colorful narrations, for example: "Now put a light bulb in each hand, hold your hands straight out to the side, pretend that your light bulbs are jet engines and run down the street for a take off!" (Eberle, 1995).

Flying High!

Wild Stories from Headlines Elicit Visualization

Another exercise guaranteed to elicit visualization (and elaboration) is a creative writing task suggested by Helman and Larson (1980): "Cut out headlines from a newspaper dealing with unusual stories and have the kids make up stories." Some recent grocery store rags included the following visualization-producing winners: "Damaged Alien Space Craft is Orbiting Earth: NASA Secretly Helping To Recover E.T. Bodies"; "5,000 Bodies Vanish From Old Cemetery"; "Baby Born Talking Gives Dad Winning Lottery Numbers"; "Bigfoot Saves Hunter Stuck in Quicksand"; "Titanic Survivor Has Been Afloat 76 Years"; "We'll Keep Our Two-Headed Baby, Say Proud Parents"; "Lightening Bolt Zaps Coffin—And Corpse Comes Back To Life!"; "Farmer Dies in Suicide Pact With 46 Cows!"; "Female Vampires Terrorize Town!"; "Teacher Picks Up Hitchhiking Ghost"; and "Amazing Duck Man Lays Real Egg (No Yolk!)." Some people do not believe these stories.

Analogical Thinking

Analogical Thinking.   Exercises for practicing analogical thinking appear in Chapter 6. Stanish's (1977) *Sunflowering* and Gordon's (1974a) *Making it Strange* are loaded with exercises in analogical thinking.

Analysis, Synthesis, Evaluation Exercises

Analysis, Synthesis, Evaluation.   These, of course, are higher-level thinking skills in Bloom's taxonomy of educational objectives. Exercises include asking students to *analyze* components, relationships, hypotheses, patterns, and causes and effects; *synthesize* parts into plans, theories, generalizations, designs, and compositions; and *evaluate* the accuracy, value, efficiency, or utility of alternative ideas or courses of action.

What's Good? What's Bad?

Other evaluation exercises ask students, including adult students, to list what is *good* about an idea (or plan or experience), and what is *bad* about the idea (or plan or experience). Students can learn to use an evaluation matrix, as described in Chapter 5 (see Figure 5.2). Parnes (1981) recommends looking at a creative problem solution from other people's perspectives or else imagining them reacting to the idea as you explain it.

Transformation

Use Visual Puzzles

Transformation. Transformation abilities are related to visualization, imagination, and creativity in general. Students can practice making mental transformations with complex visual puzzles of the type shown in Chapter 5. What else can they see in the picture? People differ vastly in their ability to "see" other meanings and perceptions (e.g., the cow in Chapter 5), suggesting that many need practice with this particular ability. Sounds, such as crumpling paper, also elicit meanings and transformations.

Predicting Outcomes: What Would Happen If?

Predicting Outcomes. Predicting outcomes is related to evaluation abilities in the sense that evaluating problem solutions amounts to predicting their utility. Also, exercises of the "What would happen if . . . ?" variety give students practice at predicting outcomes. It's a form of futuristic thinking.

Logical Thinking

Logical Thinking. Logical thinking is underrated as a central creative ability. Logical thinking is involved in clarifying the problem, figuring out solution requirements, relating proposed ideas to solution requirements, and implementing the solution. There seem to be few exercises designed to strengthen logical thinking abilities, other than syllogistic reasoning ("all A is B, all B is C, therefore all A is C") and related problems such as "If Tom is taller than Janice, and Janice dresses better than Dennis Rodman, who is the best golfer?"

An early workbook by Myers and Torrance (1966) included exercises in logic that could serve as models for similar teacher-constructed activities. For example, explain why each of the following is *true* or *false*:

Logic Exercises

If something is beautiful, it has to be valuable.

Joe has one sister, but three brothers-in-law.

An object has color or else it has no color.

Joe, a strict vegetarian, prefers fish to beef.

The twins rode into town by themselves, with Chuck in the middle.

The headlights of the oncoming car blinded its driver, causing him to run off the road.

Diamonds are more expensive than pearls, therefore pearls are more expensive than rubies.

A few thinking skills workbooks try to strengthen logical thinking with syllogistic reasoning problems and other types of deductive and inductive reasoning exercises (see, e.g., Black & Black, 1984).

The list of creative abilities in this section appears central to creative thinking, and we have described some exercises that may help strengthen them. Of course, it is not an exhaustive list. As noted in Chapter 4, it would be extremely difficult to identify a cognitive ability or style that is *not* in some way involved in the complex requirements of creative thinking. Also other lists of creative abilities overlap with our present list. In Chapter 10, for example, we reviewed Taylor's (1986, 1988) multiple-talent totem pole (creative) thinking talents of *productive thinking, communicating, forecasting, decision making,* and *planning*; and his getting-ideas-into-action talents of *implementing, human relations,* and *discerning opportunities*. These can be taught (see Schlichter, 1997). Tardif and Sternberg (1988) described as important creative abilities *decision making, independence of judgment, coping with novelty, ability to escape perceptual sets, ability to find order in chaos, aesthetic ability* (taste and judgment), and *versatility*. Many of these resemble the present creative abilities or the personality characteristics described in Chapter 4.

Taylor's Talents

More Abilities

CREATIVE THINKING TECHNIQUES

See Chapters 6 and 7

We have devoted enough space to *techniques* of creative thinking in Chapters 6 and 7. Teaching students to use such techniques not only provides them with strategies for generating ideas, but helps them to understand the nature of creative ideas and the creative processes used by others. Children's versions of the techniques are found in Davis and DiPego (1973), Stanish (1977, 1981, 1988), Gordon (1974a), and Gordon and Poze (1972a, 1972b).

As a caution, it is not easy for adults or children to quickly adopt an unfamiliar thinking or problem-solving method. Nonetheless, creative people do use such techniques, consciously or unconsciously, and the techniques work. Personally, your author found ideas for the more-or-less amusing dialogues of this book by creating checklists of well-known children's stories (Alice in Wonderland, Cinderella), movies (Rambo), famous people and comedians (e.g., Sigmund Freud, Woody Allen, Barbara Walters, Don Rickles, Rodney Dangerfield, Norm Crosby), and myths and legends (Frankenstein, the devil, an oracle), and using these as analogical sources. The morphological synthesis (matrix) technique helped generate hundreds of exercises that use creativity procedures (brainstorming, analogical thinking, "What would happen if . . . ?", visualization) to help students understand values and character (Davis, 1996a, 1996b).

INVOLVEMENT IN CREATIVE ACTIVITIES

Leonardo DaVinci did not become a great painter by practicing shuffleboard, nor did Hemingway spend much time on juggling skills. The strongest and most logically sound recommendation for strengthening creativity is to involve yourself or your students in activities that intrinsically require creative thinking and problem solving. It is virtually assured that creative attitudes, abilities, and skills will be strengthened in the course of actual creative involvement.

For example, Renzulli's Type III Enrichment and his Schoolwide Enrichment Model focus on individual or small group projects and investigations of real problems. The variety of potential projects is unlimited. Reis and Burns (1987) itemized several hundred possibilities (partly reproduced in Davis and Rimm, 1998) in the categories of visual arts and performing arts; math, science, and computers; literature, writing, and communication; social sciences, culture, and language; business and economics; and miscellaneous (e.g., bridge, chess, horses, karate, magic, and sailing). The *Future Problem Solving* and *Odyssey of the Mind* programs also involve students in real creative activity.

Gallagher (1998; Gallagher & Stepien, 1996) described *problem-based learning* (PBL), which was born in medical school programs and currently is extended to K-12 classrooms. In medical schools, students traditionally were taught content first, then given problems that required the application of appropriate treatment strategies. Precious little problem solving and reasoning took place. PBL turns the sequence around. With PBL, learning does not begin until students are given a problem to solve; learning is thus integrated with creative problem solving.

Briefly, students are given an ill-structured problem which requires them to gather new information. Consistent with Torrance's definition of creative problem solving in Chapter 3, students proceed through a back-and-forth process of "problem definition, hypothesis testing, evaluation, problem redefinition, new hypothesis testing, and so on" (Gallagher, 1998). With PBL, students become motivated, independent learners. Better yet, according to Gallagher, they learn for understanding and the knowledge typically is retained *better* than with tradi-

Direct involvement in aesthetic and scientific activities promotes creative interests and skills. These two students are absorbed in violin lessons and hygiene research. (The Museum of Modern Art/ Film Stills Archive.)

tional instruction. PBL also fosters the development of reasoning and other thinking skills, interest in the subject matter, collaborating with peers, integrating information (e.g., from different disciplines), and more flexible and adaptive thinking.

PBL seems an effective strategy for involving students in creative thinking and problem solving on a daily basis.

As another classroom involvement activity, the Lynch and Harris (1999) *refutation* method is a creativity-stimulating strategy that apparently can be used in any subject area and with students of any age. The procedure is disarmingly simple. A teacher presents incorrect information, perhaps on the chalkboard — for example, incorrect math problems (4 x 7 = 14; "The sum of the lengths of the sides of a right triangle equals the length of the hypotenuse"), incorrect historical facts ("Pilgrims landed at Plymouth Rock in 1975"; "Our first president was named Elton John"), or incorrect language arts sentences ("We wuz going the movie show to.")—and students predictably become motivated, even animated, in detecting the problems and "refuting" their accuracy.

The refutation approach stimulates creativity in the sense of exercising important underlying creative abilities, such as attending to detail, detecting problems, elaborating their original ideas, and creating and testing original hypotheses.

Comment   In addition to reviewing a few issues pertaining to "teaching creativity," along with contributions from earlier chapters plus a few infant and early childhood suggestions, the main focus of this chapter was on five core objectives of creativity training and their related strategies. As for which approach or combination of approaches produces the greatest gains the most quickly and efficiently, the variety of ages, abilities, interests, and needs of particular students—along with a virtual absence of relevant research—make it impossible to specify an all-around ideal recipe. Your author recommends using *all* of the goals/activities in approximately the order they were presented. Students need to be aware of creativity and acquire attitudes that predispose them to thinking creatively; they need to metacognitively understand creative people and creative thinking; their creative abilities and skills should be exercised; they should learn brainstorming and other idea-finding techniques; and they certainly should be involved in activities that require creative thinking and problem solving.

Very little in your own personal development or in the education of your children or students is as critical as strengthening creative potential. Creative self-actualization is much too important to be left to chance.

SUMMARY

While heredity plays a large role, creativity can be taught and learned. There is "massive evidence" for the teachability of creativity, said Torrance.

There are individual differences in responsiveness to creativity training.

Differences in motivation to create—arousal-seeking tendencies—are thought to be governed by the brain's reticular activating system.

The psychological safety (Rogers) of a receptive and reinforcing creative atmosphere is essential.

Teaching a general, self-actualized creativity can include strengthening creative attitudes, abilities, techniques, teaching the CPS model, and involving students in FPS and OM. Such training is mostly content-free. Teaching special talent creativity, however, which requires a depth of knowledge and content-specific skills, must take place within a content area. Independent projects is a good strategy.

Earlier chapters made the following contributions to the teaching of creativity.

Chapter 1 stressed the importance of creativity to the (self-actualized) individual and society.

Chapter 2 reviewed blocks and barriers to creativity, including von Oech's 10 mental blocks and a bunch of idea squelchers.

Chapter 3 looked at definitions and theories, which can increase one's understanding of creativity.

Chapter 4 reviewed characteristics of creative people, including eminent ones, many of which can be reinforced or otherwise cultivated.

Chapter 5 illustrated perceptual change as a process, discussed the effective CPS model, and noted how some eminent persons have used imagery in their creative thinking.

Chapter 6 covered the most common and useful creative thinking process/technique of all, analogical thinking.

Chapter 7, a central one in creativity training, described other creative thinking techniques.

Chapter 8 reviewed creativity tests, which contributes to one's understanding of creativity. Test content can be used as creativity exercises.

Chapter 9 summarized G/T program models and enrichment and acceleration strategies that feature creative development as a main goal (FPS, OM, Type II and Type III Enrichment, Feldhusen/Kolloff three-stage model).

Chapter 10, creative dramatics, contributes to more flexible thinking.

This chapter presented issues, suggestions for improving cognitive development and problem solving abilities in infants and young children, and emphasized five main points (goals, strategies) related to increasing creative potential.

Suggestions for babies focused on providing a stimulating environment. Babies and toddlers must learn turn-taking and sharing. Toddlers can learn the ABC's of character development: asking, patience, courtesy, respecting others' rights, helpfulness, and the like.

Responsibility is aided with age-appropriate home chores. Parenting recommendations included providing structure, overtly valuing schoolwork, eliciting thoughtful discussion, taking field trips, being a good role model, and raising awareness of educational and career goal-setting.

Parents can improve cognitive development and problem solving by encouraging exploration and simple problem solving, for example, in building things, pretending, simple planning, creating musical instruments, and using toys and blocks in new ways.

Five main points (goals, strategies) related to increasing creative potential are as follows:

First, we should increase students' creativity consciousness and creative attitudes, especially an appreciation for creative ideas and a predisposition to think creatively.

Second, we should help students metacognitiviely understand the topic of creativity, such as the importance of creativity, blocks and barriers, nature of creative ideas, creative characteristics, techniques, rationale of tests, ways to view the creative process, CPS model, definitions and theories, plus additional principles of creative thinking and problem solving.

Third, we should help strengthen creative abilities. Many divergent thinking types of exercises and brainstorming problems have been suggested for strengthening fluency, flexibility, originality, and elaboration. The newer Torrance and Urban and Jellen scoring systems suggest exercises for resisting premature closure and, at least in drawing and writing, combining figures, breaking boundaries, and adding emotional expressiveness, movement and action, unusual perspectives, and humor.

As examples of other creative abilities that may be rehearsed:

Problem sensitivity and problem finding may be exercised by having students ask questions about a phenomena.

Problem defining exercises can focus on identifying the "real" problem, isolating important aspects of a problem, identifying subproblems, or thinking of alternative problem definitions.

Guided visualization can be used to exercise visualization and imagination abilities. Also, writing stories for bizarre newspaper headlines stretches visualization and elaboration abilities.

Many analogical thinking exercises appear in Chapter 6.

Regarding Bloom's higher-level abilities, students can analyze components, patterns, causes and effects; synthesize parts into plans and designs; and evaluate accuracy, value, or utility. Students also can practice evaluation skills by thinking of what is "good" and "bad" about an object or experience, using an evaluation matrix, or looking at an idea from other people's perspectives.

Student can practice mental transformations with complex visual puzzles of the type shown in Chapter 5.

Logical thinking is important to creative potential. Some thinking skills workbooks exercise inductive and deductive logic.

Other creative thinking abilities that may be strengthened are Taylor's totem pole thinking talents and idea-implementing talents.

The fourth main goal of creativity training is teaching creative thinking techniques.

Fifth, we should involve students in creative thinking and problem solving activities.

It is recommended that creativity training proceed in the sequence in which the five points were presented.

Because creative development is tied to self-actualization, it is extremely important.

Teaching for Creative Growth

Self-Test: Key Concepts and Terms

Briefly define or explain each of these:

Responsiveness/receptiveness to creativity training _____

_____

Motivation to create _____

_____

Creative atmosphere _____

_____

Content-free creativity training _____

_____

Creativity consciousness _____

_____

Creative attitudes _____

_____

Metacognition _____

_____

Let's Think about It

1. Some people have argued that "creativity" must be taught within a subject area. The author disagrees.

   How does the author use the relationship between self-actualized and special talent creativity to help resolve the issue?

   _____

   _____

   _____

   _____

2. Which chapter in this book has helped you the most in understanding "creativity"? Explain.

   _____

   _____

   _____

   _____

3. A key part of creativity training is *involving* students in projects and activities that require creative thinking.

   a. What are some projects and activities that might strengthen a general, *self-actualized* type of creativeness (with either elementary or secondary students)?

      _____

      _____

      _____

      _____

   b. What are some projects and activities that might strength *special talent creativity* (with either elementary or secondary students)?

      _____

      _____

      _____

      _____

4. Either in schools or a business setting, how can we:

a. Raise creativity consciousness?

_____

_____

_____

b. Help people overcome blocks and barriers?

_____

_____

_____

c. Develop creative personality traits?

_____

_____

_____

d. Develop a habit of "mentally transforming" objects, ideas, or processes into creative variations?

_____

_____

_____

e. Help people think more analogically; that is, help them draw ideas from other sources or see connections between "this problem" and a related situation?

_____

_____

_____

f. Motivate people to use creativity techniques when they are stuck for ideas?

_____

_____

_____

g. Improve understanding of creativity?

_____

_____

_____

h. Exercise and strengthen important creative abilities?

_____

_____

_____

i. Involve children or adults in creative activities?

_____

_____

_____

5. Make up a paragraph about this headline: **"Our Neighbors Are Aliens! They Become Turtle People After Dark!"**

_____

_____

_____

_____

_____

_____

6. How has this book increased YOUR creative potential and/or your creative outlook on life?

_____

_____

_____

_____

If your answer is "It hasn't!" explain why not. (Hints: "I am already quite creative, thank you." "I have a rigid personality and no imagination." "I'm just interested in football." "I prefer to be a conformer." "I didn't know I was supposed to learn to be more creative." "I could be more creative if I wanted, but it's too much like work." "I just needed a 'C' in this class." "I KNOW without a doubt that creativity absolutely cannot be taught or learned—particularly by me.")

_____

_____

_____

7. Think of some problems or challenges in your life, or some things you would like to do better.

a. _____

b. _____

c. _____

d. _____

Think of one or two creative solutions for each problem/challenge/goal.

a. _____

_____

b. _____

_____

c. _____

_____

d. _____

_____

solutions to chapter puzzles and questions

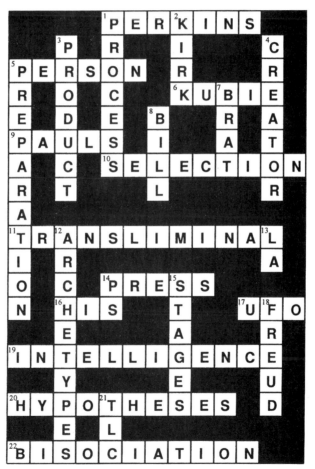

Crossword Puzzle 3.1

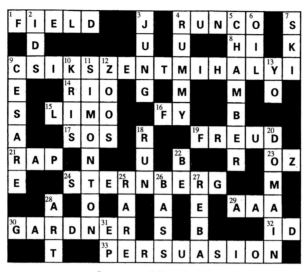

Crossword Puzzle 3.2

Answers to matching questions, Chapter 3

1. j
2. g
3. k
4. a and i
5. i
6. d
7. m
8. l
9. j
10. c
11. o
12. b and j
13. f
14. e
15. a and i
16. n

Answers to matching questions, Chapter 8.

1. i
2. f
3. i
4. f
5. j
6. g
7. c, k
8. b
9. l
10. a
11. e
12. i
13. h

Crossword Puzzle 9.1

Crossword Puzzle 9.2

references

Al-Sabaty, I., & Davis, G. A. (1989). Relationship between creativity and right, left, and integrating thinking styles. *Creativity Research Journal, 2*, 111–117.

Albert, R. S. (1990). Identity, experiences, and career choice among the exceptionally gifted and eminent. In M. A. Runco & R. S. Albert (Eds.), *Theories of creativity* (pp. 13–34). Newberry Park, CA: Sage.

Alexander, T. (1978). Inventing by the madness method. In G. A. Davis & J. A. Scott (Eds.), *Training creative thinking*. Melbourne, FL: Krieger.

Allen, M. S. (1962). *Morphological creativity*. Englewood Cliffs, NJ: Prentice-Hall.

Allen, M. S. (1966). *Psycho-dynamic synthesis*. West Nyack, NY: Parker.

Amabile, T. M. (1983). *Social psychology of creativity*. New York: Springer-Verlag.

Amabile, T. M. (1987). The motivation to create. In S. G. Isaksen (Ed.), *Frontiers of creativity research: Beyond the basics* (pp. 223–254). Buffalo, NY: Bearly Limited.

Amabile, T. M. (1988). A model of organizational innovation. In B. M. Staw & L. L. Cummings (Eds.), *Research in organizational behavior* (Vol. 10, pp. 123–168). Greenwich, CT: JAI.

Ambrose, D. (1995). Creatively intelligent post-industrial organizations and intellectually impaired bureaucracies. *Journal of Creative Behavior, 29*, 1–15.

Ambrose, D. (1996). Turtle soup: Establishing innovation-friendly conditions for school reform. *Journal of Creative Behavior, 30*, 25–38.

Andreason, N. C. (1978). Creativity and psychiatric illness. *Psychiatric Annals, 8*, 113–119.

Andreason, N. C. (1987). Creativity and mental illness: Prevalence rates in writers and their first-degree relatives. *American Journal of Psychiatry, 144*, 1288–1292.

Andreason, N. C., & Canter, A. (1974). The creative writer: Psychiatric symptoms and family history. *Comprehensive Psychiatry, 15*, 123–131.

Arietti, S. (1976). *Creativity: The magic synthesis*. New York: Basic Books.

Assouline, S. G., & Lupkowski-Shoplik, A. (1997). Talent searches: A model for the discovery and development of academic talent. In N. Colangelo & G. A. Davis (Eds.), *Handbook of gifted education* (2nd ed., pp. 170–179). Boston: Allyn & Bacon.

Barron, F. (1955). The disposition toward originality. *Journal of Abnormal and Social Psychology, 51*, 478–485.

Barron, F. (1961). Creative vision and expression in writing and painting. In D. W. MacKinnon (Ed.), *The creative person* (pp. 237–251). Berkeley, CA: Institute of Personality Assessment and Research, University of California.

Barron, F. (1965). The psychology of creativity. In F. Barron, W. C. Dement, W. Edwards, H. Lindman, L. D. Phillips, J. Olds, & M. Olds, *New directions in psychology II* (pp. 1–134). New York: Holt.

Barron, F. (1968). *Creativity and personal freedom*. Princeton, NJ: Van Nostrand.

324   *References*

Barron, F. (1969). *Creative person and creative process.* New York: Holt.

Barron, F. (1978). An eye more fantastical. In G. A. Davis & J. A. Scott (Eds.), *Training creative thinking* (pp. 181–193). Melbourne, FL: Krieger.

Barron, F. (1988). Putting creativity to work. In R. J. Sternberg (Ed.), *The nature of creativity* (pp. 76–98). New York: Cambridge University Press.

Bartlett, M. M., & Davis, G. A. (1974). Do the Wallach and Kogan tests predict real creative behavior? *Perceptual and Motor Skills, 39,* 730.

Bass, S. (1968). *Why man creates* (16 mm film). Oakland, CA: Kaiser Aluminum.

Begley, S. (1993, June 28). The puzzle of genius. *Newsweek,* pp. 46–51.

Bem, S. L. (1974). The measurement of psychological androgyny. *Journal of Consulting and Clinical Psychology, 42,* 155–162.

Benbow, C. P., & Lubinski, D. (1997). Intellectually talented children: How can we best meet their needs? In N. Colangelo & G. A. Davis (Eds.), *Handbook of gifted education* (2nd ed., pp. 155–169). Boston: MA: Allyn & Bacon.

Berlyne, D. E. (1961). *Conflict, arousal, and curiosity.* New York: McGraw-Hill.

Betts, G. (1985). *Autonomous learner model.* Greeley, COL: Autonomous Learning Publications and Specialists.

Betts, G. (1991). Autonomous learner model. In N. Colangelo & G. A. Davis (Eds.), *Handbook of gifted education* (pp. 142–153). Boston, MA: Allyn & Bacon.

Biondi, A. M. (1980). About the small cage habit. *Journal of Creative Behavior, 2,* 75–76.

Black, H., & Black, S. (1984). *Building thinking skills.* Pacific Grove, CA: Critical Thinking Press and Software.

Black, H., & Black, S. (1988). *Building thinking skills.* Pacific Grove, CA: Critical Thinking Press and Software.

Bloom, B. S. (1985). *Developing talent in young people.* New York: Ballantine Books.

Bloom, B. S., & Sosniak, L. A. (1981). Talent development vs. schooling. *Educational Leadership, 39,* 86–94.

Borland, J. (1997). Evaluating gifted programs. In N. Colangelo & G. A. Davis (Eds.), *Handbook of gifted education* (2nd ed., pp. 253–266). Boston: Allyn & Bacon.

Briskman, L. (1980). Creative product and creative process in science and art. *Inquiry, 23,* 83–106.

Bronowski, J. (1961). *Science and human values.* London: Hutchinson.

Buckmaster, L. R., & Davis, G. A. (1985). ROSE: A measure of self-actualization and its relationship to creativity. *Journal of Creative Behavior, 19,* 30–37.

Bull, K. S., & Davis, G. A. (1982). Inventory for appraising adult creativity. *Contemporary Educational Psychology, 7*(1), 1–8.

Bull, K. S., & Davis, G. A. (1980). Evaluating creative potential using the statement of past creative activities. *Journal of Creative Behavior, 14,* 249–257.

Callahan, C. M. (1991). The assessment of creativity. In N. Colangelo & G. A. Davis (Eds.), *Handbook of gifted education* (pp. 219–235). Boston: MA: Allyn & Bacon.

Campbell, D. T. (1946). Blind variation and selective retention in creative thought as in other knowledge processes. *Psychological Review, 67,* 380–400.

Cattell, R. B. (1955). *Handbook for the objective-analysis test battery.* Champaign, IL: Institute for Personality and Ability testing.

Chase, W. I. (1985). Review of the *Torrance Tests of Creative Thinking.* In J. Mitchell (Ed.), *Ninth mental measurements yearbook* (Vol. 2, pp. 1630–1634). Lincoln, NE: Buros Institute of Mental Measurement.

Clark, C. H. (1958). *Brainstorming.* Garden City, NY: Doubleday.

Clasen, D. R. (Ed.) (1985). *Teaching for thinking: Creativity in the classroom.* Madison, WI: University of Wisconsin-Extension.

Clasen, D. R., & Clasen, R. E. (1997). Mentoring: A time-honored option for education of the gifted and talented. In N. Colangelo & G. A. Davis (Eds.), *Handbook of gifted education* (2nd ed., pp. 218 229). Boston: MA: Allyn & Bacon.

Compton, A. H. (1952). Case histories: Creativity in science. In F. Olsen (Ed.), *The nature of creative thinking* (pp. 23–31). New York: Industrial Research Institute.

Conti, R., Coon, H., & Amabile, T. M. (1996). Evidence to support the componential model of creativity: Secondary analyses of three studies. *Creativity Research Journal, 9,* 385–389.

Cooper, I. (Trans.); Hamilton, E., & Cairns, H. (Eds.). (1961). *The collected dialogues of Plato.* Princeton, NJ: Princeton University Press.

Covington, M. V., Crutchfield, R. S., Olton, R. M., & Davies, L. (1972). *Productive thinking program.* Columbus, OH: Charles E. Merrill.

Cox, C. M. (1926). *Genetic studies of genius. Volume II: The early mental traits of three hundred geniuses.* Stanford, CA: Stanford University Press.

Cox, J., Daniel, N., & Boston, B. A. (1985). *Educating able learners: Programs and promising practices.* Austin, TX: University of Texas Press.

Crabbe, A. (1985). Future problem solving. In A. L. Costa (Ed.), *Developing minds: A resource book for teaching thinking.* Alexandria, VA: Association for Supervision and Curriculum Development.

Cramond, B. (1994). Attention-deficit hyperactivity disorder and creativity—what is the connection? *Journal of Creative Behavior, 28,* 193–210.

Crandall, R., McCown, D. A., & Robb, Z. (1988). The effects of assertiveness training on self-actualization. *Small Group Behavior, 19,* 134–145.

Crawford, R. P. (1978). The techniques of creative thinking. In G. A. Davis & J. A. Scott (Eds.), *Training creative thinking* (pp. 52–57). Melbourne, FL: Krieger.

Cropley, A. J. (1971). Some Canadian creativity research. *Journal of Research and Development in Education, 4*(3), 113–115.

Cropley, A. J. (1972). A five-year longitudinal study of the validity of creativity tests. *Developmental Psychology, 6,* 119–124.

Csikszentmihalyi, M. (1988). Society, culture, and person: A systems view of creativity. In R. J. Sternberg (Ed.), *The nature of creativity* (pp. 325–339). New York: Cambridge University Press.

Csikszentmihalyi, M. (1990a). The domain of creativity. In M. A. Runco & R. S. Albert (Eds.), *Theories of creativity* (pp. 190–212). Newbury Park, CA: Sage.

Csikszentmihalyi, M. (1990b). *Flow: The psychology of optimal experience.* New York: Harper & Row.

Dacey, J. S. (1989). *Fundamentals of creative thinking.* Lexington, MA: Lexington Books.

Damm, V. J. (1970). Creativity and intelligence: Research implications for equal emphasis in high school. *Exceptional Children, 36,* 565–570.

Daniels-McGhee, S., & Davis, G. A. (1994). The imagery-creativity connection. *Journal of Creative Behavior, 28,* 151–176.

Davis, G. A. (1971). Instruments useful in studying creative behavior and creative talent, Part II: Noncommercially available instruments. *Journal of Creative Behavior, 5,* 162–165.

Davis, G. A. (1973). *Psychology of problem solving.* New York: Basic Books.

Davis, G. A. (1975). In frumious pursuit of the creative person. *Journal of Creative Behavior, 9,* 75–87.

Davis, G. A. (1989a). Objectives and activities for teaching creative thinking. *Gifted Child Quarterly, 33,* 81–84.

Davis, G. A. (1989b). Testing for creative potential. *Contemporary Educational Psychology, 14,* 257–274.

Davis, G. A. (1991a). *How do you think: Administration and technical manual.* Cross Plains, WI: Westwood.

Davis, G. A. (1991b). Teaching creative thinking. In N. Colangelo & G. A. Davis (Eds.), *Handbook of gifted education* (pp. 236–244). Boston: Allyn & Bacon.

Davis, G. A. (1992). On Walberg's human capital model of learning, creativity, and eminence. *Creativity Research Journal, 5,* 341–343.

Davis, G. A. (1994, April). Discussant. In H. J. Walberg (Chair), *Notable American women: Childhood contexts and psychological traits.* Symposium conducted at the meeting of the American Educational Research Association, New Orleans.

Davis, G. A. (1995). Portrait of the creative person. *Educational Forum, 12,* 205–212.

Davis, G. A. (1996a). *Teaching values: An idea book for teachers (and parents).* Cross Plains, WI: Westwood.

Davis, G. A. (1996b). *Values are forever: Becoming more caring and responsible.* Cross Plains, WI: Westwood.

Davis, G. A. (1998). Barriers to creativity and creative attitudes. In Runco, M. A. (Ed.), *Encyclopedia of creativity.* San Diego, CA: Academic Press.

Davis, G. A., & Belcher, T. L. (1971). How shall creativity be measured? Torrance Tests, RAT, Alpha Biographical, and IQ. *Journal of Creative Behavior, 3,* 153–161.

Davis, G. A., & Bull, K. S. (1978). Strengthening affective components of creativity in a college course. *Journal of Educational Psychology, 70,* 833–836.

Davis, G. A., & DiPego, G. (1973). *Imagination Express: Saturday subway ride.* Buffalo, NY: DOK.

Davis, G. A., Helfert, C. J., & Shapiro, G. R. (1973). Let's be an ice cream machine!: Creative dramatics. *Journal of Creative Behavior, 7,* 37–48.

Davis, G. A., Kogan, N., & Soliman, A. (Submitted). *The Qatar creativity conference: Research and recommendations.*

Davis, G. A., Peterson, J. M., & Farley, F. H. (1973). Attitudes, motivation, sensation seeking, and belief in ESP as predictors of real creative behavior. *Journal of Creative Behavior, 7,* 31–39.

Davis, G. A., & Rimm, S. (1980). *Group inventory for finding interests. II.* Watertown, WI: Educational Assessment Service.

Davis, G. A., & Rimm, S. (1982). Group inventory for finding interests (GIFFI) I and II: Instruments for identifying creative potential in the junior and senior high school. *Journal of Creative Behavior, 16,* 50–57.

Davis, G. A., & Rimm, S. (1998). *Education of the gifted and talented* (4th. ed.). Boston: Allyn & Bacon.

Davis, G. A., & Subkoviak, M. J. (1978). Multidimensional analysis of a personality-based test of creative potential. *Journal of Educational Measurement, 12,* 37–43.

Davis, G. A., & Williams, B. L. (1992, April). *A field dependence/independence inventory and its relationship to left-right and creative thinking.* Paper presented at the meeting of the American Educational Research Association, San Francisco.

DeMille, R. (1955). *Put your mother on the ceiling.* New York: Viking/Compass.

Dewey, J. (1933). *How we think.* Lexington, MA: Heath.

Domino, G. (1970). Identification of potentially creative persons from the *Adjective Check List. Journal of Consulting and Clinical Psychology, 35,* 48–51.

Drucker, P. (1989). *The new realities.* New York: Harper & Row.

Eberle, B. (1995). *Scamper.* Waco, TX: Prufrock.

Eberle, B., & Stanish, B. (1985). *CPS for kids.* Carthage, IL: Good Apple.

Edwards, M. O. (1968). A survey of problem solving courses. *Journal of Creative Behavior, 2,* 33–51.

Eichenberger, R. J. (1978). Creativity measurement through use of judgment criteria in physics. *Educational and Psychological Measurement, 38,* 221–227.

Einstein, A. (1952). Letter to Jacque Hadamard. In B. Ghiselin (Ed.), *The creative process* (pp. 43–44). Berkeley: University of California Press.

Einstein, A. (1961). *Relativity: The special and the general theory.* New York: Crown.

Eisenman, R. (1964). Birth order and artistic creativity. *Journal of Individual Psychology, 20,* 183–185.

Fabun, D. (1968). *You and creativity.* New York: Macmillan.

Farley, F. H. (1986, May). The big T in personality. *Psychology Today,* 47–52.

Fekken, G. C. (1985). Review of *Creativity Assessment Packet.* In D. Keyser & R. Sweetland (Eds.), *Test critiques* (Vol. V, pp. 211–215). Kansas City, MO: Testing Corporation of America.

Feldhusen, J. F. (1995). Creativity: A knowledge base, metacognitive skills, and personality factors. *Journal of Creative Behavior, 29,* 255–268.

Feldhusen, J. F., Denny, T., & Condon, C. F. (1965) *Manual for the creativity self-report scale.* Unpublished manuscript, Purdue University, West Lafayette, IN.

Feldhusen, J. F., & Kolloff, P. B. (1981). In R. E. Clasen, B. Robinson, D. R. Clasen, & G. Libster (Eds.), *Programming for the gifted, talented and creative: Models and methods.* Madison, WI: University of Wisconsin-Extension.

Feldhusen, J. F., & Kolloff, P. B. (1986). The Purdue three-stage enrichment model for gifted education at the elementary level. In J. S. Renzulli (Ed.), *Systems and models for developing programs for the gifted and talented* (pp. 126–152). Mansfield Center, CT: Creative Learning Press.

Flach, F. (1990). Disorders of the pathways involved in the creative process. *Creativity Research Journal, 3,* 158–165.

Fleming, E. S., & Weintraub, S. (1962). Attitudinal rigidity as a measure of creativity in gifted children. *Journal of Educational Psychology, 53,* 81–85.

Flower, L., & Hayes, J. R. (1984). Images, plans, and prose. *Written Communication, 1*(1), 120–160.

Flowers, J. H., & Garbin, C. P. (1989). Creativity and perception. In J. A. Glover, R. R. Ronning, & C. R. Reynolds (Eds.), *Handbook of creativity.* New York: Plenum Press.

Freeman, J., Butcher, H. J., & Christie, T. (1968). *Creativity: A selective review of research.* London: Society for Research into Higher Education Ltd.

Freud, S. (1975). Creative writers and daydreaming. In A. Rothenberg & C. R. Hausman (Eds.), *The creativity question* (pp. 48–54). Durham, NC: Duke University Press.

Gallagher, S. A. (1998, May). *But does it work? Testing the efficacy of problem-based learning.* Paper presented at the 1998 Henry B. and Jocelyn Wallace National Research Symposium on Talent Development, University of Iowa.

Gallagher, S. A., & Stepien, W. J. (1996). Depth versus breadth in problem-based learning: Content acquisition in American studies. *Journal for the Education of the Gifted, 19,* 257–275.

Gardner, H. (1983). *Frames of mind: The theory of multiple intelligences.* New York: Basic Books.

Gardner, H. (1993). *Creating minds.* New York: Basic Books.

Gelade, G. (1995). Creative style and divergent production. *Journal of Creative Behavior, 29,* 36–53.

Gendrop, S. C. (1996). Effect of an intervention in synectics on the creative thinking of nurses. *Creativity Research Journal, 9,* 11–19.

Getzels, J. W., & Jackson, P. W. (1962). *Creativity and intelligence.* New York: Wiley.

Getzels, J. W., & Csikszentmihalyi, M. (1976). *The creative vision.* New York: Wiley.

Ghiselin, B. (Ed.) (1952). *The creative process.* New York: Mentor.

Goertzel, M. G., Goertzel, V., & Goertzel, T. G. (1978). *300 eminent personalities.* San Francisco: Jossey-Bass.

Goldman, C. (1991). Late bloomers: Growing older or still growing? *Generations, 15*(2), 41–48.

Golman, D. (1980, Feb.). 1528 little geniuses and how they grew. *Psychology Today,* 28–53.

Gorder, W. D. (1980). Divergent production abilities as constructs of musical creativity. *Journal of Research in Music Education, 28*(1), 38–42.

Gordon, W. J. J. (1961). *Synectics.* New York: Harper & Row.

Gordon, W. J. J. (1974a). *Making it strange.* Books 1–4. New York: Harper & Row.

Gordon, W. J. J. (1974b). Some source material in discovery by analogy. *Journal of Creative Behavior, 8,* 239–257.

Gordon, W. J. J. (1987). *The new art of the possible: The basic course in synectics.* Cambridge, MA: SES Associates.

Gordon, W. J. J., & Poze, T. (1971). *Metaphorical way of learning and knowing.* Cambridge, MA: SES Associates.

Gordon, W. J. J., & Poze, T. (1972a). *Teaching is listening.* Cambridge, MA: SES Associates.

Gordon, W. J. J., & Poze, T. (1972b). *Strange and familiar.* Cambridge, MA: SES Associates.

Gordon, W. J. J., & Poze, T. (1980a). SES synectics and gifted education today. *Gifted Child Quarterly, 24,* 147–151.

Gordon, W. J. J., & Poze, T. (1980b). *The new art of the possible.* Cambridge, MA: Porpoise Books.

Gough, H. G. (1979). A creative personality scale for the Adjective Check List. *Journal of Personality and Social Psychology, 37,* 1398–1405.

Gough, H. G., & Heilbrun, A. B., Jr. (1965). *The Adjective Check List manual.* Palo Alto, CA: Consulting Psychologists Press.

Griggs, S., & Dunn, R. (1984). Selected case studies of the learning style preferences of gifted students. *Gifted Child Quarterly, 28,* 115–119.

Gruber, H. E., & Davis, S. N. (1988). Inching our way up Mount Olympus: The evolving-systems approach to creative thinking. In R. J. Sternberg (Ed.), *The nature of creativity* (pp. 243–270). New York: Cambridge University Press.

Guilford, J. P. (1967). *The nature of human intelligence.* New York: McGraw-Hill. (Creativity tests available from Consulting Psychologists Press, Palo Alto, California).

Guilford, J. P. (1977). *Way beyond the IQ.* Buffalo, NY: Creative Education Foundation.

Guilford, J. P. (1979). Some incubated thoughts on incubation. *Journal of Creative Behavior, 13,* 1–8.

Guilford, J. P. (1986). *Creative talents: Their nature, uses and development.* Buffalo, NY: Bearly Limited.

Guilford, J. P. (1988). Some changes in the structure-of-intellect model. *Educational and Psychological Measurement, 48,* 1–4.

Hadamard, J. (1945). *An essay on the psychology of invention in the mathematical field.* New York: Dover.

Hamburger, M. (Ed. and trans.). (1952). *Beethoven: Letters and journals and conversations.* New York: Pantheon.

Hammerschmidt, P. K. (1996). The Kirton Adaption Innovation Inventory and group problem solving success rates. *Journal of Creative Behavior, 30,* 61–74.

Helman, I. B., & Larson, S. G. (1980). *Now what do I do?* Buffalo, NY: DOK.

Hennessey, B. A., & Amabile, T. M. (1988). Story-telling: A method for assessing children's creativity. *Journal of Creative Behavior, 22,* 235–246.

Hetherington, E. M., & Parke, R. D. (1979). *Child psychology: A contemporary viewpoint.* New York: McGraw-Hill.

Hilgard, E. R., Atkinson, R. L., & Atkinson, R. C. (1979). *Introduction to psychology* (7th ed.). New York: Harcourt.

Hocevar, D. (1980). Intelligence, divergent thinking, and creativity. *Intelligence, 4,* 25–40.

Holland, J. L. (1961). Creative and academic performance among talented adolescents. *Journal of Educational Psychology, 52,* 136–147.

Holt, R. R. (1964). Imagery: The return of the ostracized. *American Psychologist, 19,* 254–264.

Ironson, G., & Davis, G. A. (1979). Faking high or low creativity scores on the Adjective Check List. *Journal of Creative Behavior, 13,* 139–145.

Isaksen, S. G. (1987). Introduction: An orientation to the frontiers of creativity research. In S. G. Isaksen (Ed.), *Frontiers of creativity research: Beyond the basics* (pp. 1–26). Buffalo, NY: Bearly Limited.

Isaksen, S. G., & Treffinger, D. J. (1985). *Creative problem solving: The basic course.* Buffalo, NY: Bearly Limited.

Jamison, K. (1989). Mood disorders and patterns of creativity in British writers and artists. *Psychiatry, 52,* 125–134.

Jeffery, L. R. (1989). Reading and rewriting poetry: William Wordsworth. In D. B. Wallace & H. E. Gruber (Eds.), *Creative people at work: Twelve cognitive case studies* (pp. 69–89). New York: Oxford University Press.

Jones, C. A. (1960). *Some relationships between creative writing and creative drawing of sixth grade children.* Unpublished doctoral dissertation, Pennsylvania State University, University Park, PA.

Jung, C. G. (1933). *Psychological types.* New York: Harcourt.

Jung, C. G. (1959). *The archetypes and the collective unconscious: Collected works.* New York: Pantheon.

Jung, C. G. (1976). On the relation of analytic psychology to poetic art. In A. Rothenberg & C. R. Hausman (Eds.), *The creativity question* (pp. 120–126). Durham, NC: Duke University Press.

Kaltsoonis, B. (1971). Instruments useful in studying creative behavior and creative talents: Part I. Commercially available instruments. *Journal of Creative Behavior, 5,* 117–126.

Kaltsoonis, B. (1972). Additional instruments useful in studying creative behavior and creative talents: Part III. Noncommercially available instruments. *Journal of Creative Behavior, 6,* 268–274.

Kaltsoonis, B., & Honeywell, L. (1980). Additional instruments useful in studying creative behavior and creative talent: Part IV. Noncommercially available instruments. *Journal of Creative Behavior, 14,* 56–67.

Kang, C. (1989). *Gender differences in Korean children's responses to the Torrance Tests of Creative Thinking from first to sixth grade.* Unpublished M.S. thesis, University of Wisconsin, Madison.

Kanter, R. M. (1989). *When giants learn to dance.* New York: Simon & Schuster.

Kastenbaum, R. (1991). The creative impulse: Why it won't just quit. *Generations, 15*(2), 7–12.

Katz, A. N. (1980). Do left-handers tend to be more creative? *Journal of Creative Behavior, 14,* 271.

Keating, D. P. (1980). Four faces of creativity: The continuing plight of the intellectually underserved. *Gifted Child Quarterly, 24,* 56–61.

Khaleefa, O. H., Erdos, G., & Ashria, I. H. (1996a). Creativity in an indigenous Afro-Arab Islamic culture: The case of Sudan. *Journal of Creative Behavior, 30,* 268–282.

Khaleefa, O. H., Erdos, G., & Ashria, I. H. (1996b). Gender and creativity in an Afro-Arab Islamic culture: The case of Sudan. *Journal of Creative Behavior, 30,* 52–60.

Khatena, J., & Torrance, E. P. (1976). *Manual for Khatena-Torrance Creative Perceptions Inventory.* Chicago: Stoelting.

Kirton, M. J. (1976). Adaptors and innovators: A description and measure. *Journal of Applied Psychology, 61,* 622–629.

Kirton, M. J. (1987). *Kirton adaption-innovation manual* (2nd ed.). Hatfield, England: Occupational Research Center.

Koestler, A. (1964). *The act of creation.* New York: Dell.

Kolloff, P. B., & Feldhusen, J. F. (1984). The effects of enrichment on self-concept and creative thinking. *Gifted Child Quarterly, 28,* 53–57.

Kosslyn, S. M. (1983). *Ghosts in the mind's machine.* New York: Norton.

Krippner, S., & Murphy, G. (1976). Extrasensory perception and creativity. In A. Rothenberg & C. R. Hausman (Eds.), *The creativity question* (pp. 262–267). Durham, NC: Duke University Press.

Kris, E. (1976). On preconscious mental processes. In A. Rothenberg & C. R. Hausman (Eds.), *The creativity question* (pp. 135–143). Durham, NC: Duke University Press.

Kubie, L. S. (1958). *Neurotic distortion of the creative process.* Lawrence, KA: University of Kansas Press.

Kulp, M., & Tarter, B. J. (1986). The creative processes rating scale. *Creative Child and Adult Quarterly, 11,* 166–173.

Lees-Haley, P. R. (1978). *Creative behavior inventory.* Huntsville, AL: Basic Research, Inc.

Lees-Haley, P. R., & Sutton, J. (1982). An extension of Davis' How Do You Think test to elementary school students. *Roeper Review, 4*(3), 43.

Lees-Haley, P. R., & Swords, M. (1981). A validation study of Davis' How Do You Think (HDYT) test with middle school students. *Journal for the Education of the Gifted, 4*(2), 144–146.

Leff, H. L. (1984). *Playful perception.* Burlington, VT: Waterfront Books.

Lewis, J. D. (1993). Self-actualization in junior high students: A pilot study. *Psychological Reports, 73,* 639–642.

Lewis, J. D. (1994). Self-actualization in gifted children. *Psychological Reports, 74,* 767–770.

Lewis, J. D., Karnes, F. A., & Knight, H. V. (1995). A study of self-actualization and self-concept in intellectually gifted students. *Psychology in the Schools, 32,* 52–61.

Lichtenwalner, J. S., & Maxwell, J. W. (1969). The relationship of birth order and socioeconomic status to the creativity of preschool children. *Child Development, 40,* 1241–1247.

Lindauer, M. S. (1998). Interdisciplinarity, the psychology of art, and creativity: An introduction. *Creativity Research Journal, 11,* 1–10.

Lombroso, C. (1895). *The man of genius.* London: Scribners.

Lowes, J. L. (1927). *The road to Xanadu.* Boston: Houghton Mifflin.

Lynch, M., & Harris, C. R. (1999). *Teaching the creative child, K-8.* Boston: Allyn & Bacon.

MacKinnon, D. W. (1961). Creativity in architects. In D. W. MacKinnon (Ed.), *The creative person* (pp. 291–320). Berkeley, CA: Institute of Personality Assessment and Research, University of California.

MacKinnon, D. W. (1976). Architects, personality types, and creativity. In A. Rothenberg & C. R. Hausman (Eds.), *The creativity question* (pp. 175–189). Durham, NC: Duke University Press.

MacKinnon, D. W. (1978a). Educating for creativity: A modern myth? In G. A. Davis & J. A. Scott (Eds.), *Training creative thinking* (pp. 194–207). Melbourne, FL: Krieger.

MacKinnon, D. W. (1978b). *In search of human effectiveness: Identifying and developing creativity.* Buffalo, NY: Creative Education Foundation.

Maltzman, I. (1960). On the training of originality. *Psychological Review, 67,* 229–242.

Marland, S. (1972). *Education of the gifted and talented, Volume I. Report to the Congress of the United States by the U. S. commissioner of Education.* Washington, DC: U.S. Government Printing Office.

Martindale, C. (July, 1975). What makes a person different? *Psychology Today,* 44–50.

Maslow, A. H. (1954). *Motivation and personality.* New York: Harper.

Maslow, A. H. (1968). *Toward a psychology of being* (2nd ed.). Princeton, NJ: Van Nostrand.

Maslow, A. H. (1970). *Motivation and personality* (2nd ed.). New York: Harper & Row.

Maslow, A. H. (1971). *The farther reaches of human nature.* New York: Viking Press.

Mason, J. G. (1960). *How to be a more creative executive.* New York: McGraw-Hill.

May, R. (1959). The nature of creativity. In H. H. Anderson (Ed.), *Creativity and its cultivation.* New York: Harper & Row.

McKee, M. G. (1985). Review of Creativity Attitude Survey. In D. Keyser & R. Sweetland (Eds.), *Test critiques: Vol. V* (pp. 206–208). Kansas City, MO: Testing Corporation of America.

Mednick, M. T., & Andrews, F. M. (1967). Creative thinking and level of intelligence. *Journal of Creative Behavior, 1,* 428–431.

Mednick, S. A. (1962). The associative basis of the creative process. *Psychological Review, 69,* 220–232.

Mednick, S. A. (1967). *Remote associates test.* Boston: Houghton Mifflin.

Meeker, M. (1969). *The structure of intellect: Its use and interpretation.* Columbus, OH: Merrill.

Meeker, M. (1978). Nondiscriminatory testing procedures to assess giftedness in Black, Chicano, Navajo and Anglo children. In A. Baldwin, G. Gear, & L. Lucito (Eds.), *Educational planning for the gifted.* Reston, VA: Council for Exceptional Children.

Meeker, M., & Meeker, R. (1986). The SOI system for gifted education. In J. S. Renzulli (Ed.), *Systems and models for developing programs for the gifted and talented* (pp. 194–215). Mansfield Center, CT: Creative Learning Press.

Meeker, M., Meeker, R., & Roid, G. (1985). Structure-of-intellect learning abilities test (SOI-LA). Los Angeles: Western Psychological Services.

Michael, W. B., & Colson, K. R. (1979). The development and validation of a life experience inventory for the identification of creative electrical engineers. *Educational and Psychological Measurement, 39,* 463–470.

Millar, G. W. (1995). *The creativity man: An authorized biography.* Norwood, NJ: Ablex.

Morelock, M. J., & Feldman, D. H. (1997). High IQ children, extreme precocity, and savant syndrome. In N. Colangelo & G. A. Davis (Eds.), *Handbook of gifted education* (2nd ed., pp. 439–459). Boston: Allyn & Bacon.

Moss, M. A. (1991). *The meaning and measurement of Jung's construct of intuition: Intuition and creativity.* Unpublished doctoral dissertation, University of Wisconsin, Madison.

Moustakis, C. E. (1967). *Creativity and conformity.* Princeton, NJ: D. Van Nostrand.

Moyer, J., & Wallace, D. (1995). Issues in education: Nurturing the creative majority of our schools—A response. *Childhood Education, 72*(1), 34–35.

Mozart, W. A. (1952). A letter. In B. Ghiselin (Ed.), *The creative process* (pp. 44–45). New York: Mentor.

Mudd, S. (1995). Suggestive parallels between Kirton's A-I theory of creative style and Koestler's bisociative theory of the creative act. *Journal of Creative Behavior, 29*, 240–254.

Murphy, G. (1963). Creativity and its relation to extrasensory perception. *Journal of the American Society for Psychical Research, 57*, 203–204.

Myers, R. E., & Torrance, E. P. (1966). *Plots, puzzles and plays.* Boston: Ginn.

Newell, A., Shaw, J. C., & Simon, H. A. (1962). In H. E. Gruber, G. Terrell, & M. Wertheimer (Eds.), *Contemporary approaches to creative thinking* (pp. 63–119). New York: Atherton.

Nicholls, J. G. (1972). Creativity in a person who will never produce anything original and useful: The concept of creativity as a normally distributed trait. *American Psychologist, 27*, 717–727.

Norman, D. A. (1976). *Memory and attention: An introduction to human information processing* (2nd ed.). New York: Wiley.

Nunamaker, J. F., Applegate, L. M., & Konsynski, B. R. (1987). Facilitating group creativity: Experience with a group decision support system. *Journal of Management Information Systems, 3*, 5–19.

Okuda, S. M., Runco, M. A., & Berger, D. E. (1991). Creativity and the finding and solving of real-world problems. *Journal of Psychoeducational Assessment, 9*, 45–53.

Osborn, A. F. (1963). *Applied imagination* (3rd ed.). New York: Scribners.

Parke, B. N., & Byrnes, P. (1984). Toward objectifying the measurement of creativity. *Roeper Review, 6*, 216–218.

Parnes, S. J. (1961). Effects of extended effort in creative problem solving. *Journal of Educational Psychology, 53*, 117–122.

Parnes, S. J. (1978). Can creativity be increased? In G. A. Davis & J. A. Scott (Eds.), *Training creative thinking* (pp. 270–275). Melbourne, FL: Krieger.

Parnes, S. J. (1981). *Magic of your mind.* Buffalo, NY: Bearly Limited.

Parnes, S. J., Noller, R. B., & Biondi, A. M. (1976). *Creative actionbook.* New York: Scribners.

Perkins, D. A. (1988). The possibility of invention. In R. J. Sternberg (Ed.), *The nature of creativity* (pp. 362–385). New York: Cambridge University Press.

Perry, D. (1993). *Backtalk: Women writers speak out.* New Brunswick, NJ: Rutgers University Press.

Peters, T. (1992). *Liberation management.* New York: Knopf.

Peterson, J. M., & Lansky, L. M. (1980). Success in architecture: Handedness and/or visual thinking. *Perceptual and Motor Skills, 50*, 1139–1143.

Petkus, E., Jr. (1994). Ninja secrets of creativity. *Journal of Creative Behavior, 28*, 133–140

Piechowski, M. M. (1997). Emotional giftedness: The measure of intrapersonal intelligence. In N. Colangelo & G. A. Davis (Eds.), *Handbook of gifted education* (2nd ed., pp. 366–381). Boston: Allyn & Bacon.

Porshe, J. D. (1955, October). Creative ability: Its role in the search for new products. Paper presented at the Special Conference on Managing Product Research and Development, American Management Association, New York.

Prince, G. (1968). The operational mechanism of synectics. *Journal of Creative Behavior, 2*, 1–13.

Prince, G. (1982). Synectics. In S. A. Olsen (Ed.), *Group Planning and Problem solving methods in engineering.* New York: Wiley.

Pryor, K. W., Haag, R., & O'Reilly, J. (1969). The creative porpoise: Training for novel behavior. *Journal of the Experimental Analysis of Behavior, 12*, 653–661.

Puccio, G. J., Treffinger, D. J., & Talbot, R. J. (1995). Exploratory examination of relationships between creativity styles and creative products. *Creativity Research Journal, 8*, 157–172.

Ramos-Ford, V., & Gardner, H. (1997). Giftedness from a multiple intelligences perspective. In N. Colangelo & G. A. Davis (Eds.), *Handbook of gifted education* (2nd ed., pp. 54–66). Boston: Allyn & Bacon.

Rank, O. (1945). *Will therapy, truth and reality.* New York: Knopf.

Read, G. M. (1955). *Profile of human materials.* Paper presented at the Centennial Symposium on Modern Engineering, University of Pennsylvania, Philadelphia, PA.

Reis, S. M., & Burns, D. E. (1987). A schoolwide enrichment team invites you to read about methods for promoting community and faculty involvement in a gifted educational program. *Gifted Child Today, 49*(2), 27–32.

Renzulli, J. S. (1977). *Enrichment triad model.* Mansfield, CT: Creative Learning Press.

Renzulli, J. S. (1983, Sept./Oct.). Rating the behavioral characteristics of superior students. *G/C/T*, 30–35.

Renzulli, J. S. (1994). *Schools for talent development: A practical plan for total school improvement.* Mansfield Center, CT: Creative Learning Press.

Renzulli, J. S., & Reis, S. M. (1985). *Schoolwide enrichment model.* Mansfield Center, CT: Creative Learning Press.

Renzulli, J. S., & Reis, S. M. (1991). The schoolwide enrichment model: A comprehensive plan for the development of creative productivity. In N. Colangelo & G. A. Davis (Eds.), *Handbook of gifted education* (pp. 111–141). Boston: Allyn & Bacon.

Renzulli, J. S., & Reis, S. M. (1997). The schoolwide enrichment model: New directions for developing high-end learning. In N. Colangelo & G. A. Davis (Eds.), *Handbook of gifted education* (2nd ed., pp. 136–154). Boston: MA: Allyn & Bacon.

Rhodes, M. (1961). Analysis of creativity. *Phi Delta Kappan, 42*, 305–310.

Rhodes, M. (1987). An analysis of creativity. In S. G. Isaksen (Ed.), *Frontiers of creativity research: Beyond the basics* (pp. 216–222). Buffalo, NY: Bearly Limited.

Richards, R. L. (1981). Relationships between creativity and psychopathology: An evaluation and interpretation of the evidence. *Genetic Psychology Monographs, 103*, 261–324.

Richards, R. L., Kinney, D. K., Lunde, I., Benet, M., & Merzel, A. P. C. (1988). Creativity in manic-depressives, cyclothymes, their normal relatives, and control subjects. *Journal of Abnormal Psychology, 97*, 281–288.

Rimm, S. B. (1976). *GIFT: Group inventory for finding creative talent.* Watertown, WI: Educational Assessment Service.

Rimm, S. B. (1983). *Preschool and kindergarten interest descriptor.* Watertown, WI: Educational Assessment Service.

Rimm, S. B., & Davis, G. A. (1976). GIFT: An instrument for the identification of creativity. *Journal of Creative Behavior, 10*, 178–182.

Rimm, S. B., & Davis, G. A. (1979). *Group inventory for finding interests. I.* Watertown, WI: Educational Assessment Service.

Rimm, S. B., & Davis, G. A. (1980). Five years of international research with GIFT: An instrument for the identification of creativity. *Journal of Creative Behavior, 14*, 35–46.

Rimm, S. B., & Davis, G. A. (1983, Sept./Oct.). Identifying creativity, Part II. *G/C/T*, 19–23.

Rogers, C. R. (1962). Toward a theory of creativity. In S. J. Parnes & H. F. Harding (Eds.), *A source book for creative thinking* (pp. 63–72). New York: Scribners.

Rothenberg, A., & Hausman, C. R. (Eds.). (1975). *The creativity question.* Durham, NC: Duke University Press.

Rubenson, D. L. (1991). Creativity, economics, and baseball. *Creativity Research Journal, 4*, 205–209.

Rubenson, D. L., & Runco, M. A. (1992). The economics of creativity, and the psychology of economics: A rejoinder. *New Ideas in Psychology, 10*, 173–178.

Rugg, H. (1963). *Imagination: An inquiry into the sources and conditions that stimulate creativity.* New York: Harper & Row.

Runco, M. A. (1987). The generality of creative performance in gifted and nongifted children. *Gifted Child Quarterly, 31*, 121–125.

Runco, M. A. (1990). Implicit theories and ideational creativity. In M. A. Runco & R. S. Albert (Eds.), *Theories of creativity* (pp. 234–252). Newbury Park, CA: Sage.

Runco, M. A., & Albert, R. S. (Eds.) (1990). *Theories of creativity.* Newbury Park, CA: Sage.

Runco, M. A., & Bahleda, M. D. (1986). Birth-order and divergent thinking. *Journal of Genetic Psychology, 148*, 119–125.

Runco, M. A., Ebersole, P., & Mraz, W. (1991). Creativity and self-actualization. *Journal of Social Behavior and Personality, 6*(5), 161–167.

Runco, M. A., Okuda, S. M., & Hwang, S. R. (1987). Creativity, extracurricular activity, and divergent thinking as predictors of mathematics and science performance by talented students. Eric Document ED279523.

Runco, M. A., Okuda, S. M., & Thurston, B. J. (1988). Psychometric properties of four systems for scoring divergent thinking tests. *Journal of Psychoeducational Assessment, 5,* 149–156.

Santrock, J. W. (1996). *Child development* (7th ed.). Dubuque: Brown & Benchmark.

Sawyer, R. K. (1998). The interdisciplinary study of creativity in performance. *Creativity Research Journal, 11,* 11–19.

Schaefer, C. E. (1969). Imaginary companions and creative adolescents. *Developmental Psychology, 1,* 747–749.

Schaefer, C. E. (1970). *Biographical Inventory-Creativity.* San Diego, CA: Educational and Industrial Testing Service.

Schaefer, C. E. (1971). *Creativity attitude survey.* Jacksonville, IL: Psychologists & Educators, Inc.

Schatz, E. M., & Buckmaster, L. R. (1984). Development of an instrument to measure self-actualizing growth in preadolescents. *Journal of Creative Behavior, 18,* 263–272.

Schiever, S. W., & Maker, C. J. (1997). Enrichment and acceleration: An overview and new directions. In N. Colangelo & G. A. Davis (Eds.), *Handbook of gifted education* (2nd ed., pp. 113–125). Boston: Allyn & Bacon.

Schlichter, C. (1997). Talents unlimited model in programs for gifted students. In N. Colangelo & G. A. Davis (Eds.), *Handbook of gifted education* (2nd ed., p. 318–327). Boston: Allyn & Bacon.

Schubert, D. S. P., Wagner, M. D., & Schubert, H. J. P. (1977). Family constellation and creativity: Firstborn predominance among classical music composers. *Journal of Psychology, 95,* 147–149.

Schuldberg, D. (1990). Schizotypal and hypomanic traits, creativity, and psychological health. *Creativity Research Journal, 13,* 219–232.

Schuldberg, D. (1993). Personal resourcefulness: Positive aspects of functioning in high-risk research. *Psychiatry, 56,* 137–152.

Schuldberg, D., French, C., Stone, B. L., & Heberle, J. (1988). Creativity and schizotypal traits: Creativity test scores and perceptual aberration, magical ideation, and impulsive nonconformity. *Journal of Nervous and Mental Disease, 176,* 648–657.

Seidel, G. J. (1962). *The crisis in creativity.* Notre Dame, IN: University of Notre Dame Press.

Selby, E. C., Treffinger, D. F., Isaksen, S. G., & Powers, S. V. (1993). Use of the Kirton Adaption-Innovation Inventory with middle school students. *Journal of Creative Behavior, 27,* 223–235.

Shallcross, D. J. (1981). *Teaching creative behavior.* Englewood Cliffs, NJ: Prentice-Hall.

Sheerer, M. (1963). Problem solving. *Scientific American, 208*(4), 118–128.

Shields, S. (1989). *Creativity of radio announcers.* Unpublished Doctoral Dissertation, University of Wisconsin, Madison.

Shostrum, E. L. (1963). *Personal orientation inventory.* San Diego, CA: Educational and Industrial Testing Service.

Shostrum, E. L. (1975). *Personal orientation dimensions.* San Diego, CA: Educational and Industrial Testing Service.

Siau, K. L. (1995). Group creativity and technology. *Journal of Creative Behavior, 29,* 201–216.

Simberg, A. S. (1978). Blocks to creative thinking. In G. A. Davis & J. A. Scott (Eds.), *Training creative thinking* (pp. 119–135). Melbourne, FL: Krieger.

Simonton, D. K. (1988a). Creativity, leadership, and chance. In R. J. Sternberg (Ed.), *The nature of creativity* (pp. 386–426). New York: Cambridge University Press.

Simonton, D. K. (1988b). *Scientific Genius: A psychology of science.* Cambridge, England: Cambridge University Press.

Simonton, D. K. (1990). History, chemistry, psychology, and genius: An intellectual autobiography of histrionomy. In M. A. Runco & R. S. Albert (Eds.), *Theories of creativity* (pp. 92–115). Newbury Park, CA: Sage.

Simonton, D. K. (1994). *Greatness: Who makes history and why.* New York: Guilford Press.

Simonton, D. K. (1997). When giftedness becomes genius: How does talent achieve eminence? In N. Colangelo & G. A. Davis (Eds.), *Handbook of gifted education* (2nd ed., pp. 335–349). Boston: Allyn & Bacon.

Skinner, B. F. (1971). *Beyond freedom and dignity*. New York: Knopf.

Skinner, B. F. (1972). *Cumulative record: A selection of papers* (3rd ed.). Englewood Cliffs, NJ: Prentice-Hall.

Smith, E. (1985, Sept. 30). Are you creative? *Business Week*, pp. 80–84.

Smith, G. J. W., & Carlsson, I. (1987). A new creativity test. *Journal of Creative Behavior, 21*, 7–14.

Smith, J. M. (1966). *Setting conditions for creative teaching in the elementary school*. Boston: Allyn & Bacon.

Snow, R. E. (1986). Individual differences and the design of educational programs. *American Psychologist, 41*, 1029–1039.

Solomon, G. T., & Winslow, E. K. (1988). Toward a descriptive profile of the entrepreneur. *Journal of Creative Behavior, 22*, 162–171.

Solomon, G. T., & Winslow, E. K. (1993). Entrepreneurs: Architects of innovation, paradigm pioneers and change. *Journal of Creative Behavior, 27*, 75–88.

Solso, R. L. (1991). *Cognitive psychology*. Boston: Allyn & Bacon.

Somers, J. V., & Yawkey, T. D. (1984). Imaginary play companions: Contributions of creativity and intellectual abilities of young children. *Journal of Creative Behavior, 18*, 77–89.

Sosniak, L. (1997). The tortoise, the hare, and the development of talent. In N. Colangelo & G. A. Davis (Eds.), *Handbook of gifted education* (2nd ed., pp.207–217). Boston: Allyn & Bacon.

Springer, S. P. & Deutsch, G. (1985). *Left brain, right brain* (2nd ed.). New York: Freeman.

Staats, A. W. (1968). *Learning, language, and cognition*. New York: Holt.

Staff. (1995). The SOI model school. *SOI News, 17*(2), 4–7.

Stanish, B. (1977). *Sunflowing*. Carthage, IL: Good Apple.

Stanish, B. (1979). *I believe in unicorns*. Carthage, IL: Good Apple.

Stanish, B. (1981). *Hippogriff feathers*. Carthage, IL: Good Apple.

Stanish, B. (1988). *Lessons from the hearthstone traveler*. Carthage, IL: Good Apple.

Stankowski, W. M. (1978). Definition. In R. E. Clasen & B. Robinson (Eds.), *Simple gifts* (pp. 1–8). Madison, WI: University of Wisconsin-Extension.

Stanley, J. C., & Benbow, C. P. (1986). Youths who reason exceptionally well mathematically. In R. J. Sternberg & J. Davidson (Eds.), *Conceptions of giftedness* (361–387). New York: Cambridge University Press.

Stariha, W. E., & Walberg, H. J. (1995). Childhood precursors of women's artistic eminence. *Journal of Creative Behavior, 29*, 269–282.

Sternberg, R. J. (1988a). A three-facet model of creativity. In R. J. Sternberg (Ed.), *The nature of creativity* (pp. 125–147). New York: Cambridge University Press.

Sternberg, R. J. (Ed.) (1988b). *The nature of creativity*. New York: Cambridge University Press.

Sternberg, R. J. (1997). A triarchic view of giftedness: Theory and practice. In N. Colangelo & G. A. Davis (Eds.), *Handbook of gifted education* (2nd ed., pp. 43–53). Boston: Allyn & Bacon.

Sternberg, R. J., & Lubart, T. I. (1990, September). *The creative mind: An investment theory of creativity*. Paper presented at the meeting of the American Psychological Association, Boston.

Sternberg, R. J., & Lubart, T. I. (1992). Buy low and sell high: An investment approach to creativity. *Current Directions in Psychological Science, 1*, 1–5.

Sternberg, R. J., & Lubart, T. I. (1995). *Defying the crowd: Cultivating creativity in a culture of conformity*. New York: Free Press.

Sternberg, R. J., & Lubart, T. I. (1996). Investing in creativity. *American Psychologist, 51*, 677–682.

Striker, F. (Undated). *Creative writing workbook and the morphological approach to plotting*. Unpublished manuscript, University of Buffalo.

Subotnik, R. (1988). Factors from the structure of intellect model associated with gifted adolescents' problem finding in science: Research with Westinghouse science talent search winners. *Journal of Creative Behavior, 22*, 42–54.

Tannenbaum, A. J. (1997). The meaning and making of giftedness. In N. Colangelo & G. A. Davis (Eds.), *Handbook of gifted education* (2nd ed., pp. 27–42). Boston: Allyn & Bacon.

Tapscott, D., & Caston, A. (1993). *Paradigm shift: The new promise of information technology.* New York: McGraw-Hill.

Tardif, T. Z., & Sternberg, R. J. (1988). What do we know about creativity? In R. J. Sternberg (Ed.), *The nature of creativity* (pp. 429–440). New York: Cambridge University Press.

Taylor, C. W. (1963). Variables related to creativity and productivity among men in two research laboratories. In C. W. Taylor & F. Barron (Eds.), *Scientific creativity: Its recognition and development* (pp. 228–250). New York: Wiley, 1963.

Taylor, C. W. (1986). Cultivating simultaneous student growth in both multiple creative talents and knowledge. In J. S. Renzulli (Ed.), *Systems and models for developing programs for the gifted and talented* (pp. 306–351). Mansfield Center, CT: Creative Learning Press.

Taylor, C. W. (1988). Various approaches to and definitions of creativity. In R. J. Sternberg (Ed.), *The nature of creativity* (pp. 99–121). New York: Cambridge University Press.

Tegano, D. W., Moran, J. D., & Godwin, L. J. (1986). Cross-validation of two creativity tests designed for preschool children. *Early Childhood Research Quarterly, 1*, 387–396.

Terman, L. M. (1925). *Genetic studies of genius: Volume I. Mental and physical traits of a thousand gifted children.* Stanford, CA: Stanford University Press.

Terman, L. M., & Oden, M. H. (1947). *Genetic studies of genius: Volume 4: The gifted child grows up.* Stanford, CA: Stanford University Press.

Thompson, J. (1942). *John Thompson's modern course for the piano. Fifth grade book.* Cincinnati, OH: Willis Music Co.

Torrance, E. P. (1962). *Guiding creative talent.* Englewood Cliffs, NJ: Prentice-Hall.

Torrance, E. P. (1965). *Rewarding creative behavior.* Englewood Cliffs, NJ: Prentice-Hall.

Torrance, E. P. (1966a). *Torrance tests of creative thinking.* Bensenville, IL: Scholastic Testing Service.

Torrance, E. P. (1966b). *Torrance tests of creative thinking, norms-technical manual.* Bensenville, IL: Scholastic Testing Service.

Torrance, E. P. (1968). A longitudinal examination of the fourth-grade slump in creativity. *Gifted Child Quarterly, 12*, 195–199.

Torrance, E. P. (1974). *Norms and technical manual: Torrance tests of creative thinking.* Revised edition. Bensenville, IL: Scholastic Testing Service.

Torrance, E. P. (1977). *Creativity in the classroom.* Washington, DC: National Education Association.

Torrance, E. P. (1979). *The search for satori and creativity.* Buffalo, NY: Creative Education Foundation.

Torrance, E. P. (1981a). Non-test ways of identifying the creatively gifted. In J. C. Gowan, J. Khatena, & E. P. Torrance (Eds.), *Creativity : Its educational implications* (2nd ed., pp. 165–170). Dubuque, IA: Kendall/Hunt.

Torrance, E. P. (1981b). *Thinking creatively in action and movement.* Bensenville, IL: Scholastic Testing Service.

Torrance, E. P. (1984a). Some products of twenty-five years of creativity research. *Educational Perspectives, 22*(3), 3–8.

Torrance, E. P. (1984b). Teaching creative and gifted learners. In M. E. Wittrock (Ed.), *Handbook of research on teaching* (3rd ed., pp. 630–647). Chicago: Rand McNally.

Torrance, E. P. (1987a). *The blazing drive: The creative personality.* Buffalo, NY: Bearly Limited.

Torrance, E. P. (1987b). Teaching for creativity. In S. G. Isaksen (Ed.), *Frontiers of creativity research: Beyond the basics* (pp. 189–215). Buffalo, NY: Bearly Limited.

Torrance, E. P. (1988). The nature of creativity as manifest in its testing. In R. W. Sternberg (Ed.), *The nature of creativity* (pp. 43–75). New York: Cambridge University Press.

Torrance, E. P. (1990a). *Torrance tests of creative thinking: Manual for scoring and interpreting results. Verbal forms A and B.* Bensenville, IL: Scholastic Testing Service.

Torrance, E. P. (1990b). *Torrance tests of creative thinking: Norms-technical manual. Figural (streamlined) forms A and B.* Bensenville, IL: Scholastic Testing Service.

Torrance, E. P. (1995). *Why fly? A philosophy of creativity.* Norwood, NJ: Ablex.

Torrance, E. P., & Ball, O. E. (1984). *Torrance tests of creative thinking: Streamlined (revised) manual, figural A and B.* Bensenville, IL: Scholastic Testing Service.

Torrance, E. P. & Dauw, D. C. (1965). Aspirations and dreams of three groups of creatively gifted high school seniors and a comparable unselected group. *Gifted Child Quarterly, 9,* 177–182.

Torrance, E. P., & Goff, K. (1989). A quiet revolution. *Journal of Creative Behavior, 23,* 136–145.

Torrance, E. P., Khatena, J., & Cunnington, B. F. (1973). *Thinking creatively with sounds and words.* Bensenville, IL: Scholastic Testing Service.

Torrance, E. P., & Myers, R. E. (1970). *Creative learning and teaching.* New York: Dodd, Mead.

Torrance, E. P., & Safter, H. T. (1989). The long range predictive validity of the Just Suppose test. *Journal of Creative Behavior, 23,* 219–223.

Torrance, E. P., Williams, S. E., Torrance, J. P., & Horng, R. (1978). *Handbook for training future problem-solving teams.* Athens, GA: Georgia Studies of Creative Behavior, University of Georgia.

Treffinger, D. J. (1985). Review of the *Torrance Tests of Creative Thinking.* In J. Mitchell (Ed.), *Ninth mental measurements yearbook* (Vol. 2, pp. 1632–1634). Lincoln, NE: Buros Institute of Mental Measurement.

Treffinger, D. J. (1995). Creative problem solving: Overview and educational implications. *Educational Psychology Review, 7,* 301–312.

Treffinger, D. J., Isaksen, S. G., & Dorval, K. B. (1994a). *Creative problem solving: An introduction* (rev. ed.). Sarasota, FL: Center for Creative Learning.

Treffinger, D. J., Isaksen, S. G., & Dorval, K. B. (1994b). Creative problem solving: An overview. In M. A. Runco (Ed.), *Problem finding, problem solving, and creativity* (pp. 223–236). Norwood, NJ: Ablex.

Treffinger, D. J., Isaksen, S. G., & Firestien, R. L. (1982). *Handbook of creative learning.* Volume 1. Sarasota, FL: Center for Creative Learning.

Urban, K. K. (1993). *Test for creative thinking-drawing production (TCT-DP): Design and empirical studies.* Hannover, Germany: University of Hannover.

Urban, K. K., & Jellen, H. G. (1993). *Manual for the Test for Creative Thinking: Drawing Production.* Hannover, Germany: University of Hannover.

Van Gundy, A. B. (1987). Organizational creativity and innovation. In S. G. Isaksen (Ed.), *Frontiers of creativity research: Beyond the basics* (pp. 358–379). Buffalo, NY: Bearly Limited.

Vernon, P. E. (1970). *Creativity.* Harmondsworth, UK: Methuen.

Von Oech, R. (1983). *A whack on the side of the head.* New York: Warner Communications.

Von Oech, R. (1986). *A kick in the seat of the pants.* New York: Harper & Row.

Walberg, H. A. (1988). Creativity and talent as learning. In R. W. Sternberg (Ed.), *The nature of creativity* (pp. 340–361). New York: Cambridge University Press.

Walberg, H. J. (1994, April). Introduction. In H. J. Walberg (Chair), *Notable American women: Childhood contexts and psychological traits.* Symposium conducted at the meeting of the American Educational Research Association, New Orleans.

Walberg, H. J., & Herbig, M. P. (1991). Developing talent, creativity, and eminence. In N. Colangelo & G. A. Davis (Eds.), *Handbook of gifted education* (pp. 245–255). Boston: Allyn & Bacon.

Walberg, H. J., & Stariha, W. E. (1992). Productive human capital: Learning, creativity, and eminence. *Creativity Research Journal, 5,* 323–340.

Walberg, H. J., & Zeiser, S. (1997). Productivity, accomplishment, and eminence. In N. Colangelo & G. A. Davis (Eds.), *Handbook of gifted education* (2nd ed., pp. 328–334). Boston: Allyn & Bacon.

Walberg, H. J., *et al.* (1996). Childhood traits and experiences of eminent women. *Creativity Research Journal, 9,* 97–102.

Walker, A. M., Koestner, R., & Hum, A. (1995). Personality correlates of depressive style in autobiographies of creative achievers. *Journal of Creative Behavior 29,* 75–96.

Wallach, M. A., & Kogan, N. (1965). *Modes of thinking in young children.* New York: Holt.

Wallas, G. (1926). *The art of thought.* New York: Harcourt.

Warren, T. F. (1974). How to squelch ideas. In G. A. Davis & T. F. Warren (Eds.), *Psychology of education: New looks* (pp. 428–430). Lexington, MA: Heath.

Way, B. (1967). *Development through drama.* London: Longman.

Weaver, R. L. (1990). Faculty dynamation: Guided empowerment. *Innovative Higher Education, 14*(2), 93–105.

Weiner, D. A. (1992). Mentors highlight the essence. *Gifted Child Today, 15*(3), 23–25.

Weisberg, P. S., & Springer, K. J. (1961). Environmental factors in creative function. *Archives of General Psychiatry, 5,* 554–564.

Welch, L. (1946). Recombination of ideas in creative thinking. *Journal of Applied Psychology, 30,* 49–53.

Welsh, G. S., & Barron, F. (1963). *The Barron-Welsh art scale.* Palo Alto, CA: Consulting Psychologists Press.

Westberg, K. L. (1996). The effects of teaching students how to invent. *Journal of Creative Behavior, 30,* 249–267.

Williams, F. (1980). *Creativity assessment packet.* Buffalo, NY: DOK.

Winslow, E. K., & Solomon, G. T. (1989). Further development of a descriptive profile of entrepreneurs. *Journal of Creative Behavior, 23,* 149–161.

Witkin, H. A., Moore, C. A., Goodenough, D. R., & Cox, P. W. (1977). Field-dependent and field-independent cognitive styles and their educational implications. *Review of Educational Research, 47,* 1–64.

Woodman, R. W., & Schoenfeldt, L. A. (1990). An interactionist model of creative behavior. *Journal of Creative Behavior, 24,* 270–290.

Woodward, C. E. (1989). Art and elegance in the synthesis of organic compounds: Robert Burns Woodward. In D. B. Wallace & H. E. Gruber (Eds.), *Creative people at work: Twelve cognitive case studies* (pp. 226–253). New York: Oxford University Press.

Yamada, H., & Tam, A. Y. (1996). Prediction study of adult creative achievement: Torrance's longitudinal study of creativity revisited. *Journal of Creative Behavior, 30,* 144–149.

Yamamoto, K. (1963). Creative writing and school achievement. *School and Society, 91,* 307–308.

Yates, F. A. (1966). *The art of memory.* Chicago: University of Chicago Press.

Yonge, G. D. (1975) Time experiences, self-actualizing values and creativity. *Journal of Personality Assessment, 39,* 601–606.

Zuckerman, M. (1975). *A manual and research report of the sensation seeking scale.* ETS Test Collection. Princeton, NJ: Educational Testing Service.

name index

339

subject index